Spritsails and Lugsails

Frontispiece. Spritsail and balanced lugsail in one rig. The 18ft centreboard Humber canoe yawl *Viking* was designed by John Hamilton, her original owner, in the 1890s and sets 160 square feet in mainsail, mizzen and jib. *Photo – Roger M. Smith.*

John Leather

Spritsails and Lugsails

with drawings by the author

ADLARD COLES LIMITED
GRANADA PUBLISHING
London Toronto Sydney New York

Other books by John Leather

Gaff Rig (1970)
Clinker Boatbuilding (1973)
The Northseamen (1971)
World Warships in Review 1860–1906 (1976)
A Panorama of Gaff Rig (1977)
The Salty Shore (1978)
The Sailors Coast (1978)

Published by Granada Publishing in
Adlard Coles Limited, 1979

Granada Publishing Limited
Frogmore, St Albans, Herts AL2 2NF
and
3 Upper James Street, London W1R 4BP
1221 Avenue of the Americas, New York, NY 10020 USA
117 York Street, Sydney, NSW 2000, Australia
100 Skyway Avenue, Toronto, Ontario, Canada M9W 3A6
Trio City, Coventry Street, Johannesburg 2001, South Africa

Copyright © 1979 John Leather

ISBN 0 229 11517 9

Printed in Great Britain by
Fletcher and Son Ltd, Norwich

To Doris, for enthusiastically assisting the writing of yet another book.

Acknowledgements

The author wishes to thank many friends afloat and ashore who have helped to mould the contents of this book. I am particularly grateful to my colleague Harry Steenstra for information on Dutch spritsails, to Fabian Bush for his description of his modern version of the dipping lug rig, and to Roger C. Taylor for reading the chapters on American craft.

I am indebted to many contemporaries for generous help, especially with photographs, particularly W. Bolland Haxall, Peter J. Guthorn, R. D. Culler, the Rev. Alan Shaw, Les Moore, Michael Stammers, Chuck Harris, Basil Greenhill, Dick Wagner, Hervey Benham, John M. Leavens, Phil Bolger, Peter Van Dine, John Mannering, F. Gibson, and Alan Lockett. Institutions which have helped with photographs include the Maritime Museum 'Prins Hendrik', Rotterdam, the Smithsonian Institution of Washington D.C., the Mariners Museum, *Newport News*, the Science Museum, London, Museum of Fine Arts, Boston, Mystic Seaport, the National Gallery of Art, Washington D.C., the National Maritime Museum, London, and Merseyside Country Museums, Liverpool.

Any student of fore and aft craft is grateful for the inspiration and work of other researchers and practical boat sailors such as Herbert and Bevil Warington Smyth, E. K. Chatterton, Robert C. Leslie, Charles G. Davis, Arthur Briscoe, Stephen Reynolds, Bob Hunt, William M. Blake, George Holmes, Conor O'Brien, G. Soe, Herbert Reiach, Hugh V. Willyams, Howard Chapelle, Sir Alan Moore, Albert C. Ettinger, Ernest Dade, David Cabot, Phelps Soule, H. C. Folkard, H. Oliver Hill, and others.

For practical experience with the rigs I will always be grateful to skipper Charles Sheldrik of the *Leofleda* for my first sail with spritsail rig, to Bob Sainty for early instruction in sailing with standing lugsails and perhaps not least to Chief Engineer Christiansen of the *Belder*, who let me use a ship's boat and her dipping lug for my first sail under that powerful rig more than thirty years ago.

John Leather
Cowes, Isle of Wight. 1978.

7

Contents

Introduction   15

Part I. The Rigs

Chapter 1. Spritsails   45
Chapter 2. Lugsails   62

Part II. Spritsails and Lugsails in England, Wales, and Ireland

Chapter 3. Luggers in the Downs   113
Chapter 4. The Sussex Coast   148
Chapter 5. Inside the Wight   169
Chapter 6. West Bay to the Scillies   187

Chapter 7. The West Coast, Wales and
            Ireland   219
Chapter 8. Cobles, Yawls and Dusters   247
Chapter 9. Norfolk and Suffolk   270
Chapter 10. Essex, the Thames and
            Medway   300

Part III. Spritsails and Lugsails in North America

Chapter 11. Spritsails in New England   325
Chapter 12. New Jersey to the Mexican
            Gulf   342
Chapter 13. East and West coasts   364

Drawings

(drawn by the author unless credited otherwise)

Figure   *page*

A   Cornish three masted lugger   22
1   The *rua pet*   24
2   Bombay craft   26
3   Singapore racing *kolek*   28
4   Rig of a Dunkirk *lamaneur*   29
5   Somali coast *matapa*   29
6   River Nile *naggar*   30
7   Danish beach fishing pram   31
8   Greek cargo lugger   33
9   Greek 'brigantine'   35
10   The sailing and rowing boat *Bluenose*   39
11   A typical boomless spritsail   46
12   An efficient snotter   48
13   Robands   48
14   A spritsail with a boom   52
15   Another arrangement for a spritsail   53
16   Greek and Turkish spritsail arrangement   55
17   Swedish *almogjolle* or Danish *kaperboat*   56
18   Danish fishing boat   57
19   Dutch arrangement of sprit   60
20   Divided spritsail rig   61
21   Mast tabernacle for open boat   63

22   Bending a lugsail to a yard   64
23   Marlin hitch lacing   65
24   A rolling hitch   65
25   Arrangement of dipping lugsail   67
26   East coast of Scotland 'fifie'   71
27   Dipping lug foresail and standing lug mizzen   72
28   28ft gig with dipping lugsail   74
29   Typical standing lugsail   79
30   Boomless standing lugsail   79
31   16ft centreboard boat   81
32   Scotch cut standing lugsail   82
33   Sail plan of *Papoose*   84
34   Sail plan of *Red Lancer*   85
35   12ft racing dinghy   86
36   Settee rig   87
37   Dinghy with a balanced lugsail and jib   88
38   Keeping the lugsail yard close to the mast   89
39   Another method of controlling the lugsail yard   91
40   Lugsail halyard, without traveller   91
41   Gunter rig sloop   92
42   Detail of gunter rig   93

11

12

43	Variation of gunter rig	93
44	Seine gunter-rigged sloop	94
45	A current type of gunter lug	95
46	A simplified gunter lug halyard	95
47	Alternative gunter lug halyard arrangement	95
48	Jam-free luff lacing	96
49	17ft 'Jewel' one-design	97
50	Azores whaleboats	98
51	The schooner *La Reine*	99
52	Kenneth Gibbs' gunter lug	100
53	Gunter lateen	102
54	The 28ft sharpie *Crotchet*	106
55	20 square metre 'Rennjolle'	107
56	*Procyon*	108
57	Three masted Deal cutter	117
58	The Walmer lugger *England's Glory*	119
59	*Argonaut* (sail plan)	136
60	*Argonaut* (lines and construction)	137
61	*Happy Go Lucky* (sail plan)	143
62	*Happy Go Lucky* (lines plan)	144
63	Topsail on a Hastings lugger	156
64	The Spithead wherry *Woodham*	172
65	14ft fishing boat *Caprice*	177
66	*Mullett* (general arrangement)	178
67	*Mullett* (sail plan)	179
68	The racing dinghy *Water Rat*	182
69	*Sylvia* (sail plan)	203
70	*Sylvia* (lines and general arrangement)	204
71	*Ira* (sail plan)	206
72	*Ira* (lines and general arrangement)	207
73	*Cuckoo* (sail plan)	209
74	*Cuckoo* (lines and general arrangement)	210
75	*Evelyn* (sail plan)	214
76	*Evelyn* (lines and construction)	215
77	A Somerset flatner	224
78	*Seahorse* (sail plan)	232
79	*Seahorse* (profile and plan)	233
80	*Seahorse* (body sections, etc.)	234
81	28ft Irish *Pucan*	238
82	*Dora* (sail plan)	245
83	*Dora* (lines and general arrangement)	246
84	S.H. 64, a mule coble	263
85	Hull duster	268
86	Grimsby duster	269
87	*Star of Peace* (sail plan)	272
88	*Star of Peace* (lines)	273
89	The Southwold beach yawl *Bittern*	286
90	*Ossie* (sail plan)	298
91	*Ossie* (lines and arrangement)	299
92	Typical undecked gun punt	306
93	Gravesend waterman's wherry	311
94	A spritsail-rigged passenger wherry	312
95	A Medway fishing doble	319
96	Medway huffler's boat	320
97	Noman's Land fishing boat (lines)	326
98	Noman's Land fishing boat (sail plan)	327
99	The Plymouth lobsterboat *Vixen*	333
100	A typical centreboard 'Hampton boat'	340
101	Barnegat Bay sneakbox	347
102	North Carolina Sound boat	352
103	Pensacola pilot gig	357
104	The Mississippi lugger *Giacomo*	360
105	Maine spritsail wherry	368
106	Sailing a St Lawrence skiff	372
107	Coming about in a St Lawrence skiff	373
108	*Sea Serpent* and *Mermaid*	381

Photographs

Frontispiece
The Humber canoe yawl *Viking*

Plate   *page* 20

1   Armed lugger close-hauled   20
2   Bisquine fishing luggers   27
3   A variety of canoe rigs   38
4   The spritsail schooner *Rondo II*   40
5   The dory *Dancing Feather*   41
6   A 13ft spritsail peapod   47
7   *Hoogaars* from Arnemuiden   49
8   A replica of a Crotch Island Pinky   51
9   Spritsail rigged *water schepen* at work   59
10 A Penzance crabber   63
11 The Cornish mackerel driver *Morning Star*   68
12 The Lowestoft Volunteer Lifeboat *Caroline
    Hamilton*   73
13 The Essex One-Design *Tern II*   76, 77
14 *Rushton Princess*, a sailing canoe   78
15 The 5-Rater *Norman*   83
16 A small French fishing boat   90
17 *Heathen Chinee*   104
18 The *Fox* and the *Gypsy*   126
19 A Deal lugger   130
20 The Deal lugger *Annie*   133
21 A Deal sprat punt   138

22 A four-oared Deal galley   140
23 The Hastings lugger *Team*   150
24 A Hastings lugger   151
25 *New Moon*   153
26 An Eastbourne fishing lugger   158
27 A new Eastbourne lugger   160
28 *Paradox*   161
29 The Eastbourne lugger *Our Lassie*   163
30 A Folkestone lugger   163
31 Brighton hog boats   165
32 Details of Brighton hog boats   166
33 The battleship *Britannia* and Portsmouth
    wherries   170
34 Emsworth fishing lugger *Metilda*   184
35 The Devon lugger *Beatrice Annie*   189
36 Harry Conant of Sidmouth   193
37 Harry Conant's lugger *England's Rose*   194
38 A lugger beaching at Sidmouth   195
38a Devon fishermen hauling lugsail boat   196
39 A Falmouth waterman's boat   212
40 A Newlyn pilot gig   216
41 The Scilly Isles gig *Nornour*   217
42 A Clovelly 'picarooner'   220
43 An Appledore waterman's boat   221
44 A Somerset flatner   225

45   An Irish pookhaun   239
46   Three-masted Mersey gigs   241
47   Liverpool waterman's gigs   242
48   Sunderland whammel net boat   243
49   The sailing coble *Gratitude*   249
50   The Whitby coble *Lily*   250
51   *Mauretania* passing Tyne pilot cobles   256
52   Model of a Yorkshire fishing coble   260
53   Yorkshire mule   264
54   Cromer crab boats   271
55   Sheringham crab boats   275
56   A Lowestoft beach yawl   282
57   The Southwold yawl *Bittern*   285
58   Lowestoft beach yawl under sail   291
59   The Lowestoft beach yawl *Georgiana*   293
60   Model of a Yarmouth mackerel boat   295
61   A Suffolk beach punt beaching   296
62   Beachmen at Southwold   297
63   An Aldeburgh beach boat   297

64   Walton-on-Naze lobsterboats   302
65   The West Mersea winkle brig *Black Duck*   303
66   Thames peter boats   313
67   Shipping in the Thames Estuary   317
68   Model of a Noman's Land boat   328
69   The Kingston lobster boat *Annie Fuller*   332
70   A Hampton boat   338
71   A Hampton boat under sail   339
72   The beach skiff *Lizzie*   343
73   A Barnegat Bay sneak box   349
74   *Setting out after rail* by Thomas Eakins   350
75   Albemarle Sound shad skiffs under
     construction   353
76   Model of a Mississippi lugger   359
77   *Breezing up* by Winslow Homer   365
78   A replica of a Woods Hole boat   366
79   St Lawrence River sailing skiffs   371
80   Model of a Columbia River salmon boat   378

Introduction

Spritsails and lugsails are amongst the oldest types of rigs in the world and were the most widespread in use. This book offers a practical assessment of spritsail and lugsail rigs for small craft of the present, and surveys the boats and people using the rigs for work or pleasure in Britain and North America over several centuries. It will be noted that the many types of lugger from Scotland, Cornwall and the ports of Lowestoft and Yarmouth, have not been included in this survey as it was considered that these had been discussed in detail in other works, particularly *Sailing Drifters* by the late E. J. March. The English spritsail barges of Essex, Suffolk, Kent, the Thames, Sussex and elsewhere have also been deliberately omitted as these are included in the author's forthcoming book *Barges*, also to be published by Adlard Coles Ltd.

Readiness of use and minimal expense were the driving factors behind evolution of most of the spritsail and lugsail boats described; qualities which have increasing appeal to many small boat sailors as yachting is engulfed in an excess of sophistication and the effects of money inflation. In future, more and more people with a yearning to get afloat will turn to simple craft, which can be maintained and used easily and inexpensively.

The restoration of traditional small sailing craft has grown during the past twenty years to a recognisable trend in pleasure sailing. Commencing as a few enthusiasts inexpensively rebuilding old 'tore-outs' in odd corners, it has become a cult which supports the design and construction of plastic-hulled, gaff-rigged craft in several countries and causes much money to be poured into uneconomical restoration of old hulls and rigs. While the effects of money inflation and economic fluctuations increase, many see the chance to build or restore a sizeable traditional craft recede; a process complicated by the expense of material maintenance and mooring, if moorings can be found in the now crowded pleasure sailing areas. An answer may lie in these generally simpler small craft, evolved to work under sail or oar and setting simple, stowable rigs. While no less appealing in traditions of use and skills needing to be mastered in their construction and handling, they combine this with smaller size, less expense and easier handling. If under about 22ft long, such boats need not necessarily be kept on a mooring and can be trailed behind a car for launching miles from home, to explore unfamiliar waters. They can be kept on the trailer at the owner's home, when not in use, or for winter laying up and maintenance. So spritsail- and lugsail-rigged craft have much to offer those who go afloat in future.

The simplest form of spritsail needs few blocks and none or few metal fittings, which made it desirable in working boats. The quadrilateral sail does not need a halyard and is bent to a short mast. To set it, the pointed upper end of a spar termed the 'sprit' is placed in the rope cringle at the peak, and the sprit heel is supported at the mast by a rope strop termed the 'snotter'. The sail is usually boomless and can be sheeted flat for windward work. The head of this peculiar rectangular sail sags under wind pressure giving an appearance distinctive from gaff or lug sails.

Various types of lugsail were much used in many of the world's working and pleasure craft. As with a spritsail, a lugsail needs few blocks and fittings. The head of this quadrilateral sail is bent to a yard hoisted by a simple halyard on a relatively short mast which may be unstayed. The sail may or may not have a boom and the tack may or may not be set forward of, or at, the mast. Lugsails stand well to windward if sheeted correctly. Dipping, standing, balance, settee and gunter are the principal types of lugsails, basic shapes of which are shown in Figs. 25, 29, 30, 36, 37, 41, 45.

There were rigs for small boats, to which a significant increase in wind strength appears as a squall and demands reefing or dousing of some

sail. There is a great difference between reefing a larger craft, even singlehanded, which can be carried out in a relatively leisurely manner, and shortening canvas in an open boat where the sails must be capable of being lowered very quickly. So, besides limitations of materials, technical ability and expense, spritsails and lugsails appealed to many small boat sailors, to whom the best sail was the one which could be struck or effectively reduced with greatest speed and certainty, or could be quickly shifted for a smaller one. The ability to unstep masts, spars and sails in a boat which is also used for rowing, considerably reduces the air resistance under oars, even in light winds. It is also useful if the boat is to be launched or beached, particularly from or to a lee shore, and valuable too if caught in bad weather, when it is surprising how much sea a well handled and well shaped open boat will stand under oars and with the rig struck and lashed in her. Either type of sail can be made of inexpensive materials, be cut by inexpert hands and still be made to set efficiently by virtue of their quadrilateral shape and scope for adjustment. The masts and spars are not long, need not be heavy, can be made from timber of only average quality, and rigged with simple blocks and rope strops and seizings, yet function well. These truths still commend the rigs to those who like simple sailing. If a larger boat was needed they added another mast and sail of the same size as the original and adapted it to balance the jib, if one was carried. If it was desirable to increase length further a third mast and sail were added, again of similar size to the first, resulting in adequate sail area with a low centre of effort, necessary for a lightly ballasted open boat with beam restricted for rowing. Rowing was often as important as sailing in these craft, and the ability to strike and stow masts, spars and sails out of the way made standing rigging undesirable, even if it also meant a slightly larger mast diameter.

As lugsails were usually favoured in long, narrow craft of light displacement, the spritsail seems to have originated in shorter, beamy craft of greater displacement. The true origins of both sails are obscure and it is worthless to attempt definition. It is probable that the lugsail, like so much else maritime, was first evolved by Chinese and Asiatic sailors of antiquity. It may be related to or even have antedated the lateen sail of the Indian Ocean and Mediterranean, some variations of which have a short luff between the heel of the long yard and the tack. The use of lugsails may have spread to or was similarly evolved in the Mediterranean, western Europe and Scandinavia.

Spritsail evolution is equally difficult to trace. We are certain that the sail was in use by the first and second centuries AD in the eastern Mediterranean, and may have appeared earlier in Asia. Its use spread to European and Scandinavian coasts, and to Britain, whence it was carried to America, where it was widely used until the early twentieth century.

Until recent years many maritime historians considered that only the squaresail was used by the ancients. Northern seafarers probably started sailing with the squaresail and used it for centuries as a reliable and versatile rig for their

sea and wind conditions, efficient enough to propel the usually coarse-lined hulls of their craft. The square sail was inefficient to windward and awkward for sailing in confined channels but they preferred it to the long yard of the Mediterranean lanteen rig, which some had seen or had heard described. Lanteen rig was thought to have originated with the Arabs after the time of Mohammed, and spritsails and gaff sails to have appeared during the fifteenth or sixteenth centuries, probably from Dutch invention.

However, many centuries previously, sailors were using spritsails and lateens, and probably various forms of lugsail. Greek and Roman tombstones of the first or second centuries AD provide direct pictorial evidence by carved representations of craft in which the deceased sailor voyaged; a style of decoration then favoured for many vocations. A gravestone found near Thessaloniki in north Greece and preserved in the archaeological museum shows a craft carrying a spritsail and preparing to leave the shore. Two others were discovered in Asia Minor, near the site of ancient Troy; one from Lampsacus shows a spritsail-rigged boat moving smartly under sail and the other from Camberli-Tas, shows a spritsail craft running before the wind with sails goosewinged; the main spritsail is to port and a smaller spritsail is set to starboard, from the same mast. Both are preserved at the archaeological museum of Istanbul.

The rather morbid method of studying burial relics provides a further example of early spritsail on a sarcophagus of the third century AD preserved at the Ny-Carlsberg, Glyptotik in

Copenhagen. One of several detailed ships carved on its sides depicts a spritsail-rigged craft complete with a vang to trim the peak, consisting of a single line made fast at the deck, passing through a block at the head of the sprit and down to belay at the deck.

Hitherto a miniature painting by a Flemish artist, Hubert Van Eyck, dated as 1420 and showing St Julian sailing in a sprit-rigged craft, had been regarded as the earliest known illustration of the rig, but the tombstones and sarcophagus prove it was used at least a thousand years previously and possibly long before. It was not a local rig, being used in north Greece, Asia Minor, Rome and elsewhere. In its primitive form it was a square piece of matting or cloth attached at the luff by light lashings to an unstayed mast and supported at the peak by a light spar or sprit pivoting at its foot in a rope sling or 'snotter' on the mast. In eastern India such sails were used by river watermen who had no concept or intention of sailing to windward, and the rig was merely a method of sailing a vessel for running. When the mast was supported by shrouds the sail was, significantly, hoisted before them. It is possible that the Greeks also discovered spritsail rig in the eastern Mediterranean as it is doubtful if the Romans devised it, not being particularly active seafarers; perhaps it was copied from Asian craft seen by far travellers. All this is conjecture. There remains a huge gap in the evidence of its use between the third century AD and about 1420. Perhaps it went out of use and was re-discovered by the Dutch.

The lugsail may be related to the lateen sail which was generally thought to have Arabic origins, but some researchers have sought its beginnings in the East. It was used by the Greeks during the second century AD, and evidence exists in another tombstone of a fisherman born at Miletus, in Asia Minor, who died near Athens. He is carved on the stone, standing with his son on board his boat which is single masted and rigged with a lateen sail. This relic antedates by several centuries record of the lateen sail's appearance elsewhere.

At the time when ships began to be rigged with two masts, a variety of sail was tried and by the sixteenth century some seagoing vessels were rigged with a sprit mainsail, stay foresail and a mizzen mast often setting a lateen sail. Such a ship was shown several time in Lucas Waganaer's *Speculum Nauticum* of 1586, on his charts of the North Sea and Baltic. Some also set a squaresail and square topsail and a small square sail set on a yard under the bowsprit, which was also confusingly called a 'spritsail'. This was principally used to aid steering.

The principal types of rigs between 1400 and 1600 were square, sprit or lateen and most of the craft with sprit mainsails set a stay-foresail, which was apparently not then used with any other type of mainsail. Another of Waganaer's charts, which included part of Finland, showed a two masted ship with a mainsail very similar to a lugsail, a lateen mizzen and a well steeved bowsprit with a square 'spritsail' under it.

During the seventeenth and early eighteenth centuries, British coasting hoys providing a service for goods and passengers between ports were frequently rigged with a sprit mainsail, stay-foresail, jib and a lateen mizzen, a rig similar to those of the Turkish coasting *trehendire* or Greek *sacoleve*, described in Chapter I (Fig. 16). But the size of a vessel which could use a spritsail as its principal sail was limited by the height and weight of the large sprit, which in bigger craft became a huge spar having weight and windage unacceptable for working in big seas. Later, these hoys were frequently rigged with a standing gaff, often termed a 'half sprit', a rig surviving into some early twentieth-century British coasting and fishing craft.

The spritsail was taken to North America in the earliest days of settlement. The *Mayflower*'s shallop was so rigged and spritsails were widely used there during the eighteenth and nineteenth centuries. The rig is shown with vangs, sheet and mast lacing on a vessel off Fort St George at the mouth of the Kennebec River and was probably built there in 1607. A view of New York about 1700 shows a spritsail-rigged small boat, and thereafter evidence of the rig is frequent, becoming widespread in small boats during the nineteenth and early twentieth centuries.

The lug was known during the seventeenth century and was noticed and illustrated by Fortree about 1660, though it seems to have been little used in European waters. Towards the end of the seventeenth century the lugsail is recorded as sometimes being used for the mainsail of craft setting a recognisable brigantine rig. A painting by John Cleverly dated 1752 shows a brigantine with a furled lug mainsail and a square main topsail. The log of a brigantine rigged in this way

in 1718 was quoted by F. C. Prideaux Nash in his *Extracts from the log of a salt trader*. It is doubtful that these craft were then called brigantines; a term which, in the seventeenth century referred to a small galley rigged with fore and main lateen sails. During the early eighteenth century the lug or *buss* sail of the brigantine rig was replaced by a gaff sail or shoulder of mutton sail with a short headstick.

The lugsail appears to have been known in north European waters for many years but was little used before the second part of the eighteenth century when it became widespread in a very developed form, often associated with fast hulls of refined shape. Barlow's journal of 1658-1703 shows a vague representation of a two masted craft setting square-headed lugs similar to those of a Deal galley, on fore and main. Brooking's painting *Morning, or sun rising* which is probably not later than 1750, illustrates an open boat with a lug foresail and sprit mizzen. His *Light breeze* shows another two-masted boat with lugs for foresail and mainsail, also carrying a bowsprit, indicating that a jib could be set.

There is a reference to French luggers carrying oysters in 1762, but lugsails are not mentioned in Lescallier's *Vocabulaire de Marine* of 1777 and he uses 'Voiles auriques' the literal translation of lugs, to indicate the gaff sail and spritsail! The word lug is included but with explanation 'voile de fortune, ou treou'. However, contemporary dictionaries were usually twenty years behind actual usage of many things maritime and little reliance can be placed on their relationship to active use or development of any item.

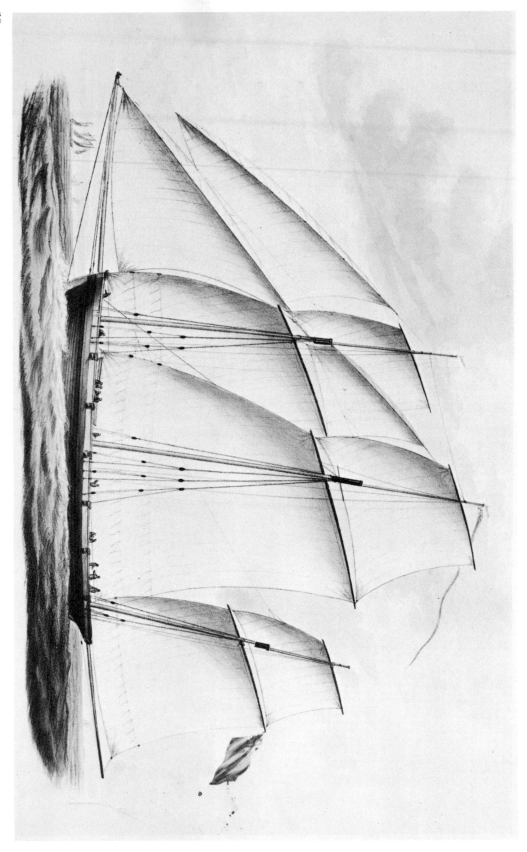

Plate 1. Armed lugger close hauled. Typical of the naval, privateer and smuggling luggers of the late eighteenth and early nineteenth century. These set topsails and were notably fast. She sets a large jib topsail, main topmast staysail and has bowlines to luffs of the main lug and the mizzen topsail. *Coloured lithograph from J. Rogers 'Celebrated Sailing Vessels', Published 1825.*

In *Traité du Grément* of 1791 Lescallier describes and illustrates a lug, referring to it as a useful sail to windward, but that the necessity of dipping it confined its use to small craft. In contrast Steele, in 1794, shows the three masted lugger with fore and main topsails.

When the lugsail became more widely appreciated it soon displaced the buss sail, probably because the essential difference was not in the shape of the sail but rather in the method of going about. The influence of the buss sail lingered in the way early luggers set their canvas, sometimes with the longer yardarm braced forward. Steele stated they were fitted with braces. He did not include the lugger amongst foreign vessels.

The nineteenth century was the time of greatest development of the fishing lugger, which name was generally given only to British craft having more than one mast. Three masted English luggers were common until about 1850 when on many parts of the coast they discarded the mainmast. Many French and Belgian luggers retained the three masted rig until the end of sail.

Lug rigs varied considerably in Britain, France, Belgium, Italy and Greece, which were the western countries principally using luggers. Generally when going about, the fore lug was dipped, or lowered and brought round abaft the mast, as was the main if carried; while the mizzen was usually a 'working', or as later termed a 'standing' lug, with its tack close to the mast, requiring no attention when tacking, and was usually sheeted to an outrigger or stern bumkin. Lug-rigged working craft usually set up the

halyards to the windward rail as a stay, another feature common to lateen rig, but this complicated tacking. The luffs of some dipping lugsails were kept taut by spars known as vargoods or foregirts, a feature found in some Asian luggers and probably of great antiquity. Some luggers carried bowsprits and jibs and many, English, French and Belgian, set yard topsails above the lugs, principally over the main and mizzen.

Although the lug was for centuries a major rig for European and Eastern small craft, it was, inexplicably, never widely used in North America.

After 1700 the spritsail tended to become increasingly a rig for small open boats, with notable exceptions in England, Holland, Germany, Denmark, Sweden, Russia, Greece and Turkey, where larger craft used it into the twentieth century, and the surviving English spritsail barges of Kent, Essex and Suffolk, now sailed for pleasure, retain the rig in its large and very efficient form. During the last days of sail, between 1910 and 1930, these craft encroached on what remained of the trade available for the more conservatively rigged British coasting ketches and schooners.

Until late in the nineteenth century the spritsail was probably the most widely used sail for small boats in northern Europe. Scandinavia, and on the eastern seaboard of North America. By the end of the seventeenth century some two masted spritsail boats had the after sail larger than the foresail, a rig of schooner proportions, and many had sails of equal size. In Britain, two masted spritsail-rigged boats with sails of about the same

22

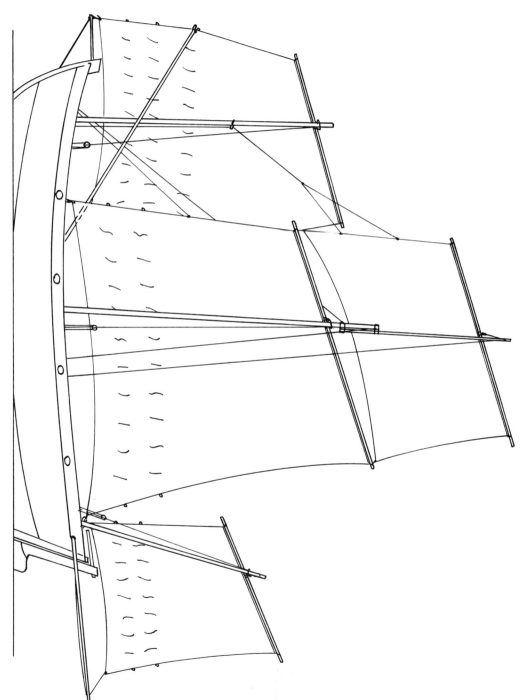

Figure A. Cornish three masted lugger with the foresail luff set taut for windward sailing with a 'vargood' or 'foregirt'. Note bowlines to luffs of main lug and its topsail, and oar ports in the sheer. Circa 1815.

area were used in some places as long as working craft sailed, but most of them had the sails disposed with the smaller aft, in the proportions of a yawl rather than ketch rig. The small mizzen was often stepped just inside the transom. During the nineteenth century the spritsail began to be replaced by the various forms of lugsail. In some boats, for instance in West Cornwall and North Devon, the sprit mainsail was replaced by a standing lug, but the sprit mizzen was often retained.

The modern sliding gunter lug probably evolved from the high peaked, boomless sail of the *houari*, illustrated by Lescallier. In 1749 Steele referred to pinnaces which 'sometimes have lateen sails, and rig with a sliding gunter like houarios' and he illustrated sails which resemble the gunter lug. Strictly, the gunter lug yard had only one traveller or set of jaws, the sliding gunter had two, or jaws and a traveller higher up the yard. The term gunter applied to this rig may have come from reference to a slide rule invented by Edmund Gunter (1581–1626), a mathematician and instrument maker, though it seems unlikely that seamen would have been sufficiently impressed to name a rig after him.

Although hull forms usually showed marked local characteristics, one cannot be so certain with rigs. For example, the small, open boats working the oyster fishery in the Essex River Roach and adjacent creeks, until about 1914 often set a single square sail which, when sailing to windward had its tack set close to the mast, almost converting it to a lugsail. Pedantry was of little use in earning a living, where the main chance had to be sought

and seized, and exact classification of one's working craft was of little interest, providing she was suitable for her task and sailed as well and as fast as possible. Just as now, when a leading builder of yachts introduces some improvement in hull form or equipment which is copied within a year by many others, so the men building and sailing small craft for a living quickly became aware of changes and improvements in hull form and rig along a coastline, and often from overseas as well. For instance, in 1848 a German seaman painted Brunschausen, on the River Elbe; a house with landing stage and a quiet creek with a sloop at moorings. In the foreground, painted in great detail, is a flat sheered sailing craft about 28ft long, rigged with three *lateen* sails set on short masts, and a small jib set on a steeved-down bowsprit. The hull shape and the stern are contemporary German. A small coach roof is shown above the flush deck. The forward and main sails are fitted with two rows of reef points and brails to the heads of the sails. Probably she was some sea captain's fancy for pleasure sailing, but she makes more plausible the origins of the Norfolk Broads lateeners which flourished for pleasure sailing at the same period.

Spritsail and lugsail rigs are so basically simple a method of setting sails that they almost certainly originated independently in various parts of the world. Many of the British and American craft and rigs described had parallels in other countries, and it is worth describing some examples to give perspective to the wide variety of craft using spritsail and lug rigs.

Lugsails may have originated in the east. The

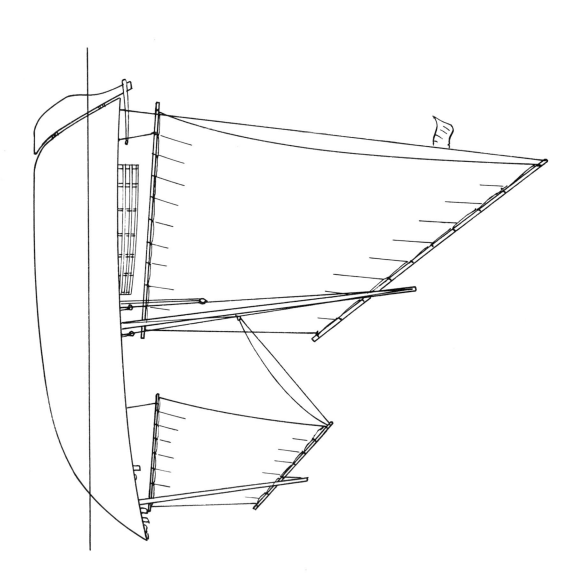

Figure 1. The *rua pet* of the Gulf of Siam set a high peaked standing lug mainsail and foresail.

two masted *rua pet* or 'duck boat' of the Gulf of Siam set a graceful, high-peaked standing lug mainsail and foresail in a shapely hull having an outreaching bow reminiscent of a modern yacht, and a pointed stern. The rudder was hung on a curved sternpost similar to many Scandinavian craft. Draught aft was deeper than forward and the keel was well rockered for turning under sail. Size varied from 20 to 50ft but an average boat was 40ft long with 15–16ft beam and 3ft 6in draught light, to 5ft 6in loaded (Fig. 1). The rua pet was a seaboat but had low freeboard aft. The best were built along the eastern shore of the Gulf of Siam, of ton takien, a heavy and worm resistant hardwood unknown in European boatbuilding. The carvel planking was fastened with treenails. Stone ballast was ceiled over and the crew of three or four lived under a non-watertight deck which stretched aft to the mainmast. Abaft this a coach roof of palm leaves and bamboo was built over the hold, and the remaining eight or ten feet of the hull was open for helmsman and crew.

The foremast was stepped in the eyes of the boat, without standing rigging. The boomed foresail had a halyard, sheet and single part vangs port and starboard to trim the peak of the yard when going to windward. The mainmast was stepped just forward of amidships and raked aft. Two shrouds on each side supported the masthead which had two sheaves for the main and peak halyards. The yard was held to the mast by a traveller made from rattan, and a downhaul from the heel of the yard was often wound round the mast to keep the yard peaked

up and to relieve strain on the luff rope. Sails were of yellow palm matting which was light in weight and open in weave. These lasted about a year but soon became holed and ragged.

However, the crews liked them better than canvas as in heavy weather the palm sails let the force of wind pass through, yet in light winds it held the slightest air. However, these sails were not very efficient to windward. When reefing, the yard was lowered to the desired height and the boom was revolved with a wooden handspike handle through a grommet at its forward end; a centuries old form of roller reefing rediscovered by British pilots and yachtsmen at the end of the nineteenth century. The reef was secured by leaving the handspike in place once the desired area was reached. The sails were furled aloft on the yards in a similar way to a lateen.

A type of sailing boat used at Bombay, India, set a long yarded lateen sail which had a short luff and a well roached foot (Fig. 2). which resembled some types of dipping lugsail. This type of sail was used in the Mediterranean, the Red Sea, the Persian Gulf, the Gulf of Arabia and on the east coast of Africa. It was possibly of Arab origin, suited to those waters and to light winds, but was difficult to reef and unmanageable in stormy conditions. Varieties of the balance lugsail were used in China for thousands of years and may have originated in the same way as the ancient Egyptian squaresail, which had a boom on its foot.

The three masted *bisquine* of La Houle, near Cancale, on the Gulf of St Malo, was amongst the most spectacular of all luggers. Originating as a

26

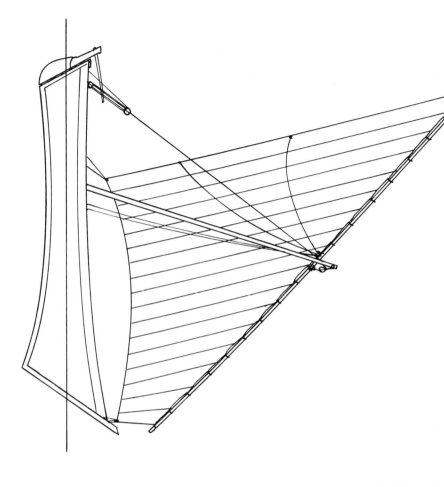

Figure 2. Bombay craft set a lateen sail with a short luff, possibly an early concept of the dipping lugsail. The keel profile was a local peculiarity for windward sailing.

two masted craft with straight stem, transom stern, long straight keel and moderate draught, for use in drift netting and in the local oyster fisheries, the type increased in size and rig to set a rectangular yard topsail above the main and a jib on an unstayed bowsprit. Later boats added a counter to increase deck area for hauling dredges and to improve speed, and a fore topsail. The final development was amongst the most shapely of French fishing craft and reminiscent of the fast English cutter smacks from the Essex River Colne, which were also developed for trawling and shellfish dredging. A mizzen was added, stepped on the counter and sheeted to an outrigger, but the most striking addition was an upper topsail on the fore and main masts. These were regularly set when working in light weather and in the keenly contested regatta racing amongst bisquines, when a large jib, overlapping jib topsail and mizzen staysail might also be set, and the working craft heeled to the puffs.

Size of these bisquines ranged to about 60ft, with draught up to about 8ft, but an average would be 42ft × 11ft × 5ft draught with about 1000 square feet in the lower sails. Bisquines spent much time drifting for mackerel and the lugger rig was not ideal for the season of oyster dredging, which formed part of the year's work. Shellfish dredging usually demands the weatherly qualities, quick handling and readily adjusted speed of the cutter rig. However, they satisfied the crews, who worked three 6ft dredges from the weather side or beam trawled for bottom fish.

Smaller French fishing luggers from Concarneau set a small dipping lug foresail on a decked, with low bulwarks and a single guardrope on stanchions around the deck; an unusual feature in fishing or coasting craft of the time.

A spritsail rig of similar proportions was set by kolek sea fishing canoes from the east coast of the Malay peninsular. These hulls were light, shallow and narrow beamed, hewn and hollowed from a large tree, opened out with fire and water to the desired beam, before framing and upper strakes were fitted. A typical kolek was 24ft × 4ft beam × 2ft depth, with a foot of freeboard. The banana-like hull form gave them the name kolek, which means rocker. The small forward spritsail was tacked to the stemhead and combined the functions of staysail. The taller mainmast raked aft and set a rectangular spritsail. Both sails were boomless. The heads of the sprits were trimmed with a single part vang set up to weather. Some set two lugsails with the tack brought to the mast, like a standing lug, others carried two dipping lugs. The rudder was a paddle held against the quarter by the helmsman, or a paddle-shaped rudder slung from a quarter post; the earliest form of rudder known. Generous sail area, low freeboard and little beam made these canoes tricky to handle for the four or five man crew, who sat them out on the weather gunwale.

Although poor performers to windward except in long tacks at sea, the kolek was developed for pleasure sailing, particularly at Singapore where a typical racing kolek was 45ft long × 5ft 10in beam × 2ft 6in depth and set a sloop rig with a very high peaked sprit mainsail and a foresail set to the stem. (Fig. 3). The sprit was 48ft long and the boom 35ft, spreading a mainsail of 970 square

Plate 2. French three masted Bisquine fishing luggers of La Houle, Brittany, carried topsails and topgallants above the lugsails and were smart sailers.

mast stepped in the eyes of the boat, and a larger main lug on a well raked mast stepped amidships. The foresail was hoisted by a single part halyard, and the main lug by a pendant and purchase set up to the weather side. The yards of both sails drooped aft when set and each had a stout luff rope which was tautened when going to windward by a spar with a fork at the end known as a vargood in English terms. The pointed stern hulls were carvel planked and averaged 30ft length with 9ft beam and about 4ft draught aft. Many boats of this size were open but larger luggers of the same type were fully

27

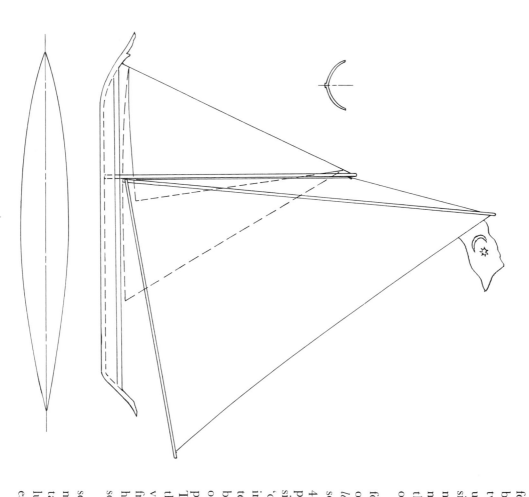

Figure 3. Singapore racing *kolek* setting a high peaked sprit mainsail. Dimensions 45ft × 5ft × 2ft 6in depth. A crew of 20 were needed to sit her up. Midship section inset.

feet and with 475 square feet in the foresail these boats almost left the water off the wind. A crew of twenty or so men were needed to keep the kolek upright in a breeze. Most sat along the weather side with a few bailing to leeward while eight or nine swung themselves out to windward by manropes from the masthead, feet braced against the gunwale in the manner of racing dinghy crews on trapezes.

The Kentish boatmen of the Downs were noted for their small boat seamanship. On the other side of the channel at Dunkirk, open boats called *lamaneurs* also launched from the beaches and beat seaward under large, single, dipping lugsails. (Fig. 4). These were very similar to the Deal galley punts and were used for similar purposes in similar waters. They were used by 'lamaneurs' or 'canoties' whose work was carrying pilots to inward or outward bound ships, and to wait and tend on shipping anchored in the roads. The boats went far to seaward when seeking work and on sighting an inward bound ship, hailed her for preference in tending when she was anchored. These luggers had the mast almost amidships and the lugsail was of exceptional width. They were very fast under ideal conditions of reaching in a fresh wind, but were tender and needed expert handling. Like many working sailing craft they soon disappeared after 1918.

The canoe-like *malapa* of the Somali coast was a seaworthy open boat with a deep forefoot, unlike most Arab craft, and carried a square sail with its tack set to the stem head, resembling a dipping lug (Fig. 5). A craft which could be compared in essentials to the galley punt of the Downs.

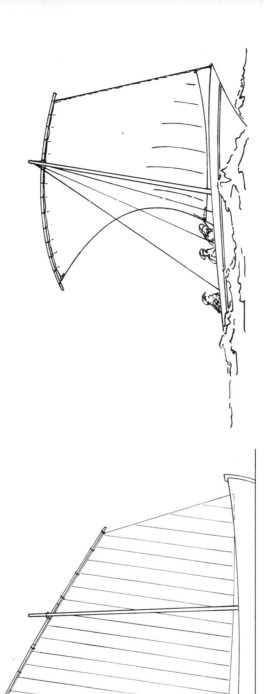

Figure 4. Rig of a Dunkirk *lamaneur*, the French equivalent of the galley punt of the Downs, showing the large dipping lugsail.

Figure 5. Soma i coast *matapa* with a square sail tacked to the stem head, in similar fashion to a dipping lug.

Ancient Egypt was a cradle of navigation and amongst the many types of river craft which survived under sail and oar into the twentieth century was the lug-rigged *naggar*, which carried cargo south of the Third Cataract on the River Nile. The low hull had a long, outreaching bow for beaching on the river banks to discharge, and the transom stern supported a large and strong rudder. Length varied from about 30–50ft and the rig was a single lug set on a mast about a quarter of the length abaft the bow. The almost

rectangular sail was set at an angle of about 45°, with the heel of the boom to the mast at deck and the yard heel brought forward of it (Fig. 6). Naggars were sailed with a fair or reaching wind and also used the rig to maintain control when descending the cataracts or rapids, using the prevailing north winds to keep the craft hovering about under control while the helmsman picked his way amongst the rocks and obstructions, adjusting the sheet to suit wind strength.

The inland water sailing of the naggar contrasts

Figure 6. The cargo carrying *naggar* of the River Nile voyaged under this variant of a lugsail, which was also used to control descent of the cataracts and rapids.

30

with the larger German kahn type barges of the nineteenth and early twentieth centuries, used in the rivers and coastal waterways of Pomerania, on the Baltic coast of north Germany; the three types, kaffenkahn, stevenkahn and mollenkahn, all set spritsails. The three masted mollenkahn averaged 150 ft length × 22ft beam × 7ft depth and was heavily built with rectangular sections in the long amidships, parallel body, ending in a bluff, pointed stern and almost equally bluff bow. These craft needed two sets of leeboards to keep them from making excessive leeway under sail, and steered with a large, semi-balanced rudder which had a long and heavy tiller. The flat sheered hull was decked forward and aft and had narrow side decks. Three large hatches were arranged over the holds which could be closed with hatch covers but were often left open for bulky cargoes like timber or barrelled liquids. The crew lived aft and the fo'c'sle was used as a store.

The rig of three unstayed masts was unusual. The foremast stepped about one seventh of the hull length from the bow, at the forward coaming of the fore hatch. The fore spritsail was laced to the mast and was spread by the sprit which doubled as a cargo derrick, the topping tackle taking the weight from the headrope of the sail. The sheet led to an iron horse immediately forward of the mainmast. The spritsails were hoisted by a halyard and the peak was set to the sprit end by a tackle, the fall of which led down the sprit. The sheeting arrangements were unique; a pendant led from the clew to a powerful purchase travelling on the horse. A vang led from the upper block of this to the head of the sprit.

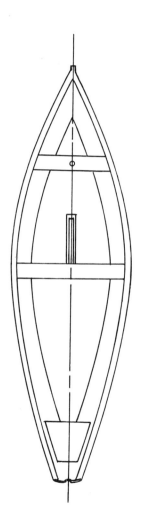

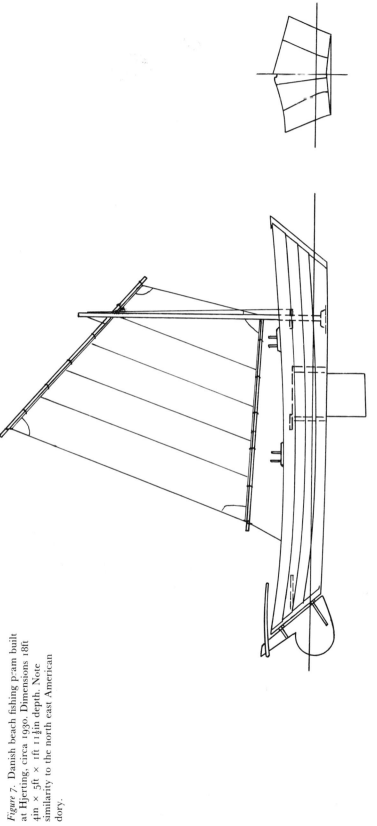

Figure 7. Danish beach fishing pram built at Hjerting, circa 1930. Dimensions 18ft 4in × 5ft × 1ft 11½in depth. Note similarity to the north east American dory.

Thus as the sheet was got in, the angle of the head of the sprit and of the sail were controlled to minimise twist. A staysail was set on a stay spread by a short bumkin, or to the stemhead. The mainmast was stepped to suit the position of the deck ties and coaming for the main hatch, about two fifths of the length abaft the stem. The mainmast and mainsail were arranged in the same way but the main sprit was longer than the other two and had a more powerful topping purchase. A small topsail with a headyard could be set from the pole mainmasthead. The mizzen was stepped at the after hatch coaming, about one seventh the length from the stern and was sheeted to the rudder head. Its size and proportions were as those of the foresail. A mizzen staysail could be set and was tacked to a strong beam dividing the main from the after hatches.

Kahns were not fast craft but were good carriers and could be compared with the English river sailing barges of the Thames and Medway. The kahns probably evolved from small, open three masted spritsail boats used for cargo carrying and fishing, and were still in use into the 1930s, fetching across the Grone Haff or the Achterwater in a fresh breeze sending spray up the foresail as they bustled along with goods for Stettin, or glided quietly upriver to berth at a village quay deep in the countryside to load timber. Small sailing *jollen* from Lynaes, facing on to the Kattegat, Denmark, set a triangular sail which was an example of the sort of link which may have existed between the lateen sail and the lug. These pointed sterned, clinker planked open boats were built as small as 12ft × 4ft 9in beam

and drawing 1ft. A short mast stepped about one third of the length from the bow carried a triangular lateen type sail, with the heel of the yard controlled by a tack rope led through a hole in a chock at the bow. The loose footed sail was spread by a light boom with jaws at the mast. Typical dimensions were head 12ft, foot 11ft, leach 9ft 3in. Jollen of this type were still built in the 1920s but the origin of use of this Mediteranean style rig so far north is another mystery.

Comparatively large daggerboards were fitted in the misnamed *prams* of Hjerting, on the North Sea coast of Jutland. These flat bottomed lugsail craft had the principal features of the north eastern American dory and averaged 18ft 6in length × 5ft beam and 2ft depth. Draught was 9in, or 2ft 6in with the broad daggerboard lowered. The stem and narrow 'tombstone' transom were well raked and the sides were planked with four or five clinker strakes, on seven or eight sawn frames and floors. The one inch thick bottom was slightly rockered for turning and for beach work. A short mast stepped about 2ft 6in abaft the stem head set a boomed standing lugsail. These prams were frequently rowed when getting off or on the beach and during fishing; they were still in use during the 1960s (Fig. 7). This type must have been originated at Hjerting by a seafarer who had observed the American fisheries, another instance of migration of a boat type.

Sailors of the Adriatic and Aegean seas were fond of the balance lugsail for working craft. It was set by the pointed sterned fishing luggers of

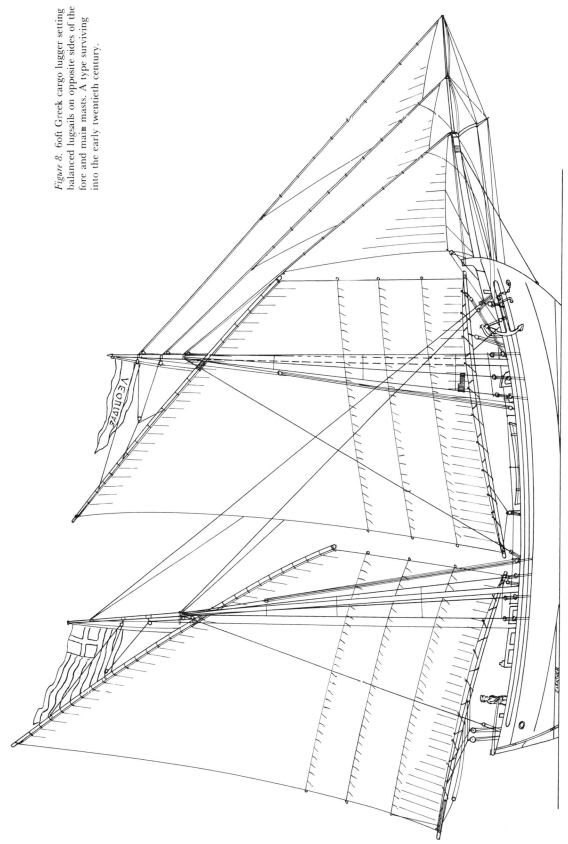

Figure 8. 60ft Greek cargo lugger setting balanced lugsails on opposite sides of the fore and main masts. A type surviving into the early twentieth century.

Ancona, the brightly painted *bargozzi* of Venice and the seaworthy *trabacola*; the principal cargo carrier of the area, and the various two masted cargo luggers and lug mainsail brigantines of the Greek coasts and islands, which had to face widely fluctuating weather conditions and uncertain anchorages. Most of the Greek craft of this type were pointed sterned and carvel planked. Shapely hulls with ample sheer and bold, curved bow setting a large balanced fore lugsail on a pole mast having three shrouds on each side and a similar sized lug mizzen or 'mainsail' on a pole mast raking aft and supported by shrouds. Size varied from about 28-90ft but most were about 60ft long and were seaworthy and well cared for craft. In many, the masts were of equal height but the larger boats usually had a taller mainmast. The mainmast stay was set up to port of the foremast by a tackle. The lugs were set with a main and a peak halyard, each was laced to a boom and had three rows of reef points. The lacing passed through eyelets hanging below the foot of the sails, which were well made and often obtained from Malta. The boats generally hoisted the foresail on the starboard side of the mast and the mainsail to port; the sails were never on the same side. To avoid the balance lug foresail getting aback against the mast and to ensure a taut luff and flat set, the tack purchase was set up to the deck well clear of the mast but almost level with it. The mainsail was set almost like a standing lug with the boom passing very little before the mast. The main yard was peaked at a greater angle than the foresail and passed well forward of the mast. The main boom extended

beyond the sternpost and the upper mainsheet block was carried on a span.

The yards were strengthened by fish pieces at the slings. The halyards were rove through two treble blocks, the upper hanging from a strop at the hounds. Sail tyers were carried hung from the yards, as in square-rigged ships. Two or three jibs might be set hanked to stays from a standing bowsprit and jib boom supported by elaborate standing rigging and a curiously shaped martingale to the bobstay. Many luggers set a single large jib to a traveller on a running bowsprit.

The crew lived in the small fo'c'sle and in the slightly larger aft cabin. The hold occupied the space between the masts, and the boat was stowed on the hatch. These shipshape little craft were tiller steered and were usually painted white, with contrasting sheer strakes and wales of different colours. Waist cloths were often rigged between the fore and main shrouds when deep loaded, to keep spray from the hatchway, in a breeze. This type was known in Greek as a 'stem head vessel' and out of it developed a hybrid brigantine style rigged small ship, the mizzen being replaced by a gaff and boom sail set on a pole mast with a jib headed topsail over. The hull was a conventional coaster form with a slightly raked stem, long straight keel and a short counter stern.

Beamy spritsail-rigged ketches worked the mackerel fisheries from Swedish ports. The hulls had a well rounded deck line and buoyant sections above water, hollow bottom lines and deep draught. Stem and stern profiles were almost identical and the hulls were clinker planked in

Figure 9. A Greek 'brigantine' sets a balanced lug foresail with a gaff and boom mainsail with a topsail above, in a hybrid but seamanlike rig. Early twentieth century.

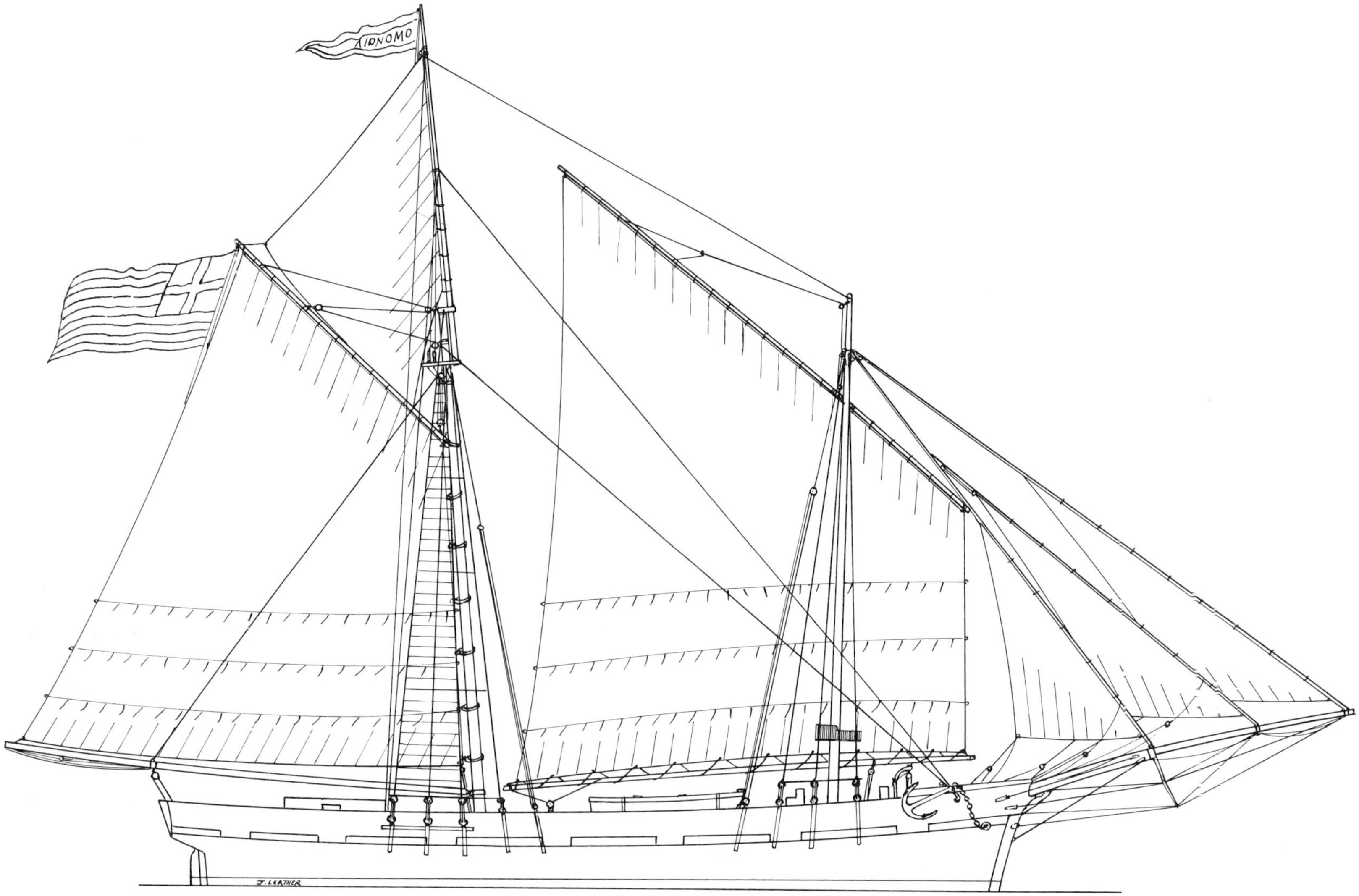

pine on sawn oak frames. The type developed from smaller sloop- and cutter-rigged skiffs to set a spritsail main, a mizzen sheeted to a short bumkin, a fore staysail, and a jib on an unstayed bowsprit. The mainmast was stout and had only one shroud on each side and no running backstays. Three sheaves at the masthead carried the mainsail halyard, sprit lift and the staysail halyard. The mainsail was set by hauling out the head to the sprit end; it could be brailed to the mast for stowing and had four rows of reef points. The sheet worked on a horse. An unusual topsail was set above the mainsail on a long yard reminiscent of a gunter sail, working on irons on the mainmast. The mizzen was unstayed and the masthead had two sheaves for the mizzen halyard and the topsail. Dimensions varied from about 28ft × 16ft × 3ft 6in to 4ft 6in draught up to 35ft × 17ft × 5ft draught. One of the most unusual spritsail-rigged boats was contrived by Archer Brading of Cowes who, in 1922 converted a float from the seaplanes built there by Whites during the 1914–18 war, to a sailing boat. Of superb wooden construction, the float was 22ft long × 3ft beam × 1ft depth and had two 'steps' across the bottom to promote lift. A 4ft × 2ft daggerboard was fitted and a rig of boomed spritsail and foresail stepped. Three people could be carried in a cockpit cut into the upper surface. She could stand rough weather and almost planed off the wind.

The three masted spritsail rig was still being used in 1910 by newly launched smakkejolle boats from the small island of Arø in the Little Belt, Denmark. These slack bilged, long keeled, open

boats were clinker planked on sawn frames and had typical dimensions of 20ft × 6ft 10in. The Danish spritsail tends to be rectangular in shape and set up with a simple snotter and luff lacing which allowed considerable drift from the mast. The mainsail and mizzen were often larger than in similar British craft. The foremast and main masts were clamped to thwarts, with the mizzen stepped through the stern bench. The foresail sheet worked on an iron horse across the amidship thwart and a jib was set on an unstayed running bowsprit. A wet well was built into the bottom abaft the mainmast thwart with a trunk brought up to thwart height. Three thole pin positions were fitted on each side for rowing in calms or when fishing. The hull form, wet well and rig make interesting comparison with the similarly shaped Doble of the Medway (Chapter 10).

The many two masted sprit-rigged Smakkejolle were similar, the mainsail being larger than the foresail by about twenty-five per cent. Masts and sails could be struck or shifted to different steps to suit increase in wind strength and these craft were a common type in the Danish sounds and bays. A typical boat from Halmø would be 16ft long × 5ft beam and 1ft 3in draught. None of these boats appears to have used a centreboard and could not have sailed well to windward. However, the three masted spritsail or lugsail rig for an open boat was more practical than many people now realise. In light winds all three masts could be stepped and maximum sail area set. In stronger winds or when working particular fishing gear or for other work, the mainmast was unstepped and could be stowed in the boat or left ashore, reducing sail area and allowing easier handling of the foresail and mizzen. For very strong winds the foresail might be taken in and the mizzen set in its place, or in a small boat the mizzen and its mast might be shifted to the mainmast step. Such flexibility was useful in boats used for pilot or waterman's work, or for line or drift net fishing, when it might be necessary to row for some time or lower sails, spars and masts quickly in order to ride easily at sea.

Lugsails almost disappeared from all except eastern working craft by the 1950s and had declined considerably in pleasure boats. Spritsails were retained in the east but were an anachronism in western working or pleasure craft, except for the English sailing barges. Now there is a resurgence of enthusiasm for building and restoring small craft of traditional form, construction and rig, particularly small, often open, boats which can be sailed or rowed when weather or fancy dictates. Because spritsail- and lug-rigged boats tend to be smaller than most types of working craft usually available for restoration, it is a much more reasonable proposition for a man to undertake on his own the restoration or construction, maintenance and sailing of such a craft. Detailed plans are available of traditional craft or new designs derived from them and there is the interest of choice of a type suited to local waters or of following well proven local craft and the research on its evolution and use. For many there is the fun, interest and occasional frustration of building their own boat and the joy of use of a characterful craft which will be long lived and demand little in time or money for maintenance, giving all the pleasure of yachting without all the expense. The simplicity of the spritsail or lugsail rig is functionally correct for these craft, as quick to rig or unrig when the boat has to be frequently launched or hauled up, or change from oars to sails, or vice versa. For similar reasons it was used when men worked for a living under sail and oar.

There is wide variety for differing waters, each of which at one time had its own local type. The huge Norfolk and Suffolk beach yawls will never again be built, but a 16–18ft lug-rigged beach punt is within reach of most enthusiasts, and replicas of the little pointed stern peter boats and dobles of the Thames and Medway make attractive rowing and sailing boats. In recent times there has been a revival of having small rowing and sailing cobles built for pleasure use and one, John Seymour's *Willmilly*, voyaged across the North Sea to Europe and the Baltic with a crew of two. A Maine man might choose a traditional rowing and sailing wherry, or a peapod; a Massachusetts enthusiast might try building a Plymouth lobster boat or one of the spritsail-rigged double enders. Further south a New Jersey beach skiff, Carolina Sound skiff or a sneak box would give rowing and sailing with traditional simplicity.

Pride of ownership of a now unusual craft gives pleasure to many and, for the ego, such boats attract the type of admiration usually reserved for steam traction engines or vintage cars. A well built, light sailing and rowing boat from ten to sixteen feet long is most generally useful of all, providing she is well designed and sets her sails

Plate 3: A variety of rigs is set by sailing canoes. The canoe in foreground sets two 'batswing' sails, a variation of the gunter lug. The other has two boomed lateen sails, which can be set on short masts.
Phot — Lingard Associates.

smartly, perhaps using a standing lugsail. Many thousands of pleasure sailors have learned to sail in such craft and a day's sail in one is always a delight from the versatility of the type which can, if necessary, also carry a small outboard motor for use in calms.

The author and his son, David Leather, have designed several. The 17ft 3in long 5ft 6in beam 7in (3ft plate down) draught, centreboard sailing and rowing boat *Bluenose,* is capable of being built at home with simple tools and is rigged with one or two spritsails, lug, or leg of mutton (bermudian) sails, stepped in a variety of positions to suit use, locality and the owner's fancy. She rows with one or two pairs of oars, will sail well to windward, can be handled by one man or carry six in comfort, is a seaboat but can wriggle up creeks and shallow gunkholes, makes a useful camping boat and can be kept ashore on a launching trolley when not in use or can be trailed behind a car.

Philip Bolger is a most versatile American designer of yachts and small craft, and has produced many boats rigged with spritsails ranging from the ingenious Thomaston Galley to thirty foot three-masters. One of these is *Rondo II* shown in **Plate 4**, slipping along by a typical Maine shore of granite and pine trees. The long, flat bottomed hull has relatively small beam and displacement to enable her to be driven by 445 square feet of sail; a rig easily handled and without any wire rope rigging, blocks, winches or special timber for masts and spars. The spritsails have sprit-booms angled down to set flat. The schooner can be handled by one with certainty

Figure 10. The 17ft 3in sailing and rowing boat *Bluenose*, designed by John and David Leather, can be rigged with spritsails, lugs or leg of mutton (Bermudian) sails and rows with one or two pairs of oars.

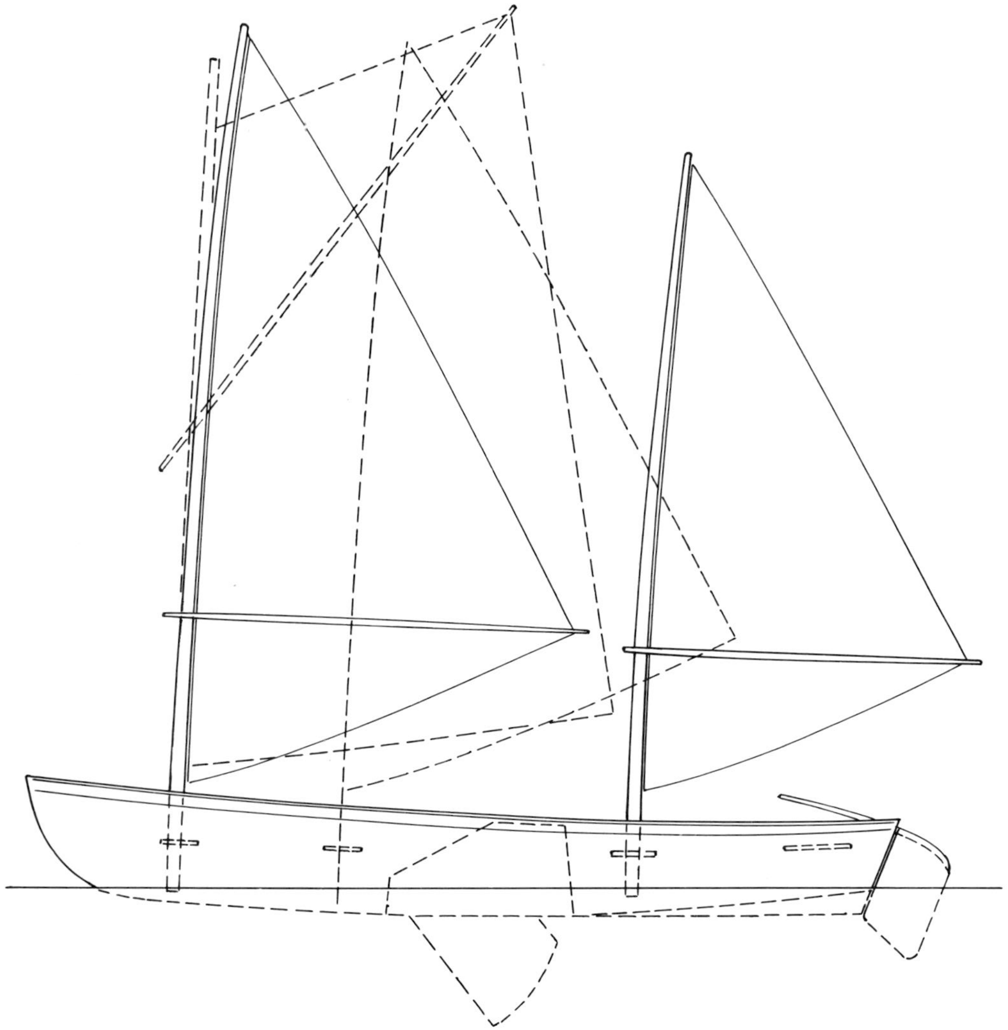

Plate 4. The 39ft 6in three masted spritsail schooner *Rondo II* slips by a Maine shoreline. This shallow draught sharpie was designed by Phil Bolger as an inexpensive cruiser.

R. D. Culler is another American producing spritsail boats, basing his designs on traditional forms. His Swampscott type, round sided dory *Dancing Feather* is a delightful craft, tender under sail but fast and interesting to handle, besides rowing well, capable of five different combinations of rig with three sails; of being launched or recovered on a trolley, of being trailed behind a car; a most characterful and versatile boat. It is good to build and own craft of varied rig and type, if only as antidote to the all prevailing efficiency of the triangular bermudian sails and particularly the predominance of bermudian sloops or ketches in yacht rigs.

Spritsail or lugsail rigs may not be as efficient, sometimes, for windward work but in small craft they offer more fun at minimum expense, as masts, spars and possibly sails can be made by the owner. A skilled sailmaker will make a splendidly setting spritsail or lug, but a careful amateur can make a useful sail for these rigs which he would not do as well for a gaff or bermudian sail. As with all rigs, the masts and spars must be as light as possible, consistent with necessary strength for the strongest wind likely to be encountered in use. There are no rules or even general rule of thumb guides for the sizes of spars for these rigs, which were evolved over many years in many localities, each having its own traditions of scantlings and methods of rigging. Now, if desired, spritsails and lugsails can be much more efficient with use of modern sailcloths and spar materials combining lightness with strength.

Plate 5. R. D. Culler's sailing and rowing Swampscott-style dory *Dancing Feather* shows her spritsail rig at Hyannis, Massachusetts. She can set seven variations of rig. *Photo – R. D. Culler.*

and without the liveliness usual in most sharpies. She is relaxing rather than exciting when sailing to windward, when she should be kept full because of the small lateral plane. The plywood planked hull has two bilge boards amidships and provides a cabin 18ft long with 3ft 2in headroom and a cockpit 10ft long which can be covered by a night tent for full headroom. Altogether this schooner displays versatile and interesting use of modern materials with well tried traditional features.

Part I

The Rigs

1

Spritsails

Spritsails are useful for small craft where a rig is needed which can be readily struck for rowing or hauling up. The rig became unfashionable, except in the 80ft sailing barges of the east coast of England, until a revival of its use in Britain and the U.S.A. during the late 1960s, which has again brought this handy rig back in traditional small boats and new craft evolved from these, using contemporary materials to advantage. The spritsail's greatest efficiency is in simplicity of gear and hence low cost, and its ability to stow mast, spars and sail in the boat, out of the way of other activities. It is an easy sail to handle, after a little practice, and will drive a well shaped craft without pressing her in the way a boomed sail can do.

The parts and arrangement of a typical spritsail are shown in Fig. 11. The sprit for a small boat should not exceed the length of the mast. Good proportions of a spritsail for small boats (where length of mast = L) are: luff of sail 0.75–0.66L; foot of sail 0.6L; head of sail 0.4L. The head of a spritsail should be perpendicular to a line from throat to clew. These proportions are general and may vary according to the cut of sail, owner's fancy and local custom.

Cutting well setting spritsails is a reviving art amongst some sailmakers and owners of small craft. Most prefer cotton canvas for spritsails as this seems to set better than polyester in rectangularly shaped sails. The cloths should be narrow and vertical, with seams parallel to the leach. There should be an aerofoil style curve of fullness in the luff and foot to get the best drive from the sail. The sailmaker will have his own feel for the shape, particularly if he has made several spritsails. A spritsail is best roped on the head, luff and foot, with the usual rat tail tapers at clew and peak, formed into beckets for the sprit and sheet. These beckets must be served or covered with leather against chafe. There is art in getting the leach of a spritsail to stand well without curling. Battens are not used in this rig, though there is no reason why they should not be except they are a complication when stowing the sail. The arrangement and proportions of the rig are best illustrated by examining the spritsail for an open rowing and sailing boat 14ft long, which could carry about 90 square feet. The mast could be 13ft 6in and the sprit 13ft.

Both will stow longitudinally between stem and

Figure 11. Arrangement of a typical boomless spritsail for a small craft. Showing sprit-end finishes for peak and snotter, and throat brail to furl sail; convenient for getting under way or bringing up.

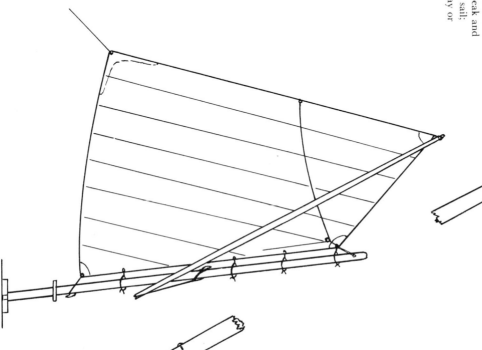

transom. The mast may be fir, pine, spruce, cedar, pitch pine (heavy but very durable) or whatever straight-grained, supple timber is available. Often a knotty pole will have to do if well shaped and treated with a mixture of linseed oil and paraffin, in the ratio of 1:2 these are efficient and can later be cleaned up and varnished.

A spar with many small knots is probably very supple and will not 'spring' or split, providing it is made from a straight-grown young tree. Alternatively a mast may be 'built' by glueing together smaller pieces of good timber; spruce or pine preferred. The 13ft 6in long mast might best be made 3 inches diameter at the heel and at the thwart or deck supporting it, with this diameter reduced to perhaps $2\frac{3}{4}$ inch, two-thirds the distance between the heel of the sprit when the sail is fully set, then tapering at the head to about two inches diameter for the last third.

The sprit for the 14ft boat is round in section to avoid chafing mast and sail. It should be about $1\frac{1}{2}$ inches diameter at centre, tapered to 1 inch diameter at the ends. The head of the sprit is shouldered down to about $\frac{5}{8}$ inch diameter to fit into the rope becket at the peak of the sail. The heel has a well shaped score or shaped hole, to receive the rope snotter which slings it from the mast, and a copper clench must be fitted below this to prevent splitting. Large sprits have a metal band around the heel for this reason, and to shackle a standing lift to support the weight in the largest rigs.

The hole in the mast thwart should not fit tightly around the mast, which should have a chafing piece of greased leather seized or sewn around it to allow the mast to rotate in the step, which is desirable with small spritsails. As with oars, the leather should not be tacked on as it can cause fracture of the mast. Two, simple wooden thumb cleats are screwed to the mast. The tack of the sail is secured to one by a becket to stop it riding up the mast (A) and the other can be fitted to prevent the rope snotter from sliding down the mast (B) though traditional rigging expects the snotter to hold without this. Whichever way it is rigged a snotter must always hold the sprit heel up in the desired position or the sprit will droop and the sail becomes inefficient, with a slack luff and baggy set. An efficient type of snotter for small boats is shown in Fig. 12. This is a long spliced eye with sufficient length to pass around the mast at the desired position and allow the thimble of brass or hardwood (oak, teak, beech or locust) to hang two inches or so beyond the tack. The thimble should be belled over or carved to fit over the splice and be very strongly seized immediately above it. Only well stretched, natural fibre rope such as manilla or Italian hemp should be used for a snotter, or pre-stretched ulstron or similar fibrous synthetic rope which will grip the mast. The snotter must be strong as if it carries away the sprit will probably plunge forcefully down and may hole the bottom of the boat.

The sprit is set up by passing the tail of the snotter through the score in the sprit heel and then through the thimble, forming a purchase which is swigged-up until wrinkles are thrown in the sail from tack to peak, as in setting a gaff sail. Take a second or third turn in the sprit score and

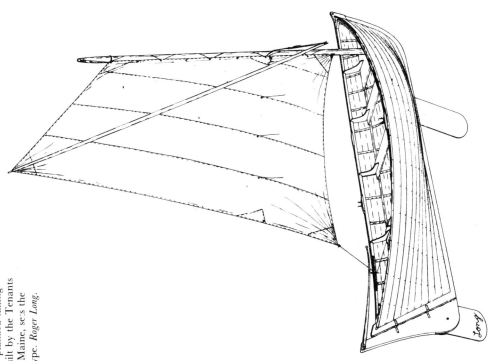

Plate 6. The 13ft cedar planked sailing and rowing peapod built by the Tenants Harbour Boat Works, Maine, sets the single spritsail of the type. *Roger Long.*

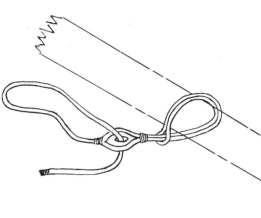

Figure 12. An efficient type of snotter for small boats.

double the slack behind the now taught snotter. Then a pull on the tail will free the snotter quickly, even under strain. The spritsail luff is kept to the mast by a lacing or by the more traditional robands (Fig. 13). The tack lashing must be taut to keep the luff close to the mast but the throat lashing may be slack when seized-on to allow the throat of the sail to align itself to the mast, with the pull of the tack lashing and thrust of the sprit pulling it aft. The robands are passed through the eyelets in the sail luff. Braided line is best for these and the ends must be sufficiently long to embrace the mast and be tied on its fore side with a square knot, alternatively the robands can be middled up and seized with twine. If laid line is used the seizing may be omitted and the robands are middled before one end is tucked through the strands, is drawn taut, and is tied with a square knot on the fore side of the mast. The luff of a well setting spritsail can stand well away from the mast and is then less affected by turbulence from it. The sails of Dutch craft which are traditionally laced to the masts, are good examples of the efficiency of this arrangement.

As a sprit may unship from the peak becket when it or the sail is being adjusted or handled, a light lashing is best passed through the eye of the becket and through a small hole bored through the head of the sprit, below the shoulder, and is set up as a preventer. This should be set up sufficiently tight with a square knot to prevent unshipping but not to distort the set of the head of the sail.

A boomless sail has the advantage of being able to be brailed to temporarily reduce area, for

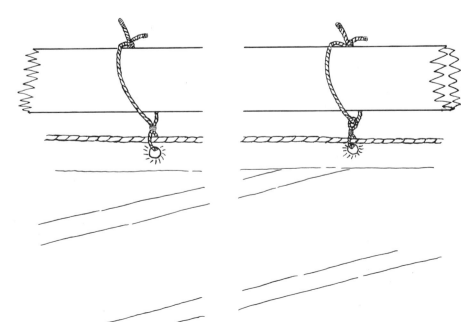

Figure 13. Robands are the traditional attachment of a spritsail luff to the mast. Upper: Roband passed through eye spliced through luff cringle. Lower: Roband passed through luff cringle and seized beyond luff rope. Ends tied around mast.

instance during a squall or when bringing up, beaching, and sometimes when getting underway. A brail for a small spritsail can be rigged with a slippery, light rope; about 1⅛in circumference or 3/16in diameter dacron or terylene is best. The rope is spliced to the throat cringle at one side of the spritsail and is carried out to the leach and through a brass or plastic thimble seized to the leach as a reinforcement. The thimble is positioned by striking an arc from the throat, with the sail peak as radius. Where this meets the leach is the best position. The brail is then brought forward on the other side of the sail to a thimble seized to the throat, through another lead thimble halfway down the luff, to avoid the slack of the brail fouling the sprit, through another thimble at the tack and then to a cleat in reach of the helmsman, perhaps on the side of the centreboard case. When not in use the brail is left slack so it will not spoil the set of the sail.

The spritsail, mast, sprit and rigging is best first tried laid out on the ground. The clew should be high and the tack low. Spritsail masts should have good rake as this seems to help the sails set well and usually improves the appearance of the rig in a small boat. Many small spritsail boats had adjustable rake on at least the mainmast.

The thumb cleat for the tack might be fitted just above the upper mast support, as low as possible, to allow adjustment of the tack position. The thumb cleat for the snotter is best positioned on the ground with the sprit 'peaked-up' at its correct angle to set the sail. This cleat should be as low as possible. The robands should be tied to the mast, not too tightly.

Plate 7. Dutch, spritsail-rigged fishing *hoogaars* from Arnemuiden set the mainsail luff well clear of the mast and in light winds also carried a bezaan (a mizzen improvised from the peak of the sprit).

49

When everything seems satisfactory on the ground, the sail can be furled for carrying or stowage by taking the sprit out of the snotter, placing it parallel to the mast and, keeping the head of the sail taut, throw the clew over the sprit, then roll the sail and sprit up to the mast, maintaining an upward pressure on the peak so it will furl tightly. The loose snotter is passed around the sail and mast and then a clove hitch is passed around all. The sheet is coiled and made fast to the tail of the snotter. The rig is then ready to be carried, stepped or stored.

With the mast stepped the sail is unfurled and set, to be checked and adjusted. In boats of reasonable beam the sheet is best led to the inside of the lee sheer and its longitudinal position is determined by trial. The sheeting of loose footed sails is critical and several vertical pins on the gunwale may be desirable so that varying positions can be tried and used, as even well used sails can vary in set, depending on wind strength, the course sailed and weather conditions. A spritsail can be sheeted in hard in smooth water but will not stand well in a seaway unless the sheet is slacked a little. A boomless sail tends to make a boat roll considerably in a fresh following wind and this is exaggerated with the sprits' movements. A spritsail can be a flat setting and powerful sail, but if it is too big for one man to handle with ease it ceases to be efficient in a small boat, and the craft would be better rigged with two or even three spritsails of more manageable area, or a gaff or bermudian rig.

A long narrow boat will probably be best with a rig of two or more spritsails. It is usually best to make these sails of different areas, with the larger as the foresail and the smaller the mizzen in a two masted rig; or the mainsail larger than the foresail, and the mizzen smallest in a three masted rig. If two masted, the full rig can be carried in light winds and in stronger breezes the foresail can be reefed. If the wind strengthens, the mizzen might be furled and unstepped and the foresail be shifted slightly aft in a second step, to preserve sail balance. This step can usefully give increased rake to the mast. In strong winds the mizzen, only, could be set up, probably in the same step and well raked. This reduction of sail area and a freshening wind will usually require the centreboard to be lowered further. In the now uncommon three masted rig the mainmast and sail is the first to be furled or struck, leaving the fore and mizzen as a useful area for stronger winds. If wind strength increases these are reefed or shifted for the two sail rig.

The foresail should have a two part sheet. It is desirable to lead the falls through a fairlead at the sheer before slipping it under the pin, to control it in stays. To take in the foresail the sheet is slackened, the helm is put down and the boat comes into the wind. The sail is rolled around the sprit and a turn is taken around all with the sheet. If a spritsail is to be reefed, as most foresails and mainsails are, but not mizzens, the reef pendant and tack pendant should be always rigged and the sail needs a halyard and a second, lower position for the sprit snotter and an additional thumb cleat, which should be positioned by trial so the foot of the reefed spritsail clears the sheer.

51

Plate 8. Peter Van Dine's 21ft 2in plastic-hulled replica Crotch Island Pinky slips along under Dacron spritsails set on spruce spars. A dayboat developed from a type of Maine fishing craft. *Photo – Peter Van Dine.*

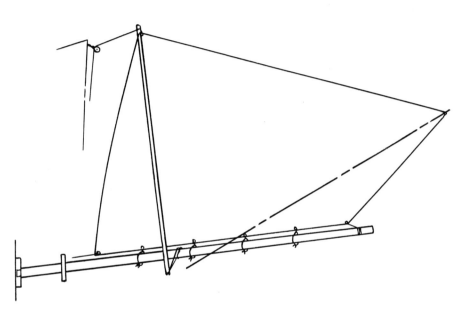

Figure 14. A spritsail with a boom to aid correct sheeting. This is set taut with a rope snotter around the mast.

The spritsail halyard may be arranged so that the fall is made fast to the throat, in the manner of sensible staysail halyards in a cutter or sloop, as the fall then cannot fly adrift and it will act as a downhaul for the spritsail.

Small boat spritsails are not easy to reef when set, as the sprit tends to swing about in a seaway. To reduce sail area in a severe squall quickly, the sprit can be unshipped from the snotter and from the peak, allowing the peak and upper leach of the sail to blow away to leeward while the triangle from the masthead to the sheet and down the luff remains partially effective, with no need to trim the sheet. However, this usually so reduces the sails efficiency that the boat may become unmanageable.

A sizeable sprit rig is not ideal for single-handed sailing, as to go forward and unship the sprit from the snotter by hand is not easy if the sprit is to leeward of the sail, and it may be difficult if it is to windward, as once the heel is out of the snotter it tends to drive down and could pierce the bottom of the boat in extreme conditions, when it is best to direct the heel overboard.

A spritsail mizzen may need a boom to set it well as the mizzen sheet will probably at least be above the stern, if not aft of it. Sometimes it is possible to lead the mizzen sheet through an eye on the rudder head, and then inboard to belay, perhaps to a cleat on the tiller, for quick release. The mizzen boom is best rigged with a rope snotter at its forward end, setting it taut from the mizzen mast (Fig. 14). The snotter should be rigged slightly above a level line from the mizzen clew. The postion is best found by experiment so that the sail sets without twist or tendency for the boom to rise. The mizzen should set flatter than the foresail and this is possible with two sprits and snotters to trim it. Alternatively a triangular or 'jib-headed' mizzen can be set, with a boom rigged to a snotter, as described, but this requires a taller mast for an equivalent area of spritsail. To take in a jib-headed mizzen, the snotter is released, the boom up-ended and the sail rolled towards the mast around the boom: a turn taken around with the sheet secures it.

When beaching a spritsail boat in a light onshore wind the sails can be allowed to rotate to blow out forward; this is possible with the rotary masts but undesirable in other conditions as retrieving the sheets and retrimming the sails would be difficult afloat. Alternatively, in a two masted spritsail boat, the mizzen is handed and the foresail is brailed up as she runs for the shore.

A useful alternative form of spritsail for a small boat can be rigged as Fig. 15. The snotter needs careful rigging: if the usual 'lark's head' becket is of natural rope it tends to slip unless constantly wetted, and needs some strength to heave it up at intervals to maintain peak in the sail when slipping occurs. In this rigging arrangement the snotter is led through a hole in the mast, then to a cleat for adjustment. The end of the snotter has a knot and is of sufficient length that if the sprit tended to carry away suddenly the knot would stop at the hole and the heel of the sprit would stop above the floorboards. A halyard is unnecessary. When stowing, the snotter is slipped, the sail is bundled round the mast and sprit and the whole rig is lifted out and stows inboard in

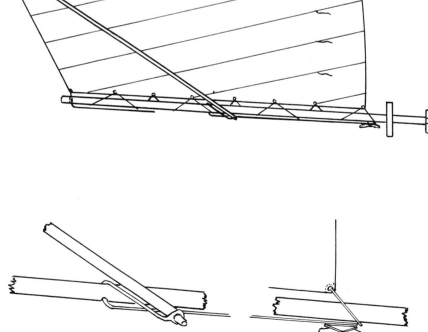

Figure 15. An alternative arrangement of spritsail for a small craft with the snotter led through a hole in the mast. Note sprit carried well up sail luff and rope becket at peak, which passes over the sprit end.

five seconds. The hole through the mast is a weakness at a point of considerable load from the sprit but this is not serious in rigs for boats up to about sixteen feet. If this arrangement is used for a sail suitable for an eighteen- or twenty-foot boat with a halyard an alternative method of striking sail is to put her head to wind, let go the sheet, release the snotter and the halyard, so the sprit and sail fall into the boat. Such a rig can set quite flat and will perform well to windward, besides standing up well in strong winds. The boomless foot is an advantage in a small boat and a well cut spritsail will stand so flat that it will not touch the sprit when the sprit is to leeward. The type of short sprit carried high up the mast may have been a stage on the evolution of the gaff sail.

A sprit for a mainsail up to about 150 square feet area can be made in two pieces joined by a metal socket for convenience in stowing within the boat when the spritsail is not in use. The socket should be a very close, tight fit on the lower part of the sprit but should not be driven on it against a shouldered down reduction in diameter of the wooden sprit as the sharp corner of the shoulder could start a split which might be disastrous in a strong wind.

In the eastern Mediterranean Greek and Turkish small craft used the spritsail for centuries with the head of the sail running on a rope or wire rope stay from the masthead to the end of the sprit, and brailing to the mast for stowing. In Greek practice the rig was called sacoleva and the mast was stepped about a third of the length from the bow and was short and steeved forward considerably, possibly a survival from the lateen

rig. It was supported by two or more shrouds on each side and by twin forestays to the stemhead, set up with lanyards. The sprit was light and long, held to the mast by a rope snotter with its heel partially supported by the luff rope of the spritsail, which was not usually laced to the mast. In some craft the sprit passed between the sail and the mast. The head of the sail was connected to the stay between the masthead and the end of the sprit by iron hanks and the foot and leach had considerable curvature. The sprit was controlled by two vangs consisting of single block purchases leading to each quarter. It was a flat setting and powerful sail of rakish appearance. A mast hoop was fitted below the throat to spread the strain from the sprit tensioning the headrope of the sail. A light topmast was usually set above the masthead.

The rig was balanced by a long-footed jib set on a running bowsprit without bobstay or shrouds, and some craft also set a lateen mizzen sheeted to an outrigger. A single part brail led from the throat across the spritsail to a cringle about an eighth of the length of the leach above the clew, to gather it in and upwards when the head outhaul was slacked and the sail furled to the mast.

The boats were between thirty-five and fifty feet long and had a pointed stern, long straight keel, well rounded and raking stem and fine sections; a potentially seaworthy and fast sailing hull form. Planking was carvel on sawn frames of Greek 'sea pine'. The flush deck had a small hatch to the fo'c'sle where the crew slept, a steering cockpit aft and a large hold amidships, usually with narrow side decks but sometimes

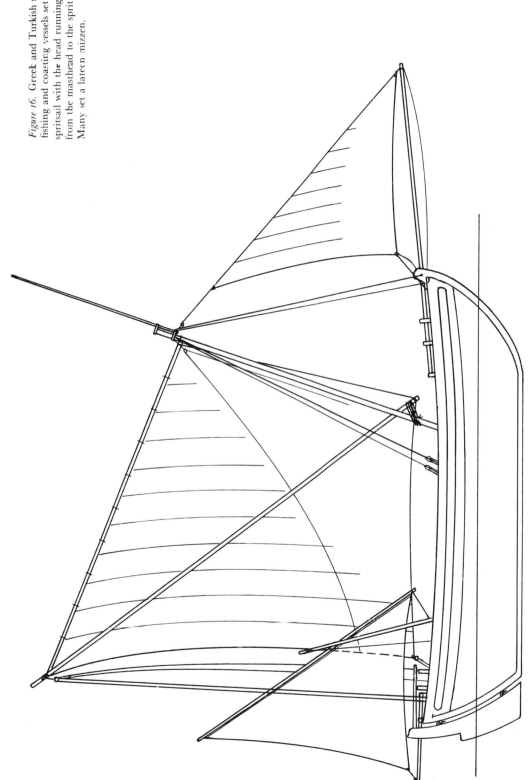

Figure 16. Greek and Turkish small fishing and coasting vessels set a brailing spritsail with the head running on a stay from the masthead to the sprit end. Many set a lateen mizzen.

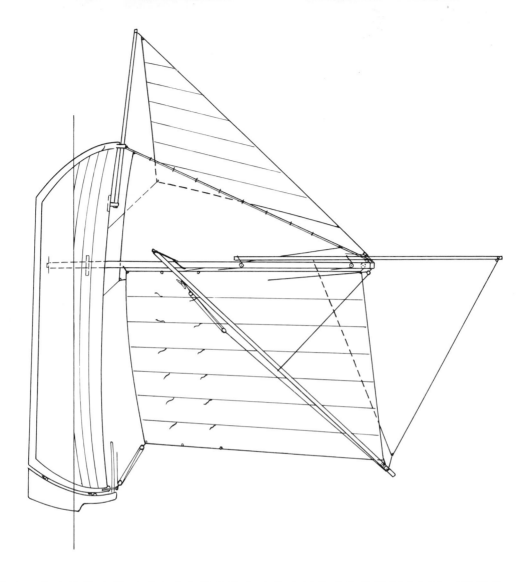

Figure 17. Swedish spritsail-rigged *almogjolle* or Danish *kaperboat* with the topsail yard set lashed to the mast or hoisted on two halyards after the spritsail has been set.

56

open to the sheer. These *trackonderi* or *trehendire* fished and coasted with general cargoes, as did the similar, pointed sterned, *tchektima* of the Turkish coast which had short forward and after decks and an open hold amidships protected by high wash strakes or bulwarks. The almost vertical mast was stepped about a third of the length from the bow and set a sprit mainsail similar to the Greek craft, a foresail on a stay to the stemhead, a jib on a bowsprit, often an outer jib on a jib boom; both hanked to stays. A topmast was rigged through a single cap iron at the masthead and although the topmast head was little higher than the head of the sprit, the heel was brought down and secured to the deck, or, alternatively, the heel was tapered and made fast to the lower part of the mast, above the deck; common methods of rigging a topmast in Turkish small craft. There were two yards crossed; for a course or squaresail and a square topsail. Braces for the yards of the squaresail led forward, close to the stemhead, and those for the topsail yard to the end of the sprit. The squaresail and topsail were furled on the yards by a man aloft. The spritsail had an outhaul running through a block at the sprit end. The end of this was made fast to a block through which a whip purchase was rove, and led down to the mast under the sprit. The sprit was carried on the starboard side of the mast and its head was controlled by two vangs having a pendant ending in a tackle on each side.

These Aegean spritsail boats can be compared with the clinker planked, pointed stern spritsail sloops and cutters of Denmark and Sweden,

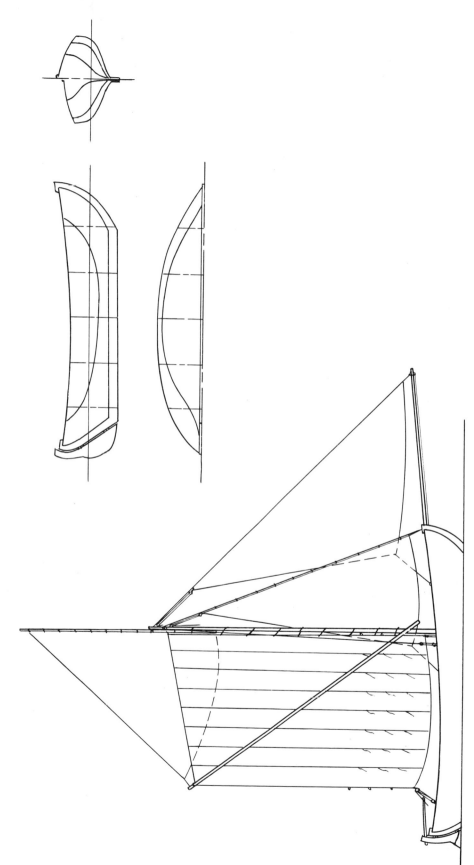

Figure 18. Spritsail-rigged Danish fishing boat of the Skovshoved herring fishery. Dimensions 24ft × 8ft 6in × 3ft draught. The hull form has the elemental characteristics of the Scandinavian sailing fishing/pilot boat types.

58

which often set a triangular topsail above the spritsail. Fig. 17 is a typical rig for a Swedish pleasure *almegjolle* with the luff of the triangular topsail set by a yard lashed to the mast after the spritsail is set and sheeted to the sprit end. These boats usually have a small foresail set to the stemhead, but some carry a jib on a bowsprit. The topsail is handed as the first reef. The mainsail usually has two rows of reef points and the foresail one.

In Denmark these are known as *kaperboats* from their use in the Sound between Denmark and Sweden by copers selling liquor and general goods to shipping in the days of sail. But they were also used by fishermen, pilots and smugglers. The Skovshoved herring fishery boats were typical of this type (Fig. 18): 24ft long, 8ft 6in beam, 3ft draught. The mast was stepped 9ft abaft the stem and stood 23ft above deck. The square headed sprit mainsail had a sprit 22ft long with its head slightly lower than the masthead. The foot of the sail was a little narrower than the head, making the leech stand vertically. The luff was laced to the mast, and the sail stood flat when going to windward. The topsail and jib were taken in when the wind increased and the mainsail and staysail had three rows of reef points. The spritsail was first hoisted up to the masthead sheave, then the head was stretched out to the peak by the outhaul. The luff lacing was tautened and the sheet tended. The sail had two brails and when brailing in the outhaul was slacked and the peak and head of the sail was snugged to the mast. These spritsails were not brailed to the sprit end, as on the British

sailing barges of the east coast and other craft.

In larger craft the sprit is left standing and the sail is brailed to the mast to reduce area, or when at anchor. It lacks the simplicity of the small boat sprit rig as the weight of the sprit has to be supported by a standing lift from the masthead to the heel, and sometimes to the middle of the sprit, as in Dutch craft.

The traditional Dutch arrangement of rigging a sprit are shown in Fig. 19. The heel was slung from the *hommer* (the hounds) at the head of the strongest part of the mast, by a tackle called the *staander* (later a chain was used), and was held to the mast by another tackle, the *talreep*, made fast to the *greelband* which encircled the mast and rested on a collar fitted around the mast.

At approximately mid-length, the sprit was suspended from the hounds by a tackle, the *trys*. A pair of vangs (*gaarden*) led from the head or *nok* of the sprit and were set up by tackles leading to each side of the deck. These controlled the sprit's athwartship movement, helping to flatten the sail in conjunction with the sheet, and also controlled it during raising and lowering.

At anchor or alongside, Dutch spritsail-rigged craft frequently lowered the sprit to a horizontal position or even with the head below the heel: See Fig. 19. This was known as *kaaien* (a term for which there is no English equivalent). First, the *voetreep* (footrope) was made fast to the sprit heel and set up to an after cleat or bitt. Then the *talreep* was cast off from the *greelband* and the foot tackle is slacked so the sprit, complete with the spritsail, swings heel forward (*kaas*) and eventually hangs

Plate 9. Spritsails at work. An early nineteenth-century Dutch warship, in camels to reduce draught, is towed over the bar at Pampus by two spritsail-rigged *water schepen* from Marken. *Drawing by I. Vos. Courtesy Maritime Museum 'Prins Hendrik', Rotterdam.*

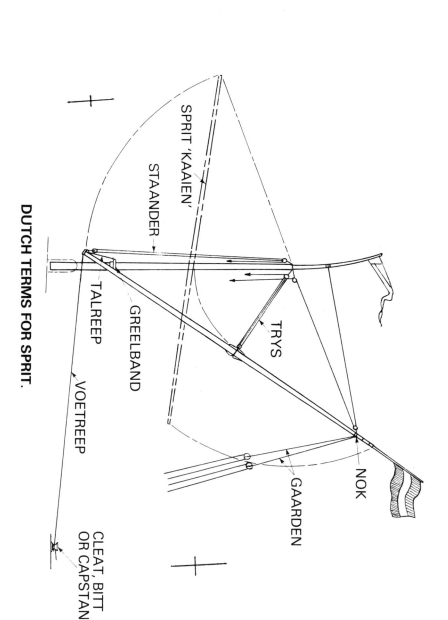

Figure 19. Traditional Dutch arrangements of rigging a sprit. Dotted lines show sprit lowered to horizontal, or *kaaien*.

DUTCH TERMS FOR SPRIT.

SPRIT 'KAAIEN'

STAANDER

TALREEP

GREELBAND

VOETREEP

TRYS

NOK

GAARDEN

CLEAT, BITT OR CAPSTAN

supported by the *trys* (sprit tackle). By hauling on the *gaarden*, the *nok* of the sprit could be held low, or down to the deck. Then the sail halyard was let go and the spritsail could be taken off or be stowed to the sprit with *beslagbanden* (sail tyers).

Usually the sprit and sail remained with head canted downward, known as *gekaaid-kaaied*. The sprit and mainsail were sent up in the reverse manner; many craft had a small capstan fitted near the helmsman to facilitate this. The spritsail

Figure 20. Divided spritsail rig with the 'mainsail' in two parts; the upper or 'topsail' and lower or 'after staysail'. An experimental rig of the 1930s.

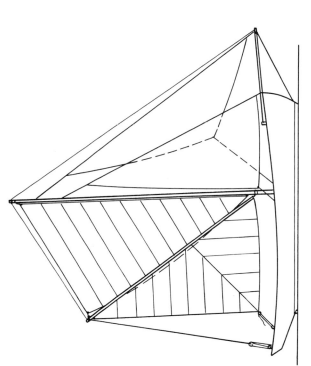

admits of few major variations but a divided spritsail rig was designed in 1935 by H. Banbury of Brentwood, Essex (Fig. 20). The 'mainsail' was in two triangular parts; the upper or 'topsail' and the lower, called the 'after staysail'. The topsail is held to the mast by slides on a track and hoists by a masthead halyard. The tack is shackled to an eye on the sprit, or is set up by a tackle to the deck. The topsail sheet and the halyard of the after staysail lead through cheek blocks at the head of the sprit and belay at its heel. The after staysail tack is made fast to an eye at the heel of the sprit and its clew is sheeted to a horse across the after deck.

The heel of the sprit pivots at the mast on a gooseneck, which is considered to relieve the usual downward thrust. A lift leads to the masthead and the sprit is controlled and steadied by vangs which are designed to relieve the strains usually restrained by the main shrouds; so runners are not fitted.

At anchor the sprit can be lowered and stowed on a gallows, projecting no further beyond the stern of an average yacht than an old-fashioned boom. In heavy weather the sprit might be able to be got down and stowed securely on the gallows, relieving top weight and windage, and a trysail can be set on the mast in the usual way. However, it is very unlikely the sprit could be lowered except in an anchorage.

This rig minimises twist, which impairs the efficiency of many sail plans and enables maximum drive to be devolped by the whole surface of the topsail and after staysail. When running, the sprit can be eased away by the weather vang and the topsail outhaul slacked away to throw fulness into the sail. The two parts of the mainsail are then adjusted to have a more lifting effect than is possible with most sail plans.

The divided spritsail sail plan can be arranged so the craft will balance under topsail and foresail, and under the after staysail and jib. Also with one reef in the after staysail and a small foresail, topsail and jib. A handy type of craft might also work under certain conditions with only the topsail set.

2

Lugsails

The principal types of lugsails used in Britain, northern Europe and in America are the dipping lug, set without a boom; the standing lug, set with or without a boom; the settee sail; the balance lug and the gunter lug. All have variations but the usual cut and arrangements are shown in Figs. 25, 29, 30, 36, 37, 41, 45.

The placing of masts in lugsail boats varies widely because of use, hull form, local conditions and prejudice. Many small luggers stepped the foremast in the eyes of the boat, setting a dipping lug foresail and a standing lug, spritsail or a triangular mizzen. These needed generous depth of hull and plenty of sheer forward (Plate 10). The Falmouth watermen's boats before about 1875, Channel Island boats and many French luggers such as those of Concarneau, were of this type, ranging in size from 14 to 40 feet long.

The masts and spars for any rig should be as short and light as possible consistent with strength and rigidity. As masts for lugsails generally do not have shrouds, the diameter needs to be greater than for a gaff or spritsail rig. The mast should be fixed against rotation with a squared shoulder, or

the halyard will lead unfairly into the sheave score at the masthead and may jamb if needed to be let go quickly. A sizeable mast which has to be raised and lowered fairly frequently at sea should have a tabernacle style step to receive the heel during the raising or lowering and is best clamped to a strong thwart or mast beam at sheer height (Fig. 21), in order to avoid having to lift the heel to sheer height before lowering it through a thwart hole and fitting it inside a step; something of a feat in a small boat dancing about on waves, and almost impossible for one man, besides risking splitting the thwart.

Efficient lugsails need a slightly longer mast than a comparable spritsail to set well and, if the mast is too long to stow in a small boat, it can be laid out over the bow when under oars, as was frequently done in many rowing and sailing small craft, or over the stern when moored. A lugsail needs a strong luff rope because peaking up the sail throws considerable strain on it and the luff must be set taut for efficient windward work. If the sail is laced to the boom a lighter spar can be used than if the foot were loose and the clew

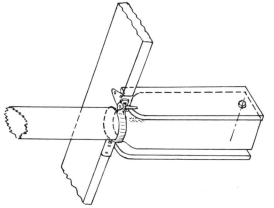

Figure 21. Mast tabernacle in an open boat. Squared mast heel secured with bolt and round part of mast clamped to thwart, with a pin for release.

Plate 10. A Penzance registered crabber beats into Newlyn, Cornwall, under dipping lug foresail and 'working' or standing lug mizzen sheeted to a typically long outrigger. *Photo – H. O. Hill.*

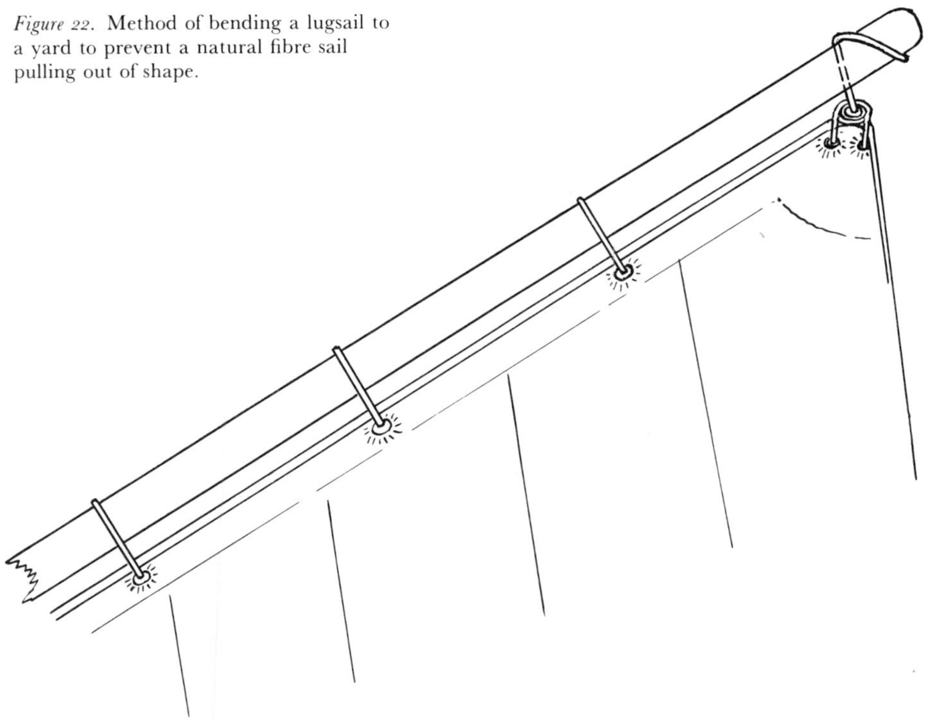

Figure 22. Method of bending a lugsail to a yard to prevent a natural fibre sail pulling out of shape.

synthetic cloth will not alter shape much but the stitching will take time to settle down, and these should be similarly treated for the first hour or two when new. Fig. 22 shows a single, simple practical method of bending a lugsail to a yard which will prevent a natural fibre sail pulling out of shape when wet, as it is only attached to the yard firmly at the peak and can be run off it easily if desired. Reefing should be avoided, if possible, until the sail has stretched and settled to shape. A lugsail can have many reefs and sometimes open boats at sea need them. Yorkshire cobles often had seven rows of reefs in one lugsail for bad weather and to control speed when working fishing gear in differing wind strengths. When bending a lugsail to a yard the throat cringle is first securely lashed to the lower end, then the head of the sail is stretched out firmly to the peak where the cringle is lashed to the outer end of the yard. The head is then bent to the yard, either marlin hitched with a continuous lacing (Fig. 23), or (particularly in larger sails) with individual robands (Fig. 13). If the sail has a boom it can be similarly attached. The yard may be served with small rope or be leathered where it crosses the mast when set, usually about one third of its length from the throat.

In British small boat practice the halyard may be made fast to the yard with a rolling hitch (Fig. 24) but many prefer a rope strop around the yard, to which the halyard is made fast. Larger British luggers used a two part halyard arrangement to ease handling, particularly for a dipping lug. The pendant or 'tye' was made fast around the yard, led through the masthead

spread with an outhaul to the boom end. However, booms laced to a sail foot were not liked on the lugsails of seaboats for various reasons, not least that if a boomed lug got overboard and filled with water it would be very dangerous in an open boat.

New lugsails cut from natural fibre canvas, now uncommon, should be bent slackly to the yard and boom and used gently until the sailcloth has stretched to its intended shape. Sails made from

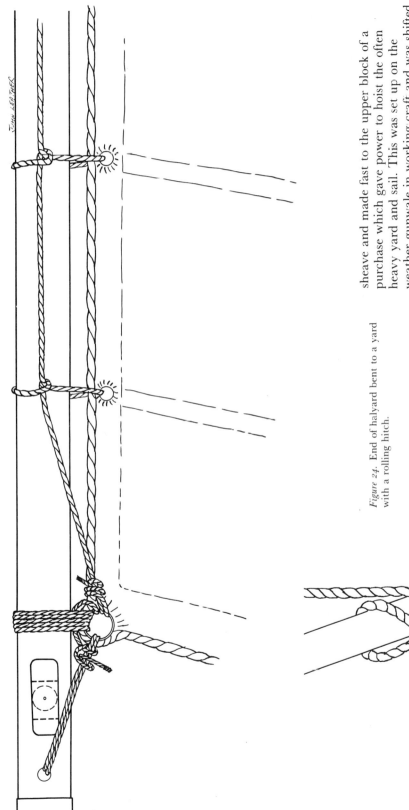

Figure 23. Marlin hitch lacing, bending sail to a yard.

Figure 24. End of halyard bent to a yard with a rolling hitch.

sheave and made fast to the upper block of a purchase which gave power to hoist the often heavy yard and sail. This was set up on the weather gunwale in working craft and was shifted to the new weather side at each tack. Some owners of small luggers use a form of becket and toggle on a lugsail yard to keep it close to the mast, the yard being well served in way of the chafe.

The simplest way to set a lugsail up to about 120 square feet area is by having a single part halyard made fast to the mast traveller and passing through a sheave or block at the masthead to belay by the heel of the mast, or at the weather gunwale in the case of a dipping lug. When the yard is hoisted to the desired height, the tack can be set taut with either a lanyard or a simple tackle. The yard of a lugsail can be peaked by setting up the halyard while the tack is held by a fixed lashing, a hook or a strop, but the leverage is inefficient. A tack tackle is not used by some small boat sailors to set lugsails but is desirable to achieve a smart set, particularly to peak a standing lug efficiently.

One downhaul arrangement for the tack of a loose-footed sail is to have a ring with a hook on it hooked into the tack cringle. A light strong rope is spliced around the mast, held against a thumb cleat, or is shackled to an eyebolt in the deck or a thwart. This passes up, through the ring and back through a small block or check sheave at the mast to be set up on a cleat. After the sail has been hoisted hand taut, this simple purchase is hauled to set the sail well. When a reef is taken, the hook is shifted up to the tack reef cringle, after the sail is lowered sufficiently for reefing.

The performance of lug-rigged craft varies considerably with choice of rig, hull form, quality and set of the sails, and not least the handling. Generally, lugsail boats must be sailed reasonably full in a seaway to keep good way on for luffing up when a big sea comes along, or to tack. Many experienced lugger sailors prefer a mizzen to a jib for help in staying round when tacking, the mizzen being sheeted in hard to assist in putting the boat's head to wind. But if she gets 'in irons', as a long keeled craft can in a seaway, a jib is useful to carry her bow through the wind to the new tack and can, if necessary, be held aback for

a few seconds to see her properly round. If she does get in irons the mizzen sheet should be let go, the helm reversed and the foot of the mainsail hauled to the side which will be the weather one when she fills on the new tack. Then, with stern way on, the boat's bow will tend to fall off so the sails can fill, and she will again make headway and be under control of the helm. Generally weight should be kept out of the bow when beating to windward or when running, as it increases weather helm and can make her plunge heavily in a seaway, though in some conditions a little weight will be beneficial forward to keep the forefoot immersed sufficiently to maintain balance and enable her to work to windward properly.

Dipping lug.

The dipping lug is a powerful sail which was much used in working craft in Britain and Europe, had one known example in America, but was used in various forms in many eastern working craft. It is a lifting sail, set with the luff well clear of the mast with its airflow eddies, and the head of the sail tends to lie fore and aft and does not sag far to leeward. It appears simple, needing only a mast, yard, halyard and sheet to set it, but it is more complex in use than a standing lugsail, much slower in stays, and can be dangerous when going about in strong winds and a sea. The proportions of luff, head, foot and leach vary with locality but Fig. 25 is a good example. The tack cringle is usually slipped over a hook at the stem head or is sometimes mounted on a short iron bumkin projecting from the stem. This is done before the sail is hoisted, to maintain control. For very small boats the halyard may be in one length. In larger boats and craft with area of an individual lug increasing to perhaps 1800 sq. ft. or more, as for instance in the Scottish herring drifters, a powerful purchase is needed and the halyard is made in two parts; the pendant or 'tye' which makes fast to the yard and leads up through a sheave at the masthead to make fast to a purchase with one or two blocks, the lower of which and the fall, being made fast to the weather side to act as a stay. The dipping lug was not usually fitted with a boom and needed a powerful sheet purchase to set reasonably flat. However, the sheet of a dipping lugsail should never be hauled in so the sail stands too flat or it will not go well to windward. These sails are sensitive to the trim of the sheet and it needs practice to get the best from them.

When going about from one tack to another the dipping lug has to be shifted, or 'dipped', from one side of the mast to the other while the craft is in stays. In this the rig is at its greatest disadvantage as, however smart the crew, the craft will be slow in stays compared to a standing lug, balance lug, gaff or bermudian sail which all swing over to the new tack unattended. Only the lateen rig is more cumbersome in small craft. Various methods of 'dipping' the lugsail were used in different localities. Perhaps the most common was to lower the sail into a quick, rough stow, unhitch the tack, carry the sail and yard around abaft the mast to lie fore and aft at the 'new' lee side of the mast, cast off the halyard or halyard purchase from the gunwale and shift it over to the 'new' weather side. Slip the tack

Figure 25. Typical dipping lugsail in an open working boat, showing halyard, sheet, and tack hooked to stem head.

Plate 11. The Cornish mackerel driver *Morning Star* was typical of the pointed stern luggers from St Ives. Built in 1880 she set a dipping lug foresail and a standing lug mizzen with a yard topsail above. *Photo – H. O. Hill.*

cringle over the hook, hoist away and see the sail goes up clear and taut at the luff before sheeting. Easy to write, difficult to do quickly in strong winds on a dark night. When making short tacks it is possible to sail one board with the yard to windward in fine weather, but to be safe it should

be shifted round the mast, as boats have been capsized in sudden puffs in this condition. It is undesirable to carry a dipping lug to windward of the mast in strong winds, even for short periods as it would be difficult to lower quickly, if necessary.

A craft rigged with a dipping lugsail is difficult

to sail single handed and, even when well manned, is inconvenient for tacking in confined waters. It also has the potential danger of being caught aback if the boat luffs into the wind's eye and the fore part of the sail between the tack and the mast is taken aback. This could capsize a small vessel, but the risk could be minimised by fitting the tack with a running downhaul instead of the hook commonly used in working boats. If the downhaul is led through a brass or nylon thimble or bullseye fair-lead in the bow of the boat and then aft to a cleat in reach of the helmsman, the tack can be quickly released and wind spilled from the sail. This accident befell one of the ferry boats which carried a large dipping lugsail working from Invergordon across the Cromarty Firth in Scotland, and afterwards the boats set a split lug with the sail divided into two, the luff of the after part being attached to the mast by hoops and the clew of the fore part having sheets like a jib. These craft were weatherly and reasonably fast in what was sometimes rough water, despite being often loaded with a horse and cart or a flock of sheep, besides passengers.

The mast of a dipping lugsail rig will stand without shrouds as the halyard is led to the weather gunwale about two feet abaft the mast, as all dipping lugs tend to pull the mast forward. A common arrangement of the staying and halyard for a large dipping lugsail in British fishing craft is shown in Fig. 26. The yard is hoisted by a 'tye' or halyard pendant which might be rope, chain or wire rope passing over a dumb half-sheave set in a score at the masthead or alternatively led through a block slung from the masthead. The other end of this pendant or tye was spliced or shackled to a double sheave upper block of a purchase leading through another double sheave block which was hooked to the weather gunwale or deck rail, the fall usually leading from the upper block to belay on the weather side, but sometimes from the lower block. In larger craft, such as fishing luggers, a burton was set up from the masthead to the weather rail. The yard was kept to the mast by a traveller of two iron half hoops joined by eyes so it would not jamb in hoisting or lowering. The tack cringle of the dipping lug was slipped over a curly hook on a short iron or steel bumkin outside the stem, or to a hook at the stem head.

When tacking, the sheet was unhooked from the sail as the helm was put down. As the lugger came head to wind the halyards were slacked and the leach of the lugsail was hauled down until the after end of the yard could be shifted round the fore side of the mast. This allowed the tack to remain hooked in and the forward part of the sail continued to act as a 'jib', assisting in paying the craft's head off. The sail was gathered in by the foot and leach and was passed round the fore side of the mast as quickly as possible. If the craft did not pay off quickly on the new tack the fore yard was kept in to the mast so only the fore part of the sail filled, and the mizzen sheet was let fly.

The only justification for continued use of the dipping lug in fishing and working craft into the early twentieth century was its lack of standing rigging, and the ability to be relatively easily stowed out of the way when fishing gear was being worked or the craft was under oars. For this reason it was particularly favoured in drift net fisheries, where most of the deck and one side of the craft needed to be clear of obstruction when hauling nets. The pointed sterned luggers designed, built and owned at the small fishing ports of the east coast of Scotland were amongst the most powerful lugsail craft and, although their evolution and use are not described in this book, it is interesting to appreciate their size and power of their rig. A typical 'Fife' type herring lugger built at Fraserburgh in 1905 was 70ft long overall, 60ft on the keel, with 21ft beam and 7ft depth. The foremast was 64ft long and 20in diameter at deck. The mizzen mast was 55ft long and 13½in diameter at deck. The running bowsprit was 54ft long and 13½in diameter at the gammon iron. The drifters used a tye of rope knotted to an iron traveller hooked to the yard about a third of its length from forward and led through a sheave about eighteen inches below the masthead to a double upper block of the halyard purchase which was rove through a single block at the gunwale, the fall being set down to tension it. When these luggers tacked, the dipping lug foresail was lowered to the deck, unhooked from the traveller, hooked on the burton stay, swung aft, then forward on the other side of the mast and rehooked to the travellers. Finally it was hoisted and the halyard and burton stay were set up to windward to support the mast.

When line fishing, many of these luggers carried a smaller, second fore-lug on the opposite side to the larger lug, to speed tacking, lowering one and setting the other at each tack. These

lugsails had reef cringles all the way up the luff and leach: sometimes twelve were fitted on a foresail. The Scotchmen did not shift the smaller mizzen forward to replace the forelug in strong winds, as did the west country drift fishermen. However, when well reefed the large lugs were heavy at the foot and did not set well. Fifies were bold, shapely and fast in their own waters and for their own work, but were not intended to make frequent tacks in close waters.

Reefing a dipping lug quickly when going to windward requires lowering the halyard so the reef cringle at the tack can be slipped over the hook forward, and the sheet can be hooked into the reef cringle in the leach. Then the sail is rehoisted and the reef points are tied in afterwards. If a smart setting sail is essential, the lugsail should be lowered and a reef be neatly taken in. When shaking out a reef, all reef points are untied before the tack or the halyard are released, to reduce time in resetting the sail. In a roomy boat it would be sensible to carry a large, light lugsail with no reefs for use in fine weather and make the working lug and its yard slightly smaller and stronger. It takes no longer to exchange them than to put in a reef and the spare yard and lug stowed on it will take up little space in the boat.

When dipping lug foresails are used with a jib, care is needed to ensure that the heel of the yard which projects beyond the mast, does not foul the leach of the jib. This may require the mast to be taller than desirable or the bowsprit to be longer than necessary for the length of foot of the jib.

The arrangement of rig of boats with dipping lugsails has been subject of argument for

71

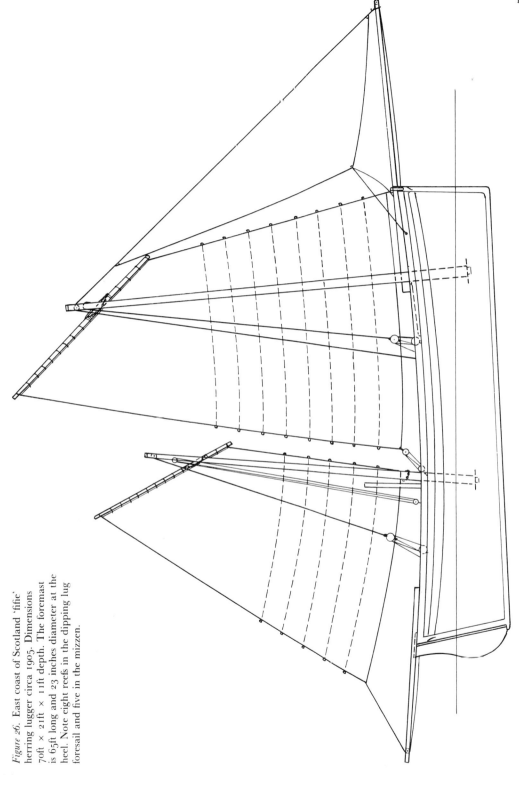

Figure 26. East coast of Scotland 'fifie' herring lugger circa 1905. Dimensions 70ft × 21ft × 11ft depth. The foremast is 65ft long and 23 inches diameter at the heel. Note eight reefs in the dipping lug foresail and five in the mizzen.

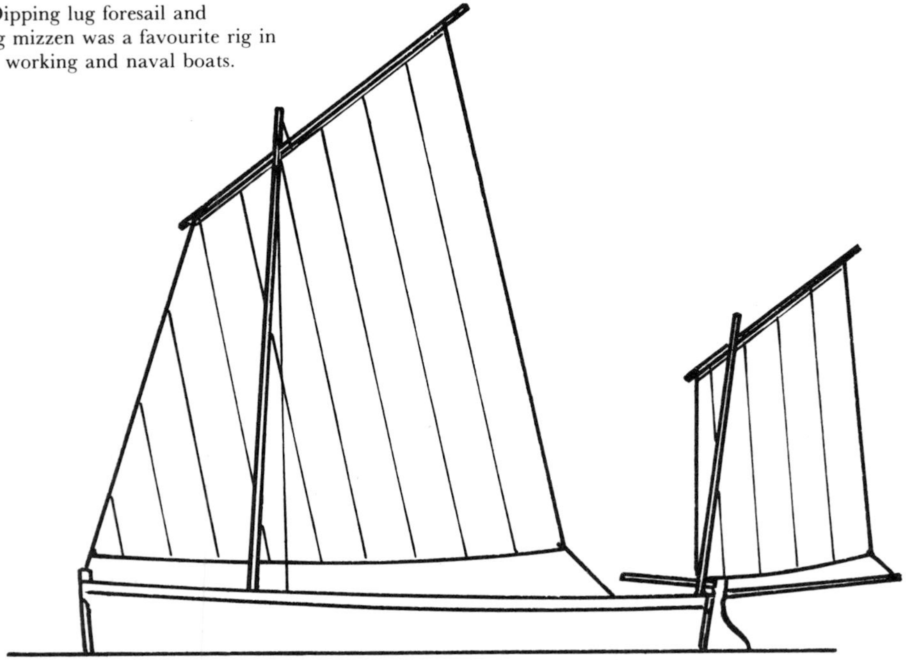

Figure 27. Dipping lug foresail and standing lug mizzen was a favourite rig in many small working and naval boats.

generations. Each locality had its favourite disposition and these could be summarised as a single dipping lug; a dipping lug with a jib set on a bowsprit; a dipping lug foresail and spritsail mizzen, with or without a jib; a dipping lug foresail and standing lug mizzen, with or without a jib (Fig. 27).

The long, narrow gigs used by pilots, beachmen, yachts and warships were often rigged with a single dipping lug of considerable area considering the boat's narrow beam for rowing of

5ft to 5ft 9in on a length of twenty or thirty feet. The mast was commonly stepped slightly forward of amidships, on the keelson or hog and clasped to a thwart so it could be got up or down quickly. The single mast and sail required minimal rigging and they stowed in the boat better than a two masted rig. Gigs sailed surprisingly well on the wind and their length, narrow beam and small displacement made them fast when reaching or running. With a dipping lugsail arranged as Fig. 28 for a 28ft gig, they will tack without a mizzen, which was commonly used in west country working gigs. Such a comparatively large sail of 200 square feet needs three or four deep reefs to reduce area drastically in strong winds. Tacking with a dipping lug having such a long yard in a narrow boat is best done by lowering the sail altogether and unhooking it from the traveller, then the mast is lifted out of its step, over the sail, and is re-stepped to windward of the sail, which is then hoisted on the new tack. A dipping lugsail of this type will need three tack hooks on each inside of the boat's bow, about six inches from each other, positioned to suit the cut of the sail; one for the whole sail and first reef, one for the second and third reefs and one for the fourth or close reef. These are necessary due to the sail's raking luff, which requires the tack to be brought further aft as the reefs are taken in, so the clew will not drop too low and result in a badly set sail. If a boat's lugsail is considered to set badly it is better to experiment with the rake and position of the mast, or the position of the tack or sheet hooks, before considering recutting the sail, as these adjustments will often cure the trouble.

Plate 12. The lug-rigged Lowestoft Volunteer Lifeboat *Caroline Hamilton* ready for her christening in the mid-nineteenth century. The leads of gear for the dipping lug foresail and standing lug mizzen can be clearly traced. A cork fender protects the clinker planked hull which is crowded with her crew and local 'worthies'. *Photo – Ford Jenkins*.

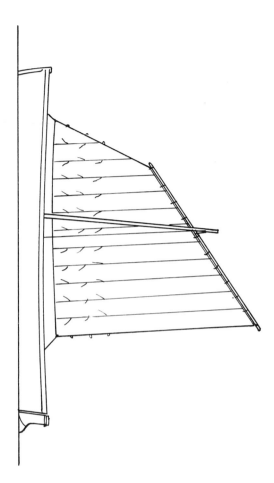

Figure 28. 28ft gig with dipping lugsail of about 200 square feet area.

An alternative rig for gigs was two dipping lugsails set on short masts and having long yards and short luffs, which allowed the sails to be dipped around the masts without slacking the halyards. These masts must be stout and reinforced at the thwart clasp or partners as there are no shrouds and the halyards are usually single part, led up and down the masts, rove from forward to aft through the masthead sheave or block, as the yards are dipped round abaft the masts. The smaller individual sail areas allow single part sheets to be used but the luffs need to be set taut, and small tack purchases or 'jigger tackles' are often fitted to bowse these taut to eyebolts on the middle line of the boat, not to the gunwales. The mainsheet can be led to a traveller on a horse at the stern but the fore sheets will need to be shifted over at each tack. Some claim that gigs from twenty-six to thirty feet long go better with this rig on all points of sailing than the larger single lug. One advantage is that when tacking, the fore parts of the sails can be carried aback to windward for a short time, though the boat sails better if they are dipped to leeward, which can readily be done with this rig without starting the halyards if the luffs are not more than five foot long, to allow the heel of the yards being reached to swing them round abaft the masts easily. This is a snug rig when reefed as the sails then become two low lateens in shape. A spare masthole should be made in a thwart just before amidships so that in strong winds one mast can be stepped there and a single lugsail set, the other mast and sail being stowed out of the way.

Dipping lugs were much used in the boats of sailing warships. British naval ships cutters were rigged with two standing lugsails until changed to a dipping lug foresail and standing lug mizzen early in the nineteenth century (Fig. 27). This rig had the advantage of being weatherly, quick to hoist and lower, and not requiring a bowsprit, but the foresail needed good handling when tacking. The boats of contemporary French warships were rigged with three masts setting a dipping lug foresail and mainsail and a standing lug mizzen; a jib was set on a bowsprit. On French boats dipping lugs were set with the tacks close to the mast, in proportion to the length of the yard, so the boat could sail to windward with the fore and main aback, without being dipped, during short tacks, though sailing would have been improved with them dipped to leeward, which was more easily done with sails of this arrangement as very little of the halyard needed to be slacked away to allow the yard to be swung around the mast. However, this rig did not stand to windward so close as the large foresail and mizzen.

Heaving-to with the dipping lug foresail and mizzen rig is difficult. It is usually attempted by easing the foresail sheet and sheeting the mizzen in hard, putting the helm a'lee. But the craft will have to be watched or she will attempt to tack, will make headway, and in light winds may get 'in irons' head to wind and unable to answer the helm. Then the mizzen sheet should be let go and the fore part of the foresail should be held out to windward while the rest of the crew keep aft to allow the bow to turn.

Few now use the dipping lug but with modern fittings and some ingenuity it might become less cumbersome. The rerigging of the 18ft Essex one-design racing centreboarder *Tern II* by Fabian Bush of Colchester, Essex, is typical of the resurgent interest in the lug rig and is particularly interesting as he chose to adopt the dipping lugsail, with improvements to its gear for quicker handling.

When bought, the hull leaked. He discarded the heavy iron centreplate and fitted a wooden daggerboard. The loss in sail carrying power was compensated by considering a rig with low centre of area to replace the large bermudian sail plan. Having sailed a boat rigged with a dipping lugsail in Scotland, he designed a dipping lugsail rig. A stout mast step was fitted well aft, and the deck in way of the mast was reinforced transversely to

take forces from it. The mast was made from a fir ladder string pole rejected from a factory. The dipping lugsail was cut from an old bermudian mainsail of comparatively heavy canvas, the upper part being cut off at an angle suitable for the lugsail yard; the sail was already stretched.

The halyard leads through a block shackled to an eyebolt at the masthead to allow it to swivel. It was considered that if it passed through a masthead sheave it would result in unacceptable chafe and torque on the mast. A smaller boat might have a rotating mast with a sheave in its head. The halyard is of stainless steel wire or prestretched polyester, and is made fast to the 12ft long yard 5ft from the luff. The nearer the luff the tauter the leading edge of the sail and the better windward performance, but the sail will have more twist than if it were attached towards the centre of the yard. Holding the yard to the mast is difficult with a dipping lug, which has to be unhooked when going about. A conventional type of traveller is of two galvanised iron semi-circular hoops linked with universal joints, but Bush preferred to make one from wire with wooden parrel balls threaded on it for movement. This helps keep the sail close to the mast when hoisting or lowering. He considers it least work to lower the sail completely.

The halyard and the tack are attached to chainplates by snap shackles, though hooks could be used. The tack can be shifted aft when running before the wind, and also the halyard, which then acts as a backstay. A refinement would be to have the tack able to run along a rope from the stemhead to the chainplate on either beam to

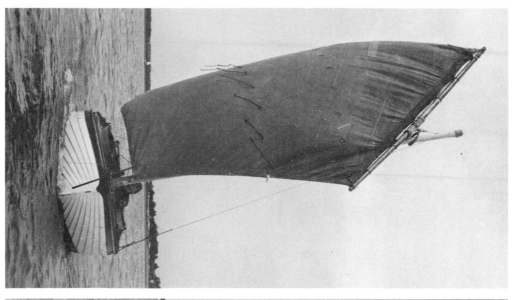

Plate 13: a. Fabian Bush re-rigged his 18ft Essex One-Design *Tern II* with a dipping lugsail for single handed coastal sailing.

b. The full set of the dipping lug is well shown in this photograph.

c. Masthead, showing traveller and halyard.

permit finer sail adjustment. Jamb cleats are fitted only for the halyard and mainsheet to avoid fouling the sail and ropes, which would occur with conventional cleats. When close hauled, sheeting the sail needs power and Bush made a purchase on one side of the boat for tautening the sail, when it has been sheeted approximately on the other end of the mainsheet. This saves a length of rope and reduces the sheet thrashing about when the sail is unsheeted. Instead of leading the halyard aft to eyes on the side decks when the wind is aft, a running backstay has been added to give further athwartships support to the mast. Normally the stay is set aft, impeding nothing and giving peace of mind when running in strong winds. For this halyard arrangement the halyard must lead to the cleat around a sharp angle of some kind rather than through a fairlead eye, as is usually fitted on cam type jamb cleats.

Fabian Bush likes the dipping lugsail for coastal sailing, particularly the ability to drop the sail quickly by the single halyard in a squall. However he recognises its limitations for narrow waters needing tacking. He has cruised with it in the *Tern II* from West Mersea, along the Essex and Suffolk coasts to Southwold and ports between. He finds that the 18ft one-design is unimpaired in performance when running or reaching but she is, of course, slower to windward. However, she makes tacks of 110–120 degrees in choppy water and the boat is better under this rig for cruising, being lighter and adequately stable with 200lbs of water ballast carried in each bilge in rubber bags. She will also sail satisfactorily when the sail is reefed.

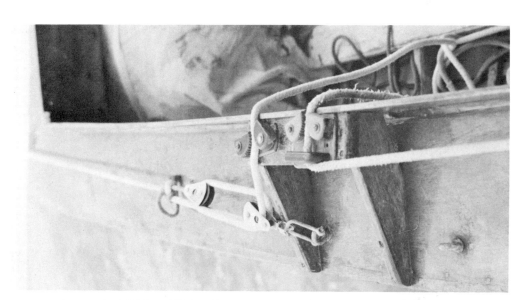

d. Halyard and backstay arrangement on deck, looking forward.

e. Halyard and backstay arrangement on deck, looking aft.

Plate 14. Dick Wagner's 14ft 2in clinker planked sailing canoe *Rushton Princess* was built in 1976 by Pat Ford at Bothell, Washington, U.S.A. Her standing lug foresail and mizzen were made by Nathaniel Wilson of East Boothbay, Maine. She is sailing off her owner's 'Old Boat House' boat livery at Seattle. *Photo – Tom Sotiris.*

Standing Lug

The standing lugsail or, as fishermen called it, the 'working lug' was a refinement of the dipping lugsail, usually rigged without a boom in fishing and working boats and with one in pleasure craft. It was probably developed out of the dipping lug by bringing the tack of the sail to the mast and dipping the heel of the yard around the mast when tacking, instead of having to lower, shift over or dip, and re-set the sail. It is a rig which was much used by fishermen, beachmen, naval ships' boats, and in small craft by pleasure sailors until the 1920's.

A standing lug is less powerful and does not lift so well as a dipping lug, but is superior in handling with a small crew and is a pleasure to sail with in a small boat, particularly if it is not necessary to have a boom. Many thousands of people began sailing in dinghies rigged with a standing lugsail or a balanced lugsail, and the standing lugsail rig reached near perfection for windward sailing in English racing dinghies between 1890–1930, and is still set by the discerning in knockabout boats and tenders.

Figure 29 illustrates the principal feature of the standing lugsail; boom fitted with wooden jaws to the mast, to keep the boom standing well and prevent the sail from riding forward on the tack downhaul and attempting to become a balanced lug. The simple standing lugsail has no boom (Fig. 30) and is set with a single part halyard, which in a small boat is best taken through a block inside the stem to lead aft and belay within reach of the helmsman. Being boomless the sail can be fitted with a single brail, rove through a

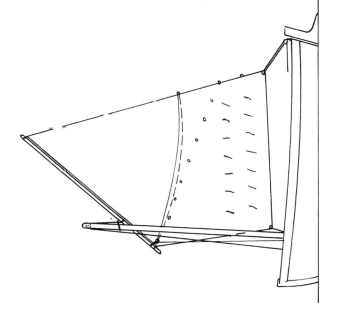

Figure 30. Boomless standing lugsail with simple halyard and brail around the sail to furl it. Note diagonal lacing eyelets for 'balance reef' in strong winds.

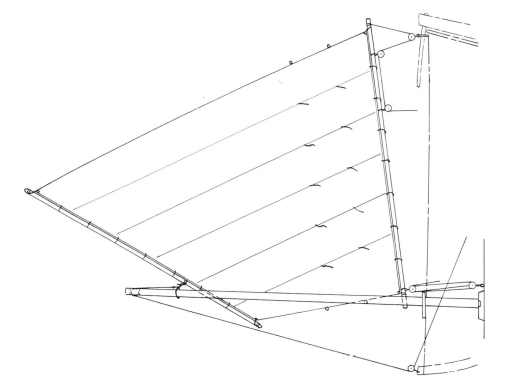

Figure 29. Typical standing lugsail with boom, as usually arranged in a sailing dinghy. The halyard has a traveller and hook to the sling (strop) on the yard and leads through a stemhead block to act as a forestay when the sail is set. The tack purchase ensures a good set to a standing lugsail. A desirable sheeting arrangement is shown.

small block seized to the heel of the yard and leading across the sail through a brass or nylon thimble at the leach, to pass across the other side of the sail and make fast to the heel of the yard. A pull on this line brails the lug in to the heel of the yard; this is useful when coming alongside, or in calms when the boat can be rowed and the sail can be carried standing but brailed, ready to be reset when the breeze comes again. The sheeting of a boomless standing lug is critical and in a 16ft boat the clew of the sail will need to be about 2ft 6in forward of the transom if the sheet is to set the sail well for windward sailing from the lee quarter of a transom of normal breadth. If this distance is less, the sail will bag at the leach and the craft will not point or go to windward well. Where a standing lug needs to extend further aft it would be an unorthodox improvement to fit a short bumkin to maintain the sheeting distance. It was to maintain after area that many British small craft setting a boomless mainsail had a small mizzen stepped at the transom.

Running is a crucial point of sailing small open boats in strong winds. The boat starts rolling, which is accentuated with a boomless mainsail because the yard cannot be entirely controlled by the sheet but swings about, allowing the sail to fill or to spill wind, thus increasing the rolling until the wind gets behind the clew and causes a gybe. A light sprit-boom can be fitted to a standing lug as shown in Fig. 14, connected to the mast with a rope snotter as described in Chapter I. This spreads the clew of the sail and can be readily shipped or unshipped, besides being higher than a conventional boom to clear unwary heads in the boat. The standing lugsail is easily reefed and if well cut is a weatherly rig. It is generally cut with a higher peak than a dipping lug, and its set depends on the position of attachment of the halyard to the yard, and on keeping the luff tight through a powerful tack purchase, without which these sails never set really satisfactorily. The position of the strop or halyard attachment is critical. An exact position cannot be calculated as it must be adjusted to suit the cut of the individual sail, but it may vary from a quarter to three eighths the length of the yard from its

forward end, many being best positioned about a third from forward; trial will establish the best set.

A standing lug for a small boat is set up by the halyard to the desired height, then the tack is bowsed down with a simple tackle or a lanyard purchasing through an eyebolt in the hog or a thwart. The tack purchase is best as it can set the luff very taut for windward sailing, and the sail can be properly peaked. Some wrinkles will spread into the sail but these should disappear when the sheet is gathered in, and the sail should set well. Do not attempt to set the halyard up after the tack downhaul or purchase is set up; the halyard should always be set up first. A standing lugsail can be sheeted flat in smooth water but needs easing in a seaway. When going to windward the heel of the yard bears against the mast and prevents the head of the sail from sagging to leeward. The yard of a standing lug should be dipped to leeward of the mast and this can be done with a light tripping line led slackly from the heel of the yard across the belly of the sail to the boom near the helmsman's reach. A pull on this will bring the yard clear to leeward on a new tack. A single part vang from the peak of the yard to the quarter will steady and trim the sail and, although not traditional practice with European or American lugsails, this was commonly used with the high peaked lugs set by craft in the Gulf of Siam. A boomed standing lug may be reefed by slacking the mainsheet, the tack tackle or lashing, setting up the tack and clew reef pendants and then tying the reef points under the sail's footrope. A boomless lug will need the sheet and tack attachments shifted to the reef cringles

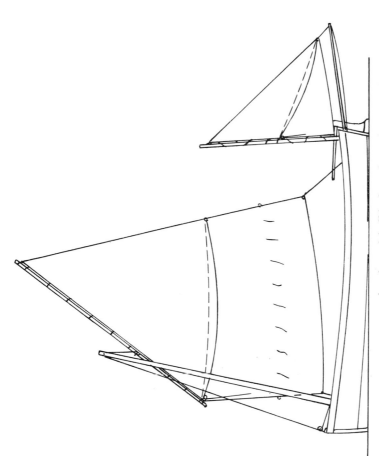

Figure 31. 16ft centreboard boat designed by John Leather has a boomless standing lug foresail and a 'leg of mutton' mizzen. Both sails have a brail.

be made fast to the forward end of the boom and are led through small blocks or nylon thimbles seized to the heel of the yard. Larger standing lugs need a purchase on the halyard, which can be arranged as for the tye and whip purchase described for a dipping lug.

Many small beach boats and other working craft were rigged with a standing lug foresail and a standing lug, spritsail or triangular 'leg of mutton' mizzen sheeted to an outrigger and set on a mast stepped on the inside of the transom, to one side of the tiller arc; a handy and practical rig for boats from fourteen to eighteen feet, leaving the middle part of the hull clear for a party of people to row or fish. Figure 31 illustrates a good example of this rig for a 16ft boat designed by the author for sea and estuary sailing; the dotted line indicates an alternative dipping lug rig. When off the wind the tack of this standing lug can be shifted from near the mast to the stem head, to give similar lifting drive to the dipping lugsail. Opinions differed on the desirability of sheeting a standing lug mizzen to a long outrigger with a boomless sail, or a shorter outrigger and a boomed sail. Beachmen and fishermen usually preferred the long outrigger and boomless sail, which they claimed was quicker to set and lower, was safer, easiest to reef and set fairly flat on the wind. Others, including naval boats and pleasure sailors, usually preferred a boomed sail with a shorter outrigger. A mizzen sheeted to an outrigger is outside the boat and the quickest way to reef it is to lower the sail, tie the reef in and then re-set it.

The Scotch-cut standing lugsail is similar but

at leach and luff before the points are tied, it being often easier to lower the sail and tie the reef in the boat; the halyard is then slacked away to the desired height of the sail foot and, if a traveller is not fitted for the yard, the upper part of the lug must be held to the mast by a running parrel or a lacing.

A double topping lift of light, strong line is useful with a boomed standing lugsail, as these gather the yard and sail as it falls. The lifts can

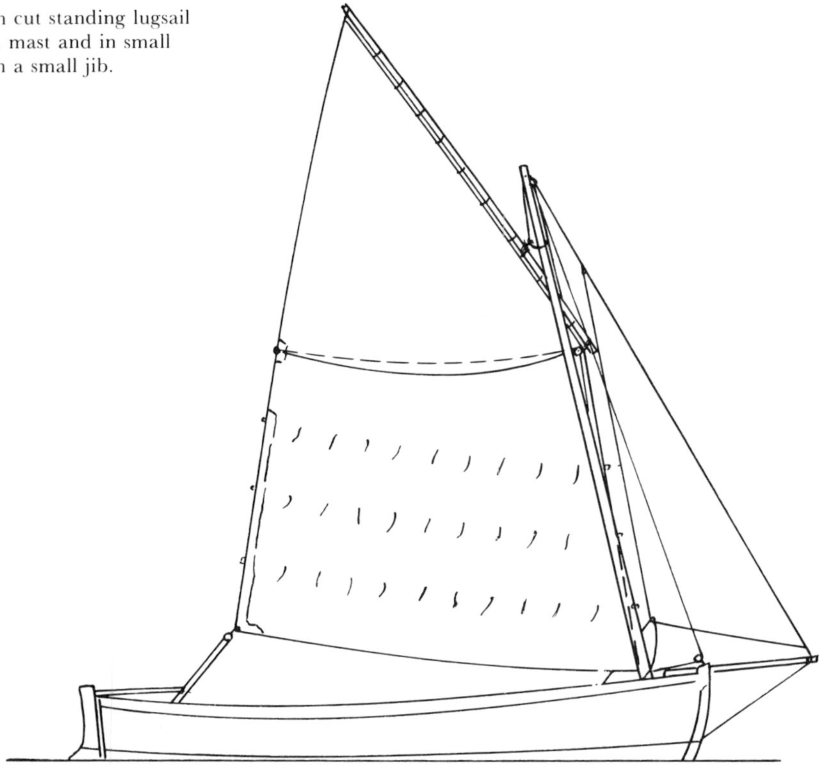

Figure 32. The Scotch cut standing lugsail is set on a well raked mast and in small boats is often set with a small jib.

has a well raked mast (Fig. 32). It was set by skiffs on the west coast of Scotland. This sail has considerable lifting power and is often used with a small jib set on a short bowsprit to aid steering and improve speed. These lugs have a 'square' head i.e. the yard is closer to the horizontal compared with the usual cut of standing lug and its leach is almost vertical, keeping the sheet clear

of the helmsman's head. The yard can be set on either side of the mast so can always be to leeward when close hauled, achieving a luff with little interference to the flow of wind. It can also be brought to windward when running, making a difference in performance in light airs, and minimises the risk of the yard jamming against the lee rigging in a breeze. The mast length must be sufficient to give the halyard adequate drift to work freely, and the sheave hole must be cut fore and aft. When deciding the length and rake of the mast, care must be taken to allow the heel of the yard to clear the forestay, if one is fitted, or the halyard if it is led to a block on the stem. Fouling usually happens during a gybe, but may be avoided by having a line made fast to the heel of the yard and leading it aft. The line can also be used to dip the yard around the mast when tacking or to trim it when running. While most British working luggers preferred to set the standing lug as a mizzen, many French craft carried them as principal canvas on one, two or three masts.

Sizeable standing lug mainsails were set by many of the small racing yachts which originated in Britain after a change in the yacht rating rules during 1887, which encouraged light displacement hulls of experimental form in a revolutionary quest for reduced wetted surface and improved windward efficiency, and led the way to the long ended yacht hull form which is still in vogue. Classes of half, one, two and a half, five and ten raters were popular on the Solent and the types soon spread elsewhere in Britain and abroad. Scores were built from 1887 until the

Plate 15. The 5-Rater racer *Norman* of 1894 set a high peaked standing lugsail and a foresail tacked to the stenhead. Her owner, C. Orr Ewing, his wife and daughter sit in the cockpit as he sails her, with the two hands on the lee deck and skipper Shawyer of Cowes keeping a wary eye from the counter as she shows off her season's prize flags. *Photo – Roger M. Smith.*

84

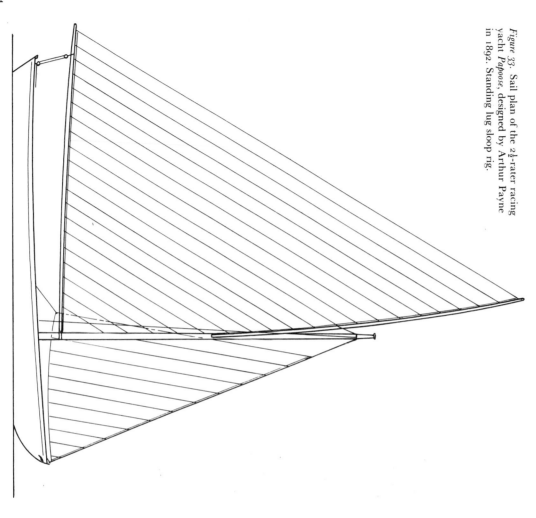

Figure 33. Sail plan of the 2½-rater racing yacht *Papoose*, designed by Arthur Payne in 1892. Standing lug sloop rig.

beginning of the twentieth century and their influence spread to the larger classes of twenty and forty rating, and the big class yachts, all of which (with the exception of the twenty rater *White Slave*) continued to use gaff rigs. 'The raters', as the small classes became known, inspired their designers, builders, helmsmen (and women), skippers and crews to become a development force in yacht racing. At the end of the 1880s the cutter rig without topsail was preferred but the lighter and, for smooth waters, more weatherly, lug sloop rig quickly became usual in these fast little yachts.

The standing lug mainsails were usually of impeccable cut and generous area, sometimes laced to the boom, sometimes not. The yard was often as long as the boom, the sail was cut with vertical cloths and had a battened leach. They were powerful well setting sails, almost equivalent to a bermudian. In contrast the foresail was usually of small size, with its tack to the stem head or slightly inboard, giving these long ended, graceful craft a strikingly modern appearance. Plate 15 is the five rater *Norman* designed and built in 1895 by Charles Sibbick of Cowes for Mr Orr Ewing. This 44ft overall craft had a 33ft waterline × 11ft beam and set 1000 square feet. Her rig and arrangement are typical, with large cockpits for working in strong winds, though her professional skipper and crew got about the deck with cat-like agility. Here she has her owner at the polished brass tiller and his wife and daughter in the cockpit. This shows how raters set the standing lugsail at the time, laced to the boom which connected to the mast with a

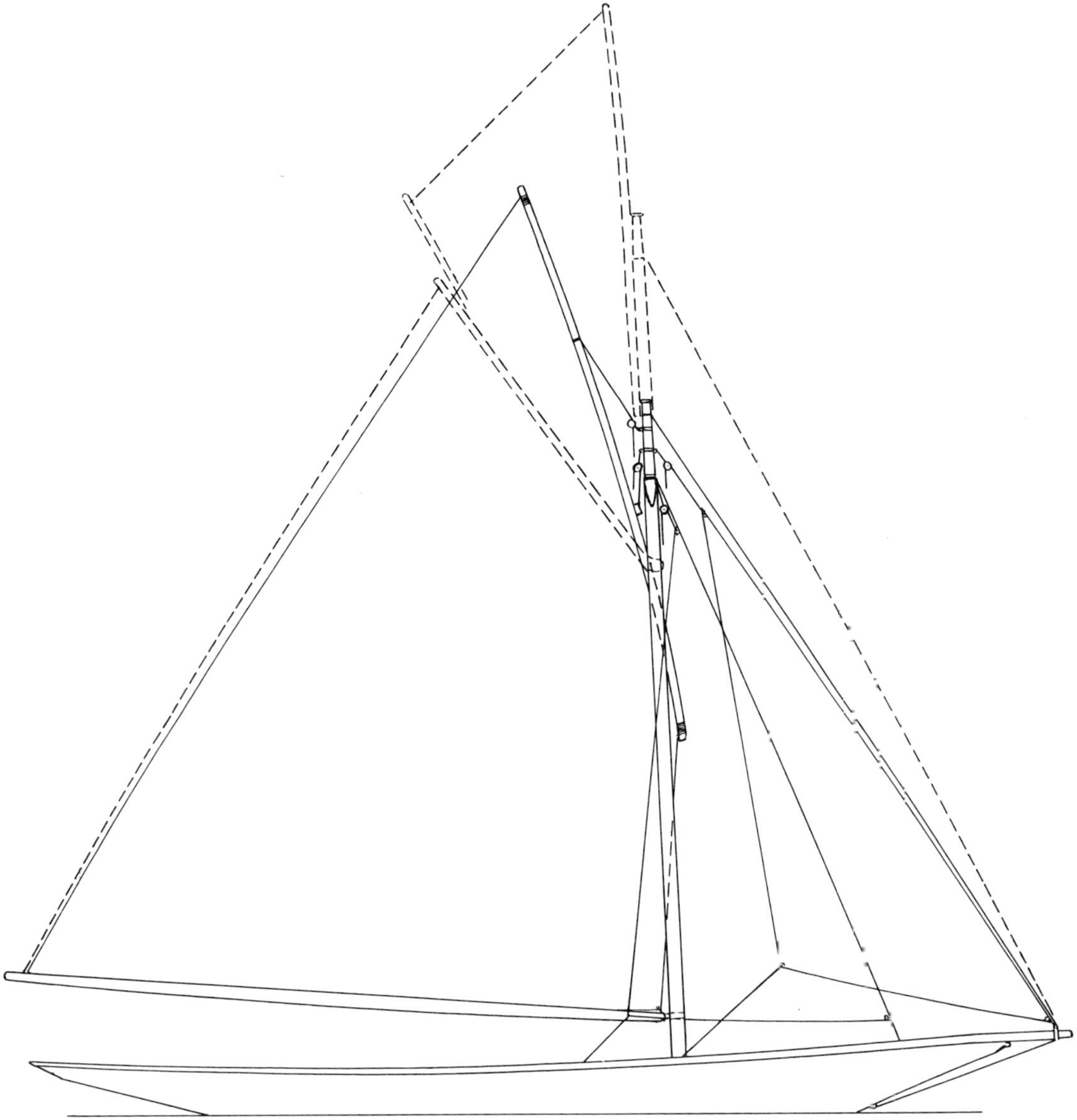

Figure 34. Sail plan of the 5-rater racing
yacht *Red Lancer*, designed by William
Fife. Standing lug cutter rig in full lines,
alternative gaff cutter rig in dotted lines.

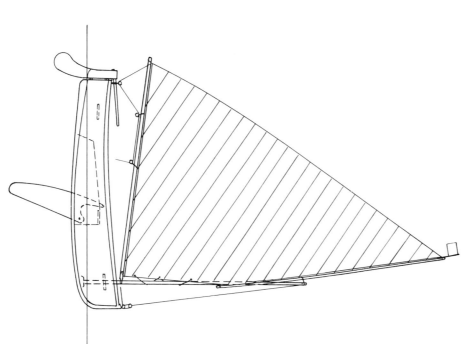

Figure 35. 12ft racing dinghy designed by F. Morgan Giles in 1920. High peaked standing lug rig. A useful type of racing and general purpose boat.

gooseneck. The long yard bent when going to windward and the leach of the sail was stiffened with battens though it remained cut with cloths parallel to the leach. The yard was probably hollow and was strengthened with bindings at the slings. The mast in these boats was comparatively short; an advantage in strong winds when the reefed mainsail brought the weight of the yard down. The shape and size of foresail is typical and here she is showing off her prize flags won that season; a record largely creditable to skipper Shawyer of Cowes, sitting on the after deck. Her two hands are amidships in the then fashionable red and white stocking caps.

Figure 33 shows the sail plan of the successful two-and-a-half rater *Papoose*, designed by Arthur E. Payne and built by Summers and Payne at Southampton in 1892 for Paul Ralli. She was 32ft 5in long, 27ft 8in waterline, 7ft beam, 6ft draught and set 543 square feet of canvas in this typical standing lug sloop rig which has a yard 24ft long and a boom of 23ft 8in. She was successful in the sixty-six races for the class on the Solent during 1892. A comparison between the areas and efficiency of the standing lug and gaff mainsails is shown in Fig. 34 of the sail plans of the Fife designed five rater *Red Lancer* of 1892, rigged with two headsails and a short bowsprit above her clipper bow. The standing lug mainsail needed a shorter mast and had a lower centre of gravity, yet performed as well as the gaff sail with topsail above.

From around 1890 until the 1920s, most class racing dinghies set a refined but still practical form of standing lugsail rig. Fig. 35 is a racing 12 footer designed by Morgan Giles of Shaldon, Devon, in 1920. The clinker planked open round-bilged hull had 4ft 7in beam and drew 7 inches, extending to 3ft 5in with centreplate lowered. The high peaked standing lugsail was typical of the final shape of the sail for racing, before it was eclipsed by bermudian rig; the halyard led to a purchase at the stemhead and the boom was very low. Such boats could be raced, rowed, or used for picnics with up to four on board and a reef in the sail; or could be comfortably sailed by one, being roomy and stable. A very desirable type.

Settee rig

Settee rig was a sail resembling a mixture of the lateen, the dipping lugsail and a low standing lug; it may have originated in India. The basic form (Fig. 36) had a short mast, a long yard, boomless foot and a short luff. It was often set with a small foresail and was used in river boats, particularly on the Thames and other sheltered waters, and often in rowing and sailing boats of narrow beam and limited stability, where its low centre of area was an advantage. It is now virtually extinct.

Balance Lug

The balance lug is similar in shape to the standing lug but a small part of the boom, yard, and luff of the sail are before the mast when it is set, hence its name. The sail does not need to be dipped when tacking. The head and foot are laced to a yard and boom which are usually of about equal length and the sail should be cut with considerable peak to stand well. The usual position for the slings is two fifths of the length of

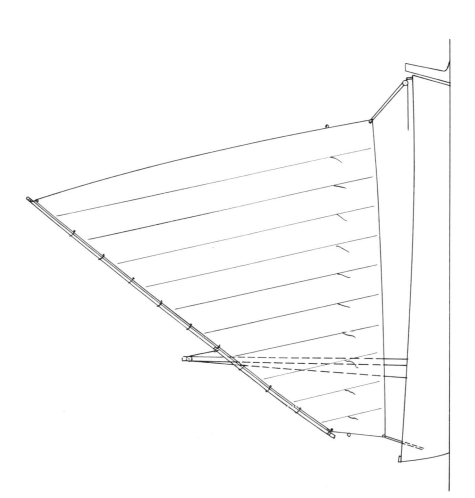

Figure 36. Settee rig resembles the lateen and the dipping lug. It was used in British pleasure boats in sheltered waters.

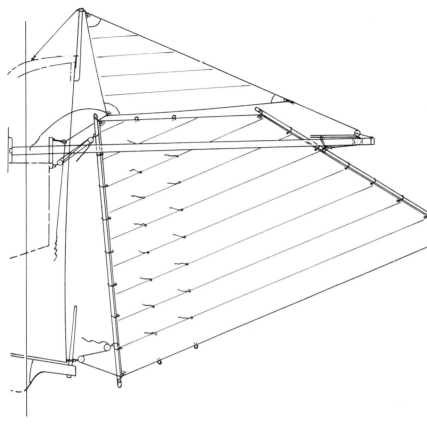

Figure 37. Balanced lugsail and jib rig in a dinghy. The tack purchase keeps the boom aft and peaks the lugsail.

the yard from its heel. Up to one seventh of the length of the foot of the sail is carried before the mast but more is dangerous in squalls because, when the boat is luffed, the wind will not readily spill from the sail. When stepped in dinghies and small boats the mast is usually unstayed.

Because the sail sets flat the balance lug is a rigid rig and it throws strain on the mast, which is noticeable in rough water. A tack downhaul is made fast to the boom close to the mast and may be a lanyard in small boats or a simple purchase leading to an eyebolt, to set the luff taut and help peak the sail. The halyard is usually set up through a block at the stem head, leading through a masthead sheave or block to a metal mast traveller to which the yard is hooked, but with this arrangement the sail cannot be fully lowered into the boat until the yard is unhitched from the traveller, or unless the tack or sheet are released. This can be troublesome when the sail has to be quickly got down in a squall or when going alongside in a breeze. An alternative method of keeping the yard close to the mast, yet hoisting the sail by a halyard hooked to the sling strop or tied to the yard is shown in Fig. 38. A line is made fast to the yard about nine inches aft of the slings and is passed around the mast on the opposite side to the yard, then leads through a nylon thimble seized to the yard about twelve inches forward of the slings, then down to belay in the boat. When the lug is set the line is hauled taut and belayed, keeping the yard close to the mast. When the sail lowers the line slackens and allows the yard to move in lowering. A simple whip purchase can be used on the halyards of a small balance lug but it should not be necessary for a sail up to about 120 square feet area. The balance lug is more efficient and less pressing if set to leeward of the mast. It is set by hoisting the yard to the desired height by the halyard, then hauling the tack taut until the sail sets flat. As with the standing lug it is best to have a tack purchase rather than a simple lanyard, to get the luff taut. When the halyard slacks after sailing for a while the tack purchase is again set up rather than the halyards.

A well cut and set balance lug will stand flatter than a dipping or standing lug sail and the tack downhaul being made fast a distance aft of the forward end of the boom reduces the possibility of the boom lifting in a breeze, and of the sail bellying out. However, the balance lug is not easy to handle in squally weather as the tack cannot be triced up or the peak rucked down, as in a gaff sail, and it cannot be brailed up like a spritsail or a boomless standing lug. It has to be lowered into the boat to be reefed. These were sufficient reasons to condemn it for use by working craft and it remains a pleasure sail.

A variation of halyard arrangement keeps the yard close to the mast (Fig. 39). The halyard is led through a small block hooked or seized to the strop on the yard and is then made fast to the traveller. Fig. 40 shows a method of slinging a balance lugsail without a traveller by leading the halyard through a nylon thimble seized to the yard, to belay at its heel.

A typical sheeting arrangement for a balance lugsail is to make one end of the mainsheet fast to one quarter of the boat, lead it up through a

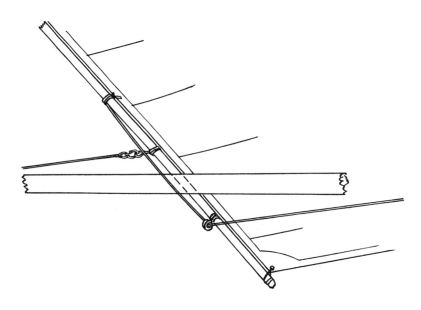

Figure 38. Method of keeping a lugsail yard close to the mast with a line led through a thimble seized to the yard and then around mast on opposite side to the yard.

89

Plate 16. A small French fishing boat sets a balance lugsail with five reef bands and a sizeable foresail. Balance lugs were unusual in British working craft but were used in many other countries. The full bows, well raked transom and long tiller were typical features of French small craft. *Photo – Douglas Went.*

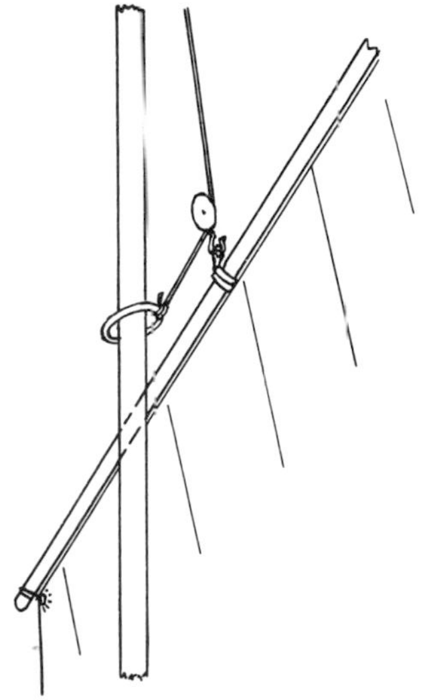

Figure 39. Another method of keeping a lug yard close to the mast. The halyard is led through a block at the strop, then to the traveller.

Figure 40. Lugsail halyard, without traveller, led through a thimble seized to yard and led around the mast on opposite side to the yard, to belay at its heel.

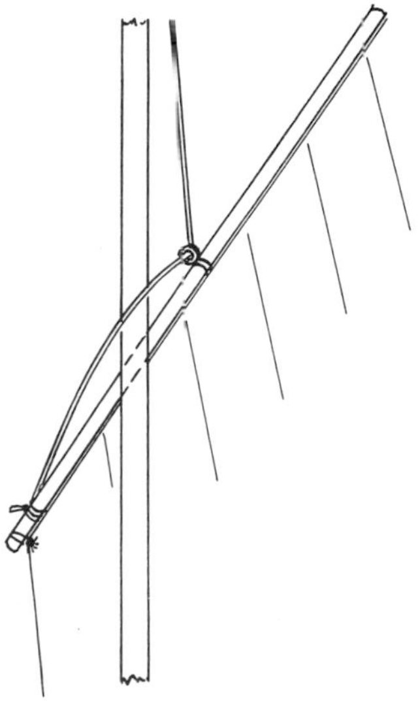

single block on the boom, then down through another single block on the opposite quarter, from which the fall leads forward to the helmsman's hand. This arrangement is awkward when changing tacks and in squalls, and a better arrangement is shown in Fig. 29, where a single block travels on a mainsheet horse. The sheet is made fast at the boom end and leads down through this block, up through another single block at the boom end, forward along the boom, through another single block ahead of the helmsman and then down to hand. This keeps the sheet forward and is a useful and safe method in a centreboard boat. If a boat rigged with a balanced lug misses stays, which can happen in a chop or light wind, the foot of the sail should be held out to the side which will be the weather one when she comes round. This will tend to stop her and press the boat to leeward, but is effective in getting her round; it should be released as soon as this occurs. As she will be almost stopped the sheet should then be eased to allow her to gather way.

The balance lug is likely to cause rolling in a small craft running before a strong wind and if, to keep the boom out of the water or to obtain vision under it, it is topped up, the part forward of the mast tends to catch the mast thwart or deck. If rolling becomes excessive it may be necessary to reef. It is also an unpleasant sail to gybe with in a small boat due to the usually long boom and yard, but is an effective and still widely used rig in small boats and yacht tenders.

The sail was much used in pleasure boats from about 1870, particularly for sailing on rivers and

lakes. Balance lugsails were much in evidence on the upper Thames where the rig was claimed to have been introduced by Alfred Burgoyne, a noted boatbuilder of Kingston on Thames, about 1870. A centreboard dinghy 10 to 14 feet long rigged with a balance lug was a common type on Britain. The author's own dinghy is a 10 foot, ex-West Mersea One Design class about forty-five years old and although the same size as his first boat, provides as much fun as any of the seventeen larger, cruising and racing craft which have been owned in between.

Some sailing canoes and knockabout pleasure boats were rigged with a balance lug mainsail and a smaller balance lug mizzen. Sometimes the mizzen was sheeted to the rudder head and moved with it so that, when the helm was put down to tack, the mizzen was forced to windward and helped the boat round in a similar way to the spritsail mizzen on an east coast sailing barge. However, the mizzen will stop her way during the tack and the helmsman cannot leave the tiller for a moment or the wind will press on the mizzen and force the rudder down, and the boat will fall off before the wind and would capsize in a strong breeze, instead of luffing up to it.

Gunter Lug
The gunter lug comes close to the windward efficiency of bermudian rig with its high peaked quadrilateral being almost a triangle. Origin of the term 'gunter' is obscure but it may have been brought to England around 1800 by seamen who observed the rig in use by craft from islands in the Molucca Sea, now part of Indonesia, where

Figure 41. A gunter rig sloop. Detail shows upper and lower gunter irons holding yard to mast, hoisted by halyard to the upper iron.

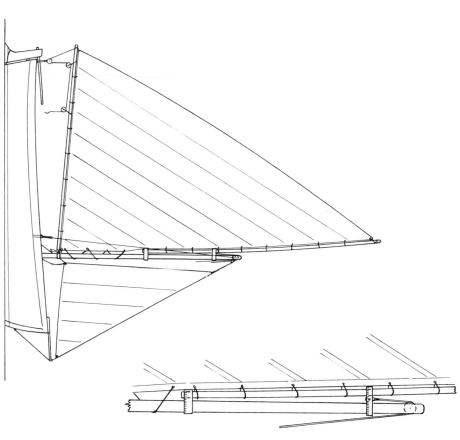

burdensome craft called 'Guntons' were in use. Gunter rig has various arrangements.

The sliding gunter rig is a triangular type of lugsail with the heel of the yard held upright and parallel to the mast by two metal sleeves, or 'irons', on which it slides almost vertically up and down the mast (Fig. 41). The halyard leads over a sheave in the masthead and is made fast to the upper hoop, or is sometimes led through an eye in the upper hoop and made fast to the heel of the yard. The head of the sail is laced to the yard and really forms part of the luff. The luff proper is laced to the mast. When reefed, the yard is lowered the required distance and when close reefed is brought almost down to the boom. This rig is snug in strong winds as, when the reefs are in, the centre of gravity of the long yard is lowered and there is no gaff to offer swinging weight and no excess of mast and rigging aloft as with the tall bermudian rig, to make windage. The lower iron should be made with a hinge and the upper one so as to unclasp from the mast, then once the luff lacing is cast off, the yard can be lowered into the boat, which is an advantage at anchor or moorings, or if the boat has to be rowed into a strong wind. A serious disadvantage is that the irons can jam when the yard is being hoisted or lowered. The irons are covered with leather, which should be greased, and a downhaul should be rigged from the heel of the yard. The two hoops should be connected by a taut line on the fore side to keep the lower iron as horizontal as possible and minimise the possibility of jamming. An alternative type of gunter iron had round sleeves on the mast and, connected to these, square

Figure 42. Upper and lower gunter iron sleeves joined by rods to minimise possibility of jamming. Heel of the gunter yard can be unshipped from the square sleeves when the sail is lowered.

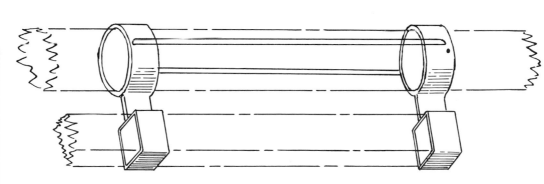

Figure 43. Variation of gunter rig with two halyards and one gunter iron with a gooseneck on the yard.
A. Cheek blocks and halyard.

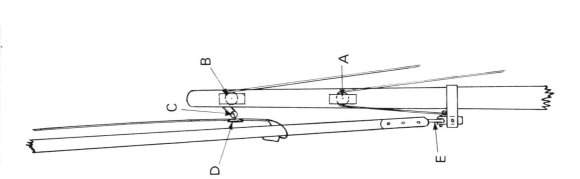

B. Cheek block and halyard.
C. Block shackled to span traveller.
D. Span traveller.
E. Gooseneck at heel of yard.

sleeves for the heel of the yard (Fig. 42), which could be unshipped from them when the sail was lowered. The sleeves were kept rigidly apart by two metal bars to minimise risk of jamming on the mast in hoisting or lowering.

Sliding gunter rig is usually used with a small foresail, as a sloop, and sometimes with two masts as a ketch.

Many of the original gunter lugs were boomless and had a brail across the sail, led to blocks hung under the lower gunter iron. The falls of the brail could also be used as a downhaul. Some boats had a boom with its after end shipped into the clew cringle or lashed to it. The forward end was set to the mast by a rope snotter eye-spliced around the mast near the tack, leading forward through a dumb sheave in the forward end of the boom, then back to be set taut around the mast, setting the boom aft hard against the clew to stretch the loose-footed sail. This saved the expense of a gooseneck and the obstruction it caused on a mast often unshipped when the boat was to be rowed. The snotter must be kept set taut if the boom end is merely shipped into the cringle as the shaking of the sail will make it fall out when the boat is in stays. It is best to lash the clew to the boom. This arrangement is similar to the sprit booms used in the sailing shrimpers of Great Yarmouth, Norfolk, the crab skiffs of Chesapeake Bay and other small working boats, now extinct.

A variation of the gunter lug with two halyards and one gunter iron was a step towards the later refinement of the rig (Fig. 43). The gunter iron was hoisted by a single part halyard led through cheek blocks on each side of the mast at (A). A

94

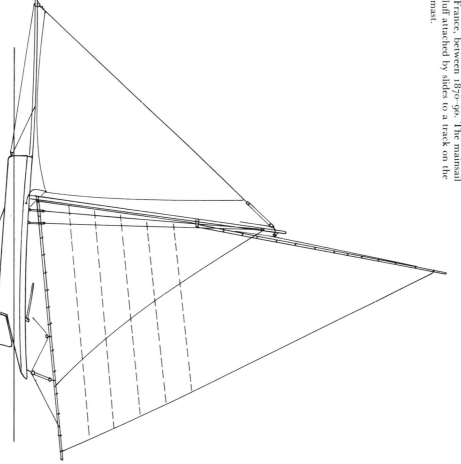

Figure 44. Excessively canvassed gunter-rigged sloops sailed on the River Seine, France, between 1870–90. The mainsail luff attached by slides to a track on the mast.

similar halyard at (B) is rove off through cheek blocks and through a small block (C) shackled to a span traveller (D) on a wire span on the yard. The ends of this span are spliced eyes, supported by thumb cleats on the yard. The heel of the yard is pivoted on a gooseneck at the upper edge of the gunter iron (E). This version of gunter rig was used by the French centreboard sloops racing on the River Seine between about 1870–1890 (Fig. 44). An interesting feature of this exaggerated rig was use of a brass mast track with slides for the luff of the sail.

Later gunter sails also developed to have jaws at the heel of the yard, with a parrel line and balls around the mast. The yard had a wire span to which the single part peak halyard was shackled via a traveller. The throat halyard was either a single part or had a simple whip purchase to increase its hauling power. When the luff was hoisted taut the peak halyard was finally set up and drew the yard close to the mast, to stand almost vertically. When the sail was reefed the throat halyard was lowered the required amount and the peak halyard remained untouched, the traveller allowing the yard to slide down the span (Fig. 45). When close reefed the heel of the yard was almost down to the boom. This became a usual form of gunter lugsail. The origin of this modified form of gunter lug is credited to Richard Perry, the sailmaker of Birkenhead, Cheshire, then prominent in canoe and small boat work, who inexplicably named it 'Perry's Medical Lug'! A gunter sail gybes as well as a bermudian but is difficult to set without the lug yard getting foul or having to be handled awkwardly in a breeze and

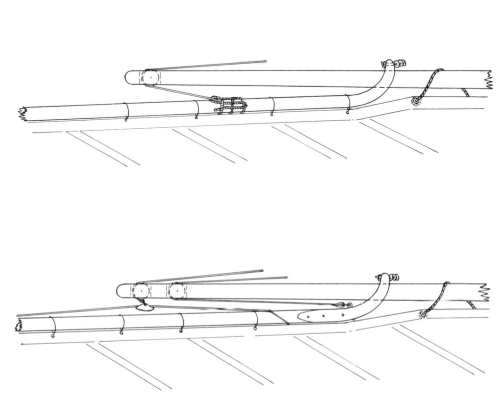

Figure 47. An alternative halyard arrangement for a gunter lug with the halyard shackled to a strop about one third of the way up the yard and a rope parrel bent to the yard and embracing the mast to keep the yard peaked when reefing or reefed.

Figure 46. A simplified but less efficient gunter lug halyard having a single part bent to the yard.

Figure 45. A now usual type of gunter lug has jaws at the heel of the yard and two halyards, the upper sliding on a wire span on the yard, allowing it to remain held close to the mast when the sail is reefed.

when setting or handing the sail. Those with experience of gunter rig tend to love it or loath it. Many will anchor or pick up a mooring before attempting to lower or reef the sail. The simplest way of setting a gunter lug is with a single halyard leading either through a sheave in the masthead or via a small block working from a short pendant from the masthead or shackled to a masthead band. The end of the halyard is made fast to the yard (Fig. 46) and hoists the sail and draws the yard to the mast as it tautens.

Hoisting or lowering this sail is relatively easy compared to the true gunter, but it will have to be lowered for reefing so the halyard can be repositioned on the yard in the correct place to preserve the set of the reefed sail. The disadvantage of this type of gunter sail is that when the halyard is slackened the yard falls away from the mast and the set of the sail is instantly spoiled. An alternative arrangement for a gunter yard, halyard and parrel is shown in Fig. 47. The jaws are set at right angles to the yard and have a parrel line with balls. The halyard shackles to a strop about a third up the yard and when hoisted the halyard block is almost up to the masthead sheave. To keep the yard peaked while reefing

96

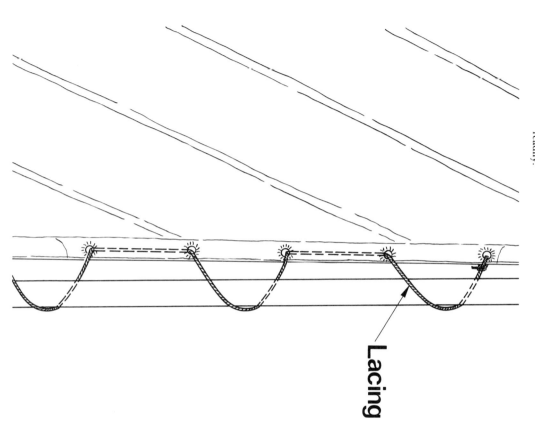

Figure 48. The best method of lacing a sail luff to a mast so it will hoist or lower readily.

Lacing

and when reefed, a rope parrel is fitted. When reefing this is slacked a little to allow the gaff to lower but not enough to allow it to sag to leeward. When rehoisting the reefed sail the slack in the parrel line is set taut. It is possible to hoist a gunter lug yard with one halyard rigged with one end made fast to a span on the yard, then led forward through one sheave of a double block at the masthead, down and through a single block at the throat, up through the other sheave of the double block and down to belay at the foot of the mast.

The luffs of gunter lugs are usually laced to the mast (Fig. 48). An alternative method of lacing the luff uses a length of lacing line spliced to the sail at the upper luff eyelet; the lower end is spliced to a lower luff eyelet. A strong brass or nylon hook is seized to the middle of this lacing line, which hangs slack while the sail is hoisted and the lug is set taut. Then the luff is secured to the mast by taking the hook around the fore side of the mast and hooking it into an intermediate eye on the luff. The length of line and position of the eye must be accurately measured to suit the rig. This lacing is quickly released and is an advantage when lowering sail.

A modified type of gunter lug with one or two full length battens across it at reef band positions was developed and used in many sailing canoes between about 1880–1905 and became known as the 'Batter' rig; apparently because all the sail was abaft the mast, whereas the balance and standing lugsails were partially before the mast. In some later racing boats the gunter yard was curved at the head to assist the tall sails to stand well to windward. In the 17ft waterline boats of the Belfast Lough Jewel class of 1898 Linton Hope designed a triangular gunter mainsail with three full length battens, and two short ones stiffening the upper leach (Fig. 49).

A hybrid type of gunter-spritsail was used by open whaleboats at the Azores and at Tonga. It was hoisted by a single halyard and was effective in sea use under very active conditons (Fig. 50). The gunter yard has a fixed band with an eye through which is rove the single part halyard, which passes through a sheave in the masthead and to a block on the stem. The heel of the yard pivots in metal jaws embracing the mast and also has eyes to pivot the heel of the sprit which crosses the sail at about 40° to extend the leach. The foot is boomless and the laced luff is set taut with a tack tackle. One or two reefs are provided. The yard, sprit and sail are all hoisted by the single halyard and the yard sets almost vertically. However, this lofty, boomless sail is inefficient when running, when it can make a boat steer badly. These whaleboats cruised under sail on the lookout for their prey or when returning to beach, but the six man crew had to be ready to lower the mast and sail quickly when a whale was to be chased, which was done under oars. The mast was attached to the forethwart by a hinged collar and the heel stepped between a pair of guide timbers forming a tabernacle, so it lowered quickly with little need of attention.

G. W. Hope, brother of yacht designer Linton Hope, owned an unusually rigged craft named *La Reine*, which proved a good single hander for his work in attending a large suction dredger in the

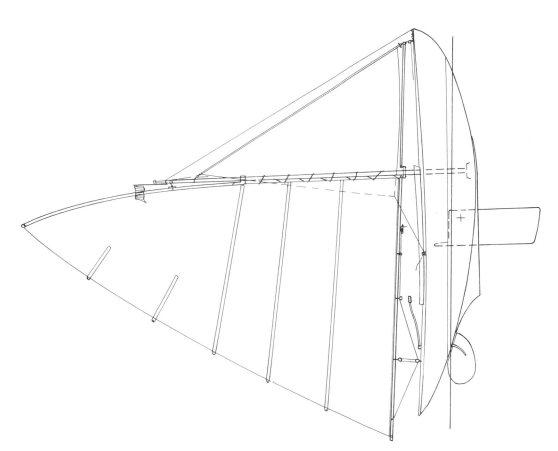

Figure 49. The 17ft waterline, centreboard 'Jewel' class racing one-designs by Linton Hope, 1898, set a high peaked, battened gunter-lug mainsail.

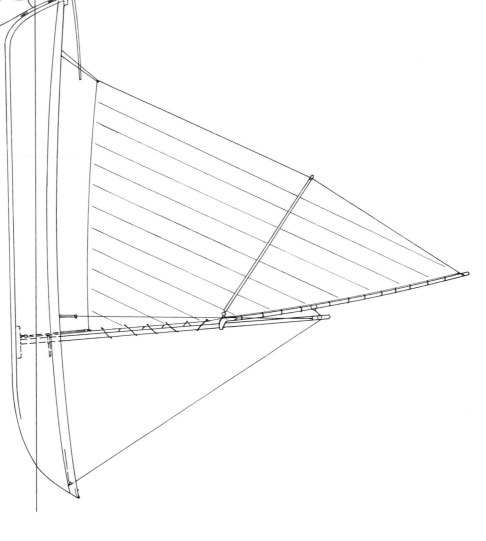

Figure 50. Whaleboats from the Azores ranged into the Atlantic seas under a variant of the gunter lugsail, having a sprit to spread the leach of the boomless sail. The boats were also rowed.

lower Thames in all weathers and seasons. Hull dimensions were 23ft 6in overall × 7ft beam × 2ft 3in hull draught (3ft 6in with plate lowered). She had a short counter stern and was rigged as a gunter lug schooner with the foremast stepped at the after end of the foredeck and the main through a thwart abaft the centreplate case. Each mast had two shrouds per side, one pair on the mainmast being spread well forward as stays.

Three sails were carried: a jib, set on a short bowsprit; the gunter foresail, without a boom, sheeting well aft and having a single brail and one row of reef points; and the gunter lug mainsail with a boom, topping lift and two reefs. When the foresail was lowered its yard overlapped the mainmast by 2ft. When the fore and main were set, both gunter yards stood at the same rake (Fig. 51).

The lugsail halyards were made fast to a travelling ring on the mast, then rove through a block on the yard, up through a sheave at the masthead and led down to a double block on the fore side of the mast, through which a purchase was rove to a deck block, setting the yard up. The luffs were set taut by tack tackles and the main boom had jaws to the mast. A combined topping lift and lazyjack was arranged for the mainsail; a line was made fast to the starboard side of the masthead and led down about two thirds of the mainsail with a thimble spliced in the end. A block at the port masthead carried a line from the deck leading down the other side of the mainsail with a thimble spliced in its end. A piece of line was similarly to the starboard side. A piece of line was led through an eye under the boom, through the thimble on the standing part, then down and through another eye on the boom about 5–6ft away from the first, then up and through the thimble in the running part, with the ends of the line knotted or spliced together. When lowering the mainsail the fall of the lift was hauled taut and the halyard let go; the sail and yard falling confined between the two parts of the lift and lazyjacks. This arrangement is most effective rigged with nylon thimbles and Terylene or Dacron lines.

La Reine sailed well in strong winds with only the foresail set; a handy all-inboard rig. As the foresail had no boom it gave a lifting effect and she would almost steer herself. Hope described her as 'the most perfect single handed cruiser anyone could wish for, and if I were going to have another, I would rig her as a schooner with gunter yards instead of gaffs on the fore and main masts, but I would have a roller jib that could be used as a spinnaker when running. I consider that a yacht up to 10 to 12 tons rigged like *La Reine* could be easily handled by a man who knew what he was doing, and if he didn't I am afraid no rig would be any better for him'.

She was later sold to Joseph Conrad, the author, who sailed her from Rye in Sussex and became equally fond of the rather unusual little schooner, which would make an excellent prototype dayboat or, with a tent rigged over hoops across the cockpit coamings, between the masts, becomes a practical estuary cruiser capable of coastal passage making in reasonable weather. The tent would provide a covered space about 6ft 6in by 6ft, closed by a zip flap and opening on to

99

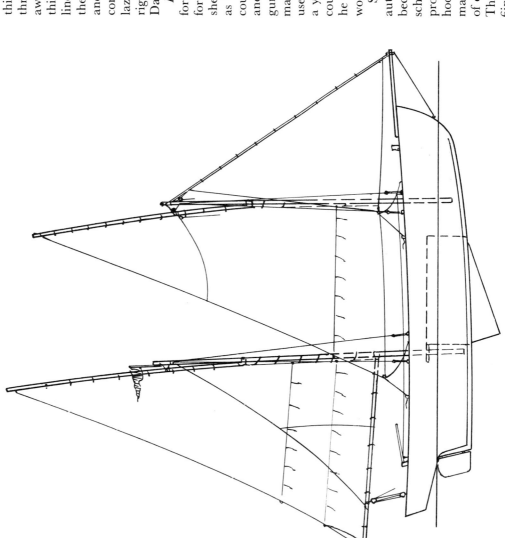

Figure 51. Linton Hope designed the 23ft 6in gunter schooner *La Reine* as a handy dayboat which would also make a camping cruiser.

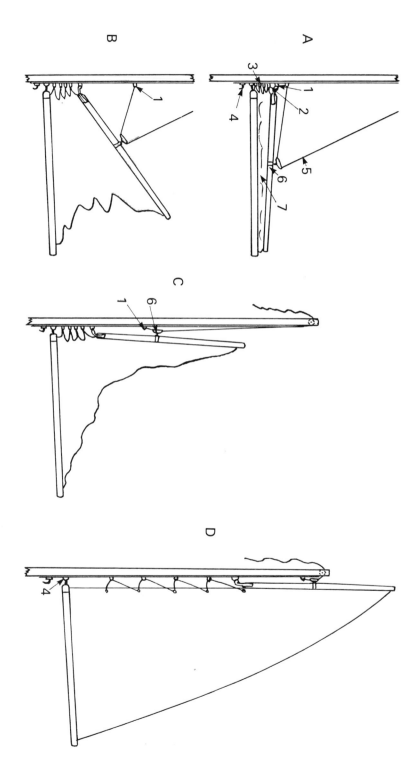

Figure 52. Kenneth Gibbs' type of gunter lug with track and slides.

1. Strong slide on mast track extending from gooseneck to halyard sheeve.
2. Metal gooseneck at heel of yard pivoted on a slide.
3. Slides for luff lacing.
4. Sliding gooseneck to boom.
5. Main halyard.
6. Span shackle attached to yard by a band.
7. Band on yard. See page 101.

the cockpit space aft for those who wished to stand up.

Kenneth Gibbs of Shepperton on Thames, a most original and enterprising designer and builder of small sailing craft, developed a version of the gunter lug which improves efficiency and keeps the sail under control during hoisting or lowering. A mainsail up to 100 sq. ft. area can be set with a single part wire and rope halyard, the luff being set taut by bearing down on the sliding gooseneck. Points or roller reefing may be used and when reefed the yard maintains its position close to the mast. The sail luff below the throat is fitted with slides engaging in ordinary mast track.

Immediately below this track a short length of standard 'C' section track clips to the mast as a magazine carrying the gooseneck, slide for the heel of the yard and slides to which the luff of the mainsail is laced, all in one unit. This allows quick removal for storage of the sail complete with yard and boom.

Fig. 52 illustrates the sequence of operation. In (A) the sail is assumed to be stowed. The numbers indicate (1) a strong slide working in the mast track which extends from a few inches above the gooseneck to the underside of the halyard sheave. (2) special jaws for the yard, also working on a strong slide in the track. (3) slides to which the luff of the sail is attached by a lacing. (4) Vertically sliding gooseneck. (5) main halyard. (6) Span shackle attached to the yard by a band (7).

Except for (1) all the fittings working on the mast track are housed in the magazine at this stage and are retained by a metal pin through the top of the magazine track. (B) Hauling on the halyard gradually raises the yard and slide (1) works up the mast track until the position shown in (C) is reached. Slide (1) is then hard up against the span shackle (6). The yard is hauled up the mast as far as it will go, the halyard is belayed and the luff set taut by bearing down on the gooseneck (4) and locking it in postion by a screw handle (D).

To roller reef, the gooseneck lock is slacked off and the boom rolled to the desired reef position; the halyard is slacked away, lowering the sail, then belayed and the gooseneck set up. The yard will maintain its angle relative to the mast as long as there is tension on the halyard and the sail luff.

To stow the sail, the halyard is cast off and the yard is lowered down on top of the boom. Luff slides and yard jaws will settle into the magazine. The span shackle is cast off, keeper pin is inserted in the magazine and the whole assembly is removed from the mast if desired to take the sails ashore.

The ultimate development in gunter rig efficiency was designed by Percy Tatchell in his twelve metre class model *Alderman* of 1907. This sloop-rigged racer had a mast of modest height. The battened gunter mainsail had a long yard, stiffened longitudinally by a jumper stay with a spreader. She proved successful in keen racing of the class by the London Model Yacht Club. However, it is believed this rig was never fitted to a full sized craft.

In 1944, J. Dudley Head, a noted six metre and Q class sailor, owned and sailed a 9ft stem

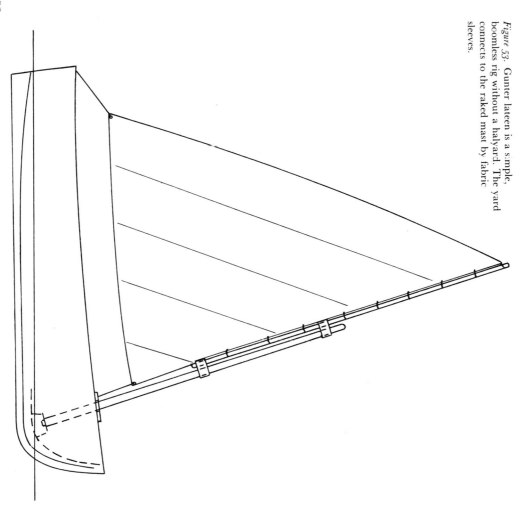

Figure 53. Gunter lateen is a simple, boomless rig without a halyard. The yard connects to the raked mast by fabric sleeves.

dinghy rigged with two gunter lugs, on separate halyards, which set flat as one sail when beating to windward but spread out, goosewinged, when running; an exciting rig in a breeze, which proved practical and gave excellent balance downwind.

The gunter lateen is another simple variation of a dinghy lugsail (Fig. 53). It needs a short mast which is set at a pronounced aft rake, stepped through a bow thwart at gunwale height; the heel fitting in a chock on the after side of the stem or deadwood. Shrouds and stays are not required in a small boat. The upper end of the mast is tapered in diameter and an eye made of plastic webbing, or similar material, is fitted around it at about half height, to receive the lower end of the yard which is of smaller diameter to suit its lesser loading. About half way along the yard a second plastic eye is permanently fitted and must be a sliding fit over the masthead. The triangular sail may be laced to the yard, or the yard is slid into a pocket in its luff. It is boomless and the sheet is a single part made fast to the clew. To set it, the sail is lifted up, the upper eye is slipped over the masthead and the heel of the yard is inserted in the lower eye.

The gunter lateen can be satisfactorily used in boats up to about 14ft length. A refinement for larger craft is to hoist the sail by a halyard, with jaws fitted to the heel of the yard. The halyard passes through a mast head sheave and, if a sheave is fitted in the bows, will serve as a forestay. A tack downhaul can be made fast to a cleat on the mast. The sail can be furled standing by wrapping it round the mast and yard and securing with the sheet.

In a further refinement the yard slides up the mast on two wire rings fitted with parrel balls and a track is fitted to its after side. To hoist sail, the yard is hauled up the mast on a halyard through a masthead sheave. Then the sail is hauled up the yard by a separate halyard leading through a sheave in the yards upper end and belaying at its heel. The luff slides easily on the track, as in a bermudian sail. The rig is light and the sail can be stowed easily, leaving mast and yard standing. The gunter lateen is a relatively safe rig; in a hard puff the sheet is started, spilling the wind instantly and with no boom to hit unwary heads.

Fully battened lugsails were fashionable in British small pleasure craft, particularly canoes, during the period approximately 1885–1914, and have again become fashionable in some small cruising yachts during the past ten years, particularly for long distance voyaging. These sails are based on the various types of Chinese lugsails used for thousands of years in eastern waters, which are claimed to have the advantages of flat setting and easier reefing, as the battens form panels of sail which fall into the topping lifts when the halyards are lowered. However, the sails are heavy, even if made of modern materials, and fully battened lugsails will not always spill the wind sufficiently when the sheets are slacked off, which can be dangerous in a squall. The multiple sheet arrangement necessary to control the leech and remove twist from the sail is complex for use when short tacking.

The principal exponent of fully battened lugsails in Britain was Landseer Mackenzie. Born in Jersey in 1849, he sailed boats from childhood

and this, coupled with their design, became his lifelong interest and his designs were original and successful. He was amongst the keen British canoeists of the 1860s and 70s and boldly carried canoe features of pointed stern, fully battened lugsails and experimental centreboard arrangements into quite large craft with successful originality.

His first larger craft was the two masted *Heathen Chinee* (plate 17). Built in 1877 by McWhirter of Limehouse, noted for his fine workmanship in larger canoes and boats; a character immortalised in Finnes Speed's book *Cruises 'n small yachts and large canoes*. Mackenzie sailed the *Heathen Chinee* as a day boat and cruiser for ten years, selling her to W. A. Beauclerk, an east coast yachtsman who had her measured for racing in the very competitive Solent two-and-a-half rating class in 1889. His racing skipper was Edward Sycamore of Brightlingsea, who handled her with young Roger Sparling of Wivenhoe. Between them they raced her hard, usually showing the grinning chinese figure on her stern to the fleet of crack Solent raters.

Captain Sycamore went on to a distinguished career in yacht racing, commanding the largest and fastest yachts. Roger Sparling, after several years as a yacht hand, became a timekeeper at the shipyard where the author was apprenticed and loved to tell of his exciting days racing the *Heathen Chinee*. Tears of laughter rolled down his cheeks when he told of the 'race' between the lugger and another Colne-manned yacht; the great racing cutter *Valkyrie* commanded by William Cranfield of Rowhedge; from Southampton Water to the Colne,

104

Plate 17. Landseer MacKenzie designed the *Heathen Chinee* in 1877 for his use as a fast day sailing boat, with Chinese lugsails. She became a noted competitor in the 2½-Rater class during 1889 and was unusual in having two centreboards.
Photo — Beken.

where both yachts were to lay up. The losing skipper was to provide the winner with a good dinner. The 27 feet *Heathen Chinee* seemed a poor match for the 117 feet racing cutter setting 10,042 square feet of canvas and with a crew of 35 men. But Sycamore used her shoal draught and drove her hard, taking short cuts denied the *Valkyrie* with her 16ft 4in draught, and he arrived in Colne just ahead of her. Captain Cranfield hailed the cold and weary 'Heathens' to luff alongside for a good meal and rest, ordering two of his crew to jump aboard the lugger and dodge her about for an hour or so. The hands sent her bowling away down Colne before the wind but when the helm was put down she refused to come round. Puzzled and angry, they could not get the *Heathen Chinee* to tack. The watch called the skippers and Sycamore realised that both centreboards were still lowered. Roger was sent away in the *Valkyrie's* gig to jump aboard and hoist the after one, when with a mischevious wink at the unsuccessful sailors, he tacked her single handed and she sailed back like a bird.

The *Heathen Chinee's* fame reached the United States of America where her lines were published and discussed. Her qualities resulted in a long controversy between Mackenzie and Dixon Kemp, the yachting authority.

Mackenzie next designed the *Crotchet*, a 28ft sharpie, for his use, intended principally for sailing in Poole Harbour. Built by J. Allen of Poole in 1885 she was plumb ended and had typical sharpie proportions of 6ft 7in beam, 2ft 7in depth and only 12in hull draught, though two centreboards were fitted. She was originally rigged with two lugsails by Ratsey and a foresail. The *Crotchet* was the simplest and least expensive of Mackenzie's designs yet, typically, she gave him considerable pleasure and he sailed her throughout the rest of his life; usually with one other hand. In 1905 she was lengthened to 30 feet to suit Mackenzie's experimental whims and in about 1927 was converted to a rig of two spritsails totalling 250 square feet made by Beaton Brothers of Poole. These were retained until Mackenzie's death in 1931. *Crotchet* represented a type neglected in Britain yet very suitable for day sailing and cruising in sheltered or semi-sheltered waters; cheap to build and maintain, characterful and capable of variety of rig.

After the sale of *Heathen Chinee* Mackenzie designed himself another shallow draught lugger, the *Fan-Tan*; 45 ft by 9ft 6in beam and having two centreboards. She was built by Allen in 1889 and Mackenzie sailed her until 1902. Her fully battened lugs were replaced by gaff sails in 1910.

In 1902 Mackenzie had built his largest and most graceful yacht which was designed on the tried principles of his earlier craft. The *Cabar-Feidh* was a seagoing lugger, 57ft overall, 46ft waterline, 12ft 10in beam and was fitted with two centreplates. Her yacht-like hull above water set off the two tanned lugsails and foresail which totalled 1750 square feet. Built at Poole by Ashton and Kilner she was used for cruising by Mackenzie until sold to a naval officer at Galway, Ireland. She was lost at sea in 1928 under unknown conditions.

The fully battened lugsail reached ultimate

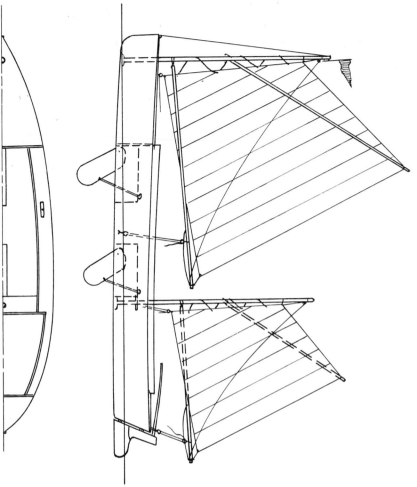

Figure 54. The 28ft sharpie *Crotchet* was designed by Landseer MacKenzie for his use from Poole in 1885. 6ft 7in beam, 1ft draught and two centreboards made her a useful shoal water dayboat. The original lugsail rig was altered to the spritsails shown here.

development in the centreboard racing classes of the central European lakes. These included the twenty square metre Rennjolle (Z-Jolle) and fifteen square metre Wander-Jolle (H-Jolle) and ten square metre Monotype. The twenty square metre class were typical and were sailed by Switzerland, Italy, Austria, Germany, France and Holland until 1939. An average boat was 27ft 6in overall length, 24ft 6in waterline length, with only 5ft 10in beam, hull draught of 6in and, with centreboard lowered, 3ft 9in. The shallow, round bilged hull had very veed sections and little stability. The sheer was often straight, or hogged, and the rudder was hung on the transom of these elongated dinghies, which were easily capsized. The twenty square metre (216 square feet) sail area was set in a gunter lug mainsail and a foresail, the luff of which was sometimes set on a spar attached to the deck and mast, to take the place of a forestay. The mainsail was high peaked and usually had eight or nine battens extending from luff to leach, and roller reefing gear.

The hollow yard was of aerofoil section and the headrope ran in a groove on its underside. Overlapping foresails of about 7.4 square metres (68.8 square feet) were carried and a spinnaker of 13.5 square metres (125.5 square feet).

Fig. 55 is of a typical twenty square metre designed in 1929 by Carl Marten of Starnberg, Germany, where many were raced on the Starnberger See (also known as the Wurmsee) 1916ft above sea level, near Munich. Although larger, these hulls were similar to the present Flying Dutchman class racing dinghies.

Few lugger yachts were built and amongst the

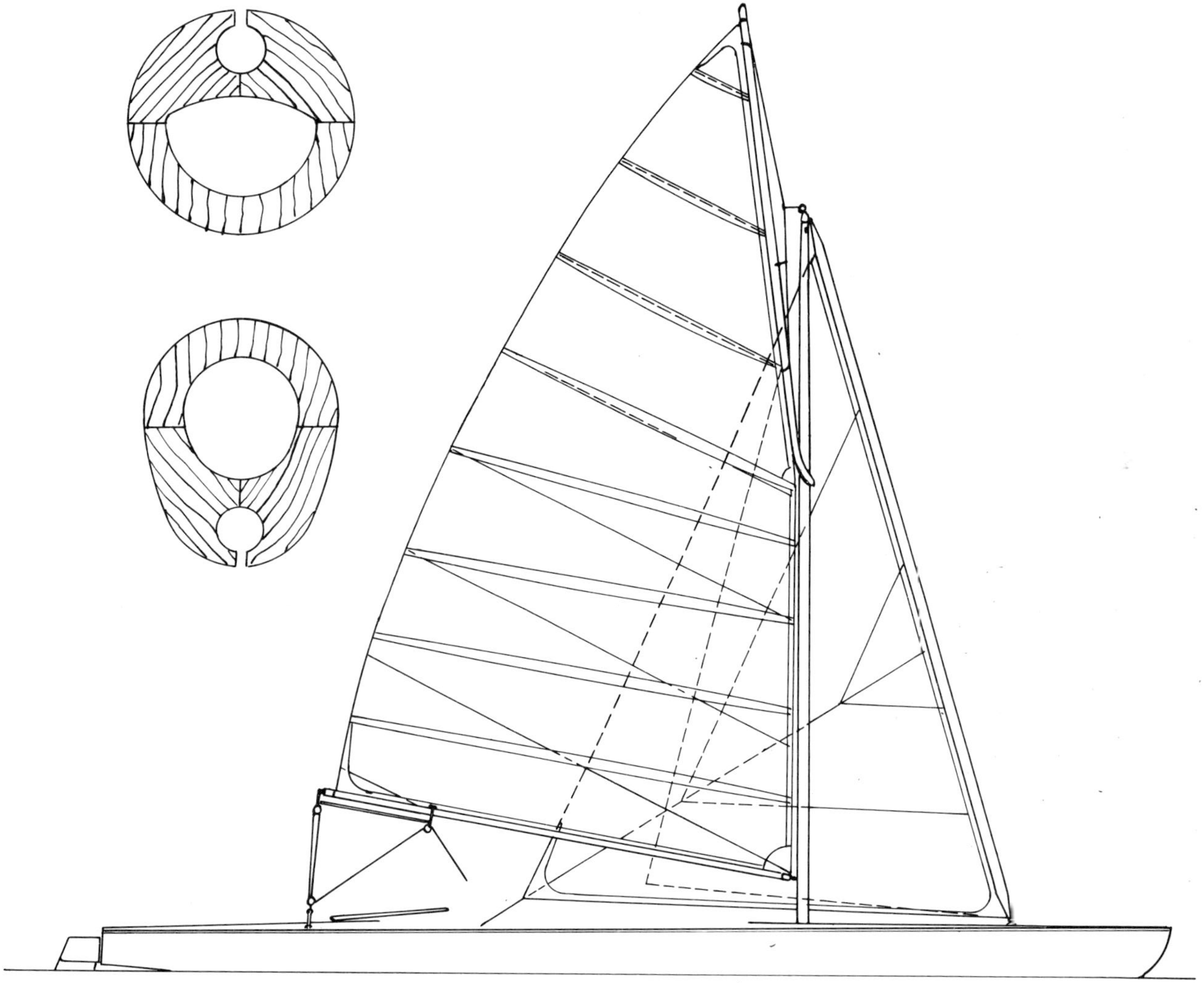

Figure 55. Twenty square metre
centreboard 'Rennjolle' designed by Carl
Marten of Starnberg, Germany, in 1929.
This shows the fully battened gunter lug
at its ultimate development for racing.
Top left: section though boom. Lower:
lug yard. Note wooden forestay spar with
groove for luff of staysail.

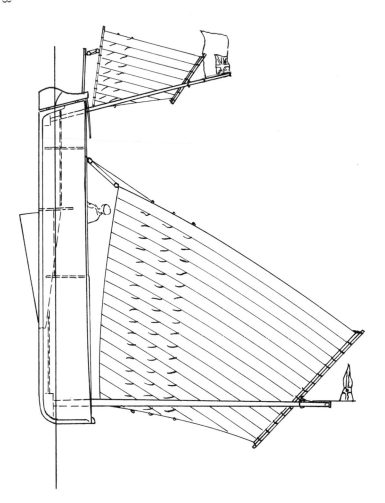

Figure 56. The 28ft 6in centreboard lugger yacht *Procyon* was built in 1867 for Richard McMullen, amongst the greatest of small boat sailors, who favoured the standing-lug foresail and mizzen rig for his cruising in the English Channel.

best remembered were the *Procyon* and *Perseus*, conceived and built for R. T. McMullen, the notable Victorian cruising yachtsman whose book *Down Channel* admirably describes his voyaging, and is one of the few true classics of yachting literature, which never palls with re-reading.

The *Procyon* was built in 1867 by Holloway of Whitstable, Kent, and was lengthened five feet by the stern in 1870. She was 28ft 6in long × 7ft 9in beam × 5ft 10in deep at the stern and 5ft 2in at the sternpost, including a 6in deep keel. Her draught forward was 2ft and aft 3ft, extended to a maximum of 4ft 6in by an iron centreplate in a case which did not protrude above the sole. She was clinker planked and fully decked, except for an amidship well and steering cockpit. The 6in diameter foremast was stepped 18in aft of the stem and was 21ft above the sheer. The mizzenmast stepped just inside the transom with 26ft between masts, which had no standing rigging.

The foresail, which McMullen termed the mainsail, was a boomless standing lugsail, sheeting 21ft abaft the mast. It was 14ft on the luff, 25ft 6in leech, 18ft 6in foot and 12ft head, bent to a 13ft yard. Three rows of reef points were fitted. It was a powerful sail which induced strong weather helm reaching and invariably brought the lugger up into the wind if the helm was released, close hauled. The sail was made of 'No 5 double, 24in canvas split ... with an upper tack tackle hooked into an extra cringle above the third reef for peaking the sail, and a lower tack tackle at the foot of the mast for tacking it.' When the lower tack was triced up, the sail worked above the head of a man standing on the foredeck.

To prevent the luff of the mainsail or the smaller storm sail, from roaching aft and losing efficiency when the mainsheet was got in turning to windward, the reef cringles on the luff were bent to hoops on the mast.

The mizzen was another standing lugsail with a boom, sheeting to an outrigger. Its luff was 7ft 3in, leech 9ft 6in, head 4ft and foot 6ft 6in. It had two rows of reef points.

The *Procyon's* accommodation was spartan. Her 'cuddy' under the foredeck was 12ft long and had 4ft height under the deck beams. McMullen disdained the locker-seats on each side and slung a hammock between the mast and the bulkhead. His stores and equipment were stowed in the 5ft long space under the after deck, probably the length added to the boat three years after launch.

McMullen thoroughly enjoyed voyaging down channel in the *Procyon*, single handed, achoring in open roadsteads, being almost independent of the shore for long periods and beating about in all conditions.

It would be possible, at reasonable expense, to reproduce a yacht-lugger similar to McMullen's *Procyon* and interesting for a keen sailing traditionalist to measure his ability and experience against him, but it is doubtful whether present-day sailing men would survive the incredible labour of lugger sailing experienced by McMullen. Hear him on reefing the *Procyon*.

'I hook the reef tackle into the fourth cringle of the after leach, lower away main halyards sufficiently, take in the slack of the upper tack tackle until it is nearly two blocks, peak the yard

again by setting up halyards, and then bowse the mainsheet aft with the reef tackle. When this is done, half the sail remains properly set, and the boat is under command during the process of reefing, or until the squall has expended its violence. If a reef is to be taken, the lower tack tackle and mainsheet have to be transferred to the cringles above and the sister hooks moused, the two hoops on the mast shifted a cringle higher, the tack and sheet rolled up and secured with short peices of manilla rope having an eye spliced in one end, eighteen reef points tied, fall of mainsheet belayed – leaving plenty of slack, so as not to interfere with hoisting the sail, reef tackle cast off, and upper tack tackle overhauled.

'Then hoist away mainsail, taking care to keep your head out of the way of the upper main sheet-block when the sail flaps in the wind, peak with upper tack tackle until the sail is girt from the tack to the peak, bowse down lower tack, throw her up into the wind and get the sheet aft. If the sail is not then as flat as it might be, I put a strop on the fall of the main halyards (which lead aft to the waist through a block at the foot of the mast), hook in a luff tackle, shake up ir the wind and bowse away until no more can be got, belay the slack of main halyards and remove the strop and tackle.

'With a strong crew – as in match sailing – the lower tack would be set up and the mainsheet hauled aft before hoisting; but single handed, the sail must be free of all impediment, to enable it to be hoisted at all. When dry, the weight of this sail with yard is 92lbs. The stormsail differs from the mainsail only in size, being 6ft or the head and

13ft 6in on the foot. The hoist is the same, and its weight with yard ½ cwt (56lbs). It is necessary to state these particulars to account for the time expended in making or taking in sail . . .'

The Deal beachmen could make little of McMullen; to them he was a new type of yachtsman who spurned their importuning offers of 'assistance', which so often could turn into a claim for salvage. They probably eventually regarded him as a thorough seaman like themselves.

After owning other yachts, in 1890 McMullen had built another lugger, the 27ft *Perseus*, by Holloways. She was to be his last boat and emerged as a carvel planked, transom sterned development of the *Procyon*, without the troublesome centreplate, Dimensions were 27ft 2in × 7ft 4in beam × 3ft 3in draught forward and 4ft 6in aft. The same arrangement of masts and rig was adopted, with 100 square feet more sail area and a jib set on a moderate bowsprit.

He cruised her single-handed in the English Channel that summer and found her thoroughly seaworthy and comfortable by his standards. In June 1891 McMullen set out down Channel for a cruise and was found by French fishermen dead at her tiller with the *Perseus* sailing herself along on a calm, moonlit sea; a fitting end for a great amateur seaman.

It is not necessary to own a large craft to explore the fascination and character of the two masted lugger. Most shapely, fine ended, moderately deep open boats of 14ft upwards are suitable.

Before 1939 the two-masted lugger *Pophyn* sailed from the Hamble River in Hampshire. Owned by Mr and Mrs Mann, *Pophyn* was a 9ft clinker rowing dinghy fitted with leeboards and a small jib set on a short bowsprit. Sails were home made from Willesden canvas and spars were shaped in the garden from stock-size softwood, supported by a minimum of rigging. As the mizzen would interfere with a conventional tiller, a Norwegian push-pull tiller was fitted to a rudder head yoke. This practical, miniature lugger bobbed about the Solent and Spithead with her elderly crew sitting on the bottom boards having tremendous fun at very little outlay, whilst being regarded with wistful interest or amusement by owners of more pretentious but more costly yachts.

Pophyn was makeshift, but she emphasises the simplicity and cheapness which the lug, like the spritsail rig, can bring to sailing. There are thousands of old dinghies like her lying for sale at low prices in most European and North American sailing areas; capable of bringing joy of ownership and enthusiasm of experiment for those wishing to sail for a few hundred pounds or dollars, instead of several thousands.

Part II

Spritsails and Lugsails in England, Wales and Ireland

3

Luggers in the Downs

The Kentish coast of the English Channel, from the Thames approaches to Dungeness and further westward, funnels the inward and outward bound merchant shipping to and from the many major ports of the North Sea and often the Baltic. The Kent coast forms the western shore of the narrowest part of the Channel, where the Goodwin Sands lie alongshore between the North and South Forelands, with the deep water anchorage known as the Downs between these sands and the beach. This roadstead was heavily used by sailing vessels until the end of commercial sail and was frequently crowded with shipping during the peaceful years of nineteenth century mercantile expansion. Vessels bound down the English Channel sometimes lay windbound there for weeks and during and after gales, ships that were sinking, damaged or in need of anchors and cables, sails and provisions, required assistance.

Opposite the Goodwin Sands the town of Deal raised houses and lookout towers along the shingle. A blustery, weatherbeaten place, its low, red brick buildings tumbled about in narrow streets and alleys, to the edge of the steep strip of beach on which the golen varnished rows of luggers, galleys and punts of the beachmen were crowded. Until the mid-nineteenth century the tree-lined farms and meadows behind the town were dotted with windmills, but the beach and its activities dominated life in Deal.

Two and three miles south were Walmer and Kingsdown, also homes of beachmen. Just round the South Foreland lay Dover Harbour; principal entry for the sailing packets from France, a commercial port and home of more luggers and galleys. A short distance south of the North Foreland lay Ramsgate, a similarly busy, man-made harbour for commercial and fishing craft, including luggers, and four miles north a few luggers sailed from the tiny harbour of Broadstairs. Immediately round the North Foreland, in the Thames Estuary, Margate harbour sheltered luggers and other fishing vessels, besides merchant shipping.

The seamanship, daring and courage of these Kentish luggermen and the bold weatherliness of their locally designed and built craft made them internationally famous; a glory tarnished by occasional extortionate demands for assistance rendered to ships in trouble.

The North and South Goodwin Sands extended almost nine miles, parallel to the coast and constantly changing, with swatchways running across them in places. At high water the sands were covered by from two to four fathoms and the eastern side was steep to, with depths of 12 to 16 fathoms close in, giving a leadsman little warning of danger in darkness or fog. Some parts dried out at low water to firm hard sand, but many areas became alive when covered by the running tides and, unless stranded vessels were quickly floated, they usually swaddled down in the sand and were eventually engulfed. This reputation as a 'shippe swallower' is as old as navigation in these waters and large ships are still sometimes lost on these treacherous shoals. When they remain firm, wrecks become menaces to other shipping until broken up by bad weather or explosives.

The bulk of sailing ship traffic passed between these sands and the shore. Before the days of steam tugs, much of this traffic was sailing ships outward bound from the Thames before the prevailing westerlies. They came fetching down from the north, through the Gull Stream channel, and in contrary winds most of them anchored in the roadstead of the Downs, which stretched approximately between Sandown Castle in the north to Walmer Castle in the south. They would be joined by ships coming up Channel with a fair wind, bound for London. These usually anchored in the Downs to await a shift of wind which would enable them to enter the Thames. In bad weather the anchorage filled with sheltering ships. Awaiting a slant might entail days or weeks windbound at anchor but this had some

compensations; passengers could shorten a long voyage by landing at Deal and others could join outward bound ships after they had left port. It was also a convenient roadstead to embark or land pilots and transmit orders for discharge or for the intended voyage.

The Downs had depths between 8 to 11 fathoms but, the bottom being principally chalk, it was not ideal holding ground for anchors. Nevertheless it was always heavily used by sailing vessels, as the mainland offered shelter from westerly gales and the Goodwins gave some slight protection from easterly winds. Huge fleets of shipping were crowded into this comparatively small anchorage after protracted westerly weather; numbers of one or two hundred being common and extraordinary fleets of three hundred or more occurring at times. Small vessels and coasters often also lay in the 'Small Downs' to the north east of Deal, where craft drawing up to about 14 feet could anchor in 4–5 fathoms on a blue clay bottom with little chance of being fouled by a large ship driving from her anchors in bad weather. In strong east by north, east north east or south east winds the land offered no protection and the Downs became a poor anchorage, so ships had often to shift for shelter elsewhere. If these winds hardened into a gale the Downs usually became a disastrous confusion of ships dragging their anchors, breaking adrift from their cables, perhaps driving foul of each other or getting ashore. Those holding on might be riding perilously to one anchor, having parted the other cable at the hawse, while many would be storm battered, leaking so badly that worn out crews could not keep the pumps going fast enough and needed assistance from fresh men. All this misery and terror often occurred when the bitter blackness of a rain-thrashed winter night seemed to deter the stoutest heart. But into the roaring darkness beyond the leaping and crashing alongshore surf, the Kentish beachmen launched their luggers, boats evolved over generations to earn part of their livelihood from disaster conditions by offering pilotage, salvage and assistance to shipping and incidentally in the course of this work saving many lives.

Much of their work was not so dramatic and luggers, with the galleys, great galleys and small punts which were also used in the beachmen's trade, found much to do in less boisterous conditions; putting pilots on board, rendering various forms of assistance, carrying out replacement anchors or sweeping for lost ones, taking off or landing people from ships in the anchorage, fishing, smuggling and other minor occupations, all contributing to picking up a living.

But hard winds brought most work in the days of sail. As ships under storm canvas came driving into the Downs anchorage from the Channel, the semaphore wagged busily, reporting arrivals and interpreting questions from captains for transmission to their owners as to whether they should accept offers of assistance with anchors and cables, or other aid from the beachmen whose luggers would be cruising about the Downs under close canvas, like attentive seabirds with an eye to the main chance. Ashore, beachmen manned tall, wooden lookout towers or peered at arrivals and sails in the offing

through long brass telescopes; steadied in the gale against tarred wooden sheds which dotted the top of the beach to serve as meeting places and stores for equipment, paint and oilskins for the crew of each lugger or 'set of boats' which lined much of Deal beach.

The site of each enterprise was known as a 'stage' and boats hauled up on the beach were said to be staged. They lay close together, sheer to sheer, sterns almost touching the houses. By ancient custom or prescriptive right each owner or group occupied had held undisputed possession of their own stage. Numbers and types of boats at each stage varied; some owners might have a large and a small lugger, a galley punt, galley and a small punt; others perhaps only a galley punt, while another, interested in fishing, might have a half-boat alongside a galley punt. At each stood a sturdy capstan, rooted deep in the shingle, the bars turned by old beachmen and boys who were paid sixpence for each haul up and received a small share of any salvage gained by the boat, for in the beachmen's heyday the lugger crews considered it beneath them to turn a capstan bar.

The crest of the ever changing beach was known as the 'full', and luggers were often launched from this to gain adequate momentum when going off into seas. Hauled up luggers were always left with bows seawards, kept upright with bilge blocks and prepared for instant launching. Rows of them lay triggered-up before their capstans, resting on greased skies called 'woods' or 'trows', like railway sleepers, which led down the beach. They were restrained from rushing down them by a chain rove through a hole in the keel known as the ruffle hole. This returned to the standing part to which it was attached by a pivoted slip hook or trigger, retained closed by an iron ring. Before a launch this ring was slipped back and replaced by a ropeyarn. During strong onshore winds or heavy breaking seas a warp was rigged to an anchor laid permanently, well beyond the low water mark. This was used when launching with a wind so onshore that the main lug could not be hoisted until the boat was clear of the first breakers. It passed over a snatch on the luggers proposed weather bow and ran clear of everything on her quarter, being used more as a spring to ensure casting the lugger on the correct tack after the sail was hoisted, than as a haul-off. The block had an opening on one side allowing the rope to be flung clear as soon as its job was done. Two of the crew tended this carefully, as the success of a launch in those conditions usually depended on its handling, though in other circumstances of wind and tide it was unnecessary.

When the crew were on board and ready to launch, with the woods greased and the mizzen set, the helmsman took the tiller, the rudder being temporarily triced up above the bottom of keel by a tackle during the launch. The helmsman waited until two or three big seas had pounded the beach and one of the launching party stood by with a sharp knife. At the shout 'Let her go!' he slashed the ropeyarn, the trigger flew out and perhaps twenty tons of lugger started down the steep beach at quickening speed, pushed by many men, roaring and rumbling on the wooden trows, the

last few of which were daringly placed by men standing at the surf, holding them down until the instant when the rushing lugger plunged into and through the first few waves, carrying her way through them, clear of the beach and into deep water, perhaps ascending high on a sea but with the great fore lug swaying up the mast, springing her to life. The rope was cast off and with sheets trimmed she bounded away seaward.

Occasionally a launch went wrong and by misjudgement or some quirk of a sea the lugger was thrown back on the beach, sometimes broadside on; termed a 'dry launch' and possibly disastrous if the lugger listed seaward and filled with breaking water. She might be carried alongshore, beating on the shingle, some distance from her capstan and perhaps stove in. An almost new lugger laden with an anchor and chain cable was once thrown back in this way and, after striking the hard beach twice, split open and smashed, leaving her dazed and cursing crew floundering in the surf.

It was difficult to launch a lugger at high water as there was insufficient distance for her to travel to gain momentum and drive clear, despite use of the warp as a haul-off. The construction of Deal pier in 1864 seriously hampered the launching of South End luggers and in heavy gales from south-west, they were sometimes swamped before getting clear. Such spectacular launching was hard on the lugger's bottoms and whenever possible, with the wind offshore or in calm weather, they were got down the beach on the trows and left to lift off with the rising tide.

Beaching could be more dangerous than

the trows, with the capstan cable fast to her stern, imposing great strain on the keel. The lugger was hauled up on the trows and prepared for launching in a few minutes, when required.

The origins of the Deal beach-boats are now beyond discovery, but they had a long history and probably went through many phases of evolution. Frederick af Chapman's accurate *Architectura Navalis Mercatoria*, published in 1768 gives a profile and sail plan of 'A Deal cutter', which illustrates the sort of craft the beachmen used before lug rig became fashionable. The term cutter indicated a clinker planked hull; 'cutter built' referring to this construction in fast craft, rather than to rig. The profile of the Deal boat was similar to the later luggers but she was rigged with three boomless spritsails. The main was largest, set on a mast amidships. It was fitted with one brail and two rows of reef points. The foresail was similar but slightly smaller, and the foremast stepped close abaft the stem. The small spritsail mizzen set on a mast stepped on the inner face of the transom. Its foot was spread by an outrigger and it had one reef. A jib with one row of reef points set from the foremast head to the end of a well steeved bowsprit. (Fig. 57). It was the developed rig of a waterman's boat, with minimum rigging to obstruct when going alongside shipping and it is easy to assume that at some time during the 18th century the spritsails were superseded by lugs, but as such surmises are often incorrect, it remains speculation.

By the early nineteenth century Deal luggers had evolved to the definite types which are best remembered. First class luggers were of two sizes.

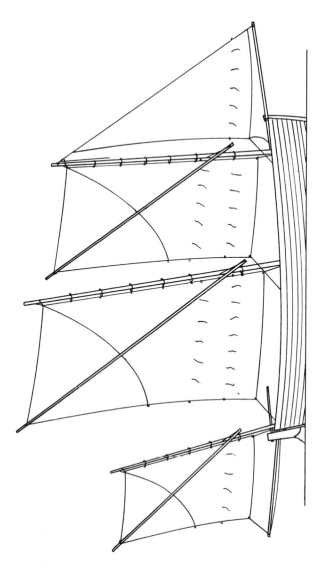

Figure 57. The three masted 'Deal cutter' of the mid-eighteenth century had a clinker planked hull and set three spritsails and a jib on a bowsprit. Note brails and mizzen stepped on inside of transom. The forerunner of the later famous luggers of the Downs.

launching, depending on the strength and direction of the wind and state and set of the tide. Luggers were sometimes 'knocked up' half full of water in onshore gales and were occasionally stove-in or even capsized on the beach before the haul up rope could be hooked in and frantic beachmen place trows in the surf. The ideal beaching was made by coming in on a wave under jib and mizzen, to run up the beach as far as possible. The shore helpers standing by with capstan cable and trows, ready to attach and place them as the wave receded. Then the lugger was hauled clear of the water and was turned on

A large boat built by Thomas Hayward and Sons of Deal in 1835 was 38ft long × 12ft 3in beam over planking and 5ft depth. This type was open except for a forward peak, decked and bulkheaded off for about 13ft abaft the stem and containing six wooden berths, lockers and a small stove. The keel was straight and narrow, of oak or Canadian rock elm rebated for the garboard planks. The stem and sternpost were slightly raked and had a small radius at the forefoot. Hull sections had considerable rise of floor with the sharp bottom carried out to fine forward and after ends, the bow being particularly hollow below the waterline (the secret of their windward ability), but full above. The transom was small, shapely and high above the waterline, leaving a clean wake. Although these luggers had a draught of perhaps only 5ft aft and 3ft 6in forward, they sailed well and were powerful seaboats.

The hulls were clinker planked in narrow strakes, usually of ¾in thick young and unseasoned English elm, copper fastened to English oak and ash timbers which were pre-bent for months before use and were then fitted close to the planking but notched over the lands. This produced a light but strong hull having a weight of about 3½ tons. 5–6 tons of shingle ballast were carried in canvas bags stowed in the bottom, under the ceiling. Thwarts were fitted but only to brace the hull and when using the sweeps in a calm the crew stood, pushing at the oar looms. A 12ft punt was often taken to sea as a dinghy, lashed upside down on the thwarts. Clinker construction of these effectively open hulls allowed them to flex and they worked in a seaway under

sail. The pump was usually going at sea in bad weather, for leakage as well as spray. Hulls were varnished or coated with linseed oil, producing a golden brown colour contrasting with the sheerstrake and transom which were painted black. The boat's and owner's names and the place of ownership were prominently painted across the transom, but only in later years did some luggers carry fishing numbers. Many luggers were boldly named: *Tiger, Success, Friend of all Nations, Queen of Sheba, North Star, Pride of the Sea, Early Morn, Renown* and *Amazon* being typical. As they were repeatedly hauled out the bottoms were kept clean, which contributed to their speed and ability. Bilge keels were fitted to protect the bilges when beaching or launching and these assisted windward sailing.

At that period the rig of many was three masts, with dipping lugsails on the fore and main masts which were stepped in tabernacles. The tack of the main lug set down well forward. The mizzen was a standing lug sheeted to a long outrigger, the mast being stepped inside the transom, offset to clear the tiller. Sometimes they were sailed with the mainmast lowered and laid along the boat with its head supported by a crutch or lashing on the mizzen, and the large main lug was set on the foremast, which was of almost equal height. This rig was particularly used in strong winds or if an anchor was to be taken off, but the main was a powerful sail and in fine weather a topsail was often set above it, some luggers carrying a main topmast sent up abaft the masthead. A jib was frequently set on a long bowsprit and was helpful when tacking in a seaway, besides drawing the lugger well to windward in a breeze. The fore lug was usually boomed out when running with a spar or the unshipped bowsprit. Sometimes a long boathook was used (Fig. 58). The hull of such a lugger then cost about £275 including spars and blocks; two suits of sails cost £45.

Due to the influence of smuggling and the earlier (Napoleonic) wartime need of speed to avoid capture, luggers built before about 1860 were finer in form and faster than later craft which were primarily used for fishing and 'hovelling', as assisting shipping came to be termed. Seven or eight men were a usual crew, but up to a score might be shipped for a special service such as a salvage job.

The small type of first class luggers averaged 33ft length by about 10ft 6in beam. These were similarly constructed and rigged, costing about £200 for hull only and a further £50 ready for sea. A crew of six was usual in summer and up to a dozen in winter. Many of these boats were rigged with two lugsails, known as 'foresail and mizzen rig', which later became general. Two masted luggers were in use in 1803 when Thomas Luny (1758–1837) painted one in detail attending a large ship entering the Downs (Painting *East Indiaman 'Cumberland' off Dover*). In three views on the same picture she is shown cruising towards the ship, lowering her sails, then has the mizzen unstepped to tow astern of the ship with the foremast still standing. Another early nineteenth-century painting shows a two masted Kentish lugger cruising off Dungeness in a strong wind and illustrates the suppleness of the lug yards

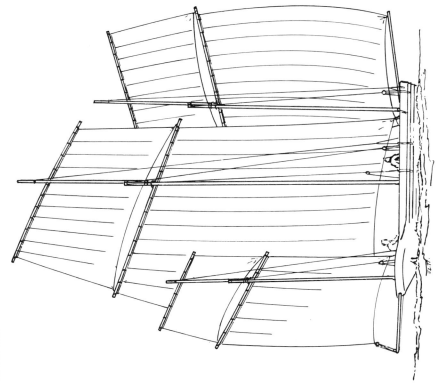

Figure 58. Three masted Walmer lugger *England's Glory*, about 1840. Topsails are set above the lugsails and the foresail is boomed out to windward with the unshipped bowsprit during a long run downwind.

which bent considerably.

Two and three masted luggers existed together until three masters died out about the 1840s. The true reason for omission of the mainmast and its lug is now obscure and difficult to define. It is probable that, as merchant ships increased in size during the early nineteenth century they needed heavier anchors and cables, so more space was needed in the lugger's waist amidships to carry them, and the mainmast, with its sails and gear, began to be an embarrassment. Also, the luggers found much of their work in strong winds, when there was no need of large sail area. The beachmen would find that having the area in a large forelug and a larger mizzen increased their windward ability, though more men were needed to set and handle the rig. In lighter weather the developing 'great galleys', later known as 'galley punts', were increasingly used for speedy errands, and this contributed to the Kentish lugger rig changing to a dipping fore lug, standing lug mizzen sheeted to an outrigger and a jib set on a bowsprit traveller in suitable conditions. The foremast was stepped at the forepeak bulkhead and the foresail tack was set down to an eye on the gammon iron. Its clew sheeted well aft and the sail needed skilled handling as it could never be allowed to be caught aback, especially when the lugger lost way, or she might capsize. This was a weakness of the rig and many luggers carried two foresails, one on each side of the mast. When going about the lug was lowered as the boat came head to wind, the traveller was unhooked to 'the other lug which was quickly hoisted as she paid off.

The beachmen knew their craft intimately and handling was superb. In very bad weather they might reduce to a double reefed foresail and, to board a wreck, they frequently beat well to windward of her, lowered the foresail and ran down alongside before the wind, under the mizzen. Easy to describe, but the awesome power of a line of heavy breaking seas on the Goodwins has to be seen to be realised; they rise in gale driven cataracts twenty feet high and thunder forward at thirty miles per hour. As momentum is checked by the sands, huge seas break and roar in across the wind with tops blown away in sheets of solid water to leeward, occasionally leaping up forty feet as they meet the long line of breakers. A cross tide runs at perhaps four knots and the dense drift of spray, the stinging rain, the tearing gripping wind and the thunder of canvas, confused all but the bravest and most experienced.

A Deal lugger might average 25 launchings each year and many had a short life of hard use but the *Hope*, built in 1859, was still sailing thirty years later and as salvaging and hovelling declined, many luggers remained in service for a quarter century. Some were built with money raised by mortgage, most by owners share subscription. When the *Cosmopolite* was lost off Dungeness in 1890 the *Cosmopolite II* was built partly from money raised by public subscription.

Some luggers and other beach boats were privately owned, usually by a boatman, but ownership of many was shared amongst several boatmen, with other shares held by shopkeepers and local businessmen, widows, retired seafarers and landlords of taverns, which naturally attracted the custom of the crews, who used these places as clubs and meeting places where business was discussed, bargains struck and often much drinking and horseplay took place. In bad weather they might sleep in the taproom to be on call if a launch was necessary.

The boatmen believed in wrapping up for winter work afloat, starting with heavy, dark coloured trousers which would almost stand up without the wearer, well greased leather boots, dark blue or brown guernseys, old pilot cloth jackets and sealskin caps of various shapes. They made sure no water penetrated down their neck by having a woollen scarf about twelve foot long wound around it by a friend holding one end while the wearer turned himself round, winding it on. Then followed wide fitting oilskin trousers reaching up to be tied under the arms. Overall went a big oilskin coat which was tied down the front. A sou'wester completed the outfit, leaving little more than nose and eyes exposed, but despite the clumsiness of this clothing ashore, the boatmen were wonderfully quick when afloat. Moss, Roberts, Riley, Rednill, Jarman, Finnis, Marsh, Gaymer, Adams, Hanger, Norris and Grigg were some of their surnames and, as ever, there were social distinctions; the North End Deal beachmen were regarded as an inferior class by the South Deal and Walmer men, and there was considerable rivalry afloat and ashore. However, this turned to solidarity when Dover and Ramsgate boatmen competed with them for the same job afloat. Many boatmen were reputedly descended from the jutes who settled in east Kent after a fifth century invasion. They had little

prospect of comfortable living and no security. A few owned ale houses, some owned bathing machines on the beach and many hawked fish around the streets in autumn but they were all able and courageous when afloat, though they drove a hard bargain for their services. Their outlook was accurately grasped by Clark Russel who asked a Deal boatman 'If you were off the sands in thick weather and you fell in with a ship so heading that she was bound to run ashore, would you acquaint her people with the peril they were in?' He answered; 'I'd hail her and ask if we should put a man aboard to navigate her. If she declined, then she might go ashore and welcome'.

The beachmen were good seamen but often knew grim poverty and seldom managed to raise themselves from humble living in those days of harsh existence. In 1833, a government return recorded 437 boatmen and concern was expressed on their prospects and employment. About 1840 several Deal boatmen went out to New Zealand, taking two galley punts. In 1841 one them, J. S. Cross, discovered Nelson Harbour, later the South Island capital, where he was eventually made pilot and harbourmaster. During 1858 there was widespread poverty and depression in Deal and many families, including the Roberts, Claysons, Corys, Bowls and Wilds emigrated to New Zealand in the ship Mystery. Six of these boatmen were employed by a wool shipper to work boats off the beach there in summer, carrying off baled wool to coasters lying in Timaru Roadstead. The beachmen rented these boats and soon mastered local conditions, improving loading times. They were paid £250 per year and were each sold an acre of land on which to build a house; New Zealand must have seemed a paradise to these hardy Kentishmen. Other Deal immigrants entered the New Zealand fisheries, though there is no record of them attempting to introduce their luggers as a type.

By the mid nineteenth century gradually rising costs and decline of work for the Deal luggers caused the building of a limited number of slightly smaller luggers which were known as 'cats', though this seems to have been a local technical term, the boatmen generally referring to them as luggers. Cats were less expensive to build and maintain but could do most of the work of the larger lugger, having the same hull form and ratio of dimensions. The two types were indistinguishable at a distance. The cats had less displacement and no decked-in forepeak. Instead a portable sleeping cabin and galley, with bunks for four men was shipped for cruising away from the beach for a day or so. This was placed between the main and fore thwarts and was effectively a watertight box with a sliding door at its after end and two sliding windows forward.

The 'half boat' was an even smaller version of the luggers, with the same rig and proportions. These were really large and seaworthy versions of the foresail and mizzen punts but were much smaller than a cat, being used almost exclusively for net fishing in the sprat, mackerel and herring seasons. For this work an iron lantern shipped on a bracket forward. Most were owned by boatmen who specialised in fishing.

In 1823 there were eight boatbuilders at Deal: Thomas Bayly, Michael Bayly, John Harrison, Morris Langely, Richard Mockett and Ratcliffe and Allen all at North End; Thomas Hayward at South End and Stephen Brown at Copper Street.

The Haywards and Baylys were noted builders of luggers. Michael Bayly was succeeded by his son Isaac. Henry Durban was their yard foreman and on Isaac's death he continued the business with his brother, thus working in the same boatbuilding shop for 62 years, one of the last boats built by Durban was the galley punt Cruiser which was awarded £90 salvage a few days after her launch. Such a boat could be built by a man and boy.

Besides local output, many Deal luggers were built at Rye, Sussex, and some at Whitstable, Kent, particularly during the first half of the nineteenth century.

The Deal and other lugger builders apparently did not draw elementary plans or make half models for design, but usually worked from three section moulds of sizes and forms to suit luggers of differing lengths and types; coupled with profiles of stems and sternposts, general proportions and sheer of hull which were evolved from years of practical experiment and experience. These moulds and other templates and data were handed-on for generations and although contributing to the 'mystery' of the boatbuilders art, mentioned in an apprentices indentures, did little to advance design.

Many luggers of all sizes, galleys and ships boats were built by the Hayward family, Thomas Hayward died in 1848 aged 80 and his son Isaac Hayward in 1887, aged 80. Between them they built at Deal for over a century in a shop at the south end of Deal and another adjoining the family house in Middle Street. Completed luggers were drawn down the street by horses and beachmen, over a track of trows. In 1866 Hayward built the 25-ton *Alexandra* for Ramsgate. With dimensions of 46ft × 15ft 3in × 7ft 9in depth she could be rigged as a lugger for winter work and as a cutter for summer pleasure tripping with passengers from Ramsgate Harbour. She was lost on the Goodwins in March 1870, salvaging mahogany from a wreck, for which she carried nine hands. The *Alexandra* was worth £700 and typically was uninsured, as companies would not accept the risk on beach boats.

The daring of the beachmen and the publicity which court awards gave to their salvage work attracted the attention of nobility, who sometimes performed the christening ceremony of a new lugger and probably contributed a few guineas towards her cost. The *Garland* was launched by the Earl of Clanwilliam. She was 35ft × 10ft and of 14 tons burthen. The following year the Hayward-built *Mary* was launched by the wife of the local member of parliament. Luggers were also built for other places; in 1867 Issac Hayward launched the *Garland* for Folkstone owners and in 1868 the *James and Thomas* for the same port.

H. and G. Gardner built at North End, Deal. In 1868 they launched the first class lugger *Albion II* with dimensions of 38ft 6in × 12ft 6in × 6ft 8in depth. In 1869 she was awarded £400 for one salvage, but this was by then becoming exceptional due to the increasing numbers of steam tugs for sailing ship towage and growth of steamship traffic.

James Nicholas, one of a family of beachmen, started business as a boatbuilder at north Deal in 1858. He built luggers, galley punts and other beach craft at a yard in Beach Street and shortly before his death in 1909, aged 83, the yard had completed a motor boat. He was typical of some lugger builders who worked afloat when business was slack. In 1878 he built a typical Deal lugger for the Australian government, to land on beaches at Freemantle, Western Australia. In 1896 he built another for the same owners; the last lugger built at Deal and with her spars made by Bristow and sails by Finnis, a typical local product. She was shipped out as deck cargo on a steamer. About 1914 Nicholas' sons moved to Chatham to build boats for warships.

Ships in trouble in the Downs often needed new sails; sometimes whole suits, and many were made in Deal by the Finnis family, who also cut the sails for luggers and other beach boats. In 1823 the loft of Philip Finnis, which had been established in the 1790s was rivalled by that of Thomas Marlow. Three Finnis sons carried on the loft, sometimes employing twenty men, but the trade declined and when George W. Finnis died in 1900 he was the last Deal sailmaker.

The work of the beachmen had a long history of change and development. In 1674 a Kentish builder launched a 25ft × 6ft 6in beam boat costing £17-10s, which was probably typical of contemporary beachboats of which between 80 to 100 then worked in the Downs in all weathers. Pepys' diary for May 11th 1660, written on board the *Naseby*, records 'It blew very hard all this night. About eleven..... came the boats from

Deal with great stores of provisions'. Supplying beach shingle for ballasting ships was then another source of income for which the patriotic boatmen charged Englishmen three pence per ton, while foreigners had to pay eight pence.

The Downs became a naval anchorage of importance, and many captains preferred to use the beachmen's boats for communication with the shore to avoid loss of pressed men by desertion. In 1703 a fierce and protracted gale caught a fleet of about 160 ships in the Downs, commanded by Sir Clowdisley Shovel. They rode it out for two weeks and, in a temporary lull, sailed for the Thames, only to be caught next day in stronger winds, which caused serious disaster. First and second rates were battered into hulks; a flagship struck the sands and was lost, and only seventy ships survived the gale. The Deal boatmen rendered whatever assistance was possible but the boats of the Customs House remained idle, despite the urgent pleas of Deal's mayor. Typically, the official mind could not make a decision in time of stress. Eventually infuriated boatmen seized the customs boats to assist in the rescue of about two hundred of the hundreds of survivors who could be seen running frantically about on the sands at low water, until most were drowned by the flood tide.

The Kentish luggermen were frequently smugglers of commodities which varied with the taxes and official restrictions. This trade was at its peak in 1737, when an inquiry revealed that over 200 open boats were landing brandy between the North and South Forelands. Cargoes of goods were being run, occasionally in daylight, with little interference, and specially fast rowing galleys, averaging forty feet in length and rowed by ten men, were regularly crossing the Channel to Boulogne, Calais and sometimes Dunkirk in calm, misty weather with smuggled goods; some extreme craft were built between 50–80 feet long and rowed by up to twenty men. These easily evaded the pursuit of revenue vessels and were often painted white; an effective form of camouflage rediscovered by British coastal forces during the 1939–45 war.

Brandy, lace, wines, tobacco and coin were smuggled, backed by financial reserves far beyond the beachmen and implicating all classes of society. The 'free trade' flourished so much that Deal boats became notorious and when a prolonged spell of bad weather kept most of them hauled ashore during January 1784, an informer advised prime minister Pitt of this and, apparently in revenge, a regiment of soldiers was sent to Deal, where naval cutters lay offshore to prevent escape seawards. The enraged beachmen were kept back at gunpoint while soldiers wielding axes smashed up luggers and burned others, leaving the community almost without means to earn a living. It was many years before Deal men forgot the depths to which the politicians had sunk, yet, being sailors, they gave their services without stint to aid the wars against France. These brought ever increasing numbers of ships to the Downs where Admiral Nelson had his headquarters in 1801 and a Deal beachman named Yawkins, a noted smuggler, became a favourite pilot to the flagship.

Salvage work continued with assistance to

naval and merchant ships, but the poor rewards for lives and equipment risked led, in October 1808, to the Deal men temporarily refusing to render assistance. In 1809 the ill fated expedition to land troops at Walcheren on the Dutch coast, brought a fleet of between 700–800 ships to the Downs, half of them transports. Two battalions of soldiers were embarked from Deal beach; fifty men each in 100 luggers, which put them on board within 30 minutes. Numbers of Kentish boats accompanied the fleet to act as landing craft.

With the war at its height the government relaxed the pursuit of Channel smugglers, probably due to the lack of preventive craft but also because of the information they frequently gleaned from French sources. With the victory at Waterloo of 1815 all this activity diminished to a trickle; few warships were left in commission but naval small craft were once more free to put down smuggling, which was suddenly again considered a serious crime. Merchant shipping was slow to recover from long years of war and the nineteenth-century trade boom was some years ahead. The beachmen faced hard times, eked out with the meagre awards for salvage and assistance to ships given by the commissioners who, as usual, were principally local dignitaries with little seafaring knowledge. Sums of £30 to £40 were awarded for taking out anchors and cables to distressed ships and this had to be divided amongst a dozen men, besides those ashore who helped to launch and haul up, and got the ground tackle on board the lugger before she left the beach.

The merchant shipping act of 1854 abolished the salvage commissioners and all claims for assistance were heard in the Admiralty court, often long after the incident. Awards were usually divided into shares by the beachmen. A lugger crew of 10 men received a share for each man, leaving 3½ for the boat (towards her maintenance) and a half share for the cost of provisions supplied by the owner, though most men preferred to provide their own. Sometimes the award was divided into equal shares, the boat receiving 1½ or 2 if she carried a cogie or punt, which was used in the service.

An instance of what these men could achieve by improvisation in adverse circumstances occurred in the salvage of the tea laden brig *Iron Crown*, ashore on the east side of the Goodwins during a south-westerly gale in February 1865. The lugger *England's Glory*, owned by William Spears, was sailed across the sands through a heavy sea by John Bailey, then stood to windward and bore away to run by the wreck. The foresail was lowered as she passed and six men from the lugger jumped aboard the *Iron Crown*, followed by six others from the Deal lifeboat *Van Kook*, on her first service. These dozen men rigged tackles to a kedge anchor on deck and swayed it out, clear of the brig, by the fore yard arm, letting it go to weather. As she moved on the sand the cable came taut and the brig rode to the kedge, head to sea. Afterwards they let go the bower anchor and as the flood made the *Iron Crown* was floated with the aid of two tugs. Sixty-two boatmen were involved in this salvage for which a record £7000 was awarded, the two tugs received £5000.

Plate 18. Beachmen's rivalry. The second class lugger *Fox* and the 'great galley' *Gipsy* racing to an American brig off the Goodwin Sands, 1831. *Drawing by William Stanton of the Fox.*

126

Such were the possible profits from disaster and death in the Downs but the boatmen's losses were often severe. From 1860–87, fifty-three Deal, Walmer and Kingsdown men were lost from luggers and twenty-three from galley-punts, leaving families in desperate poverty.

Life saving became part of the beachmen's tradition, before and after lifeboats were instituted. Between 1858 and 1880, two hundred and seventy rescued seamen were landed at Deal by luggers, besides those saved by local lifeboats. No payment was expected for saving life but, in common with other east coast salvagers, the beachmen were frequently awarded medals and rewards by individuals, societies and governments. True to their parsimonious traditions, the Board of Trade awarded the magnificent sum of £2 to be shared between eleven men who rescued eleven survivors from the wreck of the French ship *Ingolf* on the Goodwins in a gale.

William Stanton of Deal (1803–78) was a noted beachman, lugger owner, seafarer, pilot and occasional smuggler, between 1815 and 1867, during the heyday of sail. He wrote a fascinating journal, illustrated with lively and accurate drawings. Son of a beachman imprisoned for smuggling. Stanton left a then rare boarding school education in 1815 to ship as boy in a Deal-owned schooner, at the start of a typically varied career in foreign-going sloops, schooners, smacks, brigantines and ships in ocean trade and deep sea fishing. In 1824 he became a Deal beachman, buying a $\frac{1}{6}$ share of 'a set of boats', the largest a lugger named the *Ox*, also a second class lugger named *Fox* and a galley-punt, together with

equipment for working at wrecks on the Goodwins.

His journal vivedly describes a Goodwin stranding and subsequent salvage.

'On the evening of the 6th April 1830, being at a convivial party, a boatman of the middle of the town came in and said he heard some guns in the direction of the Goodwin. I, with a few more, went out of the room and got the boat ready; many did not come, as we often had a lost journey by revenue cutters firing off guns at the back of the Goodwin – signalling to one another looking after smugglers. However, we got the boat down and not quite water afloat. We found there were fourteen of us; we agreed that seven should get in the boat, the other seven to get the boat afloat, which they did with great difficulty, up to their middles in the water. If we were gone long enough to suppose we had fallen in with anything, they were to come out to the Goodwin in a large boat to assist. We stood out for the sands, wind ENE, strong ebb tide, dismal dark and bitterly cold. Worked up along the inside of the sand by the lead for some hours, and saw nothing.

'The major part was for giving it up, but the man that saw the flashes from the guns persisted that we were not far enough to the northward. We therefore made several more tacks, and had not the man been in the boat who saw the flashes, we certainly should have given it up for a false alarm, but in the standing off to the land, by the lead, we were just going about, when one man sung out he could see 'a something small'. It did not appear at first larger than your hand, but on nearing it we could see it was the vessel, with topsails set. Our difficulty now was that we could not find water enough to get to the vessel from the inside of the sand, so we had to bear up and run back again to the southward until we could find water enough to cross the sand – dangerous work on a dark night knocking about in shoal water on that sand. After we crossed we then had to work up to the northward again, aback on the Goodwin, until we could find the vessel again, and we were all this time in the greatest anxiety for fear another boat would get there before us. But, strange to say, there was not another boat came out to the sand. We got sight again of her, and run right by her, bow to bow, when 'stand by to jump' was the word. As we shot by her I fortunately jumped on her rail amidships – a very pretty treat if I had missed my hold, for I think it was never much darker. On my getting on board the decks were dreadfully lumbered, and no living soul to give the answer. I soon found that the long boat was gone, and the crew with it, no doubt. No light in the binnacle or cabin, all dark and silent except the striking of the ship heavily on the sand, and the hollow roaring of the sea flowing rapidly over the Goodwin, similar to the noise of a menagerie feeding time.

'When the boat came back and hailed me, I told them to spare me as many men as possible, for there is none here but myself. They put four men on board. Our first thing was to get a light to find the pump gear, for there was not even a lower box in the pumps. I asked them in the boat for their tinder-box and candles, when unfortunately there was only tinder-box and matches, no candles. We took the tinder box down into the cabin and struck a light, each man taking a brimstone match to look for candles about the cabin. At length we found a bundle of candles and each man then lighting his candle and blowing the sparks off the snuffs, which almost covered the whole cabin with fire. When my candle was lighted I was horror struck at seeing a cask of powder just before me on the cabin floor, with the head out. When I showed it to the others they seemed as if they were petrified with fear – how so many sparks could have escaped that cask I am at a loss to know – it must have been an entire work of providence. I took it on deck and threw it overboard. It appeared that the captain had it there for firing the signal guns, for the head of the cask lay on the cabin table. We then found the pump gear. Sounding the well, I found she made but little water. The ship's head was in the NW, with topsails set and fore top staysail, we squared the main yard and filled the fore one, when she canted off to the SE, and after striking heavily a great number of times she came afloat. We then run down aback of the Goodwin. A large Dover lugger hailed us and asked us where we were from and where bound. I told them from Petersburg, bound to Cadiz with as much foreign accent as I was master of – I was afraid if they knew how we were situated, with only five men, they might want to force some claim, but they had no suspicions, as they asked if we had seen a French ship. For a fishing smack had landed her crew at Dover, and they had come out purposely to look for her; I told them I had not seen a sail since dark. Then they asked me if I could spare them a bottle of liquor if they came on board, as the night was so cold, and with a great deal of captain this and captain that. I told them by no means to come on board as the cholera was raging so in England they would make me lay a long quarantine at Cadiz. They then said, "We wish you goodnight, captain, and a pleasant voyage", and they went away. We then hauled her in for Dover Castle and hove the ship to, waiting for water in Dover Harbour. The captain and ship agent came alongside; they were coming on board when I met them, and asked who they were and what they wanted. He told me he was the captain of the ship; I told him I could not allow him to come on board. He said he only wanted some clean linen! I told him I would not allow anyone on board, I was coming into Dover Harbour with the ship, to deliver her into the hands of the proper authorities, where he must lay his claim. He thought the case both cruel and hard, and went away with tears in his eyes. At high water, made sail and got safely into the Harbour, gave the ship into the hands of the proper officers under the Admiralty court, and proceeded home to Deal. The ship was taken into dock and discharged into the storehouse of Messrs. Latham and Co. and we were allowed to look into the cargo and open what cases we pleased, to see if everything agreed with the 'cockette', a customs house officer being present – it was great satisfaction as many things were of little value. It appears that in such cases they appeal from Dover to the officers of the Admiralty court and they considered that there was no risk of 'life', and as such £700 was a fair

remuneration. Dover court decreed as above. I received the same in sovereigns at Latham's Bank, Dover, and made the best of my way home, and divided it equally amongst my boat's crew, and it came to £52 per man.'

During the nineteenth-century heyday, fleets of anchored ships often stretched almost from the North to South Foreland. In 1858 two hundred and twenty sailing vessels sailed from the Downs between March 31st to April 4th, but only five steamers. Between April 27th to May 4th two hundred and sixteen sailing vessels and nine steamers and from June 22nd to June 28th, one hundred and ninety-seven sailing vessels and seven steamers. In January 1861 over a hundred ships passed through or anchored in the Downs during one day and one January morning in 1866 saw over five hundred vessels anchored there.

These figures and proportion of steam to sail were typical until the late 1860s when competition from steamers increased the need for speed in commerce and sailing ship voyaging. Large ships were towed up and down Channel by steam tugs, rarely anchoring in the Downs awaiting a slant. By the 1880s the once busy roadstead was often deserted, except for small vessels and the occasional windbound sailing ship.

The square-rigged sailing ship was limited in performance and her ground tackle was rarely strong enough to hold securely in very strong winds, or if it was they were unable to take the supporting actions available to a steamship. At the parting of the cable, or the threat to drive ashore, the powered craft can be brought under control but a sailing ship, however smartly

Plate 19. A Deal Lugger on the beach, showing the deep hull, fine run, narrow transom, curved tabernacle timbers, long outrigger and the bowsprit run out.

In 1867 the lugger *Albion* was stopped by a sea while launching with an anchor and chain on board; she strained badly and had to be broken up. In bad weather luggers often had difficulty in locating the vessel to which they were taking anchors and cables due to her drift from original position. By 1900 the business of taking off anchors and cables was dead. That year the barque *Elgin* required both, but none could be brought off and they were sent from London by tug.

During gales from south west or north west many ships were forced to slip their cables and make sail to avoid fouling other craft. After a gale pairs of luggers sailed parallel courses towing a warp between them to sweep for anchors. During the 1860s the Board of Trade allowed as salvage £2 for every ton weight of anchor and chain recovered, to keep the anchorage clear of potential fasts. Luggers rigged a large bow sheeve to recover cables and weigh anchors, which were landed at the anchor park at Sandown, the local name for the north end of Deal. This was in use until the 1890s. Between 1866–69, over six hundred anchors and cables were recovered from the Downs and were offered for sale by auction at the Lord Warden's depot. The work declined with the passing of sail but recovering lost anchors remained a source of income for some luggermen into the 1890s, when the government still paid 18 pence per hundredweight; little reward for the patience and skill needed to grapple and perhaps free from others a large anchor, and lift it from the bottom, but nevertheless a useful occupation in fine weather when there was little else to earn.

handled, was restricted and uncertain in her movements, in danger of fouling some of the ships about her and lucky not to go ashore. Deal was noted for the manufacture of hemp cables before 1860, after which chain cables came into general use, which was a blow to the beachmen. The old hemp cables needed constant attention when riding in bad weather and 'freshening the nip' or 'clapping a service on the cables' were vital actions on which the safety of ship and crew depended. Nevertheless, numbers of anchors were lost in every gale and hundreds of all sizes were stored in the anchor parks behind the town.

Much has been written about supplying anchors in the Downs but no one can now explain how these were quickly got on board the comparatively frail hull of a lugger lying on a beach. The men who participated are long dead and no record survives. There were no sheerlegs ready-rigged and to erect these would take time. Tackles from the lugger's mastheads may have assisted the loading but the masts were not stout enough for the big anchors, which were probably manhandled into the boat up a slope of timber and steadied down on to the burden boards. The beachmen charged £1 per hundredweight for carrying out an anchor in normal weather, and from 10 shillings to 15 shillings per hundredweight for a chain cable. As a big ship's anchor and cable might weigh six tons or more this was profitable work, particularly in winter. In January 1863 nine ships in the Downs were supplied with anchors and cables in one week. In three months of 1866, 25 anchors and cables had been supplied to vessels in the anchorage.

But the beachmen's life was not all work and waiting. When the tiny village of Broadstairs blossomed from a fishing village which built and sent a fleet of cutters to the Iceland cod fisheries, into a nineteenth-century seaside resort, many of its luggers took to 'pleasuring' with summer visitors and trippers. Some Deal men also took to this work late in the nineteenth century.

As regattas became fashionable during the mid-nineteenth century, the Kentish beachmen enthusiastically organised races for their luggers and other craft. Usually seven or eight large luggers raced at Deal for a £10 prize; the north end lugger *Early Morn* being fastest during the 1865–1881 period, winning in 1869, 1876, 1877, 1878, 1879 and 1881. The *Fly* and *Dart* were also consistent prizewinners and *Lady Bounder*, *Albert Victor*, *Briton's Pride*, and *Forester's Pride* were frequent competitors. The second class luggers raced separately and the *Faun* from north Deal was champion until she was sunk in 1864. There were also races for galley-punts and at least four eight-oared galleys regularly raced at Deal regatta for a first prize of £21 (twenty guineas). Even the humble foresail and mizzen beach punts joined in and some from Kingsdown were racing at Deal in the 'nineties.

During the mid-nineteenth century many Deal men were working as unofficial pilots and in boarding and landing pilots to vessels in the Downs. Some sailed down Channel 'seeking' ships as far as Plymouth, each lugger carrying six hands; four to board as pilots and two to sail the lugger home. They requested a testimonial from the master of each vessel piloted and these were shown to a shipmaster engaging them for the first time.

William Stanton ably stated the beachmen's experiences in pilotage work during evidence given before a parliamentary committee. The pilot cutters then cruised about Dungeness but could not board ships in strong winds, when they anchored under the lee and hauled down their pilot flags. Stanton explained that the Deal luggers could board pilots in almost any conditions and frequently put men aboard ships down Channel, often off Beachy Head or much further west. However, if that ship was subsequently boarded by a licensed pilot, the unlicensed Deal man was superseded at once and was not entitled to payment for his services. This had happened to Stanton about 300 times in 15 years; but in bad weather, when the pilots would not risk boarding from the cutters, the beachmen had the opportunity of bringing in many ships and of earning good fees. There were then about 400 men and forty luggers at Deal, but about a third of the vessels were unfit for sea because of their owner's poverty. Stanton wanted the Deal men constituted as boatmen for the licensed pilots, providing their own luggers and to be paid at 3 shillings per foot by each ship to which they boarded or landed pilots. For this sum they would be willing to cruise off Beachy Head, put a man aboard an inward bound ship to 'conduct' her up Channel to the pilot cutter at Dungeness and board the licensed pilot, later landing him at Deal, if required. The proposal was not adopted.

At that time Stanton had a limited licence to pilot vessels to and from Deal, 'three leagues from

Plate 20. Deal lugger *Annie* in 1897. A rare photograph of a lugger sailing. Unusually she had a counter stern.

the land'. He explained that as he was not a Freeman of Sandwich or Dover he had no hope of becoming an official or 'Branch' pilot, and few Deal men were until 1853. William Stanton eventually became a licensed Trinity House pilot but, like many beachmen, there was a pathetic end to his seafaring. After severely injuring a foot and enduring eight months without pay, he surrendered his licence to receive a pension of £50 per annum and ended his days as a cobbler within sound of the surf along Deal beach.

In 1853 the Fellowship of Cinque Port Pilots was dissolved and licensed pilots were transferred to Trinity House, the constituted pilotage authority. This left many boatmen, who were uneducated men but excellent Channel pilots, unprovided for as they were unable to sit the examination required. It is now too easy to dismiss such knowledge from experience in a world ridden by paper qualifications and a verbal tradition of learning, but usually such men, bred from generations of seamen and with detailed knowledge, are better fitted to handle ships than many with certificates but little experience. Most of the unlicensed Channel or North Sea pilots had spent their early years in merchant or naval ships on international voyages, before returning to own luggers, which they much preferred to decked cutters for 'seeking' down Channel. Deal luggers were often away for a week at a time, tending ships and pilots westward of Dungeness or up the Thames to Gravesend. They feared little going to windward but, as open boats, dreaded running hard before wind and sea. The large lugger *Tiger* once lay more than two weeks under

the lee of Dungeness during protracted westerly gales as her crew feared to run home through the big seas off the Admiralty pier at Dover. Had it been a head wind she would have made sail at once.

The large luggers used in pilotage work carried a small boat known as a 'cogie' and used for boarding. Typical dimensions were 14ft 4in × 4ft 10in beam with a transom 2ft 6in wide. Cogies were planked in elm on closely spaced timbers, rowed well and also carried a sail.

Luggers cruising down Channel with unlicensed pilots worked on shares; the boat taking part of the total. Four of the crew being potential pilots, the two working the lugger home shared with them. In extreme cases one man might be left to sail a forty foot lugger up Channel. In ordinary weather he could dip the foresail himself and handle her, but it was hard work and risky if the weather deteriorated.

'They might be away two or three weeks 'seeking' and turns for pilotage were determined by the toss of a coin. After 1853, most Deal unlicensed pilots brought vessels as far inward as Dungeness, then handed over to a Trinity House pilot but they frequently voyaged to Heligoland in charge of homeward bound German ships. They were regarded as cheap labour by many shipmasters, charging no scale of fees and frequently bargaining for the job. These captain's parsimony was highlighted by the loss of the East Indiaman *Earl of Eglinton*, valued at £100,000 which was driven ashore in St Margaret's Bay after refusing to take a Deal pilot who asked £8 for the job.

Piloting luggers often lay in the shelter of Dungeness, awaiting inward bound ships, and in 1874 six Deal luggers cruising in the Channel sighted the barque *Kathleen* disabled after collision with a Dover tug, and getting lines aboard they towed her into Dover under sail, cocking a triumphant snook at the steamboat men. A Deal lugger cruising in the Channel looking for pilotage work rescued the survivors from the British training frigate *Eurydice* which foundered in a squall off Luccombe, Isle of Wight, in 1878. Deal luggers frequently brought up off Shanklin, on the south shore of the Isle of Wight, for provisions and the eighteen tonner *Pride of the Sea* was lost off there during a gale in 1887. Worth £600, inclusive of her gear, she was uninsured and had been built on a mortgage.

Charles Pearson typified the Kentish beachmen's hardihood. He owned the luggers *Princess Royal* and *Friend of All Nations*, transferring the former to Walmer when work declined with the advance of steamships. Eventually his luggers became unseaworthy from lack of work and maintenence and in desperation he rowed to the Isle of Wight in a 14ft dinghy and got picked up for a pilot job. In old age he was engaged one Christmas day to pilot a barque down Channel as far as the Start. Bad weather prevented his being landed and he voyaged on to Australia, returning nine months later! Kentishmen still ranged down Channel in the nineties and the lugger *Walmer Castle* was overwhelmed off Ventnor in 1872 under storm jib and reefed mizzen, but by 1909 most pilots had left Deal for Dover, and a tradition was ending.

The Deal and other Kentish luggers were often used for fishing with lines or drift nets, as opportunity offered or when other work was slack. Some fished regularly and during the French wars many engaged in it. In June 1859 many French luggers were line fishing off Deal, and when their gear fouled the nets of beachmen the French cut the nets away, one Kingsdown lugger lost £200–£300 of nets in this way in three years. Sometimes the Frenchmen stole the nets. The crew of the lugger *Mary Blane* saw eighteen French luggers shooting lines near her nets and after requesting a French fishery gunboat to order them off, the *Mary Blane*'s crew boarded a French lugger, capturing her and her crew and brought them ashore where they were surrounded by about 400 angry and excited beach families. The Frenchmen were released next day and the Royal naval steam tender *Lizard* was belatedly sent to keep order in the Downs.

About 1870, encouraged by rail transport, craft from many parts of the Kent coast, including the luggers, began fishing for sprats using drift nets rather than the big stow nets which the Essexmen further north had used spratting for centuries. Second class luggers were often used for fishing and 60 bushels was reckoned a good catch, landings being railed away, often for hop garden manure. Luggers also drifted for herring and mackerel at the back of the Goodwins and by 1878 the decline of hovelling work caused more of them to fish regularly during the mackerel and herring seasons. That year the Kingsdown luggers earned £3000 in six weeks mackerelling; the *Flora* landing one catch worth £60. One day in 1879,

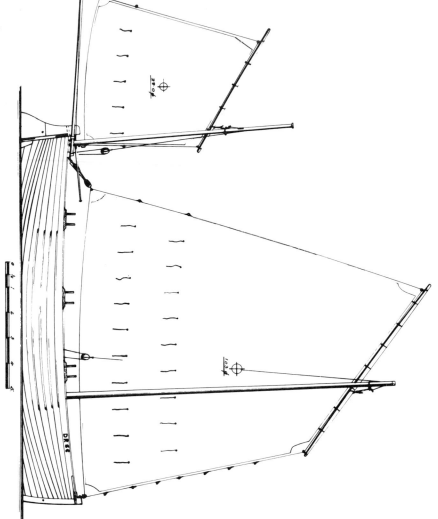

Figure 59. Sail plan of Dover fishing punt *Argonaut*, built by Nichols of Deal, circa 1880, and used for alongshore fishing. Dimensions 16ft 6¾in × 5ft × 2ft 2½in internal depth. Dipping lug foresail 103 square feet, standing lug mizzen 28 square feet. *Science Museum, London.*

55 tons were landed on Deal beach to be sent by rail to the London fish market at Billingsgate. But returns were less rosy; 26 boxes, each containing 1200 prime sprats, fetched £3-3s-6d at Billingsgate, but transport cost £1-4s-8d, leaving £1-18s-10d. from which the fishermen had to pay the merchant's charges.

During the early 1850s there were over a dozen large luggers at Kingsdown, with forepeaks and fireplaces. In fine weather some lay anchored in the Roads, otherwise they were hauled up. Names included *Victoria, Mary, Flora, British Queen, Industry, Princess Mary, Eclipse, Louise, Georgina, Active, Endeavour, Vesper* and *Pilgrim.* In 1867 there were fourteen but no galley punts, probably because this was still primarily a fishing community.

Kingsdown luggers worked in the autumn mackerel fishery off Dungeness and during ten days in 1865 they landed mackerel worth £1000, resulting in a £30 share per man. These Kingsdown craft were usually built at Deal, where in 1872 J. Bayley launched the *Pilgrim* costing £400. Two years later Henry Gardner built the *Lady Ross* which was typical in being 38ft 6in × 12ft 6in × 6ft 8in depth and registering 22 tons.

Several luggers were owned by a small fishing community at Dungeness; a desolate spit jutting into the English Channel and sustaining a lighthouse, a tavern, some small dwellings and a coastguard station. These boats were worked similarly to the Deal luggers, which they resembled. The loose, shifting shingle posed difficulties to beach activities and the fishermen wore pieces of wood fastened to their feet as beach shoes, which were jokingly called 'back stays'.

The foresail and mizzen punts were the smallest of the Kentish beach boats, varying from 14 to 18ft in length and from 4ft 6in to 5ft beam, though some 12-footers which were built for hiring to summer visitors were occasionally rigged. Many punts set a spritsail mizzen, and sometimes a bowsprit and jib were rigged in the larger ones. Most engaged in drift netting for sprats, mackerel and herring, alongshore in the Downs. The sprating season began in November and might last until March. Nets were shot at the evening change of light and they drifted one tide before hauling and returning. Landings were sometimes large, and during 1892 some punts were landing about 30,000 sprats each day, worth about 2s 6d per thousand or £3-15s to be shared between a crew of two or three. Small punts were sometimes used for hand lining and most were launched stern first, the crew jumping aboard over the bow. These punts resembled miniature luggers in form and proportions and the last of them was owned by Sir Woods Woolaston who kept her on Walmer beach for many years, sailing her single handed until she passed to a Dover school sailing club (Plate 21).

After 1880 few new luggers were built to replace those lost, and by the 'nineties hovelling was almost gone and Deal was turning from the beach for its living. However, fishing remained profitable and during 1892 a Mr Edgar opened a cannery at north Deal and contracted with thirty luggers owned at Deal, Walmer and Kingsdown and another thirty then owned at Dungeness, to

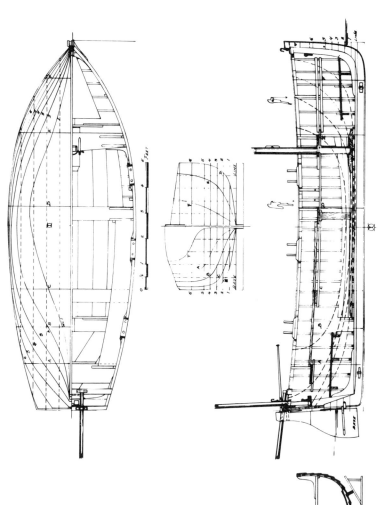

Figure 60. Lines and construction of Dover fishing punt *Argonaut. Science Museum, London.*

138

Plate 21. A Deal sprat punt photographed in 1960 setting a standing lug main and mizzen, with a jib set to a short bumkin. She was originally rigged with a dipping lug forward. *Photo — John Mannering.*

fish for sprats. Some boats earned £7 per day and the factory employed up to 300 people. The lugger *Tiger* was converted as a fish carrier, being decked over and given a lute stern. With her rig altered to ketch, she carried sprats from the cannery to London and sometimes to France.

Abnormally high tides in 1897 undermined the north Deal beach and the last luggers were unable to carry on there. This effect was blamed on construction of the enlarged Dover harbour altering coastal currents and that winter's heavy gales advanced the end of the luggers. As at many seaside towns, Deal boatmen suffered from the local council's devotion to the tripper trade. A 1911 extension of the parade drove the large boats from the south end of Deal beach. Some moved to Kingsdown and Walmer, where in 1905 there were still eighteen large luggers on the beach, but by 1914 the luggers and beachmen had disappeared from Kingsdown.

The Galley

A 'set of boats' on the beach during the period 1850–1890 was incomplete without a galley; long, lightly built rowing boats, shallow and narrow, with fine lines and a stern which had a small, heart shaped transom, high above the waterline. They were very fast under oars but the light construction allowed them to work in a seaway, and they were rarely the same shape on both sides for long. Most were four-oared, though the eight-oared *Blue Jacket* of Walmer survived into the twentieth century.

Galleys were used to carry messages, light loads and one or two passengers and often pilots,

between ships and shore in fine weather. They were usually sent if a ship entered the Downs signalling for a doctor, or for similar emergencies. Sometimes they raced luggers to a wreck and there was much robust rivalry. The lugger *Tartar* rammed and sank a galley at one wreck; she was replaced by public subscription.

Fifty-four six- and four-oared galleys lay on Deal beach in 1833, averaging 28–32ft length and costing about £45 to build. Many were used in smuggling for which two-oared galleys were favoured at one time. This reputation lasted for many years, one being condemned and sawn in half for running goods in the 1870s, the usual end for a smuggling craft.

Galleys were often given the names of favourite luggers of earlier times. The four-oared galley *Princess* was built by Nichols of Deal in 1880 for William Burwill of Dover and had typical dimensions of 29ft 1½in length × 5ft 4¾in beam × 2ft depth. Planked in English elm on ash timbers, her admidship section had flat floors but the ends were very fine and the transom small. Her normal crew was three men and she carried five 14ft oars, oak thole pins, a boathook with 45 fathoms of coir rope, and rope fenders at the stem and along the sheer in way of each thwart. The coxswain steered with yoke lines and a strong sampson post was fitted for towing, strapped to the forward thwart. She could set a large or small dipping lugsail which usually had two rows of reef points, on a mast stepped amidships and clasped to a thwart. In light weather or at regattas the sampson post was removed and a short additional mast stepped in its place, on which a small lugsail

Plate 22. A four-oared Deal galley setting a dipping lugsail in a near calm.

was set, the large lug remained set amidships. The overlapping lugsails provided a powerful reaching rig but one difficult to handle when tacking, when such a long keeled, flat floored boat without a centreboard would have to be helped round with an oar, which was probably also kept going on the lee side when sailing.

In galleys, the tye was well stretched and greased rope passing over a 'dumb' sheeve in the masthead and bent to a traveller to which a strop was hooked, placed one third of the yard's length from forward. As the tye stretched the bend was shifted and the end taken up around the standing part. The halyard was a whip rove through a single block at the end of the tye. It had an eye at each end; one was put over a pin or cleat and the other passed through a sheeve inside the gunwale and led aft within reach of the helmsman, who could let the lug down with a run, if necessary.

The lightweight galleys had to be launched down the beach at the run, the shore helpers making her bilges roar to the impulse of their grip as she shot out on a momentary smooth, then perhaps stood almost on end to an incoming breaker, before the sheet of her lugsail was hardened in and she was off, three men in gleaming oilskins huddled to windward. A galley could stand more sea than her slender hull suggested; frequently they laid-to in rough seas, waiting for a job, with sails lowered, lying 'hulling', broadside, the crew as unconcerned as though they were sitting at home.

Galleys varied in dimensions, narrowest being the 28ft *General Havelock*, launched in 1870 with only 4ft beam. The eight-oared galley *Seaman's Hope* was amongst the last built, by Nichols of Deal in 1907. Four men constructed her in six weeks and she cost £55 ready for sea. Thomas Upton used her in pilot work and occasional salvage and she was one of four galleys remaining on Deal beach during the 1950s, still in her original ownership.

Galleys made considerable use of sail whenever possible and many had new sails every second year, a few annually. During World War I, galleys had to have a coloured band across the sail and carry a red ensign on a staff at the bow.

These fast boats were raced in local regattas, rowed by younger beachmen who polished the bottoms with blacklead. Two galleys, the *Saxon* and the *Undaunted* were still used by Deal sea scouts in 1965 and kept up the regatta tradition.

Great Galleys, or Galley Punts

Great galleys, later generally known as galley punts, were as useful as the luggers and were probably the beachmen's favourite type. These developed from the galleys, incorporating the proportionate beam and more stable sections of the little beach punts to produce a seaworthy boat with considerable range of operation. Only seven were in use during 1853 but the numbers increased rapidly afterwards. Whereas galleys could do no more than carry messages, light goods or one or two passengers in fair weather, galley punts were much more seaworthy. However because the galleys remained the faster boats, there was still work for them as a separate type.

Galley punts were clench built, open boats,

which were generally sailed but could be rowed. Three principal types evolved, classified according to size: Class 1. Length overall 26–36ft. Beam approximately 6–7ft.

Class II. Length overall 24–26ft. Beam approximately 6ft.

Class III. Length overall. 22–24ft. Beam 6ft to 6ft 6in approximately. These dimensions and proportions sometimes varied but all were much deeper than the galleys.

By 1867, galley punts were replacing luggers for many jobs at Deal and Walmer, though none was owned at Kingsdown until 1869, when the newly built *Staunch* was lost. More easily handled than a lugger, they were much used in the frequent landing of letters and bulk mails from ships delayed in the Downs, and for landing and embarking passengers, ships officers and pilots. *Endeavour*, *Wanderer*, *Gipsy*, *Our Boys*, and *Hope* were some of their names, typifying the spirit of the beach.

The Walmer galley punt *Happy Go Lucky*, built by Nichols of Deal about 1880, was a good example of the smaller size, being 22ft 6in overall length × 6ft 6in beam × 2ft 10in depth inside. Her plumb stem, straight and level keel, slightly raked sternpost and small heart shaped transom were typical. The forward and aft waterlines were fine and hollowed. The amidship sections had rise of floor and a slack bilge radius enabling her to be efficiently rowed and to sail in a seaway despite lack of centreboard.

Galley punts were launched and hauled up much more frequently than luggers, and strength and durability were carefully studied. The keel was oak or ash with an iron chafing band. Frames were ash, joggled over the plank lands and spaced 6in apart. Planking was oak, ⅜in thick with fifteen planks on each side. Floors were ash and a strong keelson, which also formed a mast step, ran the length of the boat. Five wide thwarts braced the hull and there were three thole positions on each side. The third thwart, almost amidships, had a clasp for the mast and the forward thwart had one for the sampson post to which the tow rope was made fast then towing astern of a ship.

The mast could be unstepped for convenience when rowing by undoing the clasp, the men usually standing to push at the oars. But these boats were sailed, if possible.

The mast of *Happy Go Lucky* was stepped just aft of amidships, typical of many galley punts and set a dipping lugsail. The 'great sail' was 211 square feet area and had two rows of reef points. It set on the 'great mast', 20ft 10in long. The yard was stiffened by fish piece in way of the tye and was hoisted on an iron traveller. The lugsail was bent to the yard by 'knittles' instead of a lacing and the long ends of these knittles acted as tyers when the sail was lowered and stowed. It was hoisted by a tye and halyards. The tye was rigged as for the galleys but the halyard was made fast to a block on the tye and then rove from aft forwards through a block on the gunwale, then through the block on the tye, to lead down through a sheeve inside the gunwale and away aft where it belayed near the helmsman. The tack was hauled to the weather gunwale, where there were two or three hooks for use when the lug was reefed.

Galley punts usually had four rows of reef

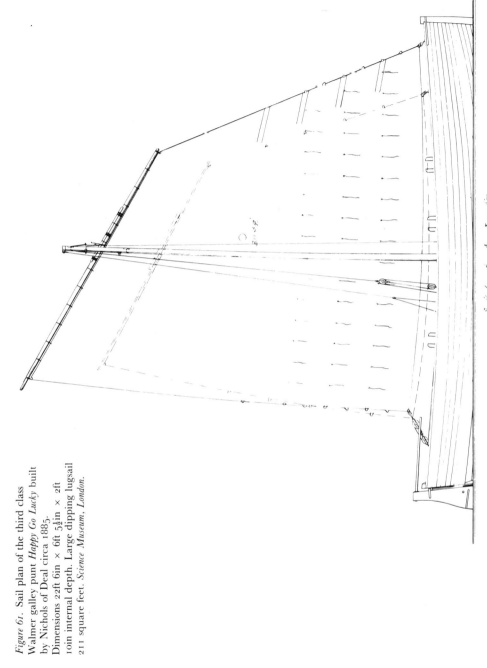

Figure 61. Sail plan of the third class
Walmer galley punt *Happy Go Lucky* built
by Nichols of Deal circa 1885.
Dimensions 22ft 6in × 6ft 5½in × 2ft
10in internal depth. Large dipping lugsail
211 square feet. *Science Museum, London.*

144

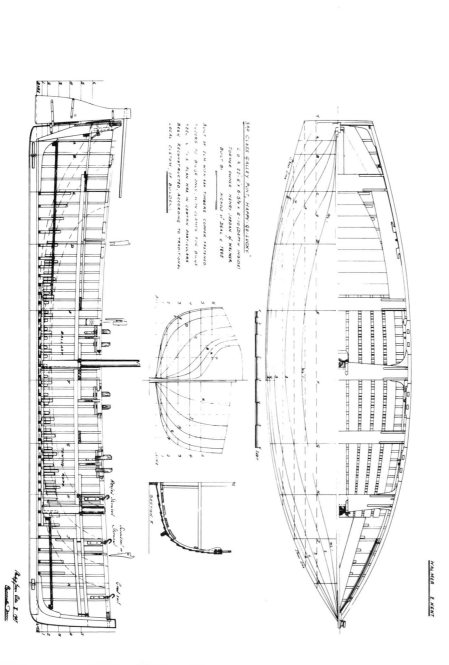

Figure 62. Lines and construction of third
class Walmer galley punt *Happy Go Lucky*.
Science Museum, London.

points in the great sail. Between the reef cringles, which were worked with the usual metal thimbles, there were other cringles, without thimbles, which were called 'stakens' and enabled a half-reef to be taken in when considered necessary to adjust sail area more exactly to the wind strength. The tack hook and sheet block were hooked to the stakens and the sail was re-set, without further tying of points. The cringle above the close reef was called the 'yardarm' or the 'mannikin' staken, but was seldom used.

The lugsail sheet consisted of two single blocks, one with a swivel hook, made fast by the steering thwart. In strong winds the 'small mast' and 'second sail' having three reefs was set in the same step, before launching off. If much turning to windward was intended, a lugsail was carried on each side of the mast, enabling the lee lug to be lowered at each tack and the opposite one to be bent on and hoisted, saving time in stays. If much reaching was expected, the crew might step a second mast and sail in the forward clasp, with the tack set to the stemhead; a rig much used by the galley punts at regattas.

The largest galley punts were extremely powerful craft, capable of considerable speed on a reach and would go to windward well, considering that a centreboard was not fitted. However, they were difficult to handle before a strong wind and sea due to the fine entry and deep forefoot, shallow hull and light draft aft. About three-quarters of a ton of shingle ballast bags was necessary for correct trim.

These boats appear to have been capable of tacking with certainty in a seaway, even under reefed small sail, but they needed careful handling in strong winds as, if the lugsail was caught aback in shifting puffs, she might capsize, so they were sailed on the sheet to keep the lee gunwale above water. In such conditions plenty of spray came aboard and one man would be constantly bailing.

Large galley punts could be launched similarly to the luggers but smaller ones were run down the beach like galleys, the crew jumping in at the water. When beaching a galley punt with a fair or reaching wind, all reefs were usually shaken out to gain speed and manoeuvrability, and bow and stern painters were prepared for flinging to shore helpers. The crew crouched aft, the helmsman watching the seas for a smooth. Then he put her at the beach, hoping to come in on the back of the sea and, as she touched, the crew leaped out and helped to hold her by the two painters until she could be hauled up. Sometimes a galley punt had to stand on and off for hours waiting for a suitable smooth on which to beach. In fine weather or an offshore wind the lugsail was lowered and the boat allowed to come broadside to the beach, opposite her capstan. One man swung himself ashore by the halyard and held on with his weight, to keep her canted towards the shore, each sea lifting her higher while the haul-up rope was being rove and passengers disembarked. Knocking up was hard on the bilge strakes and chafed the plank lands, so was done quickly.

Hovelling was the galley punt's principal work, and included anything from ranging the Downs and the Goodwins on the lookout for flotsam of value, to waiting in the track of passing ships in hope of being hailed for some errand. They were often at wrecks and in fog, if the Gull, the North Sands Head, the East Goodwin or the South Sands Head light vessels fired a gun to warn a ship standing into danger, several galley punts would immediately be launched and row or sail to the estimated position of the gunfire, finding the ship, following her and hailing to offer to pilot her clear for a fee.

Great galleys were also used to tend ships, frequently in competition with luggers. William Stanton recorded a typical incident of beachmen's rivalry: 'One morning about the year '31 (July 7th), being on the lookout, espied a brig with a large American ensign at the fore, out abaft of the Goodwin. We launched our second class boat called the *Fox*, made all sail for the brig. On looking round I saw there was only one more boat besides ourselves running at the brig, which was rather singular. This boat was a long "great galley", called the *Gipsy*, a much faster boat than we were. I waved to them to shut in together, and then we could take it easy, without driving one another to risk, but they having the fastest boat would not agree to it. All at once it struck me there was a chance left to jockey them, for they came running for my boat's stern – I suppose to show off their boat's superior speed – instead of their pointing to their object, as they ought to have done. They then tried to pass me on the port side, but I would not let them. They then tried to windward: I would not let them pass on either side. They sung out "Don't you mean to let us pass you?" Decidedly I did not, if I can

prevent it. They saw they had completely humbugged themselves and they began to be rather cross with me. I said "Had you not been so greedy we might have taken it easy". But, however, it was no use cavelling: I told them I would have the vessel if I could. We kept together that way until we came near the brig, which was lying to, when I sang out "Stand by to jump, the game is ours!" We boarded the brig on the weather quarter, they on the lee quarter, both at the same time. We got our man on board, but they could not get far enough forward on account of his boom, and what was worse, it carried their mast away. They looked both chagrined and dreadfully cross, to see that they had played with the mouse until they had lost it; they said I had served them a very pretty trick, pointing to the broken mast. By way of chaff I told them to get a new mast and send the bill to me.

'The captain of the brig was very ill and wanted medical aid. He employed us to take the brig into the Downs, and one man to stop on board to take care of her while he was on shore to get medical assistance. He was on shore about fourteen days, then he quite recovered. He gave us £50 for our services – the brig was his own. He then sailed, wind S.E.'

Galley punts were also much used in salvage; their last big haul being the sailing ship *Hazelbank*, bound home on her maiden voyage, which went on the Goodwin under all sail one fine summer afternoon in 1890. Her wreck kept the beachmen busy for weeks, landing cargo and equipment. It was an ill wind which did not bring them some gain.

The galley punt was the most useful boat of the Downs and, being adaptable to changing conditions when sailing vessels began to decline, outlived the luggers, a few even being fitted with auxiliary engines in old age. By the early twentieth century most of them were 30ft × 7ft 6in beam and the 36ft × 9ft and 24ft × 6ft types had been discarded.

As salvage and anchor work reduced, the Deal men depended increasingly on the taking off and landing of pilots from passing steamships. In fine weather the long narrow galleys were used but when it was rough the galley punts were launched. These hooked on to steamers which were flying the signal 'Pilot to drop' or 'Pilot required'; although signalling that the pilot was to be dropped frequently meant he was to be landed at Dover, so the galley punt had to sail across the track of the steamer, lower her sail and lay in the same direction as the oncoming ship which did not usually slacken speed. A towrope was then thrown up or hooked on to any fitting which would hold it, by a long ash stave having an iron hook to which about fifty fathoms of grass rope was attached. The rope was eased away until the galley punt was flying along in the wake, smothered in spray, until speed was slackened slightly to drop the pilot. Then the galley punt laid alongside and this august person was carefully seated in a sheltered part of the boat and taken ashore.

'Hooking on' was dangerous work and many men were drowned by miscalculation resulting in a punt run down, or by a jerk of the towline throwing them over. Frequently they would have sailed and rowed into the Thames as far as Gravesend or the Nore to get the job, worth £1; and that to be shared amongst a crew of three and the punt. My father recalled seeing pilots boarded or landed from ships in galley punts off Deal in rough conditions during World War I. The pilot's best clothes and cap were wrapped in canvas against the flying spray, for these boats were wet in a seaway.

Six galley punts still lay on Deal beach in 1923, many named for the old luggers, but thereafter their decline was swift and they were firewood in a few years.

Established social systems of employment, ownership and standing, types of craft, uses, customs and orderly traditions all have their days of activity and pride, then decline to be almost forgotten within two generations, the descendents often rejecting the values of their forefathers, despising in affluence their humble but vigorous origins. So it was at Deal, where the *Cosmopolite*, the last big local lugger, was presented to the town council in December 1909 to be preserved as a memorial to the beachmen. Within a few years she was neglected and she became rotten by 1925, when she was sold for £2 10s for breaking up. Deal beach was left to a handful of inshore fishermen with small boats, the gulls and the trippers who enjoy its facade of waterside houses as a piece of Georgian England still strangely unchanged.

4

The Sussex Coast

The Sussex coast forms part of the north shore of that turbulent division between England and France, the English Channel. Its steep shingle beaches are backed by chalk downs which end abruptly in bold, white faced cliffs.

Sussex men have been sailors, fishermen and smugglers for centuries and the coast now has four harbours; from east to west, Rye, Newhaven, Shoreham and Littlehampton.

But its most important fishing communities flourished in beach villages such as Hastings, Brighton and Eastbourne, which later developed into seaside resorts, to which promenades and piers, boarding-houses and bandstands, became of more importance than the simple requirements of ruddy-faced men of the beach, who were gradually harried from occupying the most inviting bits of shingle, however convenient for their livelihood.

The fishermen of the ancient port of Rye preferred the windward ability of gaff rig for working in and out of their long narrow harbour and for their principal work of trawling, but the other Sussex fishing communities preferred the lug or spritsail rigs for their craft.

Hastings
By the twelfth century Hastings men were fishing for herring and they ventured up the east coast to participate in the great fishery from Yarmouth in Norfolk, whose fortunes they helped to found. During succeeding centuries Hastings fishing craft assumed various shapes, sizes and rigs but by the beginning of the nineteenth, the larger ones were probably three masted luggers and the smaller were two masted, setting a lug on the fore and a spritsail on the mizzen. Single masted inshore fishing boats, locally termed 'punts', were rigged with a sprit mainsail and a stay foresail; a rig carried after the sixteenth century and which was used by Hastings punts until about 1900, when a fore and mizzen lug became usual.

The Hastings three-masted lug rig may have been copied from the similarly rigged French luggers across the English Channel, which were known in Hastings as 'catamarans'; probably a corruption of the French 'chasse-maree'. In common with other south coast fishermen and smugglers, Hastings men had considerable contact with their French counterparts during the late eighteenth and early nineteenth centuries, particularly in smuggling, which was then rife. After the peace of 1815, Hastings luggers were landing cargoes of fresh fish at French ports, until government duties on foreign landings stopped the trade, though many continued to sell catches to French fishing boats in the Channel. Sometimes, if the French skipper had not sufficient ready money to complete his purchase, the French lugger's boy, called 'the picaninny' was left with the English skipper as a security.

A three masted Hastings lugger at the peak of development about 1850, was 52 feet long overall × 45 feet length of keel × 15 feet beam × 6ft 3in depth of hold. The hull was usually oak planked and clean lined, with considerable rise of floor and a short counter stern. These were fast, purposeful vessels, similar to contemporary Norfolk herring luggers of Yarmouth and they represented the best of Hastings fishing endeavour and voyaging, bringing prosperity to the many Hastings boatbuilders.

The luggers had two principal fishing seasons; from September to November they went to the north coast of Kent for herring, and from mid-May to September to Cornwall for mackerel. Sometimes these 'voyages' were profitable for the crews of eight men and a boy; individual shares of £40 per trip being recorded, with the master receiving more.

100–120 mackerel nets were often worked and as hauling was laborious, the crew worked in spells of heaving twenty-five nets. When this number were boarded, the haulers shouted 'Spell – Oh' and changed places with the men at the capstan for a rest. A long 'scudding pole' was

lashed fore and aft between the fore and main masts when hauling drift nets, which were shaken out across it before being stowed below, the fish being pushed below down the 'scudding holes', or in bulk down the hatchway. Herring shoals appeared off Hastings early in November and a good season usually lasted six weeks, with record catches in one day selling for £900. If the tide was unsuitable for immediate beaching or if the shoals were running well and the luggers wished to return to sea immediately, the catch was landed, the fleet was met by 'ferry boats' which took the fish ashore.

Payment for catches was divided into shares, after expenses for food, net repairs and other incidentals. When drifting with a crew of six men and a boy the proceeds were divided into fourteen shares. Seven went to the boat in the proportion of one share for the craft's maintenance and six for the nets. From the remainder, each man took one share and the boy a half share. The skipper had an additional quarter share, and the remaining quarter share was for the beachmen looking after the boat ashore. This method came to be known as 'long sharing'. Ownership of these luggers was sometimes wholly by owner/skipper and sometimes by a number of shareholders in the town with the skipper holding many shares in his craft and generally managing her affairs. When trawling, catches were divided into five shares; two to the boat and the trawl, with the remainder divided amongst the smaller crew needed for this work. Hastings luggers took to trawling before 1850, working the prolific grounds of Rye Bay and the Channel banks, finding this more profitable than drift

149

Plate 23: The Hastings lugger *Team* beaching under reefed dipping lug foresail and small jib. The flag indicates she is beaching immediately. *Photo – Judges Ltd.*

netting as the coming of the railway ensured quick transport to London and other markets. The mainmast of the three masted rig was in the way for trawling and hastened popularity of the two masted Hastings lugger, though a few three masters were still owned there until about 1870.

The two masted Hastings lugger *Industry*, built that year, was typical of the new type of short range lugger; 32ft 8in length overall × 28ft 10in length of keel × 12ft extreme breadth × 4ft depth of hold. A shallower and full bodied craft, not fast under sail but buoyant and of manageable size for beaching and working with a smaller crew.

Until the 1880s some Hastings luggers had leeboards, similar to those of the hog boats from Brighton, further west, but these were discarded with the introduction of iron centreplates about 1885–1890. These luggers were some of the very few British small working craft to use centreplates, though most were removed when motors were first fitted in about 1912. The centreplates were a mixed blessing, enabling the bulky hulls to sail a little closer to the wind, but having a tendency to buckle when rolling heavily and sometimes being accidentally distorted when beaching.

Hastings fishermen were the usual independent inshore breed and Phillips, Gallop, Kent, White, Willis, Breach, Lepper and Dighton were some of their surnames; all with nicknames added. Many were religious men and the Hastings fishermen's church of St Nicholas, on the foreshore at Rock a Nore, was well attended. During sermon they could admire and mentally criticise a model lugger suspended from the ceiling as an offering by some local mariner who had escaped a watery end.

Along the coast they were known as 'chopbacks', – a reminder of their earlier lawlessness when a Hastings crew boarded a foreign vessel to plunder her and cut down the master with an axe.

Luggers were admired by some nineteenth-century yachtsmen, such as Lord Willoughby De Eresby, who disdained other rigs and sought out Frederick Tutt of John Tutt and Son, boatbuilders of Eastwell, Hastings, noted for fishing luggers. During 1855 Eresby ordered a 34 tonner named *Leopard*, an open boat intended for shooting and fishing. He took such interest in her building that Tutt had difficulty in convincing him she should have white canvas, not tanned like the fishing luggers. She proved fast and able at sea and two years later Eresby was back for a 100-tonner which was named *Panther*, proved remarkably fast and was used for cruising and fishing along the south Devon coast, summer and winter.

Next season Eresby decided he would have the largest possible lugger yacht, which would show the racing fleet what luggers could do. Frederick Tutt was commissioned to prepare a design for a three master, which he did by making a half model from which the lines were taken. These so pleased Eresby that the keel was laid at once.

She was enormous; 134ft overall, 128ft on the keel × 18ft beam × 12ft 2in depth forward, 16ft 2in aft and drawing 11ft aft and 6ft 4in forward. Her plumb stem, straight, raking keel, fine counter stern and deep, peg top sections followed the fashion of contemporary racing yachts, but with a

Plate 24. Hastings lugger of the late nineteenth century with mizzen topsail and mizzen staysail set. Note the lute stern. *Drawing by G. F. Campbell.*

151

beam to length ratio of 1 to 7 the lugger was one of the most extreme sailing craft built and her size was far above that of any contemporary racer.

She became an object of wonder in Tutt's yard, where the fishing community gathered to view her. The clinker planking was 1⅜ thick English oak, copper fastened, below the waterline and 1¼in Canadian rock elm above, bright varnished. Her bottom was copper sheathed and she carried 75 tons of iron ballast 'laid with cork between all the joints to impart life to it' according to contemporary account.

When launched she was decked for 29ft abaft the stem and for 18ft forward of the stern, to within 15in below the gunwales. These peak spaces were bulkheaded off as airtight compartments and the main deck was sunk 4ft below the sheer and was fitted with draining scuppers which led through the bottom, like a lifeboat. Side bench seats were arranged all round this deck, with grating tops and air cases stowed underneath. Later, the main deck was raised to within eighteen inches of the sheer; the benches and valves were removed and cabin accommodation built in. She had a Downton patent bilge and fire fighting pump and 'Newton and Smiths new anchor lift, and every novelty proved advantageous for comfort and accommodation'. She was the most expensive and exciting dayboat of her time.

The rig was powerful; the 13in diameter foremast was stepped at the forward bulkhead, the 14½in diameter mainmast stepped 76ft abaft the stem and was 85ft long, setting a lug with a 64ft yard and spreading 4,050 square feet. The fore

and main lugs were dipping lugs (imagine dipping sails of that area in stays) and the mizzen was the usual standing lug sheeted to an outrigger. A sizeable jib was set on a bowsprit (Plate 25).

When launched she was christened *New Moon* and was described with typical Victorian forthrightness as 'considered to be the ablest sea boat of her class and type in the world'. During her first trial in strong winds off Dover, she burst the main lugsail and almost carried away her masts without heeling more than six inches beyond her normal sailing angle. Later, she averaged 12½ to 13 knots, sailing in Torbay. She was used for day sailing and occasional cruises until in 1866 Eresby entered the *New Moon* for the Royal London Yacht Club 'ocean' race from the Thames to Harwich against six of the fastest racing cutters, headed by the celebrated *Lulworth*, and including two schooners and a yawl. Starting from the Lower Hope at 7 am, a fresh south south west wind sent the racers roaring out of the Thames with the *New Moon* soon leading them down Swin. She finished the 60 mile course in 5 hours 29 minutes, 30 minutes 50 seconds ahead of the fast cutter *Christabel*, and won the schooner and yawl prize by a tremendous margin. Her speed inspired an observer to write: 'Her huge lugs were ripping her along at a pace that threatened to take an aerial flight, and lift the long bright graceful hull bodily out of the sea; it was indeed a splendid sight to witness this noble vessel almost leaping from wave to wave, scattering the spoondrift in snowy clouds aloft as she swept along in stately pride to certain conquest'.

Plate 25. The 134ft three masted lugger yacht *New Moon* was built at Hastings by John Tutt and Son in 1855 for Lord Willoughby De Eresby and occasionally competed in yacht races. Sailing in Torbay on one occasion, she averaged between 12½ and 13 knots.

154

By 1900 Hastings fishing craft were all clinker planked and had two masts. The largest were then termed luggers; next were 'bogs' and finally the little punts. Luggers were fully decked and ranged from 27–30 feet on the keel. Rig was a dipping lug forward and a standing lug mizzen. A jib, mizzen staysail, mizzen yard topsail and occasionally a yard fore topsail were also set. Trawling, drift netting and lining, known as 'hooking' were the principal fisheries. Most of these boats were built in the town but some were constructed at Rye. The centreline structure, frames and beams were oak; the clinker planking usually of $\frac{7}{8}$ inch English elm, sometimes oak, and the deck pine and masts and spars of Baltic fir.

The hulls were built by eye, from experience and tradition, with the aid of an amidship mould, and the form was full; almost flat bottomed amidships with a sharp bilge radius and nearly plumb sides. However, the ends were finer but the boat was essentially buoyant, intended to lift off the beach quickly or float in on it as fast as possible when beaching in a sea. Transom sterns were usual until about the mid-nineteenth century but gradually the lute stern was used in new construction of smaller luggers, becoming usual by about 1800. Eliptical sterns were built into new luggers after about 1900, probably copied from the west country boats. These outward curving sterns were intended to keep seas from breaking inboard when beaching bow first in onshore winds.

The small lugger's hull was divided into four compartments by bulkheads. From forward these were the 'fore room', 'middle room', the 'chay'

and the 'pat', 'after place' or 'down aft'. The fore room served as a fo'c'sle, with locker seats for four sleepers and sometimes two cupboard berths above and a transverse berth for the boy, close to the bitt posts. Five or six men could be accommodated if necessary, depending on the size of lugger and intended work. Cupboard berths were not fitted in many older luggers which had shifting boards placed across the space between the locker fronts, converting the fo'c'sle into one huge bed. The fore room was entered by a small deck hatch and had an iron stove, coal locker and a food cupboard. The middle room was the fish hold and rope room. The catch was stowed each side behind shifting boards. The larger middle space held the net ropes, when these were not shot and was divided by a large centreplate case. A large central deck hatch gave access but a small wing hatch was also fitted on each side for use at sea, to get the catch below in any conditions. In addition there were small deck openings on each side of the middle room hatch, where this abutted the forward coaming of the chay hatch. These were the 'scudding holes' through which fish shaken from drift nets to the deck could be pushed to fall in the wings of the middle room; these large holes were closed tight by wood plugs when not in use.

The chay was the largest compartment and served as net room. Its hatch extended between the bulkheads and was closed by three boards. In three masted luggers the main mast passed through this hatch and stepped in a three-sided tabernacle which had heavy reinforcement around it. When the main lug was discarded with the onset of trawling, the main mast was usually cut down to about 40 inches above deck to become the tow post for the trawl warp. The chay was floored with pine ceiling on which shingle ballast known as 'beach' was carried as necessary. This was uncovered and the nets were stowed on top of it. The pat, or after place occupied the odd shaped space at the aft end, serving as sail locker and general gear store, entered by a small deck scuttle.

A capstan was mounted on deck just forward of the middle room hatch. In older luggers this was turned by handspikes but later, iron hand capstans were fitted. The deck had bulwarks all round and sweeps, spare spars, the scudding pole and a long boathook were carried on the port side, slung in raft ropes, though some luggers had lumber irons.

Hulls were usually tarred black, with perhaps a few strakes of colour about the wales, red or green being favourites.

It is now difficult to gain accurate information to judge their sailing abilities, but most latter Hastings luggers were slow, buoyant craft whose freeboard, displacement beam and modest sail area would not enable them to sail fast.

The reeving bowsprit was carried to starboard of the centreline and the jib tack was hooked to an iron traveller worked by an outhaul rove through a dumb sheave at the outboard end. Hastings luggers often passed the outhaul down over a cleat on the side of the stem near the waterline and up, to belay on deck, forming a simple bobstay. The jib halyard purchase was rove through two single blocks and the sheets

came inboard through holes in the bulwarks.

The foremast stepped about four feet abaft the stem, with the heel in a three-sided mast case or tabernacle supported at the head by curved timbers which steadied the mast during lowering or raising. The foresail was a dipping lug with three rows of reef points and the sheet rove through two single blocks; one hooked in the clew and the lower to the foresheet strap, fastened diagonally to the bulwarks at each quarter. The fall belayed to a bulwark cleat forward of the purchase.

The foremast was rigged with a halyard and a forestay called the 'fore burden', a corruption of 'fore burton'. The halyard tye passed through a masthead sheeve and this and the forestay had luff tackle purchases with a double block above and single block below. When the lug was set the halyard purchase was hooked to an iron chainplate on the weather side of the deck by the bulwark, and the forestay purchase was hooked to another, two feet further aft. When tacking, both purchases were shifted to the new weather side. After passing over the mast sheeve the halyard tye was shackled to an iron hook which passed through an eye in an iron traveller, locally called a parrel, around the mast and to which an iron strop around the lug yard was hooked for hoisting, fitted about a third of the yard's length from the forward end. The yard was strengthened with an oak fish piece on top of it. The sail was bent to the yard by robands called 'knittles' and the tack of the sail was hooked to an iron luff hook on the stem head.

Wetting the foresail to make it hold a better

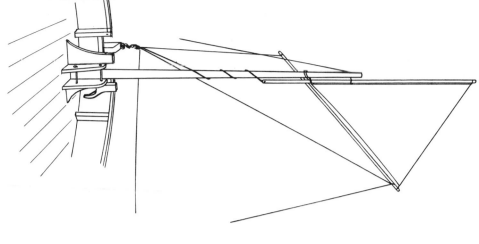

Figure 63. Method of setting a yard topsail above the fore lug of a Hastings lugger.

wind was a common task for the lugger's boy, hauling up buckets from the weather side to drench the luff.

If a topsail was set above the fore lug as shown in Fig. 63 the topsail yard was set up in an unusual manner and was locally known as the 'quant'.

The mizzen lug rigging was similar to the foremast but as it was a standing lug, the halyard and tye were not shifted when tacking. The mizzen sheet had a standing part set up with a purchase and rove through a sheeve (or sometimes only a hole in the end of a bumkin called the outrigger, protruding from the stern. The mizzen had two rows of reef points and its tack was held by a hook at the foot of the mizzen mast, which was stayed forward by a 'Tommy Hunter', set up by a purchase hooked to an eye on the centreline, almost amidships.

The mizzen staysail was set from the mizzenmast head and the tack set down to the deck about one third of the length from the stem. This sail was often boomed out when running and for an unknown reason this spar was called a 'manacle boom'. The topsail set above the mizzen was locally called the 'monk' and usually had a jack yard at its foot, with the sheet led through a hole in the gaff end.

The iron tiller was crooked to pass clear of the mizzen mast and the rudder could be drawn up by a tackle from the mizzen masthead to clear when beaching.

An attempt was made to construct a harbour at Hastings but this became ruined and all Hastings fishing boats were hauled up on the steep beach,

except in settled fine weather, when they could be anchored off for a few days. Each lugger occupied a space on the beach known as a 'stade' (c.f. 'stage' at Deal) and generally beached bow-on with the hauling-up rope or chain rove through a hole in the stem by a line, as she approached. A line was thrown ashore and the capstan was hooked on to the 'fall block' of the haul-up tackle. This heavy block rode up the shingle on a wooden sledge called a 'block slide'. The fall of the purchase led to a capstan barrel usually turned by a horse walking around it, tethered to a revolving pole above the barrel. The other end was made fast to an anchor buried in the beach, or to a strong post. As the horse rotated the capstan the purchase creaked and the bulky lugger began to move up the beach on wood 'trows', laid before the keel. Heavy bilge keels took the chafe of hauling up and down the shingle on skids, and when ashore the lugger was steadied by 'blockings' under these iron-shod keels.

In onshore winds, hauling up had to be done quickly. The older open luggers were sometimes pooped by a heavy sea and if this occurred, it might be necessary to smash a hole quickly in an after bottom plank to let the water run out and allow her to be rapidly hauled up clear of the surf, to avoid breaking up. This danger caused gradual abandonment of the transom stern for the 'lute' or elliptical counter, though even these forms could be pooped in heavy conditions, and fully decked luggers were the only safe answer. Luggers were sometimes lost in beaching and launching, and when it blew too hard onshore the Hastings men often managed to get hauled up at

Eastbourne or run into Newhaven for shelter.

Launching off was more exacting. The lugger lay stern to sea with a 'skid-chain' rove through the forefoot hole and hooked to the fall block. She stood on trows well greased with tallow and was slowly got down the beach on a way of trows placed before her, half the crew putting their backs against the bows to move her, chanting in time to heave her down to the cant of the beach; after this it became steep, and gravity did the work. With trows placed to the water and others ready to be dropped in at the tideline, the skid chain was knifed free and the lugger slid quickly down to the water. If she would not float clear a haul-off warp was led from a kedge anchor laid off and was taken to the lugger's quarter so she could haul clear and set her sails.

In 1912 one lugger had a 13 h.p. Kelvin motor installed and thereafter sail rapidly became unimportant in these craft, which were soon seen motoring with a fair wind and in a few years became powered craft with auxiliary sail.

Eastbourne

The now sedate Sussex seaside resort of Eastbourne was a vigorously thriving fishing station during the nineteenth century and probably earlier, and the Eastbourne fishermen and boatbuilders appear to have been more adventurous and progressive than their neighbours along the Sussex coast.

The decked luggers of the 'Bourners', as they styled themselves, were 35–40ft long and drifting in the English Channel for mackerel and herring was their main work, though some trawling was done, but only as a stopgap between drifting voyages which took them far away.

Eastbourne had no harbour and all craft were launched and hauled up the beach, where the 'fishing station' was on the site of the Royal Parade. When this was under construction during the 1880s it was bitterly opposed by the fishermen who hove a lugger across the contractor's light railway line. She was rammed by an engine and smashed, so the council and businessmen got their way.

The Bourners were redoubtable men and about 1886, English fishermen in the port of Ramsgate attacked French fishermen who had been stealing fish from English nets, and also taking some nets. The affray included several men from Eastbourne boats which were fishing from the port, as was their custom, and a leading part in what became known as the 'Ramsgate Riots' was taken by John French of Eastbourne.

All Eastbourne fishing vessels were registered at the port of Newhaven. The larger luggers were drifters, fishing for herring and mackerel in season as far north as Scarborough in Yorkshire, and west to southern Ireland, and frequently Plymouth. They only returned to Eastbourne between drifting 'voyages', to refit and change from one type of net to another as mackerel caught in the Channel and in Irish waters needed different sized mesh nets, as did those for herring. Although always spoken of as 'luggers', the larger ones were later dandy rigged. All sailed well and had very shapely ends, unlike the Hastings boats which were built full.

Plate 26. An Eastbourne fishing lugger on the beach, showing counter stern and working sail area.

Besides the larger luggers there were half-decked, two masted luggers called 'Shinamen', about 27–28ft long overall, 21–22ft long on the keel. They had a centreboard and a short foredeck but were otherwise miniatures of the larger luggers, rigged with a dipping lug foresail, standing lug mizzen sheeted to an outrigger and a jib set on a long bowsprit. *Bonny Kate, Crystal Spring* and *Band of Hope* were some of their names. The smaller lugsail-rigged punts drifted for sprats, went long lining, lobster potting and sometimes oyster dredging on the grounds off Norman's Bay, which was known to the fishermen as 'Norman's Bay', and Pevensey Bay village was called 'Wallsend'. The punts had a removable washstrake which was shipped in winter to increase freeboard.

Hyde, Sayers, Prodger, Mockett, Hunt, Blower, Allchon and Boniface were some of the Eastbourne fishing families and there were many characters amongst them. Bonky Jack, the bearded hermit fishermen who lived alone with a cat in his net shop (store) and went fishing alone in the punt *Peace and Plenty* was rivalled by 'Doctor' Oliver, a retired fisherman who wore a high-crowned black felt hat of a type beloved by the older fishermen; he was a herbalist with a speciality of seaweed tea.

As the town grew, brigs regularly kedged on and off the beach to discharge coal until the arrival of the railway which accelerated Eastbourne's transformation into a Victorian seaside resort. Growth of the pleasure trade caused many Bourners to start running passenger craft off the beach, taking trippers for a sail, but returning to fishing in the winter. Ben Bates had the dandy

The fishing industry of Eastbourne was given impetus by the interest of F. W. Leybourne Popham who lived at Hungerford, Wiltshire, but took great interest in Eastbourne. During the 1880s he had built several sailing and auxiliary steam drifters, two fish carriers and two yachts; one for cruising and the other racing. Popham was an ardent yachtsman who had voyaged the far Arctic in his large barquentine-rigged steam yacht *Blencathra* and had a passion for luggers.

Many of his fishing craft were built by Gausden, as were the yachts. These deep craft were launched off the fishing station on cradles, in which they were towed to Newhaven, where they were put on the gridiron and the cradles were dismantled.

Popham owned the fishing craft *Happy Thought*, *Bird of Freedom*; the dandies *Lady Eleanor*, *Rover* and *Little Florence*; built as a lugger and owned by Gausden who sold her to Popham, the last named was cut in two amidships and lengthened to emerge dandy rigged. The *Queen of Sussex* was the first lugger Popham had built at Eastbourne, this 50 footer was launched with a centreboard, which was later removed. His fleet was further augmented by purchase of the *Fred Archer*, from Plymouth. Becoming more ambitious, Popham had the 60ft × 15ft × 8.7ft draught, dandy-rigged *Nick of Time* built at Cowes in 1886, followed by the similar dandy *Free Will*, 55ft × 16ft × 9ft draught, built at Shoreham in 1883; both unusual in being fitted with auxiliary steam engines of 7 nominal horsepower.

About this time Popham became impatient with the slowness of cross channel steamer handling of fish freight for the Paris market, so he

rigged ketch *Britannia* built for this work about 1900 and she was hauled up like the luggers.

Unlike the Kentish beachmen's capstans, which were worked by men pushing numbers of capstan bars, the Sussex capstans were turned by a horse fastened to the end of a long bar and walking in circles with a little trick of stepping over the haul up rope. For a heavy haul a second bar could be rigged in line with the first, on the opposite side for another horse. Occasionally, during sudden severe gales, luggers from other Sussex ports beached at Eastbourne, as during 1896 when six Hastings luggers made emergency beachings and as the gale increased they were followed by two others. Luggers sometimes lay anchored off Eastbourne in fine weather, on a ground to the west of the pier known as the 'grasses', an area protected slightly from the Channel seas by a bank of sea grass which extended a considerable distance and broke the wave motion.

George Gausden was Eastbourne's noted builder of luggers and other craft. Later, Tom Sisk, who had served his boatbuilding apprenticeship at Worthing, joined him and the firm became Gausden and Sisk, with a yard in Beach Road. The Eastbourne luggers were clinker planked of elm on oak frames and had elliptical sterns; most of their sails were made by Hooper. The fishing punt *Pet* was built from timber scrap remaining after the lugger yacht *Paradox* was built. Some Eastbourne luggers were built in the west country, like one for 'Laddie' Simpson, which cost £100 ready for sea, and a few, like the *Rover*, had been built and previously owned at Worthing, further along the Sussex coast.

ordered two steam fish carriers to be built at Southampton. These were 136ft × 22ft × 11.2ft draught, 274 gross tons and were launched in 1888 as the *Romulus* and *Remus*. They also carried the Popham fleet's fish from southern Ireland, where there was regular drifting for mackerel out of Kinsale and Baltimore with special mesh nets.

Fred Hurd of Eastbourne sailed in the Irish fishing, starting as a boy of 13; he also fished for mackerel out of Plymouth in an Eastbourne boat for twelve seasons. He recalled that all the largest of Popham's drifters were fitted with steam capstans and boilers for hauling gear. Between drifting voyages all of them were hove up on the fishing station beach, except the two auxiliary steamers *Nick of Time* and *Free Will*, which were much too heavy to be got up.

During 1888 Popham had the lugger rigged cruising yacht *Paradox* designed by W. C. Storey and she was built at Eastbourne by George Gausden. With dimensions of 70.3ft × 20.1ft × 9ft depth she set a large sail area in a two-masted lugger rig; a dipping lug foresail and a standing lug mizzen sheeted to a long and well steeved outrigger. The mizzenmast head was higher than the foremast and in light weather she set a large mizzen staysail tacked down at the foot of the foremast. A two-cylinder inverted compound steam engine of 8 nominal horse power was installed by Guy of Cowes and the woodbine funnel was portable when sailing.

The *Paradox* was occasionally raced in the Solent handicap class during 1889, without success, but the idea of a racing lugger gripped Popham who, that winter commissioned a forty

Plate 28. The 70ft auxiliary steam lugger yacht *Paradox* was built at Eastbourne in 1888. She sets a racing rig of dipping lug foresail, standing lug mizzen, spinnaker run forward on its boom and a mizzen staysail. *Photo – Beken.*

rater racing yacht to be designed by William Fife of Fairlie, Scotland, to be built at Eastbourne by Gausden. She was to be rigged as a two masted lugger, the after mast setting the main lugsail, which caused her to be known as a lugger-schooner. The foresail was the usual dipping lug but the main was a hybrid balance lug with the luff well forward of the mast, loose footed but fitted with a boom and set from a long yard which could not be dipped and was hoisted with main and peak halyards. A yard topsail could be set above it.

The feelings of others in the forty rating class can be imagined; it comprised some of the keenest racing craft, skippers and crews in the sport and talk of a lugger competitor sent them into fits of laughter. Undeterred, Fife produced a beautifully shaped yacht, equal in form to any contemporary and Gausden built her well. She was launched and rigged for the 1890 racing season around the coast, but the lugger rig proved a failure on such a hull and she was not placed in a race. Her crew necessarily included many Eastbourne hands who well understood lugsails but knew nothing of yacht racing, and the skipper and yacht hands amongst the crew knew little of lugsails. After successive defeats her owner sent for Captain John Cranfield of Rowhedge, a noted racing skipper, to see what he could do, but even his genius could not improve the *White Slave*, as she was named. She was converted to cutter rig at Cowes in 1891, was improved but was sold the following season.

Popham's fishing interests continued to expand and numbers of Lowestoft fishermen were brought in to augment the Eastbourne crews of the fleet, which was at the height of its activity. The skipper of the *Lady Eleanor* was Henry 'Dusty' Matthews who, when introduced to King George V during a royal visit to Eastbourne said; 'I knew your mum and dad!' He became a teetoller after a fishing voyage to the westward, telling the publican 'Your watch chain's as big as a brig's anchor cable. I must have paid for every link, but now I be done!'

Sometime after 1890 Popham and all his boats left Eastbourne to make a boating headquarters at Hythe, on Southampton water. During 1892 the *Queen of Sussex* was sold to Collingwood Hughes, a Hamble yachtsman who sailed in her to the Dutch coast where she was used for pleasure fishing and shooting.

Although Popham had gone the 'Bourners' continued to flourish as late as 1914, when Jesse Hugget's lugger *Our Lassie* and Ben Bates' *Mallard* were launching off the beach on drifting voyages, along with others, fully rigged to the mizzen topsail and sailing like the wind. By the 1920s only the punts and the tripper boats remained on the beach and the vigorous old days were ended.

Newhaven

A few luggers worked from Newhaven harbour which was a frequent refuge and convenient railway landing port for fishing vessels from other Sussex ports and places much further afield, besides being heavily used by cargo-carrying sailing and steam vessels of many types and sizes.

This busy place at the mouth of the River Ouse supported a number of pilots, whose boats averaged 15 feet in length. For many years three

Plate 29. The Eastbourne lugger *Our Lassie* was built for J. Huggett by Thomas Sisk from a public subscription raised to replace a Huggett lugger lost while lobster fishing. *Photo – H. O. Hill.*

Plate 30. A Folkstone lugger with reefed dipping lug foresail, standing lug mizzen and small jib stancs out from the Kentish port to fish in the English channel with the beam trawl carried on her starboard side.

163

pilots owned one each. They were spritsail rigged on main and mizzen and set a foresail on a short bowsprit, but were frequently rowed. Generally they resembled the Cowes watermen's skiffs but were about six inches deeper.

Brighton and Shoreham

Spritsail-rigged 'hog boats' were a common type of fishing craft sailing from the beach communities of Brighthelmstone and Worthing and from the port of Shoreham, until the early nineteenth century. The type probably derived from the same concept as the Spithead and Isle of Wight wherries, further west.

Brighthelmstone men had fished and smuggled around the south and east coasts for centuries. During the eighteenth century the place became known as Brighton and was transformed from a village into a resort, made fashionable by visits of the Prince Regent and various courtiers and courtesans. At the end of the eighteenth century twenty-five hog boats were launching off its beach for trawling and forty-five others were engaged in the main fishery; drift netting in the Channel for mackerel, which around 1800 were regarded as a delicacy, fetching prices for the first landings of the season. In May 1807 mackerel were sold for 7 shillings *each* at Billingsgate market.

A typical hog boat was 28ft long × 16ft beam × 4ft 6in depth, with plumb stem, straight keel and small transom stern. The hull was flat floored and the boats sat almost upright when hauled up the beach. The forefoot was usually fine, with some flare in the bow, but they needed leeboards to work to windward. The beamy

hull provided a spacious deck, sunk below the sheer to form a footrail. The deck was of varying levels, with a long hatch or pair of hatches amidships for handling nets and a small steering hatch aft, within the tiller radius.

The hull was usually divided into three spaces by bulkheads. A small hatch in the foredeck gave access to the tiny fo'c'sle which had the usual locker seats and a fire box for cooking. Two small hatches abreast the mast tabernacle deck slot opened to the hold amidships and the larger openings, just forward of the small helmsman's cockpit, were crews' and net handling cockpits.

Large boats had two masts, each setting a boomless spritsail spread by a comparatively short and light sprit with its heel high up the mast, giving a flat set to the sails. These were cut with vertical cloths, had two rows of reef points and were laced to the masts. The sprits were held to the masts by a snotter and were set up taut by a tackle on a standing pendant from the masthead. The foremast was stepped about one third of the length abaft the stem and the shorter mizzen just inside the transom, which had the outrigger set through it. The main mast was stepped in a three-sided tabernacle and had two shrouds on each side and a forestay set up to a downward curving bumkin of rectangular, plank-like form. The foresail was laced to the forestay and was often set up to the masthead by a lanyard; another survival of their wherry origins.

Small hog boats sometimes had a single mast setting spritsail and foresail. Larger ones often set a jib on a long bowsprit run out through a gammon iron at the end of the bumkin, with the

Plate 31. Brighton hog boats of the 1820s. The chubby, clinker hulls had leeboards for windward sailing. The mainsail and mizzen were set with sprits well up the luffs and a large overlapping foresail was set in light weather from the 'plank' bowsprit. *Drawn by E. W. Cooke.*

166

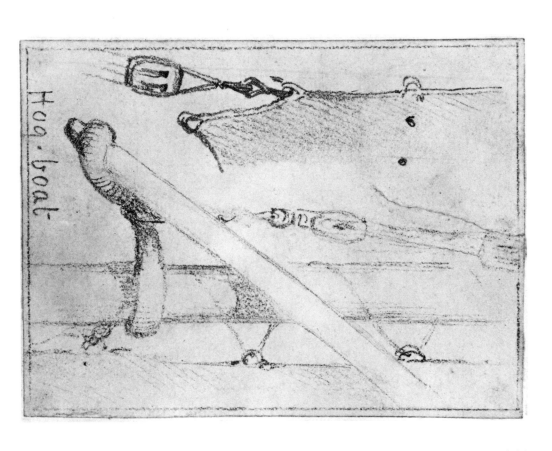

Plate 32: Sprit snotter, luff lacing and mainsheet upper block. Details of a Brighton hog boats rig drawn by E. W. Cooke early in the nineteenth century.

heel lashed to the beam across the foredeck, to which the bumkin was bolted.

Hog boat leeboards appear to have been rectangular in shape and were pivoted on a rope lanyard passing through the sheerstrake and making fast around a knee or timberhead abreast the bulkhead near the mast. The board hoisted by a single part pendant and bore against a substantial chock on the side planking, called a 'clump'. It is difficult to assess their ability under sail but from experience with a leeboard gaff cutter of similar length and profile, but half their beam, they probably sailed better than is realised; the beamy hull allowing little change of draught in strong winds.

The sprit was hoisted by a barrel winch on the side of the tabernacle. E. W. Cooke, that masterly marine artist, ably captured the buoyant liveliness of the 'hoggies' in one of his engravings of 1830 (Plate 31) and one of his drawings in the author's possession, is of the sprit heel and snotter arrangement of a Brighton boat (Plate 32).

Many hog boats were built at Hove by May and Thwaites and ranged up to 35ft length during the early nineteenth century, when popularity of the two masted lug rig spread to Sussex and they were gradually discarded, though several lingered at Brighton in the 1880s, being broken up soon after.

The Brighton luggers retained something of the hog boat's beamy hull form and a transom stern, and continued to use leeboards, but by the 1890s many had lute sterns to aid in beaching and centreboards were fitted in some, worked by a tackle from the foremast head.

Luggers were usually built locally, John Plugh building many at Brighton, where Basset made and repaired the sails. Before the turn of the century, Brighton fishermen were also buying luggers from Cornwall, though the *Elisabeth II* was launched at Brighton, fully rigged and without auxiliary engine, as late as 1910 and with the Brighton-built *Belinda* and *Victory*, were the last luggers on Brighton beach, being broken up on Admiralty orders in 1940, when invasion threatened.

Fishing and smuggling luggers were built and owned at Shoreham which, with Newhaven, was often used by Brighton luggers, particularly those built in Cornwall for Brighton owners, which were typical deep-draught drifters for extended fishing.

Worthing

Worthing was a fishing village until the mid-nineteenth century when, like Eastbourne, it also changed into a seaside resort and desirable residential area, though its fishermen and their fleet of luggers continued working for many years.

Worthing men owned fine, decked luggers up to about 50ft length and fished principally in the English Channel between Dungeness and southern Ireland, drifting for mackerel and herring, also voyaging to the North Sea in season. They were registered at the port of Shoreham and carried the letters SM before the fishing number.

Luggers were built there. During the 1850s John Belton commenced business as a boatbuilder at Worthing, constructing sailing luggers, and other fishing boats, beach tripper boats, small

yachts, oars and spars. His sons Herbert and Alfred joined the yard which launched its products down the beach and hauled other craft up it for repair. By 1900 the firm, as Belton & Co., built small yachts and beach boats in a shed just off the parade but still launched luggers for Brighton, Hastings and Littlehampton. The premises was sold during World War I.

A family named Hutchinson was boatbuilding at Worthing in 1873, and Benjamin Haslett was another during the 1870s and 1880s; he later became a housebuilder, typifying Worthing's decline into a seaside resort.

Thomas Belton was perhaps the most noted Worthing fisherman. Born in 1800, son of a fisherman, he was orphaned in 1807 but by hard work and inherent seamanship became owner of the lugger *Ebenezer*, working in the Worthing fleet principally in the English Channel mackerel fishery as far west as Cornwall and occasionally to southern Ireland. Belton was a religious man who would never fish or sell a catch on Sunday and, if his lugger made port or beached on Friday, he would not sail again until Monday. If wind or tide prevented him landing for church, he brought up or laid to and after a prayer, all hands did only necessary work and cooking for the day. Each day at sea, morning and night, he mustered the crew in the tiny cabin and read an extract from the Bible. His crew's thoughts are unrecorded but his fishing skill and seamanship were unquestionable and although he only fished five nights each week against the seven of most of his contemporaries, his landings were usually equal or higher.

167

A heavy gale once prevented him landing on a Friday afternoon during the mackerel season. On Saturday it moderated and the lugger anchored off with a big catch. The dealers were anxious as prices were high at the London market but Belton refused them, claiming the wholesalers would supply the London hawkers who he knew would be crying the fish in London on Sunday. Though he could ill afford such principle, the catch was left aboard and his crew went to their usual Saturday net washing and mending on shore. The bitter dealers and many fishermen thought he had gone too far, but abruptly the weather changed and a severe frost preserved the tons of fish, which were landed on Monday and fetched an even higher price in a starved market.

Belton prospered and had built the luggers *The Good Hope* and *The Consolation*, which were also well known in the east coast herring fishery, frequently working out of Lowestoft.

There was much contact between Worthing and west country fishermen and some settled there including the Street family, who moved from Plymouth in the 1870s, at one time working three luggers from the Sussex shore.

Seine nets were also worked by the Worthing men. In May, 1866 a great shoal of mackerel appeared close inshore and they set around them, dashing oars in the water to frighten fish into the net but, as often happens, the shoal escaped. On the same day a 'kettle net' set on large posts jutting seaward into the tideway on the sands between Worthing and Lancing caught many thousand which sold at £2 per hundred.

5

Inside the Wight

Spritsail rig was much used in small craft of the Solent, Spithead and adjacent waters in the south of England, of which the first and second class Spithead wherries are the best remembered.

Their principal work was carrying officers, baggage, stores and provisions to warships and other vessels lying in Spithead, and the occasional carriage of passengers, light general cargo and livestock between the Isle of Wight and the mainland; principally between Portsmouth and Ryde, and Southampton and Cowes.

In slack times they might fill in with fishing or assisting vessels with unlicensed pilotage, or go sweeping for anchors. Many first class wherries were used in smuggling from Cherbourg and Barfleur, and they had a reputation as able sea boats.

A naval officer serving in a sailing ship of the line during the mid-nineteenth century recalled her having to bring up to the east of the Isle of Wight with her sails blown away and shoals close under her lee; the ship plunging in heavy seas. An hour later the anxious deck watch saw a scrap of sail making towards them, tumbling from sea to sea. The wherry ran close under the warship's stern to read her name, then her oilskinned crew shot her up on a big wave and she plunged off to windward to beat back to Portsmouth and report the ship's danger.

Many of these first class wherries were owned at Portsmouth and the *Turkish Knight* was typical, being 34ft 4in overall length × 9ft beam × 5ft 6in depth from top of keelson to top of deck at side; draught forward was 3ft and aft 3ft 11in. The foredeck was 14ft 9in long and the foremast stepped 12ft 3in abaft the stem. The hull was very fine with hollow bow and stern waterlines.

The pointed stern had only slightly more buoyancy than the lean bow and the amidship section was very slack and almost semicircular in shape.

Wherries were clinker planked, usually of oak, copper fastened to sawn frames fitted when planking was completed; a comparatively light construction, but they were long lived.

Apart from forward and aft decks, wherries were open from gunwale to gunwale, but side benches were fitted for passengers and crew, with a wide thwart aft for the helmsman. A cuddy was contrived under the foredeck with a stove at its

Plate 33. Spritsail-rigged Portsmouth wherries enliven the majesty of George Chambers' painting of the line of battleship *Britannia* entering Portsmouth Harbour in February 1835 after a five-

and-a-half year Mediterranean commission. The wherry in foreground tows salvaged spars and a cutter creeps along inshore through the fine evening. *Courtesy – National Maritime Museum.*

after end and low benches for sitting and sleeping. Three or four tons of pig iron ballast were stowed under the cockpit platform or sole. About twenty half-hundredweight iron pigs with handles were stowed in a row between securing battens on the middle line amidships. In a breeze or when a press of sail was carried, these were shifted to stow in open bins under the weather side bench.

During the Napoleonic wars some wherries were rigged with three masts, each setting a spritsail in the manner of Channel Islands craft. However the amidship sail was little if ever used by the mid-nineteenth century, when wherry size may have decreased as steamships and steam towing of ships to port diminished the time spent at anchor in roadsteads.

The two masted wherry rig carried, from forward, a staysail set to the stem head and in these craft termed a 'jib'; a sprit foresail set on the foremast, which was much the tallest of the two and stepped through the foredeck; and the spritsail mizzen, set on a mast stepped immediately forward of the short after deck. The standing rigging consisted of a forestay and two shrouds each side on each mast. The foresail was fitted with brails which were generally used at anchor or alongside ships, though the sprits were sometimes unshipped and the short mastheads lay clear below lower yards and rigging. As wherries were often under sail in hard weather, two or three foresail sprits of various lengths were carried, for use with the sail when reefed. The jib and foresail were each fitted with a pair of sheets, handled at each tack. The mizzen sheeted to the top of sternpost.

Steering was by tiller lines to a yoke on the rudder head, enabling the helmsman to go forward when necessary. In calms, the wherries were rowed and three fixed crutches of oak were usually built into each gunwale for the sweeps.

Centreboards were never built into the first or second class wherries but their fine lines got them to windward through the short, hollow sea kicked up by a Spithead tide meeting an easterly wind. During bad weather, when ship's boats were kept hoisted in, wherries cruised around the fleet in Spithead or St Helens Roads, looking for a job. In these conditions weather boards were shipped forward of the mizzen to protect the passengers.

In 1822 a scale of charges was authorised by parliament. Passengers from Portsmouth and Ryde paid five shillings for passage in a single-handed wherry or seven shillings for one with two or more hands. From Southampton to Cowes a wherry or rowboat with two men cost twelve shillings and sixpence, or a guinea if manned by four men. A two-man Portsmouth wherry could be hired for the day for twelve shillings and sixpence and a four-man boat for one pound and ten shillings.

A smaller example of first class wherry was the *Woodham*; 27ft overall length × 8ft 3in beam × 4ft 9in depth. Her foremast stepped 7ft 0in abaft the stem and was only 19ft 6in long; the foresail sprit was 17ft; the mizzen mast was 15ft and its sprit 10ft 6in; mizzen boom was 7ft. She had a lower sail plan than the larger wherries, but a proportionately taller mizzen.

The *Woodham*'s lines were taken off by W. M. Blake in 1936 and show an extremely fine hull

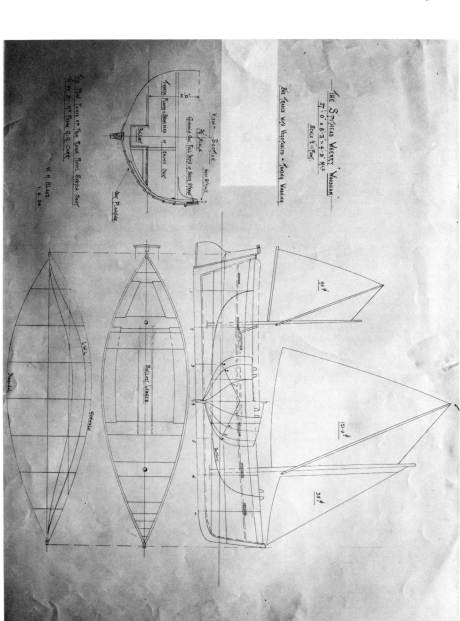

Figure 64 The 27ft Spithead wherry *Woodham* was typical of the smaller first class wherries and set two spritsails and a foresail tacked to the stemhead. The fine ends enabled these clinker planked craft to work to windward. *Science Museum, London.*

form. The stem was almost plumb, sternpost slightly raked and the keel straight; a fast craft, reaching or running, and able to go to windward well; but which would be slow in turning.

Smaller rowing and sailing 'second class' wherries were also used from Portsmouth, principally in the harbour or in Spithead when the weather was suitable; though a few are said to have been across Channel in smuggling runs under oars and sail. They were pointed stern, clinker planked open boats evolved for rowing or sailing with fine lines and considerable rise of floor which made them tender under sail and consequently the sail area was less than in most comparable working craft. Some internal iron ballast was carried and, handled with skill, they rarely capsized, except occasionally when overloaded with drunken seamen.

These wherries were fast and went to windward well, though centreplates were not fitted. Steering was by lines to a rudder yoke to clear the mizzen. The usual rig was a foresail, a boomless sprit mainsail and a small sprit mizzen stepped well inboard with its boom protruding just beyond the sternpost. The spritsails were tall and comparatively narrow, with luff and leech almost parallel. Single reefs were fitted to the foresail and mizzen, and two in the mainsail. This position of the mizzen achieved good balance of the sail plan with the staysail tacked to the stemhead, dispensing with a bowsprit which would be an encumbrance in coming alongside.

It was a handy rig to be worked by one man, but by the 1880s steam launches were rapidly reducing their trade, which continued to decline

until only a handful of Portsmouth wherries remained by the 1920s.

Some later wherries set a small, boomless lugsail for a run or reach. Some had a short forward and after deck; others an aft deck only. They were essentially shapely, finely formed rowing boats and their owners were called the 'Old Point shovellers' and were noted as oarsmen in the Solent and Spithead regattas, where they carried off most of the prizes.

Small sprit and lugsail wherries and galleys were much used by Hampshire and Isle of Wight smugglers in 'free trade' from France, which lasted until the late nineteenth century. May to September was the favourite period for Isle of Wight smuggling which was rampant between 1816 and 1842, when anti-smuggling laws strained the revenue service with the range of prohibited goods, leading paradoxically to increased participation by all classes of people, many daring runs being made.

James Buckett of Brighstone, a small village just inland from the rocky south-west shore of the Island, was typical of the smugglers. As a young fisherman during the 1820s he smuggled spirits from Barfleur on the Cherbourg peninsular, with a 20ft wherry, The Bet, rigged with a boomless lugsail and fast under oars or sail. Local farmers usually financed the run, often risking £50 in the enterprise. The voyage across the Channel and return was always made during 'the darks'; a period three days each side of new moon. Tubs of spirits were purchased complete with carrying rope joining them in pairs. The heavily loaded wherry had to weather the squally Channel and elude the watchful revenue cutters.

If a cutter was sighted, a rope girdle was laid round the sheerstrake with strops hanging from it supporting the tubs in the water, seriously diminishing speed. If chased, the girdle was cut away on both sides at once or the wherry would capsize, and the cargo sank to total loss. If undetected, the girdle was sunk on carefully taken bearings off the Island's south shore, the wherry standing on for her usual berth in the Newtown River, off the Solent. The crew returned home and next night with a shore gang swept and grappled to recover the tubs which were quickly carried inland and hidden until distributed.

Eventually smugglers became so harassed that James Buckett and others took the cross Channel packet to France and hired a French three masted chasse marée lugger and crew to run a cargo of tubs. About five miles south of St Catherine's Point a revenue cutter overhauled them and the girdle of tubs was cut away in 20 fathoms.

They were boarded and searched; their protests of innocence were disbelieved and they were jailed for trial. Meanwhile the impounded lugger was comandeered by the revenue service to cruise the Channel, but lost a mast in a squall and when the smugglers were cleared the government had to step a new one!

Later, James Buckett was caught smuggling and after trial he was impressed for five years in the navy; still a sailing service and little changed since Trafalgar. Buckett was shipped in the gun brig *Gannel*, then as ordinary seaman to the frigate *Forte*; becoming able seaman and eventually captain of the fore-top.

Returning home he eventually became coxswain of the first Isle of Wight lifeboat, stationed at Brighstone. Sometimes when the gun went to launch, coastguards and smugglers found themselves side by side at her oars or sweating-in the lugsail sheets; grim faced and silent. The boat saved 280 lives from disaster and James Buckett died a public hero.

By the 1850s the revenue men had reduced smuggling to sporadic runs. The risks were high, captured wherries or small craft being sawn in two or three pieces or else having the planks ripped from them. Larger fast craft were sometimes taken into government service.

Rufus Cotton of Atherfield, a village near Brighstone, was homeward bound with a wherry load of tubs in March 1878 when to the south of the Island he saw the capsize of the British naval training ship *Eurydice* in a squall, with loss of all but two of her large complement of boys and men. The horror stricken smugglers, battling with the same squall in the overloaded wherry, could offer no assistance without detection and stood on for home with troubled hearts.

Four-, six- and eight-oared fast rowing gigs and galleys were also for used for cross Channel runs. Lymington smugglers made one run in an eight-oared gig, returning in darkness with seventy tubs through a lumpy sea with one man bailing continuously. The exhausted crew pulled for Yarmouth, a haven at the west end of the Wight, where the cargo was to be landed for its backers. The coxswain misjudged the entrance and ran her on a pile forcing the cursing smugglers to flounder ashore, losing gig and cargo.

Watermen from Ryde and Cowes used small rowing and sailing boats for winter fishing in the Solent or Spithead with lines and seine nets. Sometimes they drifted for herring or sprats but they made a better living in summer rowing fares and light stores off to or ashore from ships and yachts in Cowes Roads and the Medina river; occassionally making a run to Southampton or Portsmouth for a belated passenger. Typical dimensions were 15ft long × 4ft 8in beam × 1ft 10in depth.

The slack midship section, fine ends and shapely transom indicate that these boats were built for rowing rather than sailing, understandably when the fierce tides of the Medina and the approaches to Cowes had to be regularly overcome in the day's work. Although the spritsail and foresail rig was really only an alternative to oars, many sailed well under it and some were fitted with centreplates, increasing draught to about 4 feet. This was unusual in British working boats, though centreboards had been used at Cowes since the American built catboat Una was brought here in 1854 and began a craze for those handy craft, which swept the Solent and led to Cowes builders imitating the type with English built 'Una' boats. Undoubtedly, the centreboard concept was copied by the watermen.

Usually the Cowes boats were rigged with a sprit foresail, set on a mast stepped through the forward thwart, and a sprit mizzen stepped close to the transom and sheeted to an outrigger; both sails being boomless. Some boats had a small foresail tacked to the stem head.

Two pairs of wooden crutches protruded above the gunwale and the sheerstrake had four vertical wooden fenders to protect the planking when lying alongside. The boats were rowed at least as often as sailed. In calm weather the watermen rowed standing, facing forward, in the manner of watermen the world over. These boats were rarely sailed after 1900 and seem to have been extinct with the 1914 war.

Similar but larger boats rigged with a sprit mainsail and a foresail worked from Bembridge and Nettlestone Point (later named Seaview) as pilot boats serving ships in and out of St Helens Road and to the east of the Isle of Wight. They were clinker planked, with good freeboard, as this can be a rough area in south or east winds. They were usually open and did not have centreboards but carried ballast and drew about 3ft 6in on a 20ft waterline.

Pilots were still boarded in this way into the mid-nineteenth century but the boats were superseded by cutters cruising on station and later by steam cutters working principally to Seaview, which rivalled Cowes as a home of pilots. The Pilot Boat inn at Bembridge echoes this activity. Spritsail-rigged open boats of the smallest size fished from the Southampton area. These outnumbered the better remembered and larger, cutter-rigged threequarter-decked boats now often called Itchen Ferry Boats by yachtsmen, but which were referred to simply as Fishing Boats in old regatta reports and were also called smacks by the men who sailed them. Their development has been recorded in the author's Gaff Rig, (Adlard Coles Ltd 1970).

In 1872 there were 141 second class and 102 third class fishing boats registered at Southampton; most of them rowing and sailing boats of a distinct and developing type. With the growth of yachting after the mid-nineteenth century, many Solent fishing boats were used only part of the year as the owners and crews spent the summer as hands in racing or cruising yachts. Boys then went fishing when 12 or 13 years of age and were serving aboard yachts at 15 or 16. A man having ability as a helmsman, by his twentieth birthday might be skipper of a small racing yacht; perhaps a five tonner or two and a half rater, with another young hand as crew and an owner to advise from his already extensive knowledge of local tides, sets and depths gleaned while fishing. So the Solent fisheries became regarded as a partial occupation by local watermen, whose years was spent yachting in summer, fishing during autumn and early winter; then the leanest period until the yachts fitted out, at a shore job, or if near Southampton, working at the docks. Those living on or near the Solent relied more on fishing.

Small boats required less outlay, were more easily laid up and cared for while the owner pursued other occupations and, in common with many of the smacks, were often worked single-handed, enabling one man to scrape a living in many local forms of fishing, though two were required to work some types of gear.

These boats were rowed more often than sailed, particularly the smaller ones. They appear to have had no distinct type name, as was typical with men more concerned with making a living afloat than with thinking what to call the craft which were the tools of a trade. Usually they were referred to by length: 'My 14 footer.' If the owner also had one of the larger decked and ballasted fishing cutters of the district, he referred to 'My little boat'; others knew them as 'rowing boats'.

Lengths varied from 12 feet to about 17 feet, rarely above. The 12–13 footers were mostly owned on the Itchen river at Itchen village, Northam or Crosshouse. Most of these were purely rowing boats. Beyond the Itchen they ranged from 14 to 16 feet, with a few up to 17ft. These belonged to Weston, Hythe, Eling, Ashlett, Warsash, Hamble, Bursledon, Lepe, Cowes and other places on the Solent and Spithead. Many were built by Hatcher or Payne, the noted Southampton yachtbuilders. Others were by individual shipwrights, constructed in outhouses or gardens as spare time jobs.

Until the end of the nineteenth century the working rig was a boomless spritsail and foresail of modest area. By 1900 many boats had discarded spritsails for standing lugs, cut with a high peak (Fig. 65) in imitation of the small rating classes racing in the Solent. Sometimes the yard was fitted with jaws and became a form of gunter lug. The lugsails were closer winded than the spritsails, but the spirt rig was still regarded as handier for fishing, when it could be more readily cleared out of the way. Some 16–18ft boats were rigged with a standing lug main and two headsails.

Several were owned at Weston on the east shore of Southampton Water, just below Woolston; a once pleasant village now overrun by the suburban sprawl of Southampton. Here a small creek, locally called a 'lake', enabled the boats to lie on moorings and they could be laid ashore on the beach at its head, where gear was stored in a picturesque building thatched with seaweed. The spritsail-rigged Weston 14-footer *Mullet* was built during the 1870s by Payne of Southampton for £11.50. Her hull and rig are typical and she is still afloat, owned by the Cozens family. With a beam of 4ft 8in and a nominal draught of 9in, the flat-bottomed and plumb-sided hull has a small bilge radius and a deep transom, with reverse curve. The forebody is fine and the stem slightly raked. Forward lower waterlines are hollow. The freeboard is high and the sheer almost level; providing ample reserve buoyancy. The *Mullet* is reputedly fast, particularly when rowed, and was borrowed for entry in local regattas. Her speed was attributed to her flat bottom and she was a handy craft, reckoned to 'work the net for you'.

Construction was red pine, carvel planking, close seamed without caulking on bent timbers. The sheerstrake overlapped the next below. Timbers were doubled in the bottom up to the bilge stringers, which were extended for half the length amidships. The rudder projected slightly below the bottom of keel and shallow bilge keels were fitted.

Boats built around 1900 and after had centreboards; a change connected with adoption of lug rig and local developments in racing small sailing boats. Some boats, such as *Mullet*, did not have a centreplate fitted as the owners considered them weatherly enough without, and her fine

177

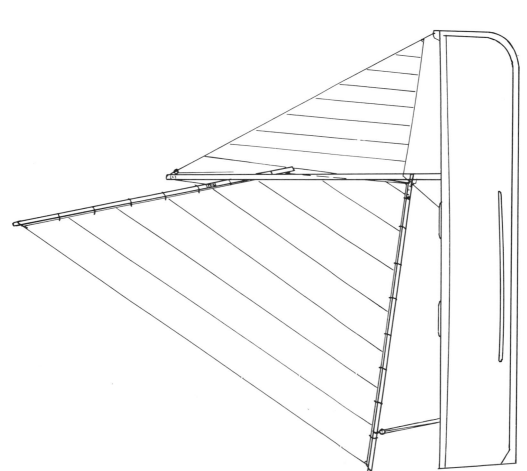

Figure 65. The 14ft fishing boat *Caprice* of Weston, nr. Southampton, set a boomed standing lug and foresail. She was also frequently rowed for her work in Southampton Water and the Solent.

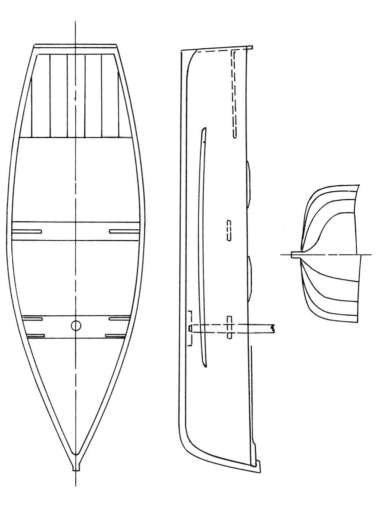

Figure 66. General arrangement and sections of the 14ft *Weston* rowing and sailing fishing boat *Mullett*, built by Payne at Southampton during the 1870s. She does not have a centreboard.

ends, stability of form and salient keel probably enabled her to go moderately well to windward.

There was a forward and an amidship thwart and a sternsheet or 'tray' into which the cod end of a trawl or a dredge was emptied. This was watertight with a low coaming at its forward end and drain holes cut in the side planking so that mud and shell could be washed overboard to avoid fouling the boats inside. Hulls were painted black or grey and in later years carried fishing numbers, which looked pretentious on such small craft.

The mast was unstayed and stepped through the forward thwart. The mainsail had two rows of reef points and when the first reef was tied, the heel of the sprit (locally termed 'spleet') which was secured by the usual snotter around the mast, was slid down the mast an equivalent depth. When the second reef was put in, a false peak was used to keep the heel of the sprit above the mast thwart.

This was a short length of rope with an eye spliced in each end; one secured to the peak and the other passed over the head of the sprit which extended above the sail peak by the length of the rope. It was necessary to unship the sprit to do this. The mainsheet block travelled on a rope horse made fast to the quarter knees; this was removed when working nets. Running in a strong wind, the sprit was unshipped and the peak of the mainsail was folded down and lashed to the truck, making a trysail.

The racing rig was of much greater area, necessitating standing rigging and, usually, a bowsprit which was held by a lashing to the

ringbolt inside the stem head and at the heel by a
lashing to the mast. Most boats had a wooden
racing keel with a lead shoe, through-bolted
under the true keel, and the rudder area was
increased by bolting an iron plate to the blade.

Most boats had two pairs of single thole pins on
which oars, with an ear piece fitted to the
loom, worked. A hole in this enabled it to be
slipped over the thole, retaining the oar if the
rower had to let go quickly to tend nets or lines.
Such oars are now rare in Britain but are still in
use amongst Solent workboats.

The *Caprice* (later renamed *Bream*) is another
14ft boat owned by the Cozers. She was built
about 1910 by G. Cozens, one of Payne's
shipwrights, for £19. Her hull has similar
proportions and characteristics to the *Mullet* but
an almost rectangular centreplate was fitted,
increasing draught to about 2ft 6in when lowered.
The *Caprice* is rigged with a standing lug, cut with
a high peak, and a foresail tacked to the
stemhead.

These rowing and sailing boats were used for
various methods of fishing in Southampton Water,
the Solent, Spithead and the tributary rivers and
creeks. During appropriate seasons they fished for
whelks, netted for mullet and other fish
frequenting the shallows with seine, trammel or
peter nets; drift netted for autumn herring and
sometimes sprats; laid long lines and speared eels
on the flats. Occasionally they were used for
wildfowling. The boats above 14ft long also
sometimes towed a small beam trawl for bottom
fish or a dredge for oysters. The plowsh or splash
net was set in a semi-circle, being held by anchors

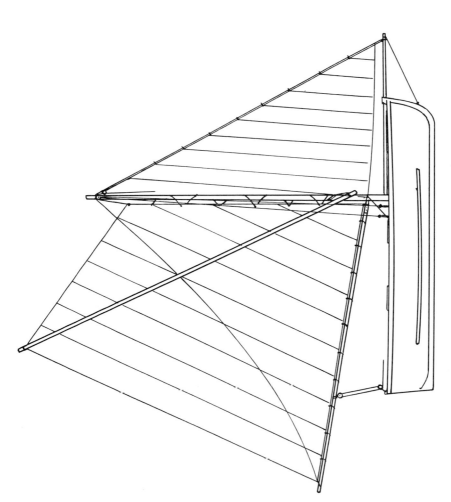

Figure 67. The Weston fishing boat
Mullett was rigged with a boomless
spritsail and a foresail for work but set
this enlarged sprit rig for local racing.

179

and allowed to bow away with the tide to form a bag. The boat moved up-tide of the net and the men splashed the surface with oars to drive fish into it. Afterwards the net was hauled aboard, being kept as baggy as possible to retain the fish. Shooting, driving and hauling usually only took about fifteen minutes.

A crew of two was necessary when working the various drift and seine nets; one to row and the other to handle the net. Typically a boat drifting for herring might be manned by father and schoolboy son, absent from class in the afternoon when the tide served, to help row a fourteen-foot boat down Southampton Water with the ebb, into the Solent; perhaps nine miles. There they shot fine cotton herring nets at the important dusk change of light; if possible when this coincided with low water. This was locally known as the 'dark shoot'. The nets were buoyed up with corks on the head rope and had leads wrapped round the footrope to make them hang like a curtain in the water, the depth of set being adjusted by rope strops at intervals along the top of the net supported by cork floats or buoys. Then they lay to one end of the net with a lantern exposed if shipping was moving, huddled in coats and oilskins against the cold and bailing the boat. If there were fish gleaming white in the lanternlight when the net was hauled, they shot again and after the second haul the net was stowed in the tray and they rowed back with the flood, or set a sail if the wind was fair. If the net was bare when the first shoot was hauled, they returned at once, reckoning further fishing useless; though in other areas, such as the River

Blackwater in Essex, where drifting from rowboats is also a traditional fishery, a barren first shot is followed by several others. Having fished in this way I can vouch for the labour needed for the usually small return of fish, but there is a thrill of expectation when the net is hauled which seems different from trawling.

By November the herring shoals might have moved up to Netley, in Southampton Water, which was dotted with small boats setting hundreds of yards of snaky curtains of net; men chaffing each other in the darkness and boat cursing boat when the tide set nets foul.

The catches were collected from the fishing villages by fish merchants with horse drawn light carts or traps, or might be landed direct at Southampton. Occasionally a fisherman's wife would row a catch to Southampton from a neighbouring village.

Races for the rowing and sailing boats were keenly contested in local regattas from the end of the eighteenth century, but there seems to have been little development in design until the 1870s when many were raced for pleasure by yacht captains and foremen shipwrights from the various Southampton and Itchen yacht and shipbuilding yards. Most villages on Southampton Water also gave races for the boats. The best of 1878 were the *Triona*, owned by one of the Paynes and the *Laura*, owned by William Shergold, Hatcher's foreman. Each flew fourteen prize flags at the season's end, imitating the custom of the racing yachts.

Enthusiasm ran high and in 1879 the Itchen Ferry Boating Club was formed, with the inevitable result that sail areas increased, the little lead keels got larger and deeper and hull form generally became more extreme. It was a microcosm of the eternal racing story in all classes. A typical 13 footer had 5 foot beam, was 2ft 9in deep amidships to underside of keel and drew 2ft 6in to the underside of the false keel; she set a sprit mainsail of 152 square feet on an 18ft sprit; a foresail of 38 square feet on a bowsprit 6 feet outboard, and carried a spinnaker of 65 square feet, spread by a 13ft boom.

One of the best known small racing boats was the *Conger*, owned and sailed by George Cozens, which invariably featured in the prize lists of local regattas until 1914, and was champion of the under 16ft class. These craft were rivalled in popularity by sailing dinghies after about 1890, many of which carried spritsail mainsails, having a short sprit with the heel set well up the mast; an arrangement which appears in many waterman's boats in old prints of the Solent area. During 1898 a development of this rig appeared in the Southampton Sailing Clubs dinghy class. The 14ft × 5ft 8in centreboard dinghy *Water Rat* was designed and built by F. Thompson and two partners. Her single chine hull with transversely curved and longitudinally rockered bottom was very similar to the Phil Rhodes designed Penguin class frostbite dinghies of forty years later, and had planing potential. Rigged with a sprit mainsail and a foresail set on a bowsprit, she set 180 square feet and had no ballast (Fig. 68). The *Water Rat* was a good all round boat and a consistent performer; reaching faster than her competitors and always amongst the leaders in

keen racing. However, her design was resented by the remainder of the restricted class who considered it too radical a departure from contemporary British practice. The *Water Rat* was probably the most interesting sailing dinghy which had then been built.

To the east of Portsmouth, on the border of Hampshire and Sussex, are two large, almost enclosed areas of salt water and marshland known as Langstone and Chichester Harbours. These stretch towards Selsey Bill and are almost divided by Hayling Island, but join by the narrow channel separating this from the mainland. The watermen and seafarers of this area preserved the ways of sail into the mid-twentieth century, but Chichester Harbour has become one of the most crowded sailing centres of the crowded south coast.

The ancient city of Chichester is slightly inland and nearby Bosham, at the top of the inlet, is an old home of seamen, rivalled by the characterful Hampshire village of Emsworth just along the coast. Both bred fishermen, coasting sailors, pilots, wooden ship and yacht builders, yacht hands and, until a century ago, smugglers. Wittering, Itchenor, Dell Quay and Hayling were other local communities contributing to harbour traditions.

By comparison Langstone Harbour was almost desolate, though only a few miles from Portsmouth and its busy dockyard. Coasters and fishing smacks worked into it and it was used by smugglers. Langstone has retained its lonely aspect and was fished by men from the hamlet of Langstone, on the channel at the back of Hayling Island.

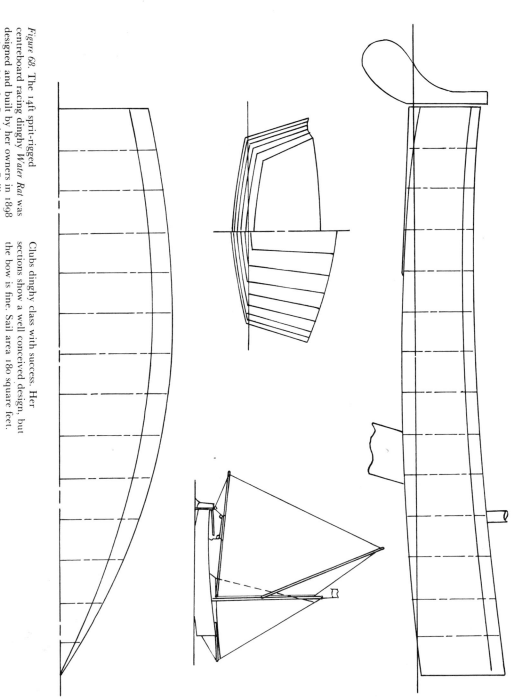

Figure 68. The 14ft sprit-rigged centreboard racing dinghy *Water Rat* was designed and built by her owners in 1898 and raced in the Southampton Sailing Clubs dinghy class with success. Her sections show a well conceived design, but the bow is fine. Sail area 180 square feet.

The entrances to both harbours are flanked by shifting banks, changing with wind and tide. At high water these are broad creeks thrusting inland through extensive marshes to once small communities, quays and watermills served by sailing ketches. At low water a maze of small channels, some deep, lead between shining mudflats and sands; a no-mans-land where an amphibious population made a precarious living. Life in the harbours was little known by outsiders before World War I, and that left them almost unchanged. The watermen were conservative, shrewd and reserved, yet enjoyed humour amongst themselves. They were suspicious of strangers and of each other, worked as hard as the tides and seasons allowed, but were not generally enterprising in extending their fisheries. They were fine watermen, handling their fishing boats and punts with natural skill. In summer some shipped as hands in the big racing cutters.

Emsworth fishermen sailed some of the finest smacks in Britain, designed and built at the Emsworth yard of James Duncan Foster, who also owned and managed them as they worked the English Channel scallop and sea oyster fisheries until the 1930s. He also built small merchant sailing ships and his story is told in *Gaff Rig*. But many Emsworth men preferred individual ownership of small luggers, which lay in a long row behind the sea wall which sheltered the village waterside from prevalent southerly winds (Plate 34). They existed almost unchanged for over a century and were still sailing during the 1940s.

Emsworth luggers were broad beamed and shallow, with slack bilge sections, usually of wide vee form. Average dimensions were 15ft long × 5ft 6in beam. A flase keel of wood or wood and iron increased draught to about 1ft 6in. There was variety of shape amongst the boats; many had fine bows and some almost semicircular midship sections. Others were chubby craft which were more stable. The hulls were decked forward, had two rowing thwarts and a fish tray aft. Two sets of thole pins were fitted to each gunwale.

A long luffed, square-headed lugsail was set, tacked down to the weather bow. This was not dipped when going about, except for very long tacks. The sails were well cut, tanned almost black and had four rows of reef points to control speed when dredging as well as for use in strong winds. The sheet led to each quarter and a single shroud on each side and a forestay, supported the mast.

These luggers were handy sized craft but the Emsworth men seldom sailed them hard to windward, preferring to down sail and row in contrary winds. If a boat missed stays in a lop she was helped round with a few strokes of an oar. Nothing would induce the harbour men to change the rig. Tradition was respected; centreboards and balance lugs were amateur fancies but of no interest to working Emsworth boatmen.

The luggers towed oyster dredges and small beam trawls for bottom fish in the harbours. If good catches of mackerel were being taken outside, they joined in with drift nets. They were unchanged in hull and rig thirty years ago, the *Matilda* of Emsworth (Plate 34) being built by Feltham of Portsmouth in 1945.

Similar boats were owned at Bosham where

184

Plate 34. Emsworth fishing lugger *Matilda* under sail. She was built by Feltham at Portsmouth in 1945. Note halyard set up as backstay; single-part sheet, shallow hull and long tiller. *Photo – H. O. Hill.*

many had centreboards to improve windward performance and regularly beat to windward. The lugsail tack rope was rove through a hole in the gunwale. Two masts were often carried; one for whole sail and a shorter for reefed conditions. They were stepped a little over one third the length of the boat from the stem.

Emsworth was the home of one of two principal oyster companies in Chichester Harbour, the other being the 'Bosham–Chichester Company'. The Emsworth company leased and worked the Emsworth Channel and the Bosham–Chichester Company the grounds from Copperas Point, south of Dell Quay, to East Head; part of Bosham Channel and most of Itchenor, except the private companies and individuals worked Thorney Creek and Snow Hill, West Wittering, until at least 1875.

In 1865 a private company obtained a parliamentary bill to enclose and drain Thorney Creek, which caused uproar amongst the fishermen. The only evidence of its efforts is a line of rotting piles from Cobnor Point (Chidham) to Thorney Island. The Emsworth Dredgermen's Cooperative Association was active into the 1960s, having maintained their lease on the Emsworth Channel and restocked the beds.

During the 1870–90 period, Chichester Harbour was busy with coasters, many bringing coal from the north of England. Some were owned and many were manned by local families, who had relations with the surrounding agricultural population. Occasionally outsiders were introduced into this close world. The Cate family of West Wittering were reputedly descended from the crew of a north country whaler who settled here about 1800. A pair of whale jaw bones and other local evidence remains. In common with many Englishmen of humble birth, some of these families have a lineage equal to any nobility. The Terneys, a family of pilots, were seafaring from the harbour in 1675, descending from hay bargement of Southampton and were connected by marriage to the boatmen of Undeynye or Pagham Harbour, to the east of Selsey Bill, who were sailing from this Sussex harbour during the mid-seventeenth century.

At high tide Langstone Harbour is a great sheet of water, sparkling blue in sun and wind, with several 'binesses', or low islands, and surrounded by low, marshy saltings rimmed with grassy sea walls. At low water the mudbanks and sands are bared, leaving a single deep channel down which the tide races to the harbour mouth, joined by tributary trickles. At all hours and seasons a living was gleaned. As the muds covered, oyster dredgers worked up and down the main channel; on the ebb, winkle pickers appeared, splashing about on mud patterns strapped to their feet.

One island had a single house built on it; the home of the oyster watchman guarding the beds. A lonely existence, living on an island 100 yards in diameter connected to firm ground by a causeway at low water. The watch house was built shortly after Trafalgar and its cellars became a smugglers caché for goods brought into the harbour by innocent looking schooners and fishing vessels.

Luggers also fished in Langstone Harbour but punts were the locals favourites. Typically they were long, low, pointed stern craft with only a few inches freeboard and a rounded deck. A pair of short oars worked in outriggers to obtain efficient spread and in fine weather a large lugsail was set. With a steering oar thrust over the lee quarter, the punts sailed with speed and weatherliness.

West of the Solent in the county of Dorset, Poole Harbour was a stronghold of spritsail rig. In 1872 most of the sixty-one second class fishing boats registered there were rigged with a sprit mainsail and a foresail; sometimes foresail and jib, set on a bowsprit. Length averaged 18ft and they fished in the extensive harbour for shrimps with a net like a wooden oyster dredge, with no scraper, called a keer drag. In winter they dredged oysters from the extensive layings and trawled fish. Gradually length increased to about twenty feet, producing a beamy, full bowed, clinker built boat, decked to the mast but capable of being rowed in calms. The rig changed to yawl with the mast stepped a third of length abaft the stem, and set a boomless gaff mainsail and a small sprit mizzen, without a boom, on a stumpy mast stepped at the transom and sheeted to an outrigger.

Miles of deeps and shallows, creeks and marsh rills make Poole Harbour a small boat sailors paradise at high water, when the distant Purbeck hills stand blue-grey in summer sun beyond the expanse of sky-reflecting water and scattered islets. It is equally fascinating to explore at low tide, between glittering mudflats with curlew calls floating downwind.

For winkling, wildfowling, wood-gathering and many other uses, local watermen developed and built flat-bottomed, chine, transom-sterned punts, often locally called 'canoes'. These were rowed or sailed with a spritsail. Typical dimensions were 15ft long × 5ft beam with a hull depth of about 18in and a draught of 2–3in. The sides were formed by one or two strakes and a centreboard or daggerboard provided lateral plane. A well-cambered deck made them moderately seaworthy for semi-sheltered waters and coamings protected a well large enough to crawl about in. They were equally at home stealing up a creek for a shot at feeding fowl, gathering bait, or out in the Channel with a brisk breeze slapping spray over the crew as, with spritsail drawing, he worked a dredge over the oyster layings.

'Canoes' were numerous; scores lay off Poole, by the stakes and the grey hulls seemed to poke out from every furze bush around the harbour. Almost all were built by the owner and there was variation of shape and dimensions which has lasted until recently.

6

West Bay to the Scillies

Beer

Lugsail and sprit-rigged craft fished and worked alongshore on the coasts of Devon and Cornwall, earning a living for shore communities. In east Devon small, lug-rigged, two masted open beach boats up to about 25 ft long fished from Seaton, where the Snells, Welches, Wilkins and Newtons were beachmen for generations, but did not seem to have the notoriety of men from the village of Beer. Beer is two miles west, sheltered from westerly winds under the lee of Beer Head at the mouth of a steep, secluded valley where a stream tumbled down beside the sandstone houses and luggers up to 30ft long were drawn up on its shingle beach.

Beer men had a reputation for boldness, particularly as smugglers. Jack Rattenbury, Beer's most colourful seafarer and smuggler, was born there in 1788. As a boy in a fishing lugger he was captured off the coast by a French warship but escaped and returned to Beer to become a noted smuggler, with quick wits and vivid imagination. He was captured a second time by the French, off the coast, but persuaded the enemy skipper that his craft was standing into danger and Jack's

pilotage was followed, which brought them into Swanage Bay, which somehow he managed to convince the Frenchmen was the coast of France! There a revenue cutter soon captured them and, ironically, released Jack for many more smuggling adventures.

But fishing was the basis of Beer life for centuries and the small open luggers had to be capable of drift net fishing for herring and mackerel, long lining for bottom fish, mackerel hooking and crab or lobster potting. The good trawling ground known as The Tenants stretches its bank south into the English Channel a few miles seaward of Beer Head and the luggers occasionally trawled there.

During the eighteenth and nineteenth centuries many Beer luggers were around 28ft long and were open, three masted boats rigged with dipping lugs on fore and main and a standing lug mizzen sheeted to an outrigger. It was a cumbersome rig, but practical for craft which did not need to make short tacks in their alongshore work. Typical hull dimensions were 28ft long × 11ft 6in beam × 5ft depth. The hulls had a plumb bow and relatively narrow transom stern

187

and were fairly sleek in form, fine-bottomed and with slack bilge sections which made them fast under sail on a reach or run, and often reasonable performers to windward in smooth water. The sheer was raised above the gunwales by a six inch washstrake which carried chocks for steel rowlocks in later boats and had oar ports in earlier ones. The open hull had four thwarts and a stern bench. A planked bow landing or 'sheet' extended from the stem to the forward thwart. Clinker hull planking was oak or English elm and the closely spaced oak bent timbers were locally called 'sturdies'. The keel was elm and the transom oak. Centreplates do not seem to have been fitted to any Beer luggers and the narrow rudder did not extend below the keel. Moveable partitions were fitted under the second and third thwarts from forward to form a fish room. Spare nets and gear were carried forward of this space. Hulls were usually tarred black inside and out, with a white strake or 'list' immediately below the sheer.

These boats were built at Beer until about 1900, when a hull cost approximately £29 and the owner needed a further £50 or so for masts and gear, with additional cost for her sails. Many Beer fishermen made their own and usually these set well. After 1900 Beer luggers were built by Lavers of Exmouth.

The foremast stepped in a tabernacle on the after side of the forward thwart. The mizzen stepped on the starboard side of the sternbench, with the mizzen outrigger passing through the top of the transom, just clear of the rudder head. The mainmast was longest, cut to just fit inside the boat. The foremast was two-thirds the length of

this and the mizzen two-thirds to three-quarters the length of the foremast.

Typical sail areas would be; foresail 570 square feet, mainsail 650 sq ft, mizzen 260 sq ft; a large rig for an open boat, even in light winds. Many Beer boats had three rows of reef points in the fore and main lugs and two rows in the mizzen. In some boats the fore and main lugs could not be reefed and as wind increased the mainsail would be stowed and in very strong winds the foresail was taken in and a smaller storm foresail, locally called the 'fore-mizzen' was set. This was often about 350 sq ft area, had three rows of reef points and was balanced by the mizzen. Essence of the rig was lightness of masts, spars and simplicity of rigging to improve stability in fresh winds, when the masts and yards bent considerably, lending a rakish appearance to these workaday craft.

The halyards of the fore and mainsails were set up to the weather side, the main halyard leading to the quarter. The fore lug tack hooked to an iron bumkin which steeved down from the stem well below the sheer and was stayed with a bobstay. The storm foresail could be hooked to a second hook halfway along it, to preserve balance.

The boats were launched off with the fore and mizzen masts standing. The mainmast was got up later, when clear of the shore and if required, the boats often sailing without the main lug set. Beer boatmen clung to the use of a wooden spar to tension the luff of the large foresail when sailing to windward. Its forward end was shipped into a luff cringle and the heel was set up to the foremast by a rolling hitch. They called it the

'Fore Good' or 'Fore Guard'; in other places it was termed the 'Fore Girt' or the 'Var Good'. The main lug luff was tensioned with a rope bowline, set up around the foremast, and the main tack was taken to the weather gunwale when sailing to windward.

During calms the boats were rowed with sweeps, the forward pair working in ports through the sheerstrake, just abaft the foremast. These were often used to help the lugger about in a lop or light weather, when these long-keeled, shallow hulls were difficult to sail round.

Beer luggers were beached broadside-on in fine weather, with sails set if the wind was onshore. The ballast and catch was put on the beach and the haul-up rope was hooked into the stem. Then the hull was put end-on to the beach and was hauled up by her capstan. The bilge lands were protected by chafing pieces against abrasion of the shingle. The Beer men were the last in Britain to use the centuries-old, three masted lug rig and the boats were raced in local regattas until 1914 and worked under sail until 1918. Plate 35 shows the *Beatrice Annie* sailing about 1910. She was 28ft × 11ft 6in beam × 5ft depth and fished under sail until 1918, when she was broken up.

The 1914–18 war brought a rapid increase in the price of fish and development of the petrol engine. In 1915 the first auxiliary engined lugger was built for a Beer fisherman and within two years the sailing boats were replaced by these smaller (21–25ft) luggers which were of the same form as the earlier boats but stepped only a foremast and mizzen. Lavers of Exmouth built many and a typical boat was 23ft × 8ft 6in

Plate 35. Three masted lugger *Beatrice Annie* of Beer, South Devon, about 1910. The fore lug is tacked to an iron bumkin and the luff is tautened by a 'vargood' or 'fore girt'. The masts are bending under the power of the lugs. *Photo – H. O. Hill.*

beam × 4ft 2in depth, and had a draught of 3ft. The general reduction in size was probably a combination of the excessive haul-up weight of a 28ft lugger if fitted with an engine and associated equipment, the ability to work a smaller boat with fewer crew, the increased space amidships for fishing by abolition of the main lugsail, and removal of utter dependence on a large sail area or oars in light weather. The Beer boats continued to carry their fore and mizzen rig into the 1930s but these were auxiliary to the engine.

Sidmouth

Seven miles west of Beer Head lies Sidmouth, now a typical Devon holiday and retirement town, but until the 1920s, the home of beach fishermen using small, two masted luggers. These were a surviving core of Sidmouth's native inhabitants who had fished there for centuries, but by the 1850s were gradually becoming outnumbered by incoming settlers of modest wealth and leisure, attracted there by serene surroundings. This growing population increased demand for fish and during the nineteenth century the beachmen were busy, but remained poor.

Sidmouth beach lies at the mouth of a steep combe or valley, running south to the sea through hills which end abruptly at the coast as 500 feet high cliffs, red with Devon earth. These frame the beach which changed every high water with the continual wash of tides and waves, which in onshore winds could become a dangerous surf. The beach stretched half a mile of shingle across the valley, between Peak Hill and the 'Ham', as the mouth of the little river Sid was called. The high cliffs west and east caused violent squalls during offshore winds.

The frenzy of civil engineering during the early nineteenth century affected quiet Sidmouth, where Rennie built a strong sea wall along the foreshore of the little town. A pier and harbour were proposed but never built, although preparations for the western arm of the harbour resulted in blowing up masses of rock which previously offered landing or launching boats some shelter from southwest gales.

The beach changed with winds and tides. Usually it descended to the tideline in a series of steps called 'cops', with slopes, flats or hollows between them. A boat would rather anchor off and wait for the tide than run in on a steep cop when loaded with nets and fish, and risk swamping before she could be hauled clear of the water. A gale from seaward, particularly from west of south, bared the shore to its marl and rock foundations, with thousands of tons of shingle stripped away, to reform later. The sea wall caused such variations in the level of the beach that at times, after a succession of southwest gales, the fishermen's boats had to be hauled up a wooden ramp on to the esplanade for safety, while after prolonged fine weather the shingle lay almost level with the road.

The capital value of a Sidmouth fisherman's boats and gear seldom exceeded £100, very rarely £200, and poor marketing arrangements and high costs of transport restricted development. However, the old Sidmouth fishing families of Barrons, Bartletts, Conants, Woolleys and others appear to have been open minded in their approach to their work, unlike the clannish and tradition-conscious Cornishmen, further west. Their working world covered perhaps 20 miles of coast and seaward to the horizon and the seasons included fishing for mackerel between May and September or October with drift nets, hooking, or with seines; catches being sold locally and sent away by rail to fish merchants, as were herring, which were taken with drift nets from November to March. Sprats were netted during the autumn and the boats worked trawls for flat fish, pots for lobsters and crabs, and skim, setting or hoop nets for prawns. Sometimes bass and mullet were seined. Pollack were caught with nets and lines and dogfish in drift nets. Skate, conger, blinn, whiting, cod, pout, and hake were caught with bottom lines and winkles were picked from the shore.

As usual, the fishermen had to sell to middle men; fish hawkers and local buyers who were only acting as agents for larger firms, but all adding handling charges to the low price the fishermen received. Some fishermen tried sending fish direct to Billingsgate market in London, but were quickly disgusted by the malpractice of city merchants, frequently receiving a pitiful sum, or even no payment for prime fish, with a statement of a 'glutted market'. One man received confirmation from Billingsgate that market prospects were good and sent up 26,400 prime herring, to receive payment of a penny ha'penny. Damage to his nets and payment for boxing cost him a pound. Naturally the merchant had covered his charges.

Sidmouth fishermen were typical smallholders of the sea, whose average earnings were only 15 shillings weekly in 1909. Sometimes a catch might fetch £10, then weeks might follow with almost nothing. Many were members of the Royal Naval Reserve and received a small retainer for the service. Like most of its contemporaries, Sidmouth gradually changed from a fishing community to a seaside resort. By the early twentieth century many of the young men were joining the navy, then at the height of its expansion and power.

All Sidmouth fishing boats were undecked and until the 1880s were rarely more than eighteen feet long and most were sixteen feet. The largest boats later increased to about twenty-four feet and fished for mackerel and herring with drift nets, but by 1910 the size of new boats had again decreased. They were usually owned by one fisherman, sometimes by two. Some local shopkeepers held shares in fishing boats and nets. The hulls were clinker planked in golden varnished English elm on oak bent timbers and centreline. During the 1850s the Sidmouth boatbuilder earned only 15 shillings weekly and worked in a shed at his home.

The old Sidmouth boats were deep-keeled, beamy and had generous freeboard. The broad-bowed, roomy hulls set a single dipping lugsail; powerful with a leading wind but tricky to manage in a seaway. They sailed badly to windward, even when helped by an oar pulled under the lee bow. In strong winds a small lugsail might be set for running, otherwise the boats were rowed, as the fishermen then said 'Better to row than to reef.' So in bad weather or calms they toiled at the long, heavy sweeps, worked cross handed in wooden rowlocks or thole pins, perhaps for hours, with labour now unimaginable.

Later, various sizes of boats were favoured; sixteen foot and eighteen foot boats being much used, with the older large boats being brought out for drift netting and small twelve foot 'punts' useful for odd jobs. Rig changed to a standing or dipping lug foresail and a standing lug mizzen sheeted to an outrigger. Some later boats also set a jib, hooked to a short iron bumkin at the stemhead: a rig locally termed 'mizzen, mainsail and foresail'. In squalls the small mizzen could be set forward in place of the large lugsail under which the boats were sometimes caught aback and almost capsized. Sometimes a boat carried a large and a small lug 'mainsail' and in fair winds on a long trip the smaller lug might be set opposite the larger on the same mast, spinnaker fashion, though used before the spinnaker was 'invented' in yachts.

These shallow draught luggers did not sail close to the wind and an oar was usually pulled under the lee bow to help them to windward. Some boats had centreplates by the 1890s, probably in imitation of the thriving club of fourteen foot sailing dinghies then also launched from the beach by the local sailing club as some of the ancestors of the now sophisticated International Fourteen Foot racing dinghy class. Many of these had a fisherman sailing in them as a hand, their skills in beaching being specially required, and they observed the fine gear and handling of the little racers.

The maximum length of a Sidmouth herring or mackerel drifter increased to 25ft. They could not be longer because of the necessity to haul up the beach, or in bad weather over the sea wall to safety. The beamy hulls had moderate freeboard, were flat-floored and had shallow wood keels to avoid heeling over and filling in a surf. A 24ft boat had about 8ft 9in beam and the 21ft *Albina* of 1892 had 7ft beam and carried sixteen hundredweight of shingle ballast bags. These boats did not sail well to windward and beating could be tedious. Their rig was a standing lug mizzen and a dipping lug forward, tacked to the bumkin; a picturesque but unwieldy sail which had to be lowered or 'dipped' around the mast every time the boat tacked. These drifters ventured up to 20 miles seaward and came to life on a reach in a breeze; one 22 footer being timed to sail 8 miles seaward in 50 minutes.

Some Sidmouth 20-footers sailed from there to Kent for seasonal fishing. One ran across Folkstone Bay during a gale under bare poles and fetched harbour amid cheers for such handling of an open boat.

About 1890, thirty or so of the larger luggers were owned and worked from the beach but by 1910 only eight survived.

The ballast of all the boats was beach shingle in forty pound coconut matting bags with a lacing allowing some to be emptied before beaching, to lighten the work of hauling up. The bags were trimmed to windward as necessary. Three feet or so of forward decking enclosed the 'cuddy' or 'cutty' in the bows. This was insufficient either for protection against pitching in a sea or for sleeping the crew when drifting, when they lay with the foresail stretched abaft the cuddy for shelter while

Plate 36. Harry Conant, a typical Sidmouth beach fisherman of 1854. Capable of keeping his boats in repair and of rigging and sailmaking.

the nets were down at night, with a riding lamp on the mizzen. During cold weather they took a few coals off in an old bucket full of holes, to make a warming fire.

When anchoring amongst rocks, where an anchor might get foul or lost, the Sidmouth boats rode to a heavy stone called a 'slingstone'.

After the 1850s, and possibly earlier, the Sidmouth fishermen's boats were raced annually as part of Sidmouth's annual regatta, which featured rowing and sailing races for the fishermen with prize money subscribed by local gentry and tradesmen to encourage a large entry and keen sport. After a few years the fishing community quietly pooled all its prize money, which was subsequently shared equally amongst the contestants, who rowed and sailed their events with unusual dignity and many mock close finishes; though how this was managed when fishermen's boats from other villages competed is difficult to understand.

Classes varied with the length of boats in use and whose owners were willing to enter. Starts were from anchor and cables were slipped at gunfire. In early years the town regatta featured a race for gigs from the area. Two worked from Sidmouth beach to tend passing shipping and also the sailing collier brigs which anchored half a mile offshore and discharged into large open boats which ferried the domestic coal ashore. Remote Sidmouth attracted artists and writers after the mid-nineteenth century and Robert C. Leslie, the marine painter, enjoyed an easy freemasonry with the fishermen of the beach and found his greatest pleasure in designing and sailing his own beach

boat for amusement, besides designing and having one of the earliest bermudian rigged cruising boats built there in 1862.

Leslie moved to Sidmouth in 1854 and quickly became acquainted with the fishermen and their boats, particularly with Harry Conant (Plate 36) owner of the fourteen foot foresail and mizzen-rigged open boat *England's Rose*, which Leslie hired for pleasure sailing. (Plate 37). Leslie's description of their first meeting is charmingly typical of his writing. 'The first of these new friends was a weather-beaten looking man I met as he landed on the beach after his night's work amongst the crabs and lobsters in a small fourteen

Plate 37. Harry Conant's 14ft lugger *England's Rose* working crab pots under the cliffs of Ladram Bay, on the south Devon coast. Typical of an inshore fisherman's work. *From the painting by R. C. Leslie.*

foot boat. He looked worn out and tired as he stepped out of his boat with a heavy basket at his back and merely dropped a small anchor on the sand, giving his boat a shove seaward left her riding to it a few yards offshore.

'It was a fine spring morning, and I asked him if he were going to sea again. He said "No; he was bound home for a nap till high-water". I had not been afloat for months, and as she lay offshore head to wind under her mizzen, the little boat looked so inviting that I offered the man a shilling for an hour or two's use of her. He answered in a simple, confiding way, "Take her, sir, for as long as you like". *England's Rose* was rigged with a lug-sail forward and a mizzen, and I had a delightful cruise in her along-shore under the lofty cliffs. Harry Conant and I were friends from that day, and I had the use of his boat for "anything I liked to give him", whenever the tide and his work suited.

'Unlike most of the local fishermen, I found that my new friend had sailed in the coal trade, and began life on board a small west country coaster, of which his father was skipper, and that, like all the old school of seamen, he was an accomplished rigger and sailmaker; he was also carpenter enough to keep his own boats in repair, besides making his own sails, and those for most of the other boats on the beach.

Like many Sidmouth beachmen, Conant also used a smaller boat, *The Friends*, of the size known as a punt.

Robert Leslie understood the beachman's life and wrote 'The work and life of a fisherman who goes down to the sea in small open boats among the surf rolling in upon an unsheltered shore is precarious in more ways than one. His boat must be small and light, yet strong and seaworthy to stand the weather and heavy strains in launching her through, and hauling her out of the surf; while in spells of bad weather he has to pass days of enforced idleness on shore, when day after day the sea rolls in upon his port in a way that defies men steered their little luggers inshore to beach, dodging the breaking combers with great skill. Spring tides were the most troublesome and a lop on the swell at springs could make landing dangerous, and the least mistake in beaching would cause a boat to sheer round, capsize and wash about in the breakers, possibly with her crew beneath her. Such possibilities meant that beach boats could not be insured, even if the owners could afford a premium from such slender incomes. Leslie describes landing a 15ft 6in boat through a sea tumbling in at high water against the steep beach. 'All sails and the mainmast were lowered, and carefully stowed and lashed out of the way, all but one bag of shingle ballast was emptied over-board, and, after the bow or cut rope had been hooked into the stem, Conant took the pair of short oars or paddles, and under them backed the boat in until within a few seas of the beach, and with an eye over his shoulder kept her there for some minutes, or until three or more larger seas than ordinary had run under us and broken upon the shore. Then with half-a-dozen powerful strokes he brought her round, and pulled in so that we were carried on the shoulder of a sea, and left almost high and dry upon the beach in from his capstan . . .'

In onshore winds they often beached through the surf under full bellied sails, trimmed by the stern and kept end-on to the seas. The cut rope was hooked on to the capstan wire and six or eight men at the capstan bars hove the boat up the beach, to be triggered and made fast. A fisherman always tried to beach before his capstan but in very strong winds and big seas the boats

Plate 38. A lugger beaching at Sidmouth, Devon. The foresail remains set while the crew get the woods under her keel to haul up. *Photo – H. O. Hill.*

any attempt to go out to his work from it.'

Each boatman had a recognised place on Sidmouth beach, headed by a hand capstan for hauling up his boats and surrounded by woods, chocks and gear. A stout, well anchored capstan and strong wire were needed to haul up the larger drifters. In strong onshore winds the Sidmouth

Plate 36a. The alongshore fisherman's labour did not end with arrival. The boat's crew, aided by other fishermen and sometimes by women and girls, had to haul up clear of the surf. In this painting by James Clark Hook, Devon fishermen haul up a small lugsail boat on wooden trows or skids.

might be forced to beach wherever possible, depending on the state of tide and sea. Occasionally they anchored off Sidmouth until it moderated, or secured to a boat which had a stout anchor, to ride it out.

During onshore gales all the boats might be forced to beach wherever possible, depending on the state of tide and sea. Occasionally they were caught by bad weather and had to beach at another coast village, relying on the help of other fishermen to haul up. This was freely given as they might need similar assistance themselves. The visiting crews were usually taken in, fed, given change of clothing and lodging until the weather moderated. Sometimes they managed themselves; a Beer lugger was forced to beach at Sidmouth at night during a heavy gale and next morning the Sidmouth fishermen were astonished to find her high up on the beach with her crew of three, one aged about 80, quietly mending nets and gear.

During onshore gales all the boats, capstans and gear on the beach were manhandled up on to the esplanade and were made fast to lamposts or sheltered in side streets; tremendous and unproductive labour for the whole community.

The writings of Stephen Reynolds give an accurate, firsthand account of the life of Sidmouth fishermen at the beginning of the twentieth century. Scientific training enabled him to see the fisheries in true perspective and ill health made him choose that locale. Reynolds was no superficial observer or musty researcher; he lived and worked with fishermen as one of them, absorbed their lore, outlook and seamanship and was gifted in expressing it in his books *Seems So*, *A Poor Mans House*, and the magnificent *Alongshore*. His perception was reinforced by the knowledge of Bob and Tom Woolley, the fishermen with whom he worked, year round.

Perhaps the mackerel fishery inspired him most. During spring the mackerel feed on tiny marine organisims but in summer they pursue and feed on the shoals of whitebait, locally called 'Brit', and could be hooked near the surface. Mackerel hooking under sail was hard and skilful work which had an element of sport appealing greatly to the fishermen. The hooking season commenced during July and might continue through August and September. The best catches were during the first hours after sunrise, when Sidmouth echoed to the tramp of fishermen bound for mackerel hooking, baskets and oilskins slung over shoulders and broad voices discussing the weather in the narrow streets. Boats were being got down the beach on the ways, with mizzens hoisted, tugging and bowing the slender masts and outriggers impatiently. They were launched off through the seas wash under oars and sail, perhaps rising and falling over a long swell left by a breeze. During fine weather in this bight of West Bay, the sea breeze of August and September days dies with evening and is followed, night and morning, by a fresh breeze off the land; a cycle often providing a leading wind out and home for the fishermen.

As soon as the little luggers were clear of the alongshore surf the mackerel lines were out. A line with a light lead to tow near the surface and called the 'bobber' was made fast to the mizzen halyard. Then two lines weighted to suit the wind and boat speed with 2–3 pounds lead were made fast on a thwart, each side amidships. A fourth line was sometimes towed from the stern, opposite the bobber, or alternatively, two bobbers were also trailed from poles projecting from the sides. One fisherman might sail his boat and manage five mackerel lines single-handed, besides the mainsheet, the boat's heading probably in the midst of several other fishing boats, tiller and sails, which might need attention at each wearing of the boat. Most boats carried two hands.

The upper part of the Sidmouth fisherman's mackerel gear consisted of two or three fathoms of stout conger line to take the chafe over the gunwale and five or six fathoms of finer line at the end of which a conical lead was attached by a clove hitch, with the short end being laid up around the standing part for an inch or two and finished off with a strong knot. A swivel, or more usually an eyelet from an old boot, ran free, just above the lead, between the clove hitch and the knot. To the eyelet was attached two or three fathoms of fine snood called the 'sid'. To this was attached a length of gut on which half an inch of clay pipe stem was threaded, and a rather large hook. If available, the first bait used was sand eel, kept alive in a bottle until hooked on. Otherwise a strip of preserved mackerel tail or a piece of clay pipe stem or red tape, threaded on the line just above the hook might lure them. After the first fish were hooked the best bait was a 'lask' or long, three-cornered strip of skin, cut from the tail of a mackerel. Older fishermen preferred a round lead cast in the shell of a gull's egg which trailed better through the water.

The lines were streamed astern of the boat as she was sailed up and down where the mackerel were thought to be. When feeding well they often bit at the pipe stem and a bare hook faster than they could be hauled on board. Considerable skill, knowledge and alertness were necessary to catch the greatest possible number of mackerel while they were feeding near the surface.

A fresh lask was a better bait than an equally brilliant salted lask. The mackerel bite at the shine of the bait and probably follow the flavour of it in the water. The fishermen constantly felt the lines for signs of a bite, the luggers spreading wider, searching for mackerel shoals, crews watching for a boat which wore round across her course once or twice, showing she was amongst a mass of fish. Then other boats were quickly there. During a fresh breeze, with fish biting, the boats were continually searching for fish, manoeuvring amongst each other in a sort of maritime country dance. Perhaps a flock of gulls hovered above, dipping and screeching, picking whitebait or fry from the surface above the feeding shoal and providing the fishermen with a clear sign of fish.

As the boats cleared the land they felt the fresh, chill offshore wind of early morning bringing the white mist or 'lerry' pouring seaward from the deep coombes of the coastline.

Stephen Reynolds caught the essence of hooking mackerel under sail from Sidmouth: 'By the time the sun is rising (it never rises twice the same) south of the easternmost headland, Tony has worked himself into a tear over self-tanging lines, and has been laughed out of it again. We are perhaps a mile or two out, and if the mackerel are biting well, we are hauling them in, swiftly, silently, grimly; banging them off the hook: going "Tsch!" if they fall back into the sea; cutting baits from fish not dead. If however, they are not on the feed, we sing blatant, or romantic or sentimental songs (it is all one out there), and laugh with a hearty sea loudness. And if the mackerel will not bite at all we invent a score of reasons and blame a dozen people and things. But there we are – ourselves, the sea, and the heavenly dawn – the sea heaving up to us, and ourselves ever heaving higher, up and over the lop. It exalts us with it. We hardly need to talk; a straight look in the face, a smile . . .'

Or again: '"Look to your leeward line," he cried, "they'm up for it!"'

He hauled a mackerel aboard, and, catching hold of the shank of the hook, flicked the fish into the bottom of the boat with one and the same motion that flung the sid overboard again; and after it the lead. Wedging the mackerel's head between his knees, he bent its body to a curve, scraped off the scales near its tail, and cut a fresh lask from the living fish. He is a tenderheart by nature, but now; 'That'll hae 'em!' he crowed.

'The mackerel bit hotly at our new baits. Before the lines were properly out, in they had to come again. Flop-flop went the fish on the bottom boards as we jerked them ceaselessly off the hooks. Every moment or two one of them would dance up and flip its tail wildly; beat on the bottom boards a tattoo which spattered us with scales, then sink back among the glistening mass that was fast losing its beauty of colour, its opalescent pinks and steely blues, even as it died and stiffened.

'Suddenly the fish stopped biting, perhaps because the risen sun was shining down into the water. The wind dropped without warning, as southerly winds will do in the early morning, if they don't come on to blow a good deal harder. The *Cock Robin* wallowed again on the water. "We'm done!" said Tony. "Lets get in out o'it in time for the early market. There ain't no other boats out. These yer ought to fetch 'leven pence the dizzen. We've made thees day guide in case nort else don't turn up."'

The Sidmouth fleet was usually joined by eight or ten larger luggers from the village of Beer, which worked six lines at once on poles right out to keep the lines clear. The Beer boats tried to lord it over the smaller Sidmouth craft and, if fishing was good, held their course through the fleet.

The art of mackerel fishing under sail was to maintain correct speed and keep the lines clear when the boats were frequently wearing round before the wind, so the lines could follow without fouling. When the fish were biting well near the surface, lines were shortened in and only one line was hauled at a time. Baits were left until only a shred remained and an excited shoal, pursuing whitebait, often took the bare hooks. The land breeze eased with the suns warmth and larger lugs were set, supplemented by a pull at the oars until the sea breeze made in.

A sixteen foot Sidmouth lugger would hook four of five hundred mackerel in a morning and two men might land fifteen hundred between 4 am and midday. Gar fish (gorbills) and shad were also sometimes hooked.

About 8 am the 'Jurners' or local fish dealers met the beaching boats. The catch was sold in 'dozens', which locally equalled one hundred and twenty fish. Then the fishermen and boys tramped home with a few fish for the table. Mackerel sold for 18 pence the dozen, in good demand, before 1910. Afterwards, the fishermen took out fishing parties by the hour, though at the height of the mackerel season every boat on the beach might be fishing at sea almost all day.

The fishermen preferred what they termed a 'mackerel breeze'; a fresh southerly wind bringing a clouded sky, provided the wind was not strong enough to prevent launching the boats. Then the mackerel were more scattered and the boats worked further offshore and were longer away, sometimes getting caught if the wind freshened to a gale, then they came swooping in to the beach, riding the seas, pausing just outside the breakers to hook a rope in the stem, leaving it coiled on the stem head, to be seized by helpers ashore when her bow touched the beach. Then it was hooked to the capstan rope and she was hauled up quickly in these conditions, with several crews assisting each other.

There are memories of huge shoals of mackerel seventy years ago. Miles of shoals alongshore, without break, flowing like a dark green river, with the flood tide, in the clear alongshore water, and being hauled ashore in tons by beach seines. Mackerel hooking could be exciting but a 'fleet' of drift nets was a beach fisherman's pride; they were hand-braided of hemp until machine-made nets of cotton were adopted at Sidmouth during the 1860s. Nets were the fisherman's greatest investment, of more importance than ownership of a craft to use them, which could usually be obtained by sharing use of the nets with a boat owner.

A fleet of nets needed constant repair, airing and tanning, to maintain condition. Often they lasted ten years but without care they quickly rotted. At Sidmouth a fleet was often nine nets, each forty fathoms long and five or six fathoms deep. When set for mackerel the headrope lay at the surface. For the deeper swimming herring the nets were suspended from buoys by strops, so the foot just cleared the bottom.

Sidmouth drift netting was a two or three man job. Eight to fourteen nets were carried for mackerel and six to ten for herring. The less fish being caught, the greater the number of nets carried. Sidmouth nets were commonly forty fathoms long by five fathoms deep, connected by a headrope. Cork buoys suspended these from lanyards which for herring were long enough to allow the foot of the net to touch bottom. For the surface and midwater swimming mackerel the lanyards were shorter, so the net's headrope lay just below the surface. A boat was kept before the wind when shooting drift nets and judgement was necessary to keep them fishing well and not fouling the bottom or another boat's fleet. Sometimes the proximity of boats, or the effect of the tides caused several fleets of nets to foul, leading to considerable cursing.

Until the 1880s, about thirty mackerel and herring drifters 22–25 ft long fished regularly from Sidmouth. By 1909 these had dwindled to ten.

The drifters caught mackerel in May and June and these fetched the best prices. July brought variable catches and August was a poor month as the fish travelled badly when landed. Good October mackerel, mixed with herring, were sometimes caught. In a glut, drifters might land several thousand mackerel from each boat and immediately prices fell. Eventually buyers would refuse to deal. Large catches were sent in waggons to Exeter, before the railway was built.

Late November was the height of the herring fishery at Sidmouth, and saw the boats drifting to sea an hour or so before sunset, returning towards or after dawn. Cruising seaward the fishermen watched for signs of the herring shoals; seabirds feeding above them or the change of colour and character of the surface of the water. Good catches were often made after prolonged strong winds by those first afloat on a sea still stained by the red earth washed from the cliffs. Sometimes the whole seascape filled with drift boats, stretching from Berry Head, eastward to the Chesil Bank; the Sidmouth men working off Exmouth in the west, to Lyme Regis eastward, their riding lights like a sea-village.

With the nets shot the fishermen ate, smoked, sang and crept under the cuddy to catch what rest they could. Usually they were too wet and cold to sleep. A Sidmouth 20ft boat might catch between twenty and twenty-five thousand herrings in a good haul, but six or seven thousand was still a good night's work. Net hauling was laborious for one man at the headrope and another at the foot. Each boat set from between two hundred and forty and four hundred fathoms of net (1440 to 2400 feet) which in a breeze might take two hours of hard hauling to get on board, holding fast when the pull of the tide was too strong, or to pick out fish. Maybe there was only a few score fish gilled in the meshes, sometimes thousands, with the nets coming over the gunwale like a glittering mat, beyond the strength of two men to get in, and help from other boats had to be sought. About twenty-five thousand herrings was the maximum capacity of a 25ft Sidmouth drifter. If she caught more, the nets were passed to other boats, or were buoyed to be recovered later. Sometimes the nets were lost. When needed, a large drifter burned a paraffin flare to bring off help. Small catches were picked from the nets as these were hauled but larger ones were picked out ashore.

Romantics who sigh for the vanished days of sail and oar should absorb the writings of Stephen Reynolds. In his book *Seems So* he gives an accurate contemporary account of herring drifting in Sidmouth's small open boats. 'When the fish are there, the thing to do is to get them quick, for soon they will go to the bottom to spawn, or the weather will break, and there are months enough of standing by. Ten days or more the three of us had been at it – rowing to the ground, shooting nets, drifting, hauling in, rowing home, hauling up, picking the fish out of the nets, counting, carrying, packing, rushing, tearing, and straining, with no time for a proper meal, not always time to wash, and every night either sleepless, short, or broken. One of our waistbelts had gone in five notches, anothers two; and waistbelts tell no lies. On the Saturday morning we finished packing

between twelve and one, snatched up a meal, and before two o'clock were aboard again. There was no wind. We had to row ten miles to the ground with heavy, warped sweeps that twisted one's wrists at every stroke; and as we passed inside the race off Beer Head, where the dead calm water boiled like a millstream, we remarked how useless it would be to try to row home against the flood tide. For three hours we rocked at the sweeps, crawling to the ground. One man was aching all over with rheumatic stiffness and indigestion. The other, who is exceptionally strong and healthy, had no pains, but his face was wooden with tiredness. To keep my own self awake I had a cold and a cough and a sort throat and a splinter under the thumbnail. Just before dark we shot our nets, put on oilskins against the cold, ate thick sandwiches, drank oily tea hotted up over a paraffin flare, looked at the nets and settled for an hours sleep. But we didn't catch off. It was too cold. "'Tis a rough 'ol shop," we complained, "and a long ways from home to be in an open boat; but a fine night, sure nuff, for to take in a taddick o' fish".

'The night wore on. We hauled in our nets, picked out a thousand or so of herrings, and shot again. We finished our food and our tea, squatted down, and with coats over our heads we tried very hard to sleep. All our old clothes were damp; the bow sheets, on which we lay, were soaking with water and fish slime, and underneath them some dirty bilge water, which we had had no time to clean out, stank like drains. I jammed myself under the cutty, in the warm; but oilskins over damp clothes, making one itch like forty thousand fleas, turned me out again into the cold. We all sat up, shivering and dithering, while the moon, muffled in clouds, spread a dull cold light over the water. One thought of feather beds, of clean warm nightclothes, and, curiously enough, not of grog, but of cooling drinks.

'The early hours were a long drawn nightmare of discomfort. About three o'clock we started hauling in for another thousand of fish, and by four o'clock we were ready to take the ebb tide homewards. There was nothing to eat on board, nothing to drink, and very little tobacco. We had drifted to a dozen miles from home, and had scarcely enough wind to fill the sail. We took perforce to the sweeps. The boat had no life in her. There was not much life in us. With eyes that closed of themselves, and parched, lumpy throats, we rowed – rowed like machines, using pain for fuel. The sun dawned late.

'Until nearly eight in the morning we rocked at the sweeps. Finally, as if to mock us, after rowing all that way, a breeze sprang up from the south-east, and we sailed the short mile home. Had we waited, the wind would have done all our work. But we weren't to know that.

'It was not finished. Most of the morning, in a drizzling rain, we picked out, counted, and packed our fish. Then, during the last hour of the last twenty-four of that week's work, we three good friends fell out, and had a miserable argument that was the roughest trip in all that roughing it. We couldn't help ourselves. Our nerves were raw with tiredness, hurry, and want of sleep.

'The weather had broken. The fishing was ended for the time. We drank beer to make us less jumpy, and went to bed.'

'With these experiences, Reynolds ordered an experimental motor beach boat during 1909, to be fished by himself and Bob and Tom Woolley of Sidmouth. She was for general purpose work including fishing, passenger carrying in summer, and light towing, usually of other fishing boats during calms. The *Puffin* was built by Hodge of Dartmouth. 17ft 6in long × 5ft 6in beam and 3ft depth. She had a four or five horsepower petrol engine. The clinker planked hull had a pointed stern, with a wooden skeg to protect the propeller when beaching. She carried a lugsail but worked as a motor boat, for Reynolds foresaw the rapid decline of the centuries old inshore sailing boats when the more profitable motor driven types were developed to ease the tremendous labour of fishing under sail and oar. Unfortunately he did not live to see the development of the power driven inshore fishing fleet to its eventual efficiency, for he died during the early 1920s.

Teignmouth and Dartmouth
The trade of small ships, brigs, schooners, ketches and sloops in and out of the Devonshire River Teign, which has a bar at its entrance, resulted in much local pilot work and several 28–30ft, clinker-planked gigs were in use, usually being rowed but sometimes setting a dipping lugsail. These were built in boatyards at Teignmouth and at Shaldon, a charming village on the opposite shore of the river entrance.

Spritsail rig was used by the fishermen of the

South Hams district of south Devon. Open boats fished from Dartmouth. The 19ft *Sarah*, built at Torcross in 1870, was typically carvel planked, with straight stem, slightly raked transom stern and generous freeboard, enabling the crew to stand braced at the side when hauling nets and gear. Four thwarts were fitted: the mast stepping through the second from forward and having two shrouds on each side. The sprit mainsail was long luffed and high peaked for windward ability when beating in and out of Dartmouth's narrow entrance between high headlands, which caused fluky winds. The mainsail foot laced to a boom and was sheeted to a transom horse. The foresail was set flying from a masthead halyard and tacked to a short iron bowsprit, which was unstayed. In light weather a yard topsail was set from the short masthead.

These boats were keenly raced in local events and by 1911 the *Sarah* had sailed in forty consecutive Dartmouth regattas always steered by her owner, George Adams, who won twenty firsts, five seconds, six thirds, three fourths, three fifths, two sixths and one seventh place.

Start Bay

Start Bay sweeps round in an arc between the mouth of the Dart and Start Point at its western end, sheltering ten miles of coastline from westerly winds. The small villages of Beesands and Hallsands were sited under the lee of Start Point. Each had broad, open beaches at the mouth of a valley and were thriving communities until the early twentieth century, fishing for crabs and lobsters.

Figure 69. Sail plan of the 16ft 6in spritsail-rigged crabber *Sylvia*, of Hallsands, Start Bay, South Devon. Built by Dornom of Salcombe in 1921. *Science Museum, London.*

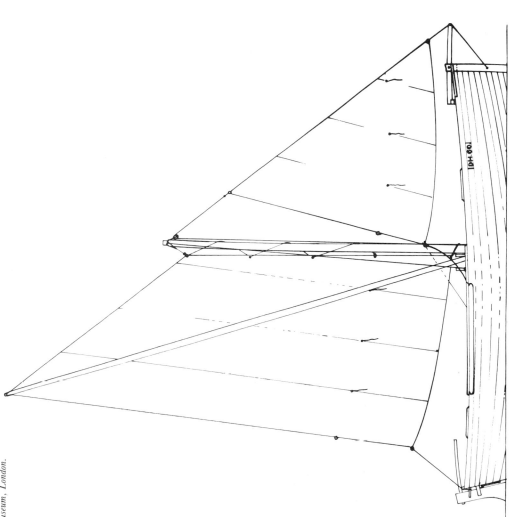

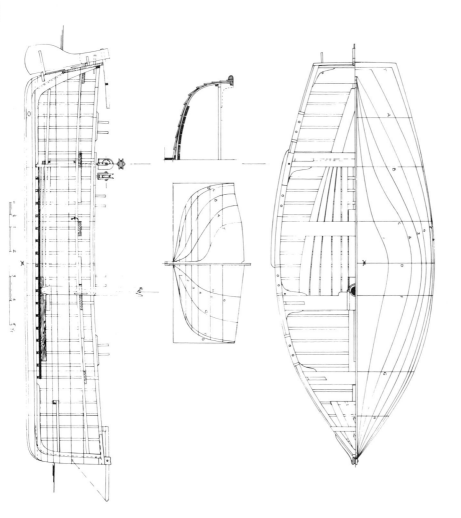

Figure 70. Lines and general arrangement of the Hallsands crabber *Sylvia.* Dimensions; 16ft 6in × 6ft 6in × 2ft 4in internal depth. *Science Museum, London.*

Harry Patey's *Sylvia* was a typical Hallsands crabber, built by Dornum of Salcombe in 1921, when a fully-rigged sailing boat was still considered economical investment. Principal dimensions were 16ft 6in length × 6ft 6in beam × 2ft 4in moulded depth. The plumb stem, straight keel and raked transom stern provided maximum internal space and adequate immersed lateral plane and although she had considerable rise of floor and slack bilges, the hull was a buoyant seaboat with fine waterlines at each end, enabling her to sail well without a centreboard. Planking was clinker on bent timbers. There were four thwarts, the mast being clasped to the second and four pairs of thole pins were fitted on each gunwale, as crabbers were frequently rowed.

The mast stepped just forward of amidships and the sprit mainsail was very high peaked, the heel of the sprit being well down the mast, just above the thwart. The mainsail luff was laced to the mast and the throat was bent to the masthead with a lanyard. The single part mainsheet rove in through a hole in the transom, to the helmsman's hand. The foresail set flying from a single part halyard at the masthead and tacked to a short bowsprit, stayed down to the stem. This almost equilateral sail had single part sheets, led aft. Both mainsail and foresail were made with four broad cloths and had a single row of reef points.

The mast was 14ft long and 4in in diameter at the heel. The sprit was 19ft 1in long and tapered from 3in diameter at heel to 1½in diameter at head. The bowsprit was 3ft 1in long and 2½in diameter inboard to 1½in outboard.

Hallsands boats hauled the pots on the starboard side, where a heavy chafing piece was added to protect the sheer as these came aboard. The crabbers were launched off and beached in the usual way, on woods, and were usually hauled up stern first. During the 1880s some boatmen trained Labrador dogs to swim out from the beach to meet an incoming boat, taking in their jaws a piece of wood to which a light line was attached, and swim ashore with it. The haul-up rope was passed with this and the boat was hove up by the shore party, stern first.

Much of the Hallsands catch was sold to welled smacks from the Hamble river, in Hampshire, which called regularly along the Devon, Cornish and Irish coasts to transport lobsters, crabs and crayfish to the extensive storage cars and ponds at Warsash. The smack anchored off with a red ensign at her peak to signal for the locals to launch off with the contents of their store pots, which were tallied into the wet well. A typical cargo was 2560 female crabs, 378 crabs, 336 lobsters, and 46 crayfish. Similar cargoes were loaded off Beesands and Ivycove and were sailed up-Channel as quickly as possible.

Tragedy came to Hallsands between 1900–1904 when there were 22 crabbers working and an assured market existed for their catches. A new naval dockyard was to be built at Keyham as part of Britain's expanding naval programme and the huge project required thousands of tons of gravel for concrete making. Government contractors prospecting the coast decided that it could be obtained off Hallsands by dredging. The villagers protested, realising as beachmen that this would undermine the shore and threaten the existence of the community. But, as ever, the official mind will not admit mistakes. When the moorings of the great suction dredger were first laid, the whole Hallsands population combined to get ropes on them and dragged them ashore shouting 'Us'll all go to prison together.'

Officialdom won. In four years the shore was undermined and subsided; a road was ruptured, houses cracked and fell down until the hillside looked as though it had been bombarded. Compensation was paid but many fisherman left. A few remained, working boats like the *Sylvia*, though those at nearby Ivycove abandoned sails in favour of motors after about 1920.

Hope

Four miles west of Bolt Head, the village of Hope nestles in the Shelter of Bolt Tail. This was another community of crab and lobster fishermen who in earlier times were also noted smugglers, running many cargoes of contraband along this rocky coast, where the rich red earth of Devon is almost purple in the sparsely populated hinterland.

In most respects their fisheries and boats resembled Hallsands and again sail lingered well into the twentieth century. The 18-footer *Ira*, owned by Henry Hurrell was built in 1924 by Chant at Salcombe; a builder with a reputation for fishing boat construction who built there for many years. The *Ira*'s dimensions were 18ft 1in length × 6ft 8in beam. Profile of keel, stem and transom were similar to the Hallsands craft but the hull was deeper and the bilges easier. There

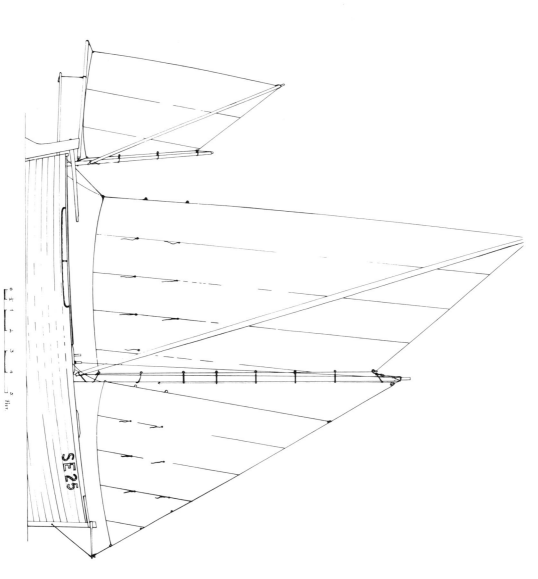

Figure 71. Sail plan of the 18ft 11in spritsail-rigged crabber *Ira*, of Hope Cove, South Devon. Built by Chant at Salcombe, 1924. *Science Museum, London.*

SE25

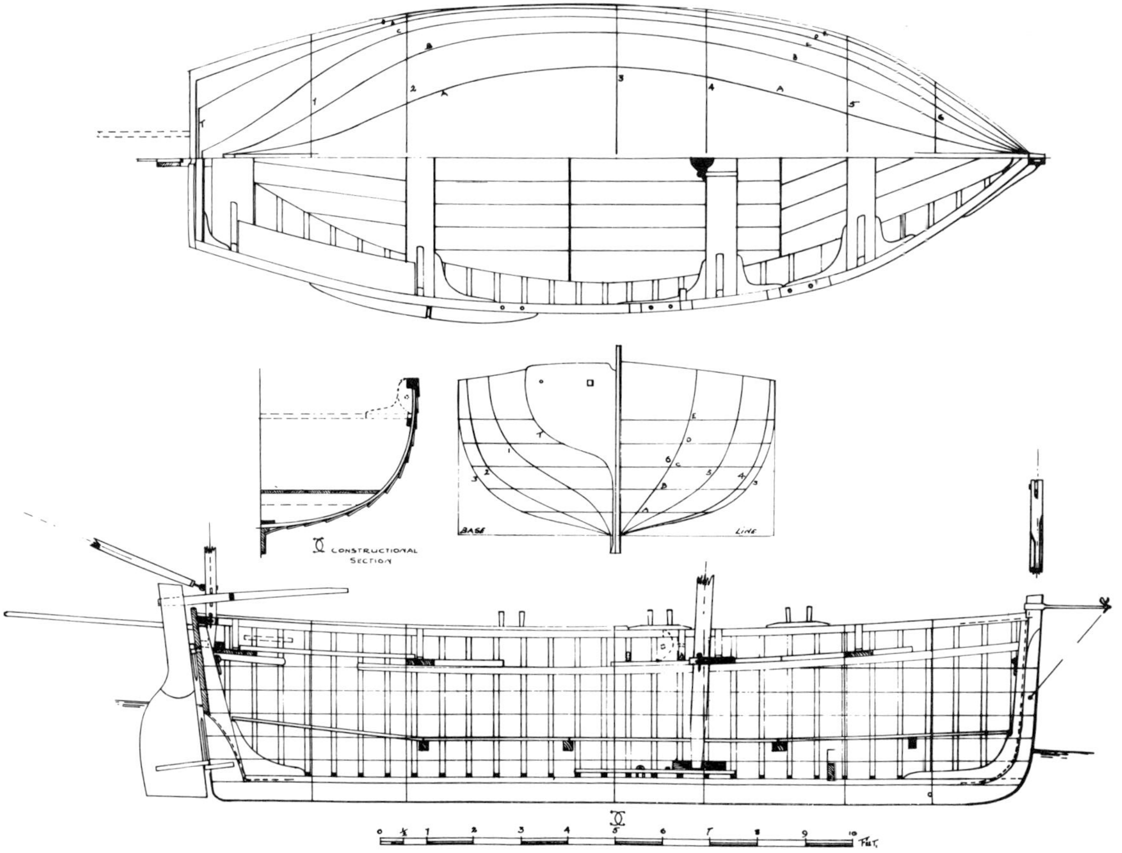

Figure 72. Lines and general arrangement of the Hope Cove crabber *Ira*, Dimensions; 18ft 1in × 6ft 8in × 3ft 2in internal depth. *Science Museum, London.*

were three thole pin positions on each side but these were boats principally intended for sailing. The mainmast stepped about $\frac{3}{8}$ of the length abaft the stem and the sprit mainsail was rigged as previously described except that it was very high peaked and the throat was hoisted by a traveller with the halyard passing over a dumb sheave at the masthead and its luff was hooped to the mast. The foresail tacked down to a short iron bumkin and both sails had two rows of reef points. The sprit mizzen was loose footed and spread with a boom sheeted to an outrigger. These boats sailed well and needed to be able to earn a living off that stormy headland.

Polperro

Over the county border in Cornwall, sprit-rigged boats fished from Polperro harbour until the end of the nineteenth century. Size averaged 28ft × 10ft beam, clinker planked and a hull which was stiff and fairly fast, with lean sections. Rig was a single mast setting a sprit mainsail and a foresail tacked to a short bumkin. Many set a yard topsail above the spritsail, with the yard sent up on a halyard to the masthead and its heel set close to the throat of the mainsail. Some had a standing lug mizzen and a bowsprit to set a jib. The boats were open except for a small decked cuddy forward and engaged in line fishing with a crew of two, or mackerel, pilchard and herring drifting with a crew of four, usually finding a living within twenty miles of home.

Many of these craft were lost in the great gale of 1891 and others were largely replaced by carvel-planked boats, rigged with a gaff mainsail which, for a time, caused them to be known as 'gaffers' in distinction from the surviving sprit-rigged boats; the sole instance of this now abused term in the nomenclature of the sea. All along the Cornish coast fishermen used open boats between sixteen and eighteen feet long; rigged with a dipping or standing lug forward and a standing lug or sprit mizzen; others having a sprit mainsail and a staysail and a standing lug or sprit mizzen. All carried considerable internal ballast and later boats often had a centreplate. Some localities developed slightly larger boats of this type for crabbing, particularly at Cadgwith, where they ranged up to 22ft long.

Gorran Haven

The Gorran Haven fishing boats were typical of this type and worked from the shelter of its tiny harbour; a crooked arm of stone breakwater built out as protection from winds from south and east.

Ashore, the village straggles up a hillside, remote to the south of Mevagissey, facing east over the Channel towards the distant Eddystone, sheltered to the west by Dodman Point.

The *Cuckoo* was an average boat; 16ft 5in long × 5ft 9in beam × 2ft 6in moulded depth and had a plumb stem and small, well-raked transom. She was undecked, built for rowing as well as sailing, with well rounded sections and steep rise of floor which resulted in very fine waterlines at the ends. Planking was carvel on bent timbers and 4 thwarts were fitted. Although centreboards were not used, the boats went well to windward due to the sharp bottom and large staysail though they needed reefing early in freshening winds.

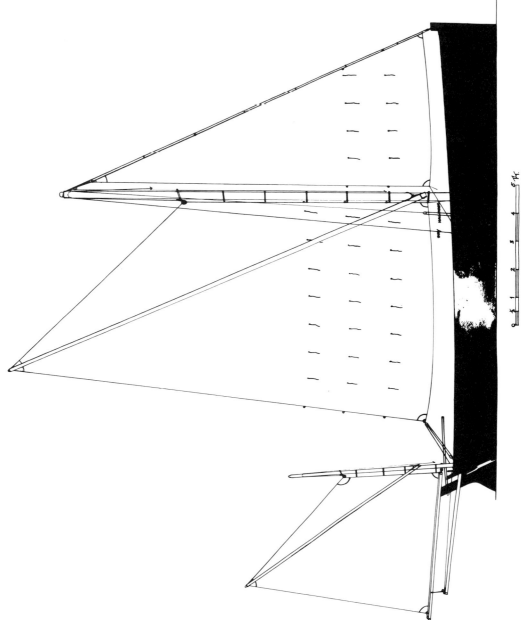

Figure 73. Sail plan of the 16ft 5in spritsail-rigged Gorran Haven fishing boat *Cuckoo*, built there by John Pill in 1881. *Science Museum, London.*

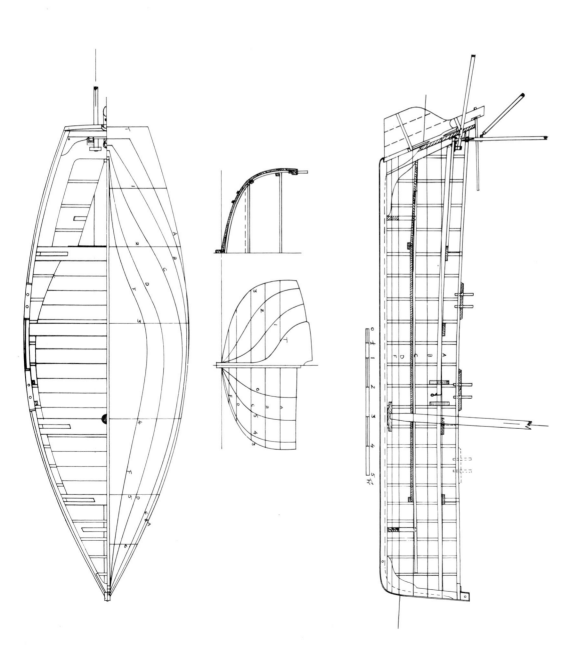

Figure 74. Lines and general arrangement of the Gorran Haven fishing boat *Cuckoo.* Dimensions; 16ft 5in × 5ft 9in × 2ft 6in internal depth. Note fine ends. *Science Museum, London.*

The mast stepped against the second thwart, and the mizzen inside the transom. Her spar dimensions are interesting as example of a small working boats spritsail rig; mainmast 16ft 6in long, diameter at heel 4in, at head 3in. Main sprit 16ft 6in long, diameter at heel 2in, at head 1½in. Mizzen mast 6ft 6in long, diameter 1¾in at heel to 1¼in at head. Mizzen sprit 7ft 9in long, diameter 1in. Mizzen boom 5ft 6in long, diameter 1in. Outrigger 5ft overall length, diameter 1½in inboard to 1in outboard.

The mizzen was offset to clear the tiller and was unstayed. The mainmast had two shrouds on each side. The mainsail was well peaked and set from hoops on the mast. It had three rows of reef points and no boom. The sheet was a simple purchase to the quarters. The single part halyard led over a dumb sheave and the heel of the sprit shipped into a snotter. The staysail hanked to the forestay, was hoisted by a single part halyard set up with a purchase by the shrouds, and had two rows of reef points. The boomed mizzen was a flat setting sail, more efficient for windward work than the boomless one used in many other local craft.

The Gorran boats worked well out from the land, principally at lobster potting and long lining but also drift fishing in season for mackerel or pilchards. The usual crew was two men, or man and boy, but some were worked single-handed. They moved well under oars and three thole pin positions were usually fitted on each side. The bilge pump or a good bailer was important as the lean bows let clouds of spray come inboard in a breeze, when the crew wore oilskins continuously.

The *Cuckoo* was built at Gorran by John Pill, and a solitary boatbuilder seems to have lived there for many years, constructing the occasional boat and repairing others, besides producing the scores of other wooden items of a remote community, from carts to coffins.

Richard Pill served his apprenticeship at Benjamin Roberts shipyard at Porthmellyn, two miles away, walking daily to and from work on the construction of coasting schconers and fishing vessels. The hours were from 6 am to 6 pm, but on Saturdays they finished at 5 pm and had Sundays off. He became respected as a good craftsman, returned to work at Gorran Haven and died in 1926 aged 72.

Later Gorran boats increased to about eighteen feet long, which seems to have remained an optimum for the dozen or so motor crabbers which now fish from Gorran Haven, some still setting a spritsail mizzen for d rectional stability in recovering pots, and perhaps to steer against in certain sea conditions.

River Fal

On the south Cornish coast a great natural harbour reaches inland from Pendennis Point and Zoze Point, some eight miles to Truro. From this main channel of the Fal, nearly a dozen creeks and arms of water cut in to the hills on either side. Farms and woods reach down to the water with green and gentle scenery. Along the edges of the channels oysters flcurish, particularly in the Carrick Roads; four miles of open water stretching from Pendennis Point at the seaward end to where the Roads narrow into the River Fal,

Plate 39. A Falmouth waterman's boat, setting a reefed standing lug foresail and a jib-headed mizzen above her carvel planked hull. A useful and pleasant type of traditional small boat.

These were generally between twelve and fourteen feet long, though some ranged to seventeen feet, beamy, with flat floors and a hard bilge but having fine forward waterlines and a shapely transom. Planking was usually carvel, of red pine on sawn frames, but some boats were clinker planked. Centreboards were not usually fitted. A boomless standing lug foresail was set on a mast stepped well in the eyes of the boat and the boomless, triangular or standing lug mizzen set on a mast stepped inside the transom and sheeted to an outrigger. The foresail had one or two reefs and the boats continued towing a dredge over the oyster grounds in strong winds and a small sea. Some were used for line fishing and lobster potting in local waters and others for carrying passengers around the estuary and for any odd jobs which made up a waterman's precarious living. The boats could be sailed and worked by one man but often carried two, and when sailed for pleasure, more.

The alternative method of dredging with the punts is still practiced in their unrigged descendants. A wooden hand windlass called a 'wink' was fitted in the bows and about sixty fathoms of warp is led around this. The anchor was dropped and the cable paid out as the punt drifted astern with the tide. After almost all the cable is let go a single dredge was cast from the stern of the punt and the cable is hauled in with the wink, back to the anchor, towing the dredge astern.

These handly little craft are amongst the most appealing of British small boat types and Herbert Warington Smyth wrote of them: 'They are a

under the cliffs of Pont Pill. The oysters are 'native' or uncultivated and have been dredged there under sail and oar for centuries. Dredging under power, common elsewhere, is here prohibited, and the Fal oyster dredgers have to work with wind and tide and muscle power on the grounds. The larger boats are three-quarter decked sailing cutters (described in the author's book *Gaff Rig*) and small open boats, locally known as oyster punts.

very smart class of neatly built little vessel, and with one or two men are handled in any weather. A dozen or more may be met with single handed on the oyster beds in the roughest equinoctial winds, kicking lightly over the flying green seas, and no finer display of fearless watermanship can be seen.'

The punts were owned at many villages and creeks of the area. In season many carried fruit from the orchards up the Truro river to market at Falmouth, where the annual regatta included a race for these river boats up to seventeen foot long. They were also used for pleasure sailing by discerning owners such as the noted artist and experienced yachtsman H. Scott Tuke who spent many hours sailing his twelve footer in those waters. Many were built at Falmouth by Burt, Jackett, Hitchens or Green; others by their owners or in little local boatbuilding shops on the quiet creeks and havens, such as Brabyn of Calennick, near Truro or Peters at St Mawes.

Some boats set a spritsail mizzen, particularly those used for crabbing alongshore from Porthscatho, in St Gerrans Bay, east of the Fal entrance. These usually stepped the foremast well aft and set a staysail to the stemhead.

A few punts are still working under the restrictive regulations of the local oyster fishery, hauling dredges by hand, though outboard motors take them to and from the grounds.

Falmouth pilots, watermen, ship chandlers, seamen tailors and runners used six and four oared gigs for boarding and tending shipping about the port and its approaches in the busy days of the nineteenth and early twentieth centuries. Most set a dipping lug on a mast stepped about one third of the length from the stem, with the tack hooked to the weather gunwale, and had a spritsail mizzen sheeted to an outrigger. The lugsail was high peaked with a luff almost prolonging the line of the yard, in the manner of a lateen, and the leach curved hollowly to the boomless foot; a dipping lug similar to those set in naval whalers and carried by Portuguese and Mediterranean craft; a sail perhaps evolved from or older than the lateen.

Similar gigs were used from Fowey, Charlestown, Penzance, Newlyn and Mousehole, on the Cornish south coast, and from St Ives, Newquay, Hayle and Padstow on the north coast. Gigs were also much used in the Scilly Isles, twenty-eight miles off the Lands End. Length averaged 26–32ft and from 4in–5ft 6in beam. The dimensions, particularly depth, varied for the types of work for which the gig was to be used. Those likely to be working at salvage were beamier and deeper than the pilot or ship chandler's gigs. Weight was as light as possible consistent with strength, though some gigs, particularly in the Scillies, were very light so a seven man crew could carry them to launch, or when beached.

The planking was usually selected English Elm in long lengths and $\frac{1}{4}$ or $\frac{3}{8}$in thick. Timbers were oak or Canadian Rock Elm, and keels of oak or pitch pine. All members were carefully put together and well fastened. These long, narrow boats flexed, but rarely leaked seriously. Oars were 16–18ft long of ash or clear pine, working in thole pins of oak or iron, or in rowlocks in later boats.

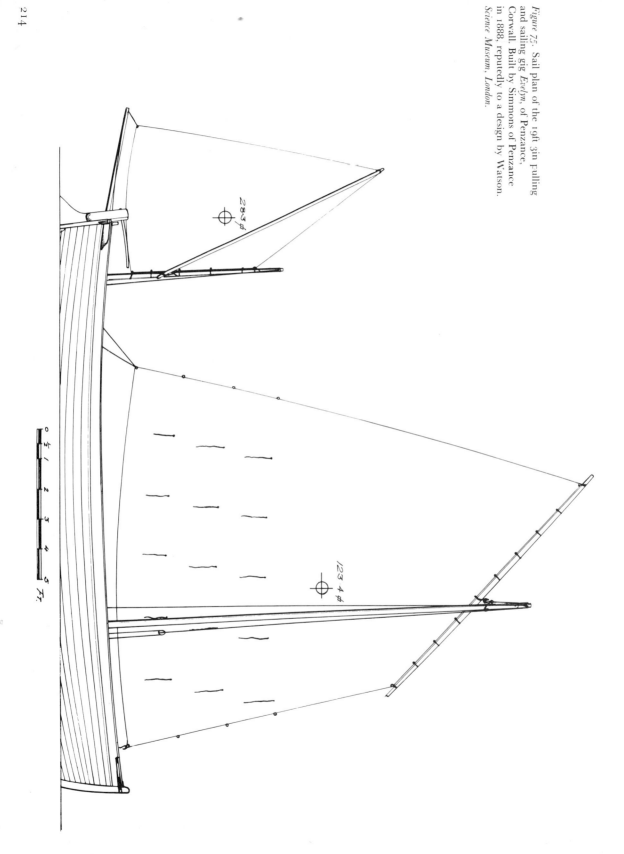

Figure 75. Sail plan of the 19ft 3in Fulling
and sailing gig *Evelyn*, of Penzance,
Corwall. Built by Simmons of Penzance
in 1888, reputedly to a design by Watson.
Science Museum, London.

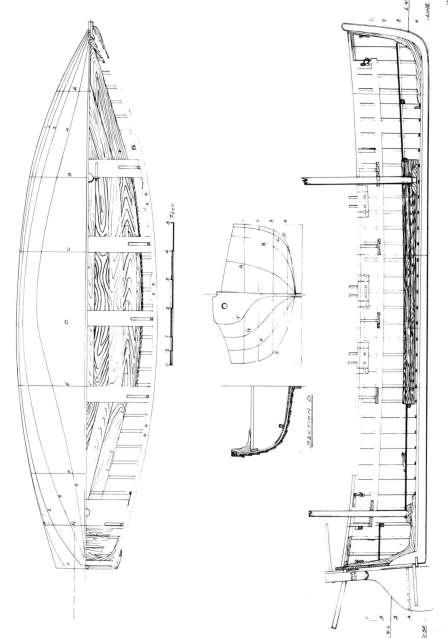

Figure 76. Lines and construction plan of the **Penzance** gig *Evelyn.* Dimensions: 19ft 3in × 5ft × 2ft 1½in internal depth. *Science Museum, London.*

Plate 40. A Newlyn pilot gig, rigged with standing lugsails, going off with a pilot sitting amidships. A boy pulls the lee bow oar and the helmsman steers with a typical Cornish short tiller. *Photo – H. O. Hill.*

gig was so shapely that her builder refused to paint her and she was coated with linseed oil, polished to a shining finish. After launch her top-hatted crew rowed her around Falmouth harbour, where the captain of a warship ordered the ensign to be dipped in salute to this fine workboat.

For two years the author owned, sailed and rowed a 28ft 6in × 5ft 3in gig surviving from the old steam yacht *Normania*. She was re-rigged gig-fashion, with a large dipping lugsail set from a mast about one third abaft the stem, using all the original hull fittings. The tack hooked to the weather gunwale and the sheet belayed aft by the helmsman. She had no centreplate, as few gigs did, but the extremely fine lines of the yellow pine planked hull by Husk of Wivenhoe enabled her to reach and run with amazing speed. Her hull twisted longitudinally reaching in strong winds but hardly leaked through her sweeping strakes which were almost all in one length. We had to row her to windward, as I suspect did most of the crews of working gigs, and she turned slowly under sail. She was fast under oars and would stand a sea providing she was kept bow on to it.

Mounts Bay

Mounts Bay pilot gigs were usually between 19–27ft long and many were built at Penzance by Simmonds. In winter these carried a small rig, often a standing lug foresail with a boom, a staysail hanked to a forestay, and a small sprit mizzen. In summer the foresail and mizzen might be two standing lugs and a staysail was set to the stemhead. Plate 40 is of a Newlyn gig taking off a pilot, who sits contentedly amidships. A boy pulls

Although all the gigs set a lug foresail, the mizzens differed. Spritsails were used at Falmouth, Penzance, Newlyn and Mousehole. Standing lugs at St Ives and a triangular 'leg of mutton' in the Scillies.

Many gigs were built at St Mawes by the Peters family, with hulls planked in English Elm, copper fastened. In 1843 the *Treffry* was built there for Newquay owners and this 32ft × 4ft 9in

Plate 41. The Scilly Isles gig *Nornour* under oars with a dipping lug and mizzen set, 1971. Built at St Marys by Tom Chudleigh, who continues the island boatbuilding traditions. *Photo – F. Gibson*.

on the lee bow oar and the helmsman steers with a typical Cornish short tiller.

Besides pilot work, Mousehole gigs also put off barrelled pilchards from Penzance to the regular London-bound steamers; typical of the varied uses of these craft. Gigs often participated in salvage work on wrecks, usually when the weather had moderated and until the mid-nineteenth century were much used for smuggling as, although the customs cutters could overhaul them running or reaching under sail, a gig could be rowed to windward much faster so long as there was not too much sea. A smuggling crew might be thirty hours at the oars and pull perhaps 250 miles in the round trip. Having pulled a gig for six hours at a stretch myself, I know how tired they were afterwards. Eight-oared gigs were also built for smuggling, but government regulations at the height of the smuggling era forbade the building of eight-oared gigs or galleys.

Scilly Isles

Scilly Isles rowing and sailing gigs were used for many purposes from pilotage to salvage and at times some carried potatoes and cut flowers to Penzance. Some were built by Samuel Tiddy who was apprenticed at Peters yard before establishing himself in the islands: a tradition of craftsmanship continued today by Tom Chudleigh in his St Marys workshop, where fine-lined gigs and other craft take shape under his hand for local rowing enthusiasts.

Several six-oared gigs were attached to the pilot cutters cruising in the vicinity of the Bishop Rock lighthouse to put pilots aboard ships which were

to await orders at the Scillies for destination of their cargoes. The Scilly gigs also landed pilots from outward bound ships and there was generally considerable rivalry amongst these gig crews to get jobs.

St Ives gigs were also used for pilotage and salvage, line fishing and regatta racing. Some of these gigs had the foremast stepped with pronounced forward rake which, when the sheet was started before the wind, gave them the appearance of Mediterranean craft. Eventually the type evolved into a carvel planked motor boat with narrow beam which retained a spritsail mizzen for fishing.

Further along the coast, Newquay gigs sometimes rowed and sailed 50 miles to Lundy Island, further up the Bristol Channel, in hopes of finding a vessel to pilot to their harbour, and of securing her mooring, discharging and ballasting work. At Padstow the two shipyards each had a gig in davits, ready to launch to any ship in need of repair.

These gigs were in use for many years and some very old ones survive for regatta racing, particularly at Newquay and in the Scilly Isles.

7

The West Coast, Wales and Ireland

Clovelly

On the north coast of Devon, to the east of the rugged cliffs of Hartland, is the curiously un-English village of Clovelly, almost theatrical in its steep setting in a cleft of high-wooded cliffs. The close packed houses tumble down to the shore and the tiny Quay Pool, protected by a stone breakwater. Like many of the little havens on the south shore of the Bristol Channel, Clovelly faces north and lies in shadow during winter. Clovelly Roads provided rare shelter on that coast for small sailing merchant ships. A fleet of small cutter-rigged trawling and oyster-dredging craft, locally called skiffs, worked from the village where most of the population were fishermen or went to sea in coasting or deep sea ships. The 200 ton schooner *Juniper* was probably the largest vessel ever to enter the pool, with cement for building the new breakwater in 1893.

Until the early twentieth century Clovelly was noted for its herring, landed from 20ft luggers setting the usual dipping lug foresail and standing lug mizzen. These half-decked boats had a reputation for seaworthiness and laid to drift nets at night, hauling over the starboard side at dawn and sailing home to shake the nets out on the quay at the pool. Herring were counted three to a cast, which was pitched into a larger round basket called a 'maund'. Forty cast made a long hundred, with a further ten cast added and one cast for luck; then the counter shouted 'Tally'. Four such measures made a 'mease' and filled the maund basket. A mease was sold, sometimes for as little as ten shillings, to the fish hawkers called 'dowsters' or 'jowders', who called the fish around the surrounding district. Sometimes there were gluts and prices were very low. Long spells of easterly winds brought hardship to the community and found fishermen warming their backs by the lime kiln along the quay, which was another staple industry of that remote place.

When deep-loaded with herring the luggers had often to wait for water into Clovelly's shallow pool, which almost dries out at low water. About 1880 some enterprising fishermen ordered a fifteen foot boat of modest draught from the usual Appledore builder, with the customary carvel planking on grown or sawn frames and with the locally necessary flat bottom at the middle line to keep her upright when grounded on the pebble bottom of the pool. The hull was roomy, seaworthy and well shaped, with a fine run and a pleasing, heart-shaped transom. The dipping lug foresail and standing lug mizzen sheeted to an outrigger were retained and the boat could be more readily rowed in calms by her crew of two, which made her more economical than the three men usually needed in the twenty footers.

The new type lugger could berth before the deeper, older boats and sometimes got a better price for the catch, besides being more economical. Others were soon ordered, from thirteen to sixteen feet long and they called them 'picarooners', perhaps after the Spanish word for 'sea robber'. Soon these boats outnumbered the old luggers and as brightly painted drift net boats, also used for occasional taking of summer visitors for a sail, lasted well into the twentieth century (Plate 42).

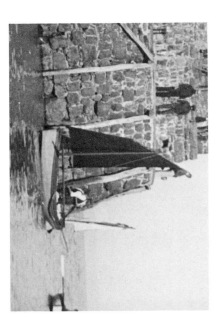

Plate 42. A Clovelly 'picarooner' is sculled round the harbour breakwater with her lugsails still set. 1934. Photo—V. C. Boyle.

Many were half-decked, which was unusual in such small luggers much used for drift netting, but made them very seaworthy. A distinctive feature was the white painting of the transom; a fashion also common amongst the Leigh bawleys of the Thames Estuary. In summer the picarooners found work in landing passengers from the Channel passenger steamers which anchored in the Roads.

The last sailing picarooners were built before 1900, but similar motor boats still drift for herring in season. Many Clovelly mariners became masters of large, deep sea ships yet hardly a seafarer now lives there and summer visitors provide the village's income. Three miles eastward the fishing hamlet of Bucksh Mills stood above a rocky shore. At the end of the nineteenth century sixteen carvel planked, seventeen foot luggers launched from the narrow sandy strand above the boulder strewn beach, each manned by two men, who drifted for herring up to four miles offshore and trawled hake and other fish in season. Most of this was sold to the country people inland, the herring being salted down for preservation.

The oldest fisherman of the community was known as the 'King of Bucksh' and three centuries ago emigrants from the hamlet took this custom with them on settling in Newfoundland. These beachmen worked against many difficulties and were very poor, but enterprising, and in spring and summer found a berth on board merchant ships.

In 1859 James Braund of Bucksh sailed the small cutter smack Surprise from Bideford to Australia and his family had a song about the

Plate 43. A spritsail rigged waterman's boat at Appledore, north Devon, circa 1900. A handy rig for a rowing and sailing boat. *Photo – Basil Greenhill.*

Bucksh men which began; 'The Braunds of Bucksh! They swim like ducks,

A race of hardy men.
So full of courage that their pluck
Eternally remain.

No haven have they, not a pier,
Wherein to moor their craft;
But up and down the rocks with care
They launch them fore and aft.'

Like beachmen everywhere, the Bucksh men never sold or broke up a boat past useful life, but laid her on the shore to decay. A handful of twelve foot boats still launch down the beach but the stone houses are now mainly the homes of week-enders.

The Taw and the Torridge
The north Devon Rivers Taw and Torridge divide from a common estuary inside the notorious Bideford Bar and were the homes of coastal shipowners, shipbuilders, seafarers and watermen using many small boats. The small schooners, ketches, sloops and cutters of Appledore, Bideford, Barnstaple and Braunton have, in recent years, attracted much attention in reminiscence, but the small boats of the estuary are worth recording as an ever present background to the watersides. Spritsails and lugs were used well into this century in the boats always coming and going about Appledore's ferry slip and 'the parlour' nearby. A favourite rig was a boomless sprit foresail and a small boomed sprit

mizzen sheeted to a short outrigger. Both sails were cut flat and set well apart (Plate 43). The drift of the luffs from the masts probably assisted the set. The mizzen was stepped to starboard of the awkwardly short tiller beloved of westcountry men.

Until the 1930s there were about twenty ferrymen working in the estuary under sail and oar; Bill and Jack Bailey, the Fishwicks, Ted Raffel, Mr Powe, Mr Smallridge, Charles Fishleigh, Wally Short and others. The village of Instow faced the town of Appledore across the River Torridge and was connected by a sailing and rowing ferry which could work at all states of the tides as the river was then deep scoured. The Johns family of Appledore were well known ferrymen and the fourth generation of them continue to operate a ferry to Instow with motor launches. Seventy years ago William (Daddy) Johns plied for hire with a handy clinker planked fifteen footer rigged with a sprit foresail and mizzen, distinctive in his broad-brimmed black felt hat and blue Guernsey, locally termed a 'frock', with shoulders embroidered with moss stitching, as padding when carrying oars or a sail bent to a yard, down to the boat. Such Guernseys were the mark of the 'Bar men' as local seafarers were termed on the west coast, though their coasting voyages earned them the nickname of 'Down homers' by Bristol sailors. Salmon were netted in the rivers and sold to hotels or were sent away by rail. Appledore salmon boats carried the spirt foresail and mizzen rig when sailing to and from their sets with the seine net, and with their best suit of sails bent and a clean bottom, were

ready for the local races. One competitor decided to experiment with a deep false keel, screwed to the long straight keel of the boat. He also replaced the forward spritsail with a large standing lugsail and won so convincingly that to maintain a chance for the more orthodox working boats, the racing committee introduced a rule of 'one man one lugsail'. As the boats sailing ability improved, centreplates were introduced in the working salmon boats after about 1900 and the most common rig thereafter was a boomless standing lug, a small spritsail mizzen and often a small foresail tacked to the stem head.

The locals loved sailing their small boats and however long they had been seafarers, never seemed to tire of being afloat. Tom Taylor, a coasting skipper, was typical in owning the small lugsail boat *Lottie*, which he raced in local events. One afternoon he set a very large lugsail, caught a puff before the start and the boat filled and sank. The spluttering Tom was hauled out by a passing boat shouting 'Never mind me, save my *Lottie!*' Other boats arrived and began to search for a drowning girl but a competitor knew better and searched for the tip of a submerged lugsail yard. Appledore men continued to set a lugsail for work until the late 1940s and a few are still seen on the Taw and Torridge in pleasure craft.

Somerset
Further east along the coast of the Bristol Channel small, spritsail-rigged open boats called flatners were built and sailed from the rivers and coast of the county of Somerset. The Rivers Parrett, Brue, Axe and Yeo wound through flat,

marshy hinterland to discharge on a shore of mudflats and sands, with flat landscapes and wide horizons. Tides are strong with a range of thirty or forty feet. The small populations were relatively isolated from larger centres, Bristol being the nearest city and Bridgewater, on the River Parrett, the principal town.

Fishing was largely a part time occupation in the area and local men evolved the flatner as an inexpensive boat capable of being rowed or sailed and of working with a crew of two. It is an old type, the earliest known picture being a painting dated 1795 in the Admiral Blake Museum at Bridgewater.

Early nineteenth-century flatners had a single chine hull form and a pointed stern with a heavily raked sternpost. The outreaching stem was slightly rounded in profile and the sides had considerable flare. Rig was a spritsail and small foresail. Usually there was a crew of two and the flatner could be rowed with one or two pairs of oars working in thole pins.

This basic type of flatner has survived amongst watermen from Combwich, Stretcholt, Dunball and Bridgewater, on the swift flowing, muddy River Parrett which flows into Bridgewater Bay. They were also owned at Burnham and Berrow at its mouth, and at Highbridge on the River Brue.

There were two principal sizes of Parrett fishing flatner; the 'Gore boat' or 'Foreboater' and the 'Bay boat', which had less freeboard. A typical Gore boat was 19ft 6in overall length, 5ft 6in beam at chine, 3ft 10in gunwale to bottom amidships and 1ft 10½in at the bow. Draught 4in. Daggerboard 4ft × 1ft.

The rudder was about 1ft 6in below the bottom. Gore boats shipped a washstrake when fishing for sprats, when they hoped to be deep-loaded homeward bound and faced winter winds and seas. Later flatners which carried washstrakes were called 'Gore boats' irrespective of size.

Early Bay Boats were about 17ft 6in long and 4ft 6in beam but length gradually decreased to 15–16ft.

As with a dory, flatner construction commenced with shaping the bottom. The type name suggests a flat-bottomed boat but the Parrett type had about 2in of transverse camber in the bottom sections, combined with about 4½in longitudinal curvature or rocker. This shape allowed a flatner to be easily pushed or turned over mud or sand, as a flat-bottomed boat could not be. It also helped her to come about quickly under sail. The 1¼in thick English Elm bottom planking was fastened to the oak floors with wooden treenails, steeved at an angle for improved holding power. Repeatedly the bottom planks were once hollowed to achieve the required transverse camber of bottom, indicating a possibility that the craft evolved from a dug-out lower hull with planked sides. As part of the Somerset coast was largely underwater in early times and small craft were necessary for transport and communications, there may be substance in this theory. Pine and other softwoods have been used for bottom planking for the past eighty years.

The shaped oak stem was cut from a grown crook but the oak sternpost was straight. Sometimes, for convenience of available timber,

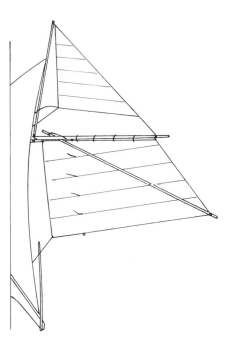

Figure 77. 19ft 6in flatner from the River Parrett, Somerset, showing the sweeping sheer and cambered and rockered bottom. The small spritsail rig was sufficient for these narrow bottomed craft. Dimensions: 19ft 6in × 5ft 6in × 1ft 9in internal depth.

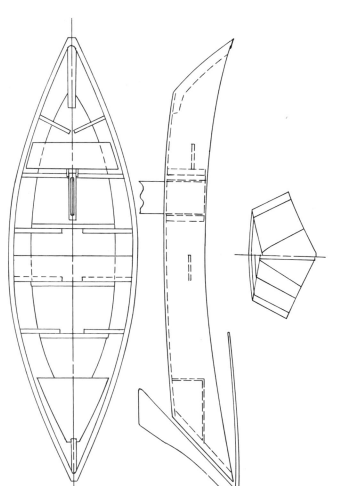

stem and sternpost were made with cheek pieces, fitted to suit the intended shape of the side planking. Stems were often constructed with a false forward nosing piece to avoid rebating for the side planking, which was cut off flush before fitting the nosing.

Each side was made from two ¾in thick English Elm planks cut from the butt of a tree to obtain sufficient width and thus needing to be scarphed amidships before erection. The upper edge was straight before bending to shape, which

determined the boat form and sheer and the angle of flare from the chine. Flatners were shaped by eye, without moulds, the grown frames and floors being fitted when planking was completed. Typically there were five frames, the forward one being a cant (i.e. normal to the hull planking, not square to the centreline) and the others lapping to the floors stiffening the bottom.

A daggerboard of elm, about a foot wide and four feet long shipped in a case immediately abaft the mast. Wooden leeboards were sometimes used

There were usually two thwarts, the after one being portable to stow the nets and catch as low as possible and aid stability of these lively craft. Raised pads were fitted to the thwarts to preserve a dry seat for the rower. A $\frac{5}{8}$in diameter tie rod was fitted under the fore thwart to reinforce the boat in way of the mast, which stepped immediately before it. A roomy stern locker or 'box' was permanently fitted to the hull to stow gear and food.

The flatner men made and butch-tanned their own sails. Modest sail area was necessary for these relatively tender boats. A typical summer sail plan was; mainsail 62 sq ft with one reef, foresail 16 sq ft, with one reef. Winter mainsail 44 sq ft, foresail 8 sq ft. The boomless spritsail was laced to the mast and the throat was lashed to the masthead. It had one or two rows of reef points and if further reduction of area was necessary the sprit was unshipped, allowing it to set as a crude triangular storm sail, with the peak flapping to leeward. The sprit was usually as long as the boat and was secured to the mast with the usual rope snotter. The mast was about three-quarters of the boat's length. When the sail was reefed a rope strop at the peak was lashed to the head of the sprit and the eye slipped over the shoulder at its end. This could be further adjusted for the second reef.

In boats with a long tiller the mainsheet was hitched under a thole pin on each quarter. Later tillers were shorter and the mainsheet sometimes led to a short horse on the aft locker. The small foresail was set flying, lashed to the masthead, and could be tacked to the stemhead or to a short bowsprit improvised from a stave about 5ft long

Plate 44. A Somerset flatner, restored during 1968 for the Bristol Museum. Compare the rudder and tiller with those of a coble (Chapter 8.)

until the 1870s, hung from each side in way of the mast, from a rope strop round a thole pin. Lateral resistance was aided by the rudder projecting up to eighteen inches below the heel of sternpost. The tiller shipped over the rudder head and was about five feet long, enabling the helmsman to sit almost amidships and vary the vertical movement when the helm was put over.

226

with a two-pronged fork at one end. This was also used as a boathook, for holding on to a bank or for raising sprat nets. As a bowsprit it was laid on the mast thwart and secured to it and to the bow painter ring by lashings. (Fig. 77).

Flatners beat to windward well for a small working boat, due to the narrow midship section, fine bow and comparatively light displacement and were reasonably stiff, but needed to be sailed with care in a breeze. Iron or stone ballast was carried amidships. They came about quickly but were wet in a short sea because of the smooth sides. When running in strong winds and broken water, an empty fish basket or some other drogue, was towed astern to prevent broaching.

Sailing in shallow water, one man steered and tended the mainsheet, the other worked the foresail sheets and kept an eye on the daggerboard. A scoop bailer carved from a block of willow or English Elm was essential in flatners, which shipped much spray sailing to windward in a breeze and also leaked from frequent racking and pulling over mud. Oars were made of larch or red deal, often 4in × 1in in the blade and 2in × 4in at the loom end, tapered to 2in square. These boats were difficult to row for long distances single-handed because of the bottom shape and light draught which made it difficult to maintain a steady course.

A four-tined grapnel anchor was used, made by the local blacksmith and let go on a warp. Parrett flatners were traditionally painted pale blue with red gunwales and buff inside, like a farm cart.

An early specification for a flatner has survived in the Port of Bridgewater Custom House letter books where George and Henry Wilkins of Pawlett, at the mouth of the Parrett, quoted for 'A flat boat for the boarding station at Burnham' in 1852, 'length overall 21ft 6in; width amidships 5ft 6in; depth of sides from inside of boat to gunwale 2ft; elm plank for sides ¾in; 3 thwarts with knees each side 1½in; bottom plank 1½in; ribbs 1¼; timbers in bottom of boat 2in; bow and stern of boat constructed alike; from fore part of after thwart to back board 17ft; iron pintles and gudgeons; standing ring at bow; 6 timbers in bottom 2in; 16 timbers in sides 1¼in; three coats paint; iron nails rove, £9. 10. 0.'

If copper nails instead of iron £11. 0. 0.'

Evidently she did not last long as in early 1859 Henry Wilkins, now of Combwich, was quoting for another flatner for the same service:

'length from exterior at both ends 20ft; width in amidships 5ft 2in; depth of sides in admidships 1ft 11in; thickness of elm plank for sides ¾in; do for bottom 1½in; thickness of three thwarts (double kneed) 2½in; thickness elm gunwale 1¼in; 14 timbers in sides of oak 1½in; five floors of oak square 2in; from the fore part of after thwart to backboard 6ft; bow and stern alike; ring in bow to be a standing one of iron; iron pintles and gudgeons to have arms and fixed with screws; rudder and tiller, mast and spirt with clamp for mast; centreboard of elm; copper nailed; three coats paint, £9. 10. 0.'

The interesting points of the last quotation are the use of a 'centre board' in so small and remote an English working boat in 1859, referred to as a commonplace and the use of a 'clamp' on the mast instead of the usual spirt to attach it to the mast instead of the usual rope snotter. Flatners and their gear were usually built as cheaply as possible. In 1914 a new flatner cost £15. F. J. Carver and Son Ltd of Bridgewater built them for many years and in 1918 wrote that they were unaware that the type was peculiar to Somerset. In later years the best flatners were reputedly built at Coombwich, on the Parrett. For over forty years many were constructed there by the village carpenter, until his death about 1916. Other locals built them but could not achieve the sailing ability of his boats which averaged fifteen foot long with beam between four and five foot (more often five foot) and six inches draught. He could build one in two weeks. Some flatners were also built at Highbridge, on the River Brue between the Parrett and Weston by H. J. Kimber who was building rowing flatners in the 1940s. Many were also built by fishermen and by farmers and smallholders who used craft with less depth and sheer on the Parrett above Bridgewater and for gathering withies, peat and reeds on the moorlands around Bridgewater and Yeovil and in the ditches and rhines draining the extensive, marshy plain of Somerset.

Flatners were left alongshore all year round and withstood considerable usage and neglect. Many were shortlived as without bottom boards they wore through at the rowing and net handling positions. The elm sides tended to split and most boats were patched. Temporarily unwanted flatners were often sunk in summer and stood capsized in winter to reduce effect of sun and frost. Some flatners fishing in the estuary or alongshore were in use throughout the year.

Many others were used by part-time fishermen. The Bay boats worked mainly in the River Parrett and Bridgewater Bay. Gore boats usually took the last of the ebb down to the tail of the Gore Sand; a bank extending about six miles westward from the north of Burnham on Sea. There were about twenty-six Gore boats working during the 1890s and about seven by the 1920s. Ground fish, sprats, shrimps and sometimes cod were taken. Nets called 'lugs' or 'stake hogs' hung between stakes set on the extensive mud flats along the coast were worked and tended by flatners. In season the stakes supported salmon buts, which were tapered wicker baskets about six feet long. Similar but larger and narrower ones called 'Hullies' were used for eels, which were a staple catch of the area. Some flatners sailed to Burnham in the sprat season and bought in bulk to sail back to Bridgewater and retail them there.

Dabs, whiting, shrimps and grey mullet were caught in the swift flowing river where flatners could be held at bow and stern by iron-tipped stakes called 'geds', pushed into the river bottom. The boat could be worked across the river by progressive movement of the geds. Either dipping or pitching nets were used. The dipping net resembled a shrimping net and was about six feet across the mouth, spread by 'stays' of willow and supported on an ash handle called the 'spill'. These were used from the bow of a flatner under oars which followed the salmon as it sounded and hopefully caught it with a dipping movement of the net. The triangular pitching net was formed by two poles and was about twelve feet across the mouth. Unskilful use of it might capsize a flatner if the current swept it beneath her. Flatners were dayboats which returned on the flood to land the catch at Burnham or carried on to Combwich or Bridgewater.

Tom Came, a flatner fisherman, was described in a poem by James Jenning in 1852:

'Now who is there that han't a hir'd o' one young Tom Came?
A fisherman of Huntspill, an' a well-known name.
A knaw'd much moor o' fishin' than many vawk bezides;
An a knaw'd much moor than mooast about tha zea and all tha tides.
A knaw'd well how to make buts, an hullies too an jitch,
An up an down tha river whaur that best place vor ta pitch.
A knaw'd all about tha stake-hangs tha salmon vor ta catch,
Tha pitchin an tha dippin net, tha slime and tha mud-batch.
A handled too iz gads well his paddle and iz oor;
A war atways bawld an fearless a, when upon the Goor.
O' heering, sprats and porpuses o' all fish a cood tell;
Who bit he amangst tha fishermen a always bear'd tha bell.'

Why Tom bore the bell is difficult to understand, unless it was significant in the ritual of a fisherman's guild to which he may have belonged? Tom Came was found frozen to death at Black

Rock after refusing to abandon his expensive nets and make for shelter at Burnham. His companion, Albert Dowden, survived the ordeal.

The flatner men were always on the lookout for flotsam and jetsam which could be sold or used. Some flatners had a local reputation as seaboats, going off to inshore wrecks which a lifeboat could not reach.

Anything which swam was game for the flatner men; they even rounded up porpoise shoals and drove them inshore to strand on the ebb and be killed for skins. Possibly they were cut up and tried down for oil. A friend of the author once did this and distilled a foul smelling liquid which was liberally smeared on ropes and gear on board his smack as a 'preservative'. It rapidly transferred itself to everything and everybody on board and could not be removed for months.

On this coast there is a sense of desolation and in some parts, almost unreality. At Kilve, between the River Parrett and Watchet, the villagers used dogs to fish for conger eels! At low water the vast foreshore was an expanse of mud with many large boulders under which the eels lurked until flushed out by terriers and spaniels, to be knocked over the head with a stick.

At Stolford, between Kilve and the Parrett, the tide recedes for about a mile and the fishermen hung nets on tall stakes at low water. These were carried out on curious wooden sledges which also brought back the catch to the stony beach, where the sledges were left until the next trip, ballasted to sink at high water. There are now no sailing flatners in use, but in 1970 there were a few Gore boats surviving, used under oars or with outboard motors for netting an occasional salmon and to tend stake nets. One fished from Combwich, five from Stretcholt and two from Dunball. A restored River Parrett sailing flatner is displayed at the Bristol City Museum.

The Parrett flatner type would be very suitable for those seeking a small, practical, traditional sailing craft, easily built and needing little maintenance. She would be useful in many waters if sailed with care.

Weston Super Mare

Twelve miles north at Weston Super Mare, the flatners were very different and seem to have been a variant of the English rowing and sailing wherry. Weston Bay faces west into the Bristol Channel. It dries out at low water and is three miles between Birnbeck Island to the north and Brean Down in the south. The River Axe flows into it near Brean Down and off this the creek of Uphill provided moorings for many fishing flatners and was reputedly an ancient port. Weston men were fishing in the fifteenth century and by the start of the nineteenth, Weston was a remote fishing village of 138 people, existing in near feudal conditions.

In 1808 a hotel was built there and during the 1820s nearby Knightstone was developed to exploit the fashion for sea-bathing. This included construction of a causeway for access to the baths and houses built on this rock, which created a small haven for coal-carrying coasters and the local flatners, which were supplementing fishing by taking visitors for a sail. Weston flatners varied from ten to thirty feet

long, had flat bottoms but clinker planked sides on sawn oak frames, narrow, deep transom sterns and a fine run, enabling them to row and sail well. A typical twenty foot flatner had three thwarts and the mast was clamped to a forward thwart at sheer height. A few retained the pointed stern. Most had a daggerboard for windward sailing and moderate beam, providing a stable sail for the trippers. Rig was a single spritsail (locally a sprit was called a 'split') with a foresail added when fishing. The flat bottom and flaring,

rounded sides made the Weston flatners dry in a sea and suited to the exposed, shallow bay. The light draught aided beaching and launching, where a boat with a keel would have stuck. It was customary to walk in the flatners on a rising tide over the flats, to get the catch ashore quickly. Parallels may be made with the New Jersey beach skiffs (Chapter 12), and in form and construction with the New England wherries (Chapter 11), which were also frequently built by their owners.

The Weston men always referred to their boats as 'flatners' and to have the River Parrett type as 'dories'. Some larger Weston flatners had two spritsails and in 1831 Thomas Clarke recorded a trip in one to the island of Steep Holm, five miles away. The boat was twenty-seven foot long and the boatmen had to row her all the way in a calm.

Weston was central to the cities of Bristol and Bath and to South Wales, so it rapidly developed as a resort for seaside holidays. By mid century the fishing village had become a thriving town of 4000 inhabitants, known as Weston-super-Mare, offering as one of its attractions trips round the bay in flatners, with day excursions to bays, headlands and alongshore.

The influx of newcomers included some professional boatmen and boatbuilders. In 1845 Thomas Price built the large *Haidai* on the lawn of the Belvedire Hotel. Her launch needed horses as well as many men and she was queen of the fleet for several years. Thomas Price later moved to Pill, on the River Avon, and became a noted builder of pilot cutters.

Two masted flatners up to thirty feet in length increased in numbers with the growth of Weston. Some were rigged with spritsails, others had a gaff mainsail and a sprit or lug mizzen clamped to the transom and sheeting to an outrigger, others were rigged as gaff cutters, sloops or yawls and about a dozen were working in 1900. All had relatively narrow beam to enable them to be rowed when necessary. These boats frequently made trips to the islands in the Bristol Channel and to Cardiff in South Wales, when chartered by a pleasure party. During 1867 a pier was built and passenger steamers gradually took away the flatners long-distance trade, but landing passengers and luggage from steamers brought some trade for smaller flatners, particularly the dinghy-sized ones known as 'punts'.

By the 1880s most Weston Flatners had narrow and well tucked up transom sterns but a few had pointed ones. Craft sixteen to eighteen foot long were known as 'Clevedon boats' and were dual purpose flatners which carried holidaymakers from the beach in summer and fished in season.

The *Silver Spray*, built and owned by John Watts in 1903 was twenty-three foot long with a maximum beam of about eight foot and three foot at the widest part of the bottom which had a two inch longitudinal rocker. Maximum beam was well forward. She was licensed to carry sixteen trippers. Such flatners were built on three moulds with shape determined by the owner's fancy. The elm bottom or 'slab' had slight transverse camber, perhaps two inches, and was made of one, two or three pieces depending on the bottom width. Construction commenced bottom up, with the slab laid on the moulds and the stem and sternpost. After shaping, the slab was rebated amidships for the garboard planking and was bevelled at the ends. After the garboard strake was fitted a second, thinner slab was added to the bottom over a layer of tarred brown paper. This took the chafe of grounding and was renewable. Then the boat was turned right way up and planking continued to the sheer. About seven strakes each side being usual. The sawn frames and floors were then fitted and the gunwales, thwarts (usually three), knees, side benches, and daggerboard case were installed. Around 1900 some flatners were built with bent frames instead of sawn frames.

The daggerboards were often in three separate pieces for ease of removal and replacement if broken. Most Weston flatners were painted white with a sheerstrake of contrasting colour. The bottom was black and thwarts and bottom boards buff.

Flatners used for tripping had side benches from the amidship thwart aft and shipped a washstrake aft to protect passenger's clothes when going off stern first from the beach.

Many flatner sails were made by the owner.

Some were supplied by tobacco manufacturers with advertising lettering on them.

Winter fishing was a staple for the flatner men, with sprats and herring landings being sent by rail to Bristol, Bath and Taunton. Most fishing was done by flatners about twenty foot long as these could be worked by two men; the larger boats needing up to six. In January and February they spratted with swing (Stowboat) nets off Brean Down. Sprats were prime fish and some were used as bait for long lines shot for cod and skate. By March and April the boats refitted for the tripping season which lasted until the end of September, but boarding-houses and hotels needed fish and some flatners worked trammel nets for dabs and other fish until August, when many went shrimping until October.

Most boatmen had other occupations. Some made sails, canvas blinds or awnings and others did odd jobs. A few owned small boatyards.

There was a good spirit amongst the Weston boatmen. When J. Counsell lost his flatner his contemporaries secretly raised a fund and commissioned F. Webb to build the *Surprise* for him.

During the 1920s there were several flatners between twenty and twenty-four feet long still sailing. The *Silver Spray*, built and owned by John Watts, who also built the *Empress* for F. Webb. Webb had built and owned the *Pride of the West*. J. Urch's *Shamrock* was by an unknown builder and the *Surprise* was then in use.

Eventually motor launches took over the flatners tripper trade, though some flatners had engines installed. In 1970 there were five surviving Weston flatners, all having transom sterns and all used as yachts.

Tenby

On the opposite shore of the tide-ridden Bristol Channel, on the Pembrokeshire coast of South Wales facing Carmarthen Bay, Tenby fishermen used luggers for the old established herring fisheries which existed in the fourteenth century, and also for line fishing and dredging oysters in and to the south of Carmarthen Bay.

Few luggers were owned at Tenby in 1800 but sixty years later there were about twenty-five and by 1891, forty-nine, half of which were from twenty to twenty-two feet long on the keel, with full-bodied, clinker planked hulls and transom sterns, an almost vertical stem and sternpost and straight keel which extended well below the rebate line to provide lateral plane.

The largest lugger, named *Eileen*, had a keel length of twenty-seven feet. The deep hulls were open except for a cuddy under a short foredeck and had three or four thwarts which served for rowers in calms. Draught was around three feet and all ballast was in the bilge. The rig was a dipping lug forward, a high-peaked sprit mizzen and a jib. The foremast was stepped about one third of the lugger's length abaft the stem and clamped to a thwart at sheer height, at the aft end of the foredeck.

The fore lug of about 250 sq ft was tacked down to the stemhead and sheeted to the quarters. It had three reefs. The mizzen mast was half the length of the foremast and stepped to one side of the rudder in clamps on the transom,

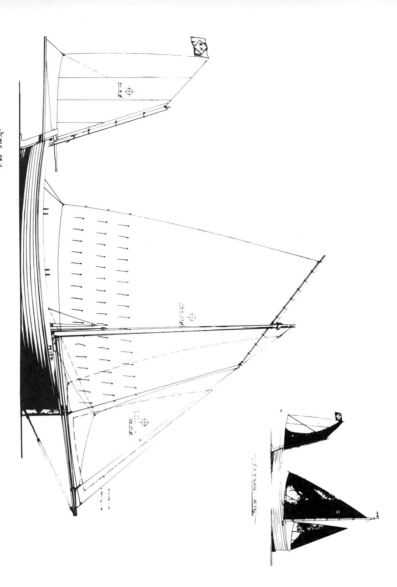

Figure 78. Sail plan of the 24ft fishing lugger *Seahorse* of Tenby, South Wales. Standing lug foresail and spritsail mizzen. Inset is trysail rig with a staysail set to the stemhead. *Science Museum, London.*

following its rake. The mizzen was about 60 sq ft area and the high-peaked sprit made it an efficient sail for windward work. The boomless foot sheeted to a long and downward steering ash outrigger. A long bowsprit shipped through a gammon iron at the stemhead and its heel rested in a chock at the after end of the foredeck. Two or three sizes of jibs could be set to suit conditions; all set flying by masthead halyards. In strong winds a triangular trysail was set in place of the fore lug.

Tenby luggers had crews of two men and a boy or, if drift netting for herring, three men and two boys. Some fishermen owned two luggers, using one for line and the other for net fishing. In summer most of them turned to taking the increasing numbers of holidaymakers for a sail; a more profitable and pleasant way of earning a living. For many years during the nineteenth century Tenby was a port of call for large numbers of trawling smacks, mainly from Brixham in Devon, which sent the catch away by a carrier smack to Bristol and elsewhere. When the railway came to Tenby fish landings there increased but after the end of the century the rise of the steam trawling port of Milford Haven started a decline of Tenby fisheries, which were extinct by the 1920s.

Across the St Georges Channel, in southern Ireland, flat-bottomed spritsail-rigged fishing boats having some similarity to flatners were used from the shoal harbour of Wexford, about 120 miles from Somerset. These 'cots' drift netted for herring from October to the end of December and were laid up the remainder of the year. A typical cot was 30ft long × 7ft 6in beam × 2ft deep with a flat bottom which had longitudinal rocker, raked stem and sternpost, clinker planked sides and a rig of three spritsails and sometimes a foresail. Two shallow bilge keels ran along the bottom of the chine for three-quarters of the length and small flase keels were fitted at each end. The bottom and side planking was pine on elm framing, stem and sternpost. The 1½in thick

Figure 79. Profile and plan of the Tenby lugger *Seahorse*, built by James Newt of Tenby in 1886. Dimensions; 24ft 10in × 3ft 8½in internal depth. *Science Museum, London.*

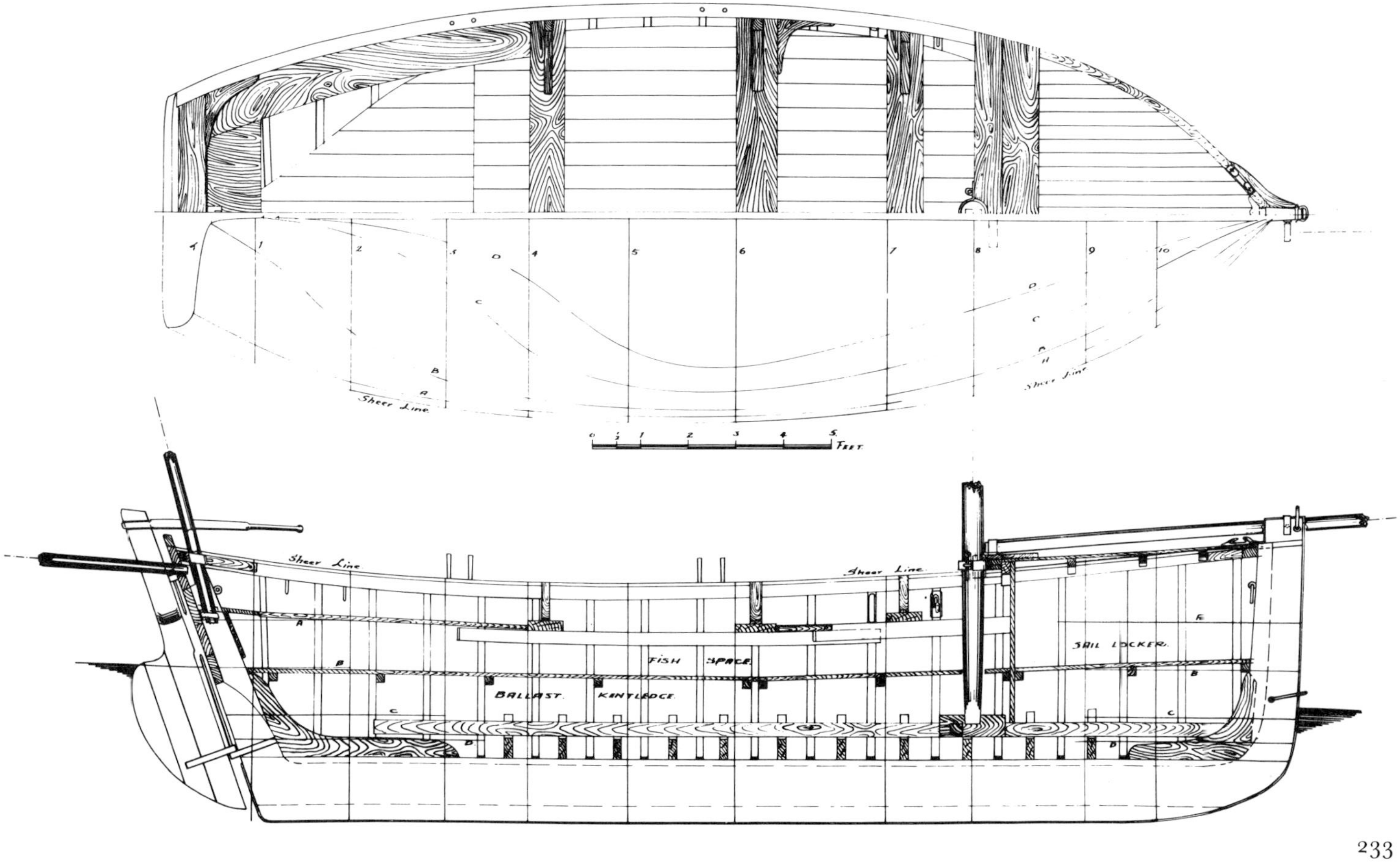

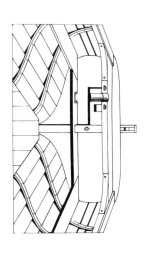

Figure 80. Body sections, structural section and detail of after end; Tenby lugger *Seahorse. Science Museum, London.*

PROJECTION of TRANSOM ─────
SHOWING
MIZZEN STEP & BOOM DETAILS

SECTION #6 CONSTRUCTION

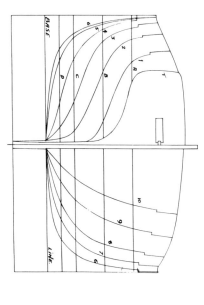

bottom was treenail fastened to the floors. The side framing was iron fastened to the frames. A daggerboard about two feet wide and one inch thick extended about five feet below the bottom and assisted sailing to windward.

Four men formed the usual crew. They rowed off while the spritsails were set, the fore and main being of about equal size and having two reefs. The much smaller mizzen stepped inboard, abaft the helmsman, and was fitted with a boom which sheeted to the head of the sternpost. A small foresail was sometimes set to a short steering bowsprit which had a simple bobstay.

A good catch would be 8000 herrings for a night's drifting and often forty or more cots would be in sight of each other, but it was hard work on an exposed coast. It is tempting to speculate what if any connection there was between the flatners of Somerset and these cots, but it seems the boats developed independently.

Aberystwyth

Various types of small fishing boats worked from the Welsh port of Aberystwyth during the nineteenth century, including rowing and sailing boats rigged with three spritsails: a rig reputedly introduced there by fishermen from the neighbouring village of Borth in about 1840. These boats averaged 23–25 feet length and were transom sterned, clinker built and had little sheer. They did not sail well to windward but although resembling purely rowing boats, were sailed whenever possible, but when beating to windward had to be helped round with an oar. Planking was yellow pine sides and larch below water, on bent timbers. There were four thwarts and the foremast stepped through the forward one, the mainmast clamped to the fore side of the amidship thwart and the mizzen stepped through a hole in the sternsheets, about a foot forward of the transom. Fore and main masts were the same length and the mizzen about two-thirds of their height. When herring drifting the mainmast was not carried and the boats sailed under the foresail and mizzen. It is interesting that this widespread discarding of the mainmast was practised even in these elementary drifters. No foresail, jib or topsail was set.

Some boats had three lugsails instead of spritsails and later boats developed with short gaff fore and main sails, but retained the sprit mizzen which set flatter than a lug for drifting.

Standing rigging was not used but the halyards led to the gunwales to give support. The foresheets were double and led to the after thwart. Mainsheets were single, as were the mizzen sheet which led through a sheave in the end of the long outrigger. This was clamped to the transom and secured inboard. All sheets were made fast to the thwarts with hitches, which could be quickly cast off.

Sails were made of light canvas and had two rows of reef points. The luffs were seized to mast hoops. Two pairs of oars were carried, worked in rowlocks. The ballast was beach shingle in bags. The crew of three needed the usual small boat gear and a jar containing water.

By the end of the nineteenth century these boats were increasingly used to carry passengers during the holiday season and were always

beached bow first, which allowed waves to break over the transom stern, so new boats with pointed sterns were developed and as most adopted gaff rig, will not be followed further.

A lighter and faster type called a herring gig was evolved, with narrow, clinker planked hulls and small transom sterns, like the west country gigs. Keel length varied between sixteen and twenty-one feet and the usual rig was a spritsail main and mizzen. No headsails were set. Masts and spars were very light for ease of stepping and unstepping and the mizzen sheeted to a long outrigger. These were indifferent sailers and centreplates were not used, so they were under oars

as much as sail. A crew of two or three men worked them when herring drifting, when the boat lay to the nets with the mizzen set. The smaller gigs often carried only a mizzen for riding to the nets and were rowed to and from the grounds, sometimes using the mizzen as a steering sail. These boats were mainly pleasure tripping in the summer, with the increasing numbers of holiday visitors coming to Aberystwyth.

By the 1890s a further class of small, pointed stern boat developed from the success of the larger beach tripper boats. Many were built in the town by David Williams and Sons and averaged eighteen foot long and six foot beam. Clinker planked with light scantlings and good finish, these were principally rowing boats for carrying holidaymakers off the beach, but a standing lugsail was set for reaching and running and they were used for herring and long line fishing in season. The Aberystwyth men thought a great deal of these boats and ventured considerable distances in them when fishing. Two men worked six to eight nets from them when herring drifting.

Whiting were caught with hand lines in summer on grounds five to seven miles south of Aberystwyth. Each boat worked three lines with two hooks on each, baited with herring or mussels. They sailed from the town at dawn and returned to sell the catch by 11 am. Sometimes they returned for a second trip. In June, mackerel shoals came in and the boats trawled for them about ten miles offshore. Later, the shoals came inshore, but were usually small fish.

The Aberystwyth boats were worked on shares and a crew of three divided five shares; one for each man and one each for boat and gear. They wore sealskin caps or tam-o-shanter hats, thick jerseys and heavy trousers but as the town increased in popularity as a resort, many found it more profitable and congenial to sail or row visitors off the beach, and their summer rig became white cotton trousers, smart blue guernseys and often a bowler hat.

Three rowing boats were still fishing for whiting in 1928 and several lasted into the 1950s.

Herring drifting commenced in September and usually ended in December. The three masters fished the shoals alongshore between Newquay in the south to Borth and Portmadoc in the north, though often they were caught only a mile or two off Aberystwyth. The herring nets were thirty yards long and four fathoms deep with 1¼ in mesh. The top of the net was suspended below the upper tant, which was attached to a line called the buoy rope by strops about two and a half fathoms long, varying according to the depth at which fish

were expected to be caught. Along this at about six foot intervals were cork floats. The foot was secured to the lower tant which had stones sewn to it as weights to keep the net vertical in the water. The larger boats carried fifteen to twenty nets each but the smaller gigs and double-ended beach boats only set six or eight nets.

During the herring season a score of boats sailed to the grounds in company and shot the nets at dusk. After an hour or so the first net was lifted to see the catch. If it had sufficient fish the other nets were hauled and piled in the boats bottom with the fish still in them, as there was insufficient space to clear the nets on board. They returned to port, where the catch was shaken out on the beach, a method which restricted the fishing to one shoot each night. The buyers were there to meet the boats and much of the catch went to Liverpool by rail but some was sold locally, often by fishermen hawking it through the town on barrows.

Catches varied but it was frequent for a three-man-boat to land one hundred 'miese' of herring, or 6300 fish in one night. Catches were reckoned in long hundreds; 126 fish making one long hundred and five of these equalling one miese. One boat fishing in Portmadoc Bay made a record catch but had to leave five nets at the bottom to struggle into Pwllheli 'loaded so the oars floated out of the rowlocks' as her crew joyfully exaggerated.

Ireland

In Ireland, two and three masted spritsail-rigged open yawls were the principal type of alongshore fishing boat on the north and north east coasts during the late nineteenth century. The yawls from Moville, near the mouth of Lough Foyle, were typical with pointed sterns, clinker planked hulls, twenty-four foot long on the keel and six foot beam. A foresail was sometimes set and the narrow hulls were slack bilged and tender, and needed sitting out by their three or four man crews. The two masts were stepped through the forward and third thwart, with alternative stepping holes in a fore and aft plank between the thwarts. The boats were often rowed with well-shaped oars and drift netted for herrings alongshore, in season. In winter the Moville men dredged oysters in the Lough.

Lug rigged sailing and rowing yawls from 20–30 feet long sailed from Belfast Lough harbours and foreshores. Many had pointed sterns and the larger set two dipping lugsails, unusually close to each other. The main mast stepped against a semicircular cut in the after side of a thwart, without a mast clasp. The shorter foremast stepped through a hole in the fore thwart. Both were heavily bowed forward by forestays but there was no other standing rigging. The tack of both lugs was secured to hooks on the gunwales, about five feet forward of each mast, but were brought further aft when running. The halyard was the usual tye and single whip purchase, with the standing part and the falls made fast to cleats on the thwart risings. As with many other luggers, the Belfast Lough men preferred a fixed 'dumb sheave' for the tye as there was little chance of it jamming when hoisting or lowering. The mainsheet was a single

part rope, passed through an unusual swivelling bullseye on the sternpost. The sails were spread by light booms which had a pin through the aft ends which was placed against the cringle in the clew of the lugsails. The other end was set up with a lashing against the mast. The sail clews were cut high to prevent them catching wave crests when rolling in a seaway. The crews of five men were quick at handling the lugs and the yawls sailed fast on a reach or off the wind, but were slow to windward. In squalls the sheets and halyards were let go and if she bored by the head when running hard before a sea, the halyards were eased. Sometimes the lugs were flattened for windward work by rigging a bowline to each luff. In strong winds only, the fore lug was set in the main lug step. Some yawls stepped only one mast permanently. Steering was by rudder head yoke and tiller lines and the crew concentrated their weight amidships to keep her lively. From two to five hundredweights of ballast stones were carried and some of this might be used as sinkers for long lines when fishing, which was a principal use of these boats.

Until the early 1930s the watermen of Dublin Bay sailed seawards from the River Liffey in similar open 'skiffs', seeking inward-bound ships which they often met seven or eight miles south of the river. These hobblers set a large tanned dipping lugsail on a reach or run, but were often rowed to windward with sixteen foot ash sweeps, the boatmen standing facing forward, a practice known as 'sheaving' on the east coast of England. These tough and hardy boatmen hooked on to ships with a large boathook, like the Deal men

237

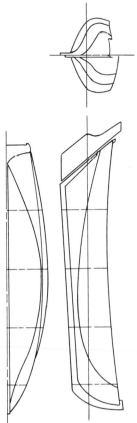

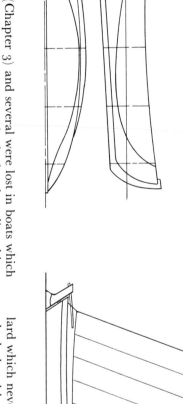

Figure 81. 28ft Irish *Pucan* with dipping lug set similarly to a lateen sail. Dimensions: 28ft × 8ft × 3ft draught aft.

(Chapter 3) and several were lost in boats which were cut down or capsized when boarding ships.

On the west coast of southern Ireland, strong westerlies bring a mountainous swell rolling in from the Atlantic to break thunderously on the jagged black rocks and clean sandy beaches of the coasts of Connemara, County Galway and County Mayo, where bold shaped open boats from twenty to thirty feet long called 'pucans' lobstered, seine and line fished inshore and cut and carried seaweed and light goods between the islands and coastal communities. Pucans set a dipping lugsail of lateen-like appearance made of coarse fabric called bandle linen, saturated with a mixture of tar and butter or coal tar and hogs

lard which never dried. Pucan hulls were carvel planked and had a shapely yet curiously old-fashioned appearance (Plate 45). Dimensions of the boat shown (Fig. 81) were 28ft overall length × 8ft beam × 3ft draught aft and 1ft 9in draught forward. A large false stem added perhaps a foot to the natural length of the fine bow. There was considerable tumble home at the sheer to keep the gunwale clear of the seas as long as possible. The rise of floor, long run and easy waterlines and buttocks enabled them to slip along easily under the large sail area. The hulls were tarred and most were not formally named. The heavy mast was unstayed and when going to windward the fore end of the yard was dipped

Mweenish Island, near Carra, Rosmue, Roundstone and elsewhere. Many were built by travelling carpenters at waterside sites. Plans were not used and the form was handed on through builders families or was copied from existing boats. Timber was brought from inland County Mayo, east Galway, or further south. Many pucans were built by Casey of Nyrush, Carna, who also constructed the larger, cutter-rigged hookers up to forty foot long, used for coastal carrying and fishing, alongshore and to the islands. Slightly smaller cutters, between twenty-six and thirty foot long were also built, called 'gleotogs' and some of these set a lugsail. The hull shape of all these craft was very similar and when afloat they appeared bluff and clumsy, but the underwater lines were clean and inherently fast. Ballast was beach stones. Construction was heavy, with sawn frames, larch planking up to 1⅛in thick and a stout elm keel to take the chafe of grounding alongside tidal quays.

Several of the last pucans were owned at the island of Inishbofin, off the coast of County Mayo, where a small community of farmers and fishermen used them for subsistence living and where many were built. The decline of working sail on this coast commenced during the 1920s with the introduction of motor lorries which quickly eroded the work of the coastal carrying cutters, though some survived to carry turf and supplies to the islands and return with cattle for sale on the mainland. The cutters were often laid up for long periods. The last pucans and hookers were built about 1930. In 1955 about twenty-five gleotogs and a few more pucans were in use for

Plate 45. An Irish pookhaun building by John O'Donnell at New Docks, Galway, June 1932.

round it in tacking and the boat was sailed round. In strong winds the man at the tack brought it round abaft the mast with a rush and it was belayed and the boat was off on a fresh tack in a minute or so. Besides the dipping lug, pucans also often set a jib on a running bowsprit. The heavy mast was unstayed.

Pucans were rowed in calms and three strong thwarts were well kneed to the sides. The boats were built to last and were constructed at Galway, Carraroe, Lettermore/Lettermullen.

fishing and odd jobs. The wooden framed, canvas covered light surf boats of various forms generally called curraghs or 'canoes', which were rowed off this coast with incredibly skilful watermanship, also sometimes set a small lugsail on a short mast for a reach or run in fair weather, though the boats relied on oars to get to windward, or in strong winds and rough water.

Liverpool

Construction of an enclosed dock for shipping at Liverpool and rapid subsequent growth of the port led to need for small boats for watermen to meet incoming ships and assist them to lock through and berth in the docks.

By the end of the eighteenth century there were large numbers of watermen, who also ferried off passengers and crews to and from ships lying in the River Mersey. An engraving dated 1797 by J. T. Serres, shows shipping in the Mersey and a transom sterned, clinker planked gig sailing under a large sprit foresail and smaller mizzen, with three men on board. Many gigs had three masts, the main setting a slightly smaller spritsail than the foremast. The mainsail was probably only set in fine weather as all the masts, sails and gear could be quickly unstepped so the gig could be rowed.

Typical dimensions of these gigs might be twenty feet by six feet six inches, but many were larger, up to twenty-eight feet or so. The hulls were deeper than a contemporary yacht or ship's gig and most had six thwarts. The sides were usually varnished, often with a black bottom and sheerstrake with a gold caveta line around the

sheer. In later years an official number was painted on each bow in black or white on black, and sometimes a painted owner's flag.

A crew of three was usual but an extra hand was sometimes shipped in bad weather. A boatman interviewed in 1887 said 'Them gigs are just as safe as an Atlantic boat and I'll just as leave be in one of them when it was blowing a gale; They can't sink if they're properly managed, but if they ain't, you're a goner' ... 'A smart fellow who has seen a bit from the dock walls can learn in a few weeks, but of course the management of a gig in a rough sea needs a lot of experience. Then the sails and steering must be attended to every second. A good deal depends too on what the boatman knows about the tides and currents.'

During the early nineteenth century the gigs and boatmen multiplied with Liverpool's trade expansion. Large numbers of small wooden sailing ships were entering and contrary winds might delay fifty ships, which, when the wind came fair, would all wish to enter on the tide. The gigs were often sailed into Liverpool Bay, seeking inward-bound ships, all needing watermen's assistance to berth. Gigs also sailed to Holyhead and sometimes to the Caernarvon Light Vessel, off the north coast of Wales. The first gig to reach an inward-bound ship was regarded as having the right of her waterman's work during her stay in port. This led to keen competition under sail and oar. Having been engaged by the ship's master, her crew went on board as she was towed astern of the ship. On arrival, the gig might be used to pass mooring ropes or wires when docking and the runner in the gig took the seamen to the boarding-housekeeper who advanced them money for a spree until their wages were paid, then shipped them off in an outward bound ship as soon as the money was gone.

In 1861 the Mersey Docks and Harbour Board required registration of all watermen's boats in the river and licence numbers were issued. This display of officialdom included fines for inefficient mooring of a gig, use of offensive language and instituted scale of charges for attending ships. However, in 1888 the boatmen were charging their own fees. One said, 'we get as much as we can. We sometimes dock a ship for thirty or thirty-five shillings. At other times we get forty or fifty shillings. Other parts of river work are where we pick money by taking people aboard ships in the river. For this we get five to seven shillings or ten shillings and sixpence a trip. We often have to wait half-a-dozen hours for gentlemen who are spreeing with the captain. Of course we get extra for this, but its terrible cold work at times. In the summer time we run parties down to Wales or anywhere they wish to go, and as a rule, this sort of work pays us.'

The period 1850–70 was the most prosperous. A boatman might average £2 between Thursday and Saturday but by 1888 this was reduced to twenty to twenty-five shillings each week and competition became keen, gigs regularly sailing to Holyhead and staying at sea perhaps twelve days, hovering about the coast, buying food from coastal villages or the light vessels, often at extortionate prices, and sleeping in the gig as best they could. Even when a ship was found they

Plate 46. Three-masted Mersey gigs sailing to meet inward bound shipping in Liverpool Bay. The barque has a paddle tug closing alongside. Watercolour by G. Stevens, Merseyside County Museums Collection.

boatmen often acted as unofficial dock or river pilots. Some acted as runners for the notorious Liverpool seamen's boarding-houses, for which they received a thirty shillings weekly wage and some perks. The runners would board an inward-bound ship and ply her crew with drink to persuade those eager to go ashore as soon as possible to go in the gig, which was in charge of one boatman. The other boatmen left on board did the seaman's work for the few remaining miles of the voyage for a fee of five or ten shillings. The

242

Plate 47. Three-masted Liverpool waterman's gigs preparing to race in the river Mersey at the end of the nineteenth century. *Photo – Merseyside County Museums Collection.*

could not be certain of engagement as by then many shipowners maintained their own boatmen and then the freelance gig lost her turn and had to wait until all her rivals in sight had found a ship.

The establishment of company boatmen and growth of the large steamship companies caused the waterman's decline, though a few sailing gigs survived until about 1920, when large shipping companies had been using motor mooring launches for over a decade.

Many gigs were kept at the old Chester Basin, near Liverpool Pierhead, heart of the ports

shipping activity. A wooden hut, stacks of masts and oars and a dozen gigs bobbing in the swirling brown tideway was the headquarters of the watermen who with 'rough tanned faces, dilapidated guernseys, have pilot cloth pants patched and darned in every part; ugly but usually well-polished bluchers and soft peak caps ... their conversation, generally mixed up with a flood of tobacco juice, is as a rule on the prospects of trade, the ships off the port and their chances for the week'. By the mid 1920s they were gone and spritsails faded from the Mersey.

Morecambe Bay
The standing lug was not often used as a principal sail of British working craft but is still set by fishermen of Morecambe Bay, on the north Lancashire coast and was earlier carried by craft in the Solway Firth, further north.

Beach pleasure boats from Blackpool and the ferry boats between Knott End and the port of Fleetwood, across the River Wyre, set lugs for a living and slightly further north, fishermen of the swift flowing River Lune developed two types of lugsail boat. Most were owned at the villages of Overton and Sunderland Point, at the mouth of the river which enters Morecambe Bay by a steep-sided channel which can be rough in some conditions of wind and tide. Salmon are attracted to this confused water and special 'tank boats' were built to work in it, mainly for Sunderland Point fishermen. These carvel planked twenty footers were rigged with a standing lug and a foresail and had airtight wooden buoyancy chambers built into the hull; an unusual feature then hauling it ashore to land the catch. These boats had to row and sail well and were usually twenty foot long with five foot beam, drawing about nine inches, sometimes more. The rig was a standing lugsail (Plate 48) and the hulls had pointed sterns.

Many Sunderland Point whammel boats were built at Overton by the Woodhouse family who also constructed gaff-rigged shrimpers and pleasure boats for Fleetwood and Morecambe. Others were built there by Gardner.

Similarly rigged mussel boats collected mussels from the rocky outcrops or 'skears' scattered amongst the sands of the Bay. These were beamy twenty footers with transom sterns, a flat floor, clinker planking and a centreboard for windward work. Rig was the local standing lug and a foresail tacked down to a short iron bowsprit. These shallow hulls were ideal for drying out on the skears, usually near Heysham, to be loaded almost to the gunwales with mussels raked from the skears, before sailing home with the flood. Woodhouse built some superior mussel boats for Sunderland Point owners which sailed well and were also used for summer salmon netting. The steep-to skears at the edges of the Lune channel allowed a deeper keel to be used and catches were landed at Glasson, for rail carriage. Mussel gathering was hard on the hulls and fishermen preferred to use older craft for the job, if possible.

The channels of Morecambe Bay altered radically after Heysham Harbour was completed in 1904 and many mussel skears were silted over, killing the trade. Whammel boats from the Lune

Plate 48. Whammel net boat from Sunderland Point, at the mouth of the river Lune, Lancashire. She sets the standing lug rig of the type. *Photo – Alan Lockett.*

for fishing boats. The two men crews lashed themselves on board when fishing this rough water. During the 1920s one tank boat was lost by the forward tank hatch washing off.

Salmon were also taken in less exciting conditions by whammel netting, which involved staking one end of a seine-like net inshore and rowing in a wide arc, paying out the net and raced in local regattas at the turn of the century and the north west coast fishermen were always keen to show the performance of their craft in competition. Boats might be raking mussels on Friday but Saturday afternoon would see the big foresail set and the owner in shirt sleeves and braces steering his workhorse to victory against his fellows in a hotly contested race. Regattas were held at Sunderland Point at the commencement of the nineteenth century and the Morecambe fishermen's regattas were first organised during the 1840s, in imitation.

Three whammel-net boats were still working from Sunderland Point under sail and oar in 1975, the owners feeling that engines would not improve their fishery.

Scotland

Whammel boats were used further north, along the coasts of Westmoreland, Cumberland and the Solway Firth. Salmon were caught by fishermen from Annan Waterfoot, on the north shore of the Solway, where Scottish fishermen worked a small fleet of cutter-rigged trawling smacks and spritsail-rigged, open clinker-planked whammel boats about fourteen or fifteen feet long and five foot beam, which worked the tide-ridden Solway with its miles or desolate sands at low water. Each set two or three hundred yards of drift or 'hang' nets. Whammel boats also sailed from Luce Bay, Wigtown Bay and Kircudbright Bay, on the Scottish shore of the Firth and others from the Cumberland side.

The Annan boats grew in size and developed into small, shallow draught versions of the Scottish fishing skiff. Although not intended for use in deep water, the hull form was seaworthy.

By the 1870s there were four boatbuilders at Annan Waterfoot, all of whom built whammel boats, besides smacks and undertaking repairs. Shaw, Neilson, McCubbin and Wilson built there and the 19ft 3in whammel boat *Dora* built by J. Wilson in 1900 was typical of the fully developed type. She had 6ft 3½in beam and 2ft 9in depth moulded, the keel was straight and the straight stem was almost upright, contrasting with the well raked sternpost. Carvel planking became general in these boats which frequently took the ground in the Solway and at moorings and construction was robust with ⅞in thick planking on 1⅝in × 2¼in frames as typical. The wood keel was deep and to it was bolted a small cast iron keel of about two hundredweight, rockered on its lower edge and there principally as a chafing piece against abrasion of the locally harsh sand. Ballast was also carried in the bilge.

The boats were decked except for a narrow, tapering cockpit abaft the mast, extending almost to the stern. There was a small cuddy forward of the mast, with side seats, lockers and a stove, where the crew of two could creep in out of the cold or while awaiting a tide.

A short mast stepped at the forward end of the cockpit, about a third of the length from the stem and it is interesting that all these north west coast whammel and mussel boats carried their mast well into the boat for this lug rig, which was probably a relic of their rowing boat origins. The *Dora*'s mast was 15 feet and the diameter at the heel was 4½in. The yard was 10ft long and the

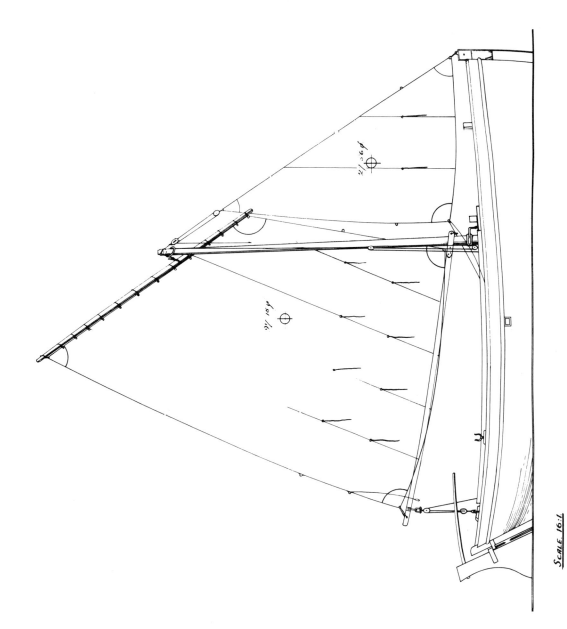

Scale 16:1

Figure 82. Sail plan of the 19ft 3in
whammel net boat *Dora* from Annan,
Solway Firth. Built there by James
Wilson, 1900. *Science Museum, London.*

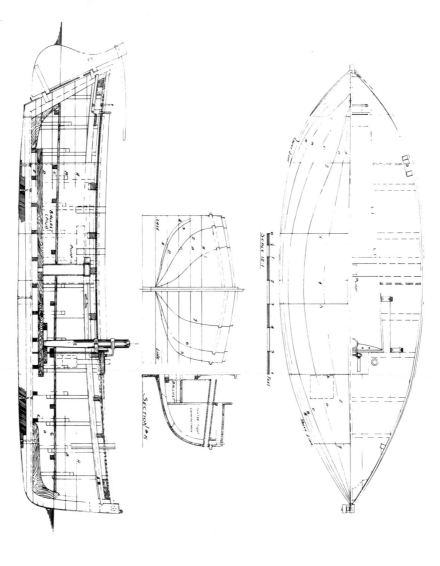

boom 11ft 4in. The standing lug main was 97 sq
ft and the foresail 28 sq ft, tacked to the
stemhead; a low rig of modest area which could
not have sailed well to windward. A rowlock
chock on each quarter enabled the helmsman to
also row the boat in a calm or help her round
with an oar when tacking in a sea. A pair of stout
bitts protruded above the deck on either bow, to
make fast nets or moorings. Some Solway
whammel boats had airtight buoyancy
compartments built in under each side deck,
similar to the tank boats of the River Lune and
presumably for similar reasons. Whammel boats
took in plenty of water when hauling nets on
board and a wooden box pump was provided
amidships discharging on each side through slots
in the side planking. Some Annan whammel
boats were fitted with engines during the 1930s
and a few rigged examples worked in 1939 but
the type is now extinct.

Figure 83. Lines and general arrangement
of the Annan whammel net boat *Dora*,
1900. Dimensions: 19ft 3in × 6ft 3⅜in ×
2ft 9in internal depth. *Science Museum,
London.*

8

Cobles, Yawls and Dusters

The Coble

The alongshore waters of the rough and stormy north east coast of England were fished by small sailing and rowing craft called cobles, working from beaches or small harbours in the Counties of Northumberland, Durham and Yorkshire. They were rigged with lugsails and the name of the type is of ancient origin. The word coble is pronounced with a long 'o' in Northumberland but as 'cobble' in Yorkshire. It probably comes from the Celtic 'Ceu' or 'Cau', meaning hollow.

An observer in Elizabethan times recorded a coble carrying three men and their fishing lines venturing twenty to forty miles seaward; a craft perhaps twenty-two feet overall with five feet beam.

He noticed that each of the three men pulled a pair of oars which they 'governe by drawinge one hande over the other', a long-standing peculiarity of rowing a coble, where narrow breadth at gunwale is determined by the tumblehome of the upper planking, making it necessary to work the oar looms hand over hand; a difficult method, perfected by long practice.

I believe the coble originated as a rowing craft with hull form resembling the upswept-bowed cobles used for salmon netting on the east coast of Scotland in recent years; a type sharing common characteristics of light construction and buoyant outreaching bows with the Fries and Norwegian coastal praams and the perhaps later Irish curragh, which were amongst the lightest and most seaworthy of small seaboats in skilled hands.

The Elizabethan observer also mentions that the three man coble was very lightly built as 'two men will easily carry yt on lande' and noticed that these boats were beached at speed, bow first on an incoming wave, which is the method favoured for a praam bowed boat in many conditions.

The coble was not a settled boat type, varying along the north east coast from the River Humber upwards and also appearing at Yarmouth, and elsewhere along the Norfolk coast, with isolated examples in Suffolk, a little further south.

The sailing coble developed to be a good sea boat. Some were of size and lightness to be launched or beached on exposed beaches where surf could be expected; others evolved for use from harbours. All had to contend with the strong winds and rough seas of an inhospitable coast and the Dogger Bank, where many Yorkshire cobles line fished in association with larger luggers and yawls.

Basically, the hull had a bold, sweeping sheer and rounded, outreaching stem with flare in the lower side planking forward to produce lift in big seas. Below the waterline the forefoot swept down to form the lowest point of the hull; a finely formed hollow gripe to split seas and provide the hull's principal lateral resistance for windward sailing, balanced by the deep narrow rudder which extended some distance below the flat shallow after body with its heavily-raked, 'U'-shaped transom and tumbled-in quarters. The foregripe also kept the coble head to sea when beaching stern first under oars.

The after bottom was protected by two bilge keels called 'draughts' or 'skorvels' which kept her upright when beaching or launching off. When shipped, the sailing rudder extended well below the bottom.

The wide sheerstrake had exaggerated tumble home throughout its length, which broke water away from the hull at its lower land, before most of it climbed to gunwale level and fell aboard. This also increased the hull's strength. These features were retained in the various sizes and types of coble evolved to suit local conditions. There were generally three types of Yorkshire coble and one type used from the Tees northwards.

Some large cobles had a pointed stern, causing them to be called mules. Pointed stern cobles were preferred by pilots and fishermen who could moor in a harbour, where the quarters of transom sterned cobles were damaged. Transom sterned cobles were faster to windward and had more stability under sail than the pointed stern type. They were usually towed, and sometimes rowed, stern first. Cobles were built as small as ten feet. The largest were about thirty-five feet long overall and were known as 'two stroke' cobles, because their sheerstrake was sixteen or eighteen inches wide and the one below it only slightly narrower. These were probably evolved in herring fishing.

Cobles had a reputation for seaworthiness and were able craft in big seas and strong winds, if handled by experienced men. Many were also fast for their length and sail area and had a comparatively easy motion at sea. Cobles cut through waves without pausing but at speed the bottom pressure often caused them to vibrate. In light airs they were slow. The long, flat run made them fast off the wind, but contributed to their tendency to broach-to in extremely bad weather. In normal strong winds the helmsman had to concentrate on his steering but there was then little danger of broaching. Many cobles were lost by being rolled over by a breaking sea and wind; a fate of many open seaboats.

In very bad weather a coble could be left to ride without sail set, lying head to wind as the deep forefoot gripped the water while the shallow stern draught lay away from the wind, riding like a duck.

Cobles were beached and hauled up on skids in many places and on large diameter, wide wheels in others, for example Boulmer. Horses were sometimes used for hauling up and at building time. They were comparatively cheap to build, which ensured their survival as a type on a coast knowing generations of poverty.

A twenty-seven foot coble cost about £90 in 1914 and another £25 for her sails. The coble hull was clinker planked on oak sawn frames which were fitted when planking was completed. It was formed without moulds, relying on the builder's eye and experience for its shape.

Naturally the owners took great interest in the construction of their coble and outlined their requirements in comparison to cobles built by or known to, the builder. 'Give her a few inches more on the mast thoft and a good fall in there,' or, 'Not so much sheer, keep her up amidships, we're not old men yet.' (crabbing cobles had little freeboard amidships so the older men could lift the heavy pots over the gunwale.) Capacity was another concern; 'We want her to carry a couple of last, so give her a good big stern.' 'A couple of last!' snorted the boatbuilder, 'What you want is a collier brig.' Two last of herring might weigh two tons.

The coble hull had no keel and the principal centreline member was the 'ram plank', extending from the stem to the transom. The 'ram', a term for keel, also used in Norfolk and north Suffolk, was flat at the aft end but swept down towards the stem, where it was iron shod for beaching.

Fastenings were galvanised spikes dumped into frames or clenched on rooves. Until the mid-nineteenth century hull planking was oak, often Russian oak. Later larch was used, but an oak bottom was used if available, to be more durable for beaching.

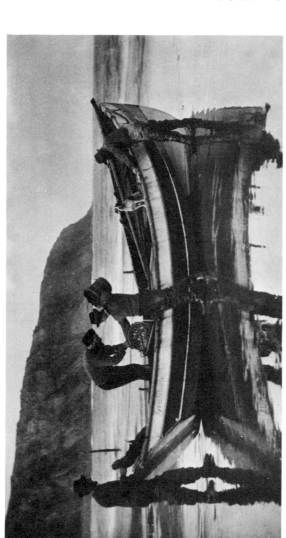

Plate 49. The beached, transom sterned sailing coble *Gratitude* shows the characteristic hull shape of the type, to facilitate beaching. *Photo – G. Nixon Duck.*

Flamborough a steam capstan in a wooden hut on top of the steep slope hauled cobles up the landing.

Launching or beaching on a flat or gently shelving beach in a moderate sea is dangerous. Swamping, broaching or capsizing were possible but were accepted as everyday hazards to be overcome as part of coble seamanship.

Approaching shoal water on a lee shore in a breeze the coble was usually turned head to sea and backed in under oars until she beached stern first.

Many cobles were built by boatbuilders working alone and six months was an average

Plate 50. Whitby coble *Lily* under sail with one reef in the dipping lugsail. Note the hollow entrance and strakes of planking painted in contrasting colours.

The garboard strakes were lapped over and clenched to the ram plank at its after end but were rebated forward, where it became narrow at the sharp, bow entrance. The next plank was at an angle to the garboard and very wide, the following one was narrow and almost at right angles to the bottom.

Oak transverse floors were fitted on the bottom planking before the two or three bilge and side planks were added, the sheerstrake (locally 'stroke') was widest of all; eighteen inches in a large coble and always considerably tumbled-in.

Trees selected for planking usually had a slight turn at the heel. These were cut into lengths of about twelve feet and then into inch thick planks. Three might be used for a large coble, so the curve met the required sheer. There were usually from seven to nine planks each side and these were not steamed into place but were twisted and nailed during fitting.

The sawn frames were then fitted to the planking, notched over the plank lands and scarphed to the arms of the floors and the horseshoe-shaped, transom fashion pieces were placed. The facing pieces of the stem and forefoot and the two bilge keels or draughts were added. These were carried up around the after side of the transom for about twelve inches, and curved upward in a distinctive manner, providing protection for the transom during beaching.

Risings were bent in to support the thwarts (thofts) and gunwales were oak, or later Canadian rock elm, steamed round the upper edge of the sheerstrake. Sometimes the hull was turned over to fit the bilge keels and the continuation of the forefoot, which extended several feet, overlapping the bilge keels at their forward ends.

The English elm rubbing strakes were termed 'binns', as in Norfolk.

Some cobles, particularly the few built for pleasure, were carvel planked, but retained the peculiar coble hull form.

Working cobles were almost invariably rigged with a square-headed, dipping lugsail, the leach and foot being only slightly longer than the luff and head. It had four or five rows of reef points.

Large cobles sometimes also set a smaller, dipping lug mizzen. Many also set a jib on a running bowsprit.

A complete suit of sails for a typical single masted Yorkshire fishing coble, consisted of: lugsail, big jib, second jib, third jib, storm jib or 'spitfire'. Working cobles setting a mizzen often made this double as a storm lugsail. Great care was taken in the set of the lug which was cut flat for windward efficiency. The canvas was dipped in a mixture of cutch and oak bark, not for preservation but as a filler to close the open weave for improved sailing efficiency, in the manner of the filler in many present synthetic fibre sailcloths.

The lug was made fast to the yard by 'rovings', instead of a lacing, and was hoisted by a strong and well-greased rope tye and a whip purchase. The tye was set fore and aft in the masthead and the lug yard was hoisted to be full on the side which was likely to be the longest tack.

Coble masts were usually of Riga white pine, if possible with a spiral grain and free of clustered knots and weather shakes. After the bark was removed the mast was shaped and stepped, usually needing no preservative coating. A single sheave of lignum vitae carried the tye or halyard which attached about a third of its length from the forward end of the tapering yard. Some cobles had two or three mast steps allowing its rake to vary by wedges. In light weather it was plumb, in a good sailing breeze the second step was used giving some rake and in strong winds the third

step, heavily-raked aft to ease the coble driving in a seaway.

Length of the working mast was slightly less than the overall length of the coble and the yard was half the length of the mast, or slightly more.

There was no standard rigging, but the halyard was set up to weather, around a vertical pin, projecting downward from the outside gunwale, the fall being jammed between the standing part and the gunwale, so a quick tug would allow the sail to fall – necessary in squalls or bad weather. The tack was held by a hook in the centre of a length of rope, the ends of which led in through holes in the sheerstrake on each side of the bow, about midway between stem and mast. Small hooks at each end of the tack rope drew the tack to the weather gunwale. The sheet was taken around the rising, just abaft the after thwart and was held in the hand, having to be shifted at each tack; cumbersome but safe in these open seaboats. The lugsail luff was tautened by a bowline hooked into the appropriate reef cringles and led aft through a block at the stemhead. A line called a backrope led aft from the heel of the lug yard to hold it steady when running. When going about the fall of the halyard was slacked, the tack was unhooked and the halyard let go, the yard was passed round the mast and the tack hooked in on the opposite bow. The halyard was shifted to the new weather side and the sheet was shifted over by the helmsman.

During all this, the coble made considerable leeway unless she was sailed full and fast beforehand. For short boards to windward the lug was not usually dipped and set well enough to windward of the mast when its tack was hauled a'weather. A shorter mast, about nine feet long, was often carried to step for a well-reefed or smaller sail. In light breezes the second mast might be used as a bowsprit. General practice was to increase the rake of the mast when reefed, to increase the lug's lift and ease the thrust forward. Pilots appeared to be fond of this practice which came to be regarded as obsolete by fishermen.

On the wind the helmsman sailed by the sheet and kept the coble going through the squalls, without luffing, as they would have quickly lost way and been knocked down. Sail area was reduced in good time to reduce angle of heel but, despite these defects, cobles were reckoned amongst the most seaworthy of British open boats when in experienced hands.

Cobles sailed best in a two reef breeze, some best of all with the short mast stepped. They were vulnerable when running as they steered badly then and might broach-to unless carefully handled. One hand was always ready to slip the halyard from its pin in these conditions and the mainsheet was never made fast. A coble which sailed badly was called a 'bruzwater'.

Cobles were frequently under sail and oar with a moderate foul wind. A typical three man crew had two men forward with a single oar each and the helmsman pushing an oar, keeping his eye on the luff of the lugsail.

For pleasure use a gunter lug and a foresail would probably improve the sailing qualities of a coble as she would point higher and be handier when tacking for river and estuary use. Cobles were often rowed, requiring knack of

stroke and strength of arm. The oars had a strap around the square loom with an eye on one side which fitted as a pivot over a metal thole pin in the sheer. Coble oars were heavy, made in two pieces; the rectangular loom of pine with a hand grip and the 'wash' or blade of ash, fitted at right angles to the oar. In small cobles the loom was heavy to balance the oar. In small cobles the oars overlapped so the rower crossed hands or took hold of the port side oar with the right hand and the starboard with the left, or vice versa. If possible they were rowed with the rudder shipped and one man steering. In a beam wind without the rudder the deep bow continually griped up into the wind. For this reason they were often rowed stern first and almost invariably were towed that way. The pointed stern of the mules enabled them to row more easily without a rudder, or to be rowed efficiently stern first.

A coble is very difficult to row single-handed and really needs another person to steer, as the forefoot tends to gripe and continually sheer her off course.

All pulling and sailing cobles were finer lined than their present motor-propelled successors and carried several hundredweights of ballast just abaft the mast step or under the second thwart; iron or lead pigs in pilot or pleasure cobles but generally bags of beach shingle in fishing craft, as with a large catch of fish these could be emptied overboard. Cobles were cranky without ballast and some was often shifted to windward on a long tack or a reach. Some had iron pigs or granite blocks, with five or six bags of shingle for trimming, totalling perhaps one and a half or two tons. The coble men expected to get the best performance from their craft under sail and liked the boat's structure and rig to be resilient rather than rigid and the ballast was sometimes bedded on scrap rubber for this reason.

The large rudder extended well below the waterline for a distance equal to about a sixth of the boat's waterline length and its breadth was about a twentieth of waterline length. Its effect sailing to windward was similar to a centreboard and was balanced in lateral plane by the fine deep forefoot.

Tiller and rudder were readily unshipped for fishing or beaching and a spare tiller was carried. The rudder had a keep rope attached to prevent its loss while being shipped or of it unshipped accidentally during sailing in a seaway. Many sailing cobles were painted in bright colours above the waterline, each strake contrasting with the next, sometimes green, yellow and red. Fishing cobles were named, numbered in later years and sometimes had the port of registry painted on.

Unlike beach boats in other parts of Britain, the cobles were usually hauled up or launched off beaches on a pair of large wheels, the axle of which was got under the bow as the coble lay in the surf and was worked aft until she balanced. Then the coble was hauled up by men or horse power.

The Coble Fishermen
Between the River Tweed, just south of the Scottish border with England, and the River Tyne, many small communities launched cobles

for herring drifting, crabbing and long lining. These cobles did not carry a bowsprit or jib.

By 1900 about 700 fishermen worked from these places and there was considerable loss of life amongst them, usually from broaching-to and capsizing. If a coble was filled by a sea she sank at once, usually with loss of life.

The physical harshness of this coast and its waters was reflected in the often stark poverty of its fishermen, particularly before railways and improved distribution of fish enabled the markets of many large northern industrial towns and cities to be reached quickly. The fishermen's wives and daughters usually shared the toil. Gathering bait for line fishing, clearing, baiting and coiling lines were accepted as part of their duties, besides managing usually large families on erratic and meagre incomes. Perhaps above all, the coble fishermen valued their independence compared with the employed toil of most of the crews in the fleets of sailing smacks and steam drifters and trawlers working from North Sea ports.

South from the Tweed, Holy Island lay close alongshore. In 1838 about sixty cobles, each about twenty-six feet long fished from the Island, where two thirds of the seafaring population were pilots for the coast to Newcastle. The local herring fishery flourished in July to September and at other seasons they landed cod, ling and halibut by long lining.

At Holy Island and at North Sunderland further south, the fishermen evolved lug-rigged open boats, larger than the cobles and called 'keel boats', setting a single, tall, square-headed lugsail on a mast stepped in the eyes of the pointed-sterned hull which might be clinker or carvel planked and about thirty feet long. The deep hull, with rise of floor in the bottom and long straight keel, contrasted with the cobles and merited the term 'keel boat'. There were three or four thwarts and the helmsman was partitioned from the rest of the boat by a transverse bulkhead, on which a crutch was mounted to receive the lowered mast when drifting for herring, which was the chief use of the keel boats. The lugsail had seven or eight rows of reef points and some boats also set a smaller mizzen lugsail. These boats worked alongside the Scottish luggers which also followed the herring shoals and the smaller salmon schools, from the Firth of Forth to the Tyne.

Further down the Northumberland coast were scattered Coble-owning villages; Bamburgh, Seahouses, North Sunderland, Beadnell, Newton, Craster, Boulmer, Alnmouth, Amble, Hauxley, Cresswell, Newbiggin and Cullercoats.

In these hardy villages, during an era when working people had to work or starve, the heavy, seaworthy cobles were launched off and hove up by muscle power in a community effort, twice daily by men and women drenched in the surf. Line fishing in the deep water alongshore was the mainstay and they also drifted there in the herring season, using a brazier of coals as a flare and to warm the crew shivering through a night watch.

Mid-nineteenth century Cullercoats was typical in launching thirty-eight transom sterned cobles from its beach on two-wheeled carriages. When not in use the boats sat on them with bows in the

air and sterns on the sand, like strange monsters. The village herring cobles were larger than the line fishing cobles; both had three man crews. Sea salmon were also netted in the season and the enterprising fishermen built a breakwater to protect the village landing.

Cullercoats was a village of single-storey fishermen's cottages but is now swallowed by the large, modern holiday resort and Newcastle suburb of Whitley Bay, and its once famous fleet of cobles has dwindled to one or two.

The nearby salt producing port of Blyth also had a fishing community, keeping their cobles at the shallow river mouth until local coal mining and shipping led to improvement of the river and eventual dredging during 1869 and harbour construction. Fishing was soon overshadowed by coal shipping, leading to considerable employment in loading and for pilots and watermen to assist the large numbers of ships using Blyth and the other coal ports of the Rivers Tyne, Wear and Tees, further south.

The foyboat men

Watermen of the coal shipping ports of Sunderland, South Shields and Blyth in north east England, were known as 'foyboat men', a name they believed to be of Scandinavian origin but which may have derived from the fee then paid for 'habbing' as assisting vessels was termed. The term 'foying' was also used for watermens' work from Broadstairs and Ramsgate, in Kent. Their principal work involved going off in small foyboats to meet inward-bound ships at the mouth of the harbours, or further seaward, and help moor them in the harbour or at quays, coaling staithes or shipyards.

During the seaborne coal traders heyday of the late nineteenth and early twentieth century, several hundred foyboat men acted also as tug crews, pilots, lumpers and dockers, besides those permanently employed as watermen. Trimmers and teamsters loaded the ships which ranged from 'geordie brigs' to large steamships. In the River Tyne the 'keelmen', who had earlier done this work with their pointed sterned, square sailed keels, were displaced when the growing size of ships and need for quicker turnaround of steam colliers caused the river to be dredged and coaling staithes to be improved, leading to direct loading from railway trucks and other means.

The foyboat men sometimes used small cobles but also developed specialised foyboats worked by two men, usually partners in ownership. These clinker planked craft had transom sterns and ranged from fifteen to eighteen feet in length. Hull form varied from port to port. At Blyth they were about seventeen feet long, beamy, planked with narrow strakes and they set a square-headed dipping lugsail with the tack taken to the weather bow. These were rowed as often as sailed and the foy men had to be ready for work day or night; sometimes there might be several ships to attend in twenty-four hours, at others none for several days. Competition was keen and foy boats met inward-bounders well seaward, to secure the watermens' work. During the 1920s a rota was introduced and this survived until recently.

At Sunderland, foyboat men used eighteen footers resembling cobles in construction and appearance. Tyneside foyboats developed to an almost standard type, 15ft long × 4ft 6in beam, deep hulled with a fine run and narrow transom stern. They were clinker planked in elm or ash; many were constructed by Eales or Michelson of South Shields who turned them out for £35 until 1939. Two thwarts and bow and stern landing boards were fitted. In the old competitive days, before the work rota, Tyne foyboats voyaged well seaward to meet ships, sailing under a dipping lug set on a ten foot long mast stepped at a twenty degree rake and clasped to the forward side of the fore thwart. The sheet led through an eye splice on each quarter, which allowed the sheet to flow to leeward when off the wind. Halyards were made fast with a jambed hitch which could be released instantly at a pull from the helmsman; often needed in a squall or a gust amongst shipping in the river. Centreboards or leeboards were not used in foyboats, which were not usually very manoeuvrable under sail. For river work they were often rowed, each man taking an oar, or were sculled with an oar over the stern. When towing astern of a ship the stout bass towline passed through a rope termed the 'snotter stop' at the stern head, which had a thimble spliced in its outer end and was made fast around the fore thwart with a jamb hitch which could be instantly cast off by a man in the stern in any difficulty.

Outboard motors have replaced sails and oars in the few foyboats remaining at the north east coast ports and their work is now inside the rivers and harbours.

Plate 51. Tyne pilot cobles are passed by the Cunard liner *Mauretania*, leaving her builders, Swan Hunter, in 1907. The coble in foreground has her lug set on the mooring. *Photo – Cunard Line.*

The Tyne

For centuries Newcastle upon Tyne was a centre of north east England in many commodities, particularly coal, which was shipped from local mines in large quantities. Much of it went to the City of London, prior to the Industrial Revolution, when coal production increased vastly to meet the huge demand and shipping crowded the Tyne and the coal ports of North and South Shields.

This vast trade needed many pilots, who used cobles to board and leave inward and outward-bound ships.

The South Shields pilot cobles were noted sailers. Manned by a pilot, one man and one 'boy' (who might be quite elderly), they cruised seaward to board inward-bound ships and frequently boarded ships off Flamborough head, perhaps having laid-to all night huddled in the bottom of the coble under the lugsail.

Many Tyne pilot cobles had pointed sterns, however, some pilots used transom-sterned cobles.

Pilot cobles were named, numbered and often had a pilot flag painted on the bows or quarters.

These pilot cobles sailed well and fleets of them raced each other in and out of the Tyne until the First World War, the flat cut lugsails straining on the wind (Plate 51). All cobles from this area had a tackle bowline to set the luff taut and five or six reefs were common in the working sails, which indicates the winter weather of this coast.

The masts were set up into a slot cut in the mast thwart, being retained by a diamond-shaped piece of wood, with a rounded face to fit the mast, which fitted into a rebate in the thwart.

Fishing cobles also worked from this locality and cobles were built at North and South Shields and much sailmaking was done there.

Before 1914 the North Shields men sometimes raced their cobles on Sundays, blackleading the bottoms for improved performance and carrying shifting ballast.

Sunderland and Hartlepool

Just south of the Tyne, fishing and pilot cobles sailed from Sunderland, at the mouth of the River Wear, in the county of Durham, a shipbuilding and coal shipping port. Hogdon was a noted builder of cobles at Sunderland in the mid-nineteenth century and local tradition maintains that the Wear men originated the coble.

The River Tees which divide the borders of Durham and Yorkshire also became an industrial centre during the nineteenth century with coal shipping, shipbuilding and iron and steel making bringing shipping which crowded the river. This increased the number of local pilots and their cobles, most of which were owned at Hartlepool and West Hartlepool, at the north end of Tees Bay. These were fishing communities until the mid-nineteenth century after which many Hartlepool men became coastal pilots, though fishing revived again later with the growth of industrial population in the area increasing demand for fish, caught with the usual long lines and herring nets.

In the early years of the twentieth century Cambridge was a noted Hartlepool builder of fast sailing cobles.

Hartlepool pilot cobles were often twenty-five feet

long overall and set the usual dipping lugsail, which had a hook at the tack. When the sail was reefed, the cringles were hooked on as necessary. The clew had a reef earring.

The mainsheet was a length of rope with a cringle spliced in one end. This hooked on a pin, and the sheet passed through the clew cringle, then back to the helmsman's hand. To make a single part sheet, the cringle was cleared from the pin, then run out and stopped at the clew cringle. This was simple and effective for these boats, which did not make short tacks, and the arrangement without blocks did not damage the helmsman when tacking.

When going about in fine weather, the helm was put down and when head to wind the tack was cast off and a gun tackle purchase, just above the tack hook, was hauled down. By then the boat was 'in irons' and an oar was got out to pull a few strokes and cast her away on the right tack. This brought the halyard and mast on the lee side of the sail, which was only acceptable for a short tack. On long tacks or in strong winds the sail halyard was set up to the new weather side, and she was soon jumping to windward with wake streaming past the quivering rudder.

Some Tees pilots worked from Redcar south of the river mouth, in pointed sterned cobles, racing each other to secure the job for a ship bound to the river.

The Yorkshire Coast
The Yorkshire coast, from the Tees to Spurn Head, at the mouth of the river Humber, had

many coble fishing communities. Both transom and pointed stern cobles were used, all rigged with dipping lugsails and many also set a jib on a bowsprit.

At the beginning of the nineteenth century there were seventy cobles working from Staithes, and thirty-five each from Runswick and Robin Hood's Bay, which, with those from Scarborough, Whitby, Sandsend, Skinningrove, Saltburn (which had a reputation for smuggling), Marske, Redcar and other places, totalled about three hundred on the Yorkshire coast. A total of twenty-eight large, 'five man boats' in which the crew actually varied between five and six men, worked from Staithes, Runswick, Robin Hood's Bay and Scarborough.

Staithes was a small town, isolated by moorland. Early in the nineteenth century its 1400 inhabitants depended on fishing for a living. In 1865 four hundred men and boys were fishing and seafaring and several hundred reputedly engaged in boatbuilding. There were sailmakers, coopers, fish merchants and curers, all busily based on a drying harbour fed by a narrow creek and faced by a vicious alongshore surf most of the year.

The Staithes five man boats laid up in winter, when the smaller (about twenty-four foot) three man cobles were used until March, long lining along the coast for the fresh fish market, with the surplus of about a quarter of the catch salted for sale. Crabs and lobsters were also caught in hoop nets and sea trout and salmon were taken with fine mesh nets.

Cobles had to be well handled to survive the often heavy surf at Staithes where they were hauled up by hand, the oars sometimes being used as skids, as the looms were made specially heavy.

Staithes men were noted long liners, fishing throughout the year for cod, haddock halibut and coalfish.

The village bait gatherers walked up to fifteen miles on the rocks between Scarborough and Robin Hood's Bay in search of limpets, walking back with perhaps a seventy pound load.

Staithes fishermen used transom sterned cobles called 'Sploshers', over thirty feet long with well raked stern. These were principally herring drifters, putting to sea at dusk and sailing about with one man hitting the bow planking with a ropes end to 'raise the herring', which on a calm night showed in phosphorescent shoals. The herring catch was counted locally in a peculiar way; a fisherman picked up two herring in each hand and this was termed a 'warp'. Thirty-two warps made a 'hundred' (actually 128) herring. Merchants bought by the quarter cran basket, four of which made a cran: one thousand herring.

Much curing of fish was done there before improved transport enabled catches to be sent inland as fresh fish.

The ancient port of Whitby stood on the River Esk, overshadowed by high cliffs crowned by ruined Whitby Abbey. Whaling and merchant seafaring bred a race of hardy, deep sea sailors and many pilots, whose pointed stern cobles were usually painted black.

Whitby was a centre of the herring trade with kippering houses, net stores, sail lofts and boatbuilding sheds along its quays, which were crowded with fishermen and seafarers, merchants and fish hawkers.

Whitby cobles were similar to those at Staithes and a typical transom sterned Whitby fishing coble is shown in Plate 50. Smallwood built many and was noted for his 'sploshers': many laid in the harbour and the river, some were hauled-out up the grooved slips called 'coble sleds' on the harbour pier.

The herrings came close inshore at the end of the nineteenth century and many inshore cobles caught them for the smokehouses on the point.

Large thirty-five foot cobles also worked from the port. Sometimes in spring they went 'netting and overing'; setting a few fine meshed drift nets to catch bait which was used on long lines which they shot for cod or haddock. The crabbing cobles were of similar form but were much smaller.

At Whitby and Scarborough, where craft could berth in the harbours, a type of large, pointed stern mule was introduced during the 1880s. These had the stern lines filled out to carry a big catch but still had less tendency to broach when running hard in a seaway than the transom sterned type whose full buoyant stern was lifted by a sea, depressing the fine forefoot.

Most mules had a well raked sternpost and the heel of the keel was curved up slightly for beaching, which was dangerous for a mule: when the stem touched the sand without the steadying effect of the draughts of the transom sterned coble, she might be thrown broadside in the surf. Mules were more sensitive on the helm than transom sterned cobles which had to have at least four feet of rudder below the stern when sailing

Plate 52. Model of a three-masted Yorkshire fishing lugger of the early nineteenth century. The fore and main topmasts are fitted on the after side of the mastheads. The mizzen mast is stepped to port, to clear the tiller, and the shapely, clinker planked hull has a lute stern. *Crown copyright. Science Museum, London.*

compared to the mules' usual two feet.

A mule's lugsail was cut with considerable peak compared to the square-headed shape of the transom sterned cobles and many carried a small lugsail for strong winds, to avoid the heavy bunch of reefed sail spoiling the set of the big lug. Small centreplates were sometimes fitted in mules, which lacked the deep foregripe of the transom sterned type and sailed better with a plate to increase the lateral plane. Some of the big mules were forty-two feet long with a beam thirteen feet and the depth of hull allowed the net room, aft of the foredeck cuddy, to be covered by loose floorboards. The net buoys and other gear were stowed aft.

Herring mules had a crew of four and carried a small coble. These large craft were even more gaily painted than the smaller cobles. Large mules were also owned at Filey and Flamborough, where their size and weight made them difficult to beach. Most were laid up in winter. During the herring season Whitby was much used by luggers from Scotland, East Anglia and Cornwall and by the Yorkshire 'yawls', many of which were owned at Scarborough and Filey.

Robin Hood's Bay

A few miles south of Whitby the village of Bay Town or Robin Hood's Bay as it is more widely known, clings to a steep hillside falling to a rocky coble landing, now deserted. The jumbled houses were once the homes of whalers and shipowners, mariners and fishermen. Bay Town had many cobles and in 1817 five large man boats were owned there, each about forty-six feet long with sixteen foot beam, clinker planked, decked, three masted, with a lugsail on each and costing about £600. Crewed by five or six men these boats carried two or three small cobles on deck and in winter fished on the Dogger Bank in the North Sea; a simple statement but evocative of the greatest hardship.

These luggers sailed on a Monday morning and hoped to return on a Friday or Saturday. On the grounds the luggers anchored, the cobles were launched and with one or two men in each, the crew set long lines in 'pieces' sixty fathoms long. Six of these made one line three hundred and sixty fathoms long and each coble set fifteen lines. As each line had hooks on a 'snood' or short piece of line spliced to the main line and set from 2ft 6in to 6ft apart, the number of hooks to be baited were a great labour to be done on the heaving deck of the lugger after a hard day's work. Halibut, turbot, cod, ling and skate were the principal catch and six tons might be taken by one boat. When landed, the catch was prepared and salted by the crew's wives and daughters and some, after sousing in brine, was dried in the sun and wind, but most was sent to markets inland.

These large luggers laid up at Christmas when the Dogger became too rough for even these hardy seamen, who then fitted out their large winter cobles to continue long lining inshore.

Each man in the coble had three lines, each two hundred to two hundred and forty fathoms long and with up to three hundred hooks. These were baited ashore, usually by their wives and daughters and were carried on an oval wickerwork 'skip'. The lines were fastened together and stretched about two and a half miles when shot, with a stone anchor and buoy at each end; all hauled by hand, in deep water alongshore during the winter and the shallower parts in summer and spring.

The crab cobles were small, as these had to be hauled ashore on wheels. Crab and lobster pots were made by the fishermen from withies and wood, to local traditional design, each attached by a rope strop about one and a half fathoms long to a rope 'tow' at eight or ten fathoms spacing. A coble might set fifty pots in a 'fleet' of gear.

In summer, when the herring season commenced, the luggers were recommissioned, sometimes sailing north to meet the herring shoals or waiting until these arrived in the area, then following them up the coast as far as Yarmouth in Norfolk, where the great autumn herring fishery attracted luggers from all parts of the east and south coasts.

The life of the Bay Town coble fishermen was well caught by Leo Walmsley in his book *Three Fevers* – the finest study of the outlook and work of inshore fishermen.

Scarborough

Scarborough was the home port of many cobles and a centre of the Yorkshire herring fishery which attracted craft from far away. The town, which developed to a northern resort, was built up the steep slopes above the man made harbour. About 1900 there were eighty sailing cobles owned there, with hulls painted in varied colours. During the 1870s the Scarborough fleet had also included about the same number of yawls and fifty trawling smacks, so it was a busy harbour, flanked by the frames and hulls of new craft building in its yards.

Many large herring cobles averaging thirty-five feet long and twelve feet beam were owned there. These were partly decked forward and were also used for long lining. A crew of four worked them for herring. Some were pointed sterned mules of large size.

By the 1840s Yorkshire coastal fishermen were ordering larger fishing craft for North Sea herring drifting and long lining. Some of the earliest of these lug rigged 'yawls' were owned at Filey and had clinker planked hulls about fifty feet long with a lute type stern. Rig was a boomless dipping lugsail set on a mast well forward, which could be lowered into a crutch when lying to drift nets, and a standing lug mizzen sheeted to a long outrigger. The mizzen had a fidded topmast and yard topsails could be set above the main and mizzen. From forward, the hull was divided into a net room, a fish well amidships, a warp room and a cabin aft with berths for four men and one large berth across the stern called the 'hullock', in which the boys slept tumbled together with the rudder stock groaning in the trunk by their heads. A crew of six was usual.

A wooden capstan was mounted abaft the warp room hatch and a twenty-three foot coble was shipped on deck when long lining at sea. Much of the lining was on the Dogger Bank and if the trip was to last more than three days, they carried ice to preserve the catch. Great quantities of bait were needed; mussels, sand eels and fish offal. In summer the yawls had to catch their own bait on the grounds with small mesh drift nets which were set from the coble. These fish were solely for baiting lines. After a day spent shooting and hauling several miles of lines by hand and clearing thousands of hooks, mostly from the coble, every man had to clear, bait and coil lines ready for the next day's fishing. With a good catch or if ice was running low, the yawl sailed for home, setting as much canvas as possible. The skippers feared calms much more than the fierce North Sea gales which made the seas on the Dogger break heavily. Nearing home in a calm, the coble was launched to tow the yawl under oars to land the catch as quickly as possible. Often the yawls anchored off the home port or the place where the highest prices were currently being obtained and put the catch ashore in barrels via the coble. At ports such as Whitby or Scarborough the yawls could berth in harbour, if the tide served.

When the yawls drifted for herring the one and a half mile long train of nets was hauled by a hand capstan with its bars turned by four or five hands who might tramp seven miles around it to grind in the dripping warp.

In September, large numbers of luggers arrived from east Scotland, Yarmouth, Lowestoft, Penzance, Newlyn and Porthleven for the herring fishery, following the shoals along the coast with the Yorkshire yawls. The concentrated hundreds of craft made a remarkable sight putting to sea for the night's drift fishing and their return brought trade and bustle to Scarborough. During the early 1880s some Yorkshire fishermen bought old Scottish luggers of fifie type from coastal ports south of Aberdeen. These were about fifty foot long and were sold cheaply, being locally called 'keelboats' to distinguish them from the cobles. On arrival at Scarborough, which was the principal port of use, the fore lug was discarded and a gaff mainsail, foresail and jib were substituted, though the lug mizzen was retained. These boats drifted for herring in summer with the fleets of large herring cobles. Other keelboats were owned at Filey, which was also prominent in the local herring fishery.

By 1900 progressive Whitby and Scarborough fishermen were turning to the steam drifters which were making the fortunes of many driftermen from other English and Scottish east coast ports. Scarborough fishermen made their

own oilskins by tanning sheepskins and then oiling them. Many coble fishermen tanned their working smocks and trousers when the sails were being 'barked'.

When Scarborough grew in prosperity as a seaside resort, some local cobles took to sailing pleasure parties in summer and the many hotels increased demand for fresh fish. Some Scarborough mules used for sailing with pleasure parties had brightly varnished sides and white bottoms.

Filey

Eight miles south, Filey shelters south of the cliffs at Filey Brigg. Cobles large and small have launched from its landings for centuries and in the past a large number of North Sea luggers and

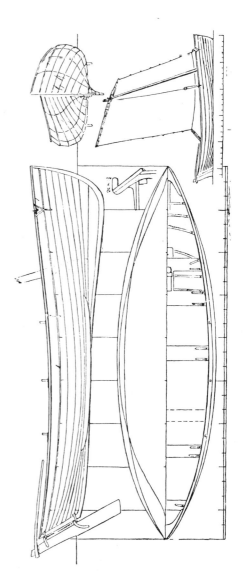

Figure 84. Lines and sail plan of S.H. 64, a Filey pointed stern 'mule' coble. Dimensions 26ft × 7ft. Drawing by George Holmes.

yawls were owned there. There were two coble landings and three coble builders including Cambridge, whose cobles were notably fast.

Filey cobles were hauled up on wheels by two or three horses which went well into the sea to be hooked on. Sixty-four cobles were owned there in 1866, long lining, drift netting and potting for crabs and lobsters. Some had pointed sterns and *SH, 64*, a typical small pointed stern mule coble from Filey is illustrated in Fig. 84. Principal dimensions were twenty-seven foot long with seven foot beam, and her hollow keel line is noticeable. Such a coble would set nine long lines which stretched three miles along the sea bed with 2500 hooks which had to be cleared, baited and re-coiled each night. Baits varied for different fish; liver or snails were used for haddock, whelks for cod and limpets for other fish. At low water the Filey fishermen's wives, daughters and young sons were out on the rocks gathering limpets for bait.

A man and a boy could work a twenty-seven foot sailing coble at inshore line fishing but many Filey men preferred to fish offshore in large cobles, some transom sterned but most of them pointed stern mules. Some of these worked on the Dogger and carried a 10ft long, deep hulled dinghy called a 'corfe' (calf) which had coble-like features. On the cod fishing grounds this could hold three men and a mile or so of long line and could carry a ton of fish, besides being able to live in rough water.

Filey cobles were painted blue inside and externally had each strake painted in a colour different to the adjoining ones.

Plate 53: Yorkshire 'mule' under sail, showing the types pointed stern. The rakish dipping lugsail has six reef bands and the luff is set taut with a bowline.
Photo – H. Cartlidge.

The 22ft 8in rowing and sailing coble *Joan and Robin* of Filey, built in 1930, was the last commercial coble to regularly use sail into the 1950s. Filey now has a large fleet of big motor cobles and remains a home of fishermen.

Flamborough
Flamborough village lies on the top of Flamborough Head and cobles were launched from the North Landing and the South Landing, on either side of the Head. So, whatever wind direction, one landing was sheltered and cobles could launch from it. In 1895 thirty large and eighty small cobles worked from the two landings.
The bay at the north landing is narrow and beaching there needed decisive handling. The

worst sea conditions were from the north, and a north east wind blew straight in. A steam driven capstan hauled cobles up the beach at the north landing, sliding up greased 'woods', and catches were also hauled up the steep slope from the beach in a box on skids. During northerly gales the cobles were hauled further inland.

Flamborough cobles were usually about twenty-seven feet long and were built with five planks each side. Baker Siddall built there and many of his cobles had centreboards. Others were built by Hergreaves Hopwood. These were painted blue inside and white outside, with a red sheerstrake.

As Flamborough village is two miles from the landings the fishermen used donkeys to carry their lines and gear; in the summer they were used to give donkey rides on the beach to trippers.

Two or three cobles were lost each winter from Flamborough, with loss of life, yet the fishermen carried on, for there were no other opportunities locally. Flamborough coble fishermen contributed to a coble 'club' and sickness payment fund and on the last Saturday in June a coble was taken round the village on a horse drawn cart, in a procession led by the village brass band, with fishermen carrying a banner depicting a sailing coble. This club provided insurance against loss of a coble and functioned until recent years for the few modern motor cobles still working here. The first engine was fitted in a Flamborough coble in about 1920.

Bridlington

Bridlington was a drying, tidal harbour, sheltered to the south of Flamborough Head, on the sweep of Bridlington Bay. Although the fishermen had no need to beach, the cobles retained the usual features and several Bridlington cobles had centreboards, but many were removed and these were probably difficult to position correctly in such strangely shaped craft.

Besides cobles there were a few smaller, pointed stern crab boats of the type common further south, particularly on the North Norfolk coast. The larger Bridlington cobles were at first pointed sterned mules but later ones were built with a transom stern. These had a foredeck enclosing a small cuddy and ranged up to thirty-five foot long and ten foot beam and were unsuitable for beaching, being intended for harbour moorings. These fished for herring during October and November using twenty-four nets to a boat, each sixty yards long by perhaps 5 yards deep. Line fishing started in November using whelks as bait.

The Bridlington trawling cobles were about thirty feet long and sometimes set a lug mizzen and jib on a bowsprit, which was generally used there in conjunction with a lugsail having greater peak than elsewhere, the yard being at the same angle as the jib luff and halyards, which it cleared.

Bill Raddings was the Bridlington sailmaker, followed by Bill Broadmeadows, who settled there from Burnham on Crouch in Essex and introduced better setting and stronger lugsails to Yorkshire.

About 1900 Bridlington cobles were often used to bunker steamships sheltering in the bay during periods of bad weather. Six or seven tons were taken off at a time and were whipped up in baskets to the ships' bunkers. They also took off provisions and swept for lost anchors.

As Bridlington grew in popularity for seaside visitors, many cobles were used to take parties of trippers for a sail.

In 1970 there were a dozen ex-sailing cobles, now fully powered, working from the harbour, the *Sunflower* being the most shapely example.

Spurn Point

Hornsea and Withernsea were fishing villages along the low shore which stretches south to Spurn Point, at the mouth of the River Humber. Cobles and crab boats launched from the beaches, the Hornsea craft being fitted with a keel and iron keel band as they were hauled up on 'skeats' (skids).

Crab and lobster fishing was the mainstay at Spurn Point, the curiously curving shingle spit at the Humber mouth, where the crab boats were indistinguishable from the North Norfolk type.

Probably the strangest use of lug rig occurred at Spurn where in 1914 a London firm of contractors laid a light railway line to carry materials from Spurn Point to Kilnsea Fort. It was worked by a steam tank engine. Until after 1919 there was no road along the Point and the light railway provided communication between the fort at its tip and the inhabited hinterland. When the solitary engine broke down the fort garrison and the local lifeboat crew used a four-wheeled railway flat car 'bogey' on which a large, borrowed standing lugsail was set, the mast being held upright by the 'crew'. Trim was adjusted by moving the mast heel across the deck. With a beam wind the car attained considerable speed. The lifeboatmen could sail it with the wind ahead but in gusts there was danger the car would derail and the sail was then usually stowed and the car pushed. When the lifeboat gun went it was all aboard the sailing rail car, sea boots thrusting into the sand to get her started while others 'set' the lugsail, the coxswain took the sheet, his other hand resting on a crude wooden brake. If the gale roared fair or allowed a fetch, this strange lugger click-clacked her way along the warren, heavily-loaded with men, sparks flying as she screeched to a stop. Running before a fresh breeze the car could attain twenty-five miles per hour and once hit the buffers at that speed, throwing the lifeboat crew overboard. By 1930 the sailing railway was abandoned and covered by the shifting sands.

Lincolnshire

Along the barren, flat Lincolnshire coast small cobles trawled whelks which were sent to other fishing ports as live bait for cod fishing. Cobles were owned at Skegness by the Grunnills and other families of Lincolnshire fishermen. Trawling smacks and larger craft used nearby Wainfleet Haven where one of the Grunnills later kept a steam launch used for long lining. A solitary motor coble now works from there.

Great Yarmouth

Cobles were unsuitable for the narrow, shoal channels and roaring tides of the Wash but the moving shoals of herring brought them south to East Anglia in autumn. Diaries of the bailiffs of the Cinque Ports of the sixteenth and seventeenth centuries refer to Yorkshire fishermen and their cobles which visited Yarmouth for the autumn herring fair. Larger ones were hired by the season to fish for merchants at Yarmouth which was for centuries the Norfolk centre of the herrings most profitable fishery. By the 1840s about sixty north east coast cobles were working from the port.

E. W. Cooke, the marine artist, found locally owned cobles at Yarmouth when he was preparing his *Shipping and Craft*, published in 1828, and cobles appear in several paintings of the Yarmouth district during the nineteenth century, though they seem to have become extinct by 1900. These were small craft, ranging from ten to perhaps twenty-five feet, with narrower strakes of planking than the cobles of the north east. Half models of cobles have been found on the Norfolk coast and at Pin Mill and Ipswich in Suffolk, so they must have been built in both counties. During the 1930s a lone Yorkshire sailing coble, sold south, was working off the beach at Felixstowe, Suffolk.

The Coble in the twentieth century

Improvement of motors after the 1914–18 war soon made the sailing coble obsolete and many were fitted with engines. Northumberland motor cobles carried a mast and lugsail into the 1950s, for emergency use, though probably none of their crews had ever handled a coble under sail. By that time the Yorkshire coble fishermen had long since discarded sail even for this purpose and preferred half decked cobles. They expected the lifeboat or a fellow fisherman to tow them in if the engine failed.

Motor cobles are still being built in the traditional way but without sails. These are single screw craft with the propeller working in a semi-tunnel for beaching, with an inspection cover at its crown. Alternatively the propeller is two bladed and its shaft has a universal joint, arranged to be retractable when launching or beaching, the propeller fitting snugly under the bottom, protected by the bilge keels.

Yorkshire cobles are now frequently tunnel sterned and half decked and are larger than those used in Northumberland. Many are still built with mule sterns. They remain a fascinating sea boat, but the lugsails are long since gone.

The Dusters of Grimsby and Hull

Watermen from the ports of Hull and Grimsby used spritsail and lug-rigged open boats in the swift, windy and rough tideway of the River Humber and its approaches, to tend ships lying in the roads or going in or out of dock. These smartly kept craft were known as 'gold dusters', or 'dusters' and were busy in sailing ship days.

Early Hull dusters averaged twenty-two feet length and had generous draught and wineglass sections, but these were gradually replaced by lighter boats which could be sailed or rowed. A typical Hull duster was 18ft long × 5ft 6in beam and had a plumb stem, long straight keel and a full midship section which blended into fine ends with hollow waterlines and a shapely transom stern. Centreboards were not used and the boats were often rowed in confined waters or in calms, which was more efficient than attempting to beat over a foul tide. The bow oar sat facing aft, the stroke

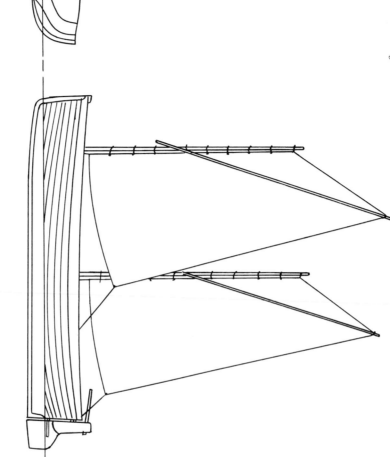

Figure 85. Hull waterman's boat or 'duster', with two spritsails. Dimensions 18ft × 5ft 6in. Circa 1900.

facing forward, the oars working in thole pins. Such a boat had four thwarts and a stern bench. Going alongside ships demanded a strong boat, well provided with fenders at the stem head and in way of each thwart. Dusters were locally built from a few moulds and differed in form and size. The clinker planking was half inch thick larch or oak on Canadian rock elm steamed timbers spaced six inches apart.

Hull dusters were rigged with two spritsails of almost equal area, set on masts of similar height and two feet shorter than the boat to permit stowage on the thwarts when lowered. Each sail had two reefs and a masthead brail to quickly furl them when going alongside a ship under way. The mainsheet was a single rope belayed to a pin in each quarter knee. Foresheets were double and belayed on cleats by the helmsman. In strong winds dusters sometimes sailed under the forward spritsail only, but usually needed help from an oar to get them round in stays.

Gold dusters went seeking ships down the Humber and sometimes as far outside as Hornsea, along the Yorkshire coast. When a likely inward-bounder appeared the watermen lay in her track and gaffed her with a large hook on a twelve foot stave having a length of rope attached. This was hooked to rigging or bulwarks and the boats crew eased away the rope to let the duster tow astern of the ship; a manoeuvre needing nerve and skill. Often dusters raced each other for the ship and the first to 'gaff' secured the ship's boating work during her stay in the Humber.

Grimsby dusters were more powerful than the Hull boats, as they needed to be working in the lower reaches of that tide racked estuary. A typical Grimsby boat was 21ft overall × 6ft 10in beam, slack in the bilge sections and fine at the ends with a false keel about a foot deep. Five thwarts were fitted, the mast being clamped to one just forward of amidships Although these boats could be rowed they were intended for serious sailing and early examples set two standing lugsails. Later, most adopted a single dipping lug having four rows of reef points and made from 'five stripe'; a strong, unbleached calico worked in nine inch cloths, hand sewn and well cut by J. Powell the local sailmaker. The lugsail was hoisted by a tye, usually of flexible steel wire rope with a single whip purchase set up to the weather gunwale. The masthead sheave was set fore and aft and the lugsail tack hooked inside the weather gunwale, the forward hook being about sixteen inches abaft the fore side of stem, the second twenty-two inches, followed by two others each eleven inches apart. (Fig. 86). Off the wind a light boom was used to extend the lugsail clew, shipped to the mast with jaws.

Eight to twelve heavy pigs of iron ballast were carried and a few boats had about three hundredweight of lead run into their false keels, making them stiffer and more weatherly. The watermen took great pride in their boats, which were smartly painted and varnished, with gear of the best. They enjoyed an annual race or two, which were keenly contested and the boat with lead on her keel usually won.

The dusters work declined with the passing of sailing ships, but some survivors lingered at Hull and Grimsby into the 1920s.

Figure 86. Grimsby waterman's boat or 'duster', rigged with a single dipping lugsail. Dimensions 21ft × 6ft 10in. Circa 1905.

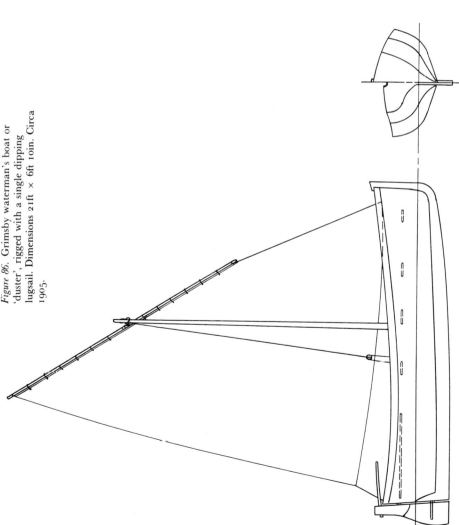
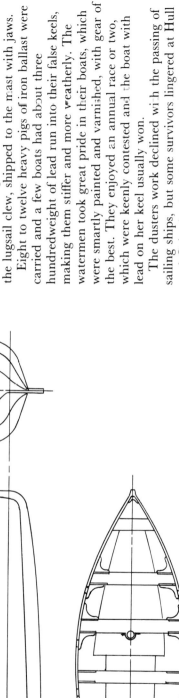

9

Norfolk and Suffolk

Norfolk's ninety miles of coastline faces the Wash and the cold, grey North Sea. Much of it is bounded by beaches, with scattered villages and small towns of hardy beachmen who evolved light, sailing and rowing boats to launch off for fishing, tending ships or salvaging.

Crab Boats

Amongst several types of lugsail-rigged inshore fishing craft working from Norfolk's north coast, the most characteristic were the crab boats of Sheringham, Cromer, Overstrand, Mundsley, Trimingham and Bacton. Their origin is uncertain but a map of 1586 shows a similar, pointed stern craft and there were a number of illustrations of them after about 1750. In 1828 E. W. Cooke drew one which hardly differed from those now in use (Plate 54).

The rocky sea bottom off that coast is ideal ground for crabs and lobsters. Local beach boats worked this fishery with circular hoop nets baited with fish offal, which were hauled up quickly at intervals to catch feeding shelfish. Catches were sold locally, mainly to buyers from Norwich, Norfolk's inland city. Crab pots were introduced

about 1850 when there were about fifty small luggers launching off Cromer beach, each manned by two men and setting between thirty and thirty-five pots. The railway reached the north Norfolk coast towns and villages soon after and transformed Cromer and Sheringham into seaside resorts, with hotels and boarding houses requiring lobsters and crabs in quantity, and rail carriage encouraged increased catches, particularly crabs, to be distributed to other resorts and customers far away.

By the 1870s the crab season lasted from April to June and the lobster season from mid-July until September. The fishermen voluntarily agreed not to land a crab less than four and a half inches across the shell under a penalty of £1, then a considerable sum. Anyone landing a reproducing lobster was liable to a heavy fine.

Form and construction

Crab boats varied in size and form, the boatbuilder altering both to the owner's briefly worded request for 'A boat like so and so's, but with a finer entry' or 'Three inches more beam, I reckon.' The resulting craft were frequently built without moulds, or with very few. Length varied from fifteen to nineteen feet and beam from five to seven feet. Rig was a single dipping lugsail without a boom. A typical boat was twelve to fourteen feet long on the keel and from sixteen to eighteen feet overall length with seven feet beam and two foot nine inches draught. The pointed stern hull had considerable rise of floor and fine ends, with hollow waterline endings. The bottom and stern shape enabled the boats to be beached in a sea, when they were allowed to slew broadside on and cant towards the beach, allowing the seas to wash around the hull instead of breaking inboard, as would happen with a flatter bottomed boat. This form also enabled the crab boats to have sufficient draught for windward sailing with minimum ballast.

Centreplates were not used and the boats made long tacks. The keel and the rounded stem and sternpost were of oak, the garboard strake, locally called the 'sand strake' was of English elm, the sheerstrake was oak and the remaining clinker planking was half inch thick oak, though later boats which were also much used for whelking had larch planking, to facilitate repair to the damage often suffered in that trade. Some later hulls were planked in pine, with sheerstrakes of English elm. The bent timbers were joggled over the plank lands to give maximum support to the planking. Many crab boats had floors of the same scantlings as the bent timbers, placed between these throughout the bottom and extending to the thwart risings. Some had six sawn floors, locally termed 'wrongs' (probably from the Dutch *vrang* = floor). Timbers were one and a quarter

Plate 54. E. W. Cooke drew these pointed-stern Cromer crab boats in the 1820s. The hull shape and arrangements remain almost unaltered in their motor powered descendants.

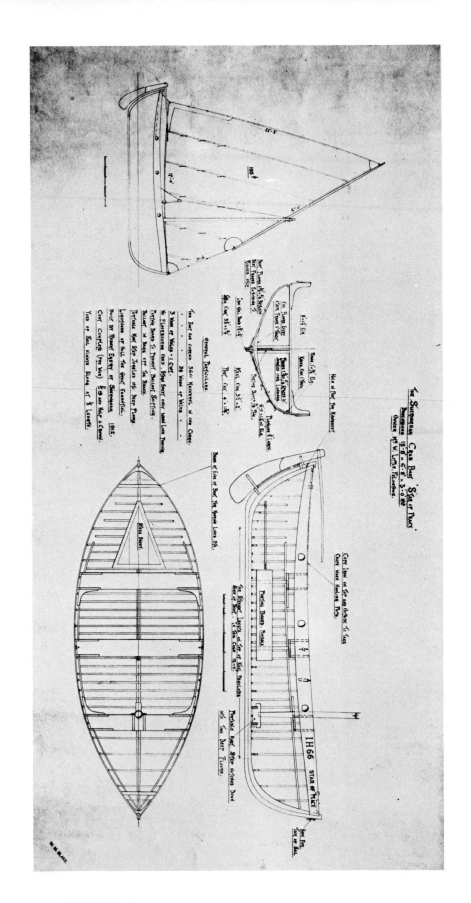

Figure 87. Sail plan and arrangement of the 18ft 8in Sheringham, Norfolk crab boat *Star of Peace.* Plans taken off when she was fishing from Felixstowe, Suffolk. *Science Museum, London.*

272

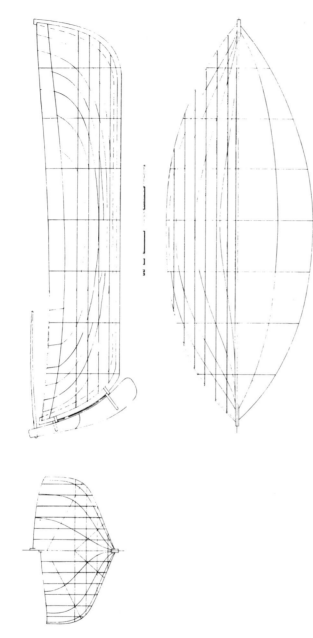

Figure 88. Lines of the Sheringham, Norfolk crab boat *Star of Peace.* Dimensions 18ft 8in × 6ft 8in × 3ft depth. *Science Museum, London.*

suggestive of the similarity of early lugsails to the lateen. The tack secured to a hook on the face of the stemhead when going to windward, but when running was shifted to one of the hooks inside the washstrake, two or three feet abaft the stem on each side. The single part sheet led through a hole through the head of the sternpost, along the side and in through the after arruck hole, to be held in the helmsman's hand.

A typical eighteen foot crab boat had a fourteen foot mast and an 18ft fin yard for the lugsail. The yard hooked to an iron mast traveller and hoisted by a single halyard through the masthead sheave, leading to a purchase of two

inch square oak or ash, spaced about five inches apart. A gunwale was not fitted but the boats had a washstrake, capped with convex iron to take the chafe of fishing gear. Oar ports known as 'arruck holes' were cut in the sheerstrake, usually three on each side. These prevented the oars from unshipping when pulling through a surf. There were three thwarts, the mast stepping through the forward one.

The usual rig at Cromer and Sheringham was a single dipping lugsail of 100–120 square feet, short in the luff but high peaked and having three rows of reef points. It was dressed for preservation until almost black. The shape of the sail was

273

single blocks. The halyard was the only rigging supporting the mast and was always set up to windward. Mast and yard were of spruce or pine, though in later years a bamboo yard might be used for lightness, particularly if racing in the coast regattas.

Ballast was four or five canvas bags of beach shingle stowed on the weather side of a fore and aft shifting board, fitted on the centreline amidships. These were shifted at each tack and were emptied overboard on beaching. The boats sailed surprisingly well to windward in long tacks and strong breezes but could have been improved by the fitting of a centreplate. This was successfully tried in one sailed for pleasure, but the fishermen would not adopt it, if only that its case would interfere with fishing operations, and relied on the sharp rise of floor and fine ends, plus the rudder which projected down about two feet below the heel of the keel to provide further effective lateral plane.

When working fishing gear the sail was stowed on the yard and with the mast, which was often unstepped, was placed forward out of the way while hauling, emptying and shooting crab pots or hauling and shooting long lines. The helmsman stood in the stern sheets but no other floorboards were fitted, to reduce weight of handling ashore. He had to stand or lean against the boat's sides, or a beam which braced the quarters. A wooden trunked, simple bilge pump was usually installed on the port side.

Like beachmen in many parts of the world the Sheringham and Cromer men liked colour. Typically the sheer and the next lower strake might be red or blue, the next white and the lower strakes black.

Handling

Early each morning in the fishing seasons, unless a gale was blowing or threatened, the north Norfolk crab fishermen launched off the beaches. This was a community effort, sometimes running the boats down on rollers, sometimes lifting them by oars passed through the arruck holes. In fine weather the two man crew pushed her off, a pair of oars projecting like wings from the arruck holes, ready for the pull offshore (Plate 55). In boisterous conditions with one man on board, the boat was poised by the alongshore wash, waiting a suitable wave. Then half a dozen men thrust her out while the boatman pulled a pair of oars to row clear of the surf and anchor off to await his mate, lashing the oars forward out of the way, to the sheerstrake or an oar port. In 1807 two Sheringham boats were overwhelmed in a sudden gale after leaving the beach and seven men were drowned.

The last boat brought off all the crews for the boats already launched, besides his own. The lugsails went up and the boats sailed or rowed seawards to the grounds which might lie in sight of the shore. Each crew scanned for marks and buoys defining their pots. Having sighted their buoy marking the first 'set' of pots, both men tied on oilskin aprons to protect clothing and depending on weather and tide, the sail might be lowered and stowed. The helmsman fetched the buoy on board, to be stowed forward with its anchor. Then he hauled in the line hand over had oak bottoms with four hazel hoops covered with netting and an entrance spout. Each was ballasted with a stone or piece of scrap iron. There were twenty-five pots in a 'shank' and each pot was separated by fourteen fathoms of rope known as the 'tow'. A boat might work six shanks, all of which were hauled by hand. Twenty large pots filled available space in an eighteen footer and needed careful stowing; four flat, five on edge, five more on edge fitting between the second row, four on top, high above the gunwale and the last ones in the sternsheets. The hauler rarely paused except to pass a pot to his mate who usually dealt with one pot, including quick repairs to its mesh, just in time to receive the next.

Hauling twenty or twenty-five ballasted pots was hard work and after the last pot came the second anchor. The boat was then rowed or sailed back to approximately the previous position for shooting the pots in a long line. When all the shanks were shot the crab boat returned with the catch.

When beaching, the boats were usually rowed in. The crew jumped overboard as she grounded and hauled up as far as possible, then hauled her round broadside, if the wind was onshore, leaving her canted towards the shore for the waves to push her up further. Rollers were fetched and helpers assisted in getting her up. Sometimes they passed oars through the arruck holes from side to side and crooked one arm under the oar loom and with the other reached over the washstrake to grasp the risings, or longitudinals supporting the thwarts, inside the boat. With four or six men on each side the boat would then be carried up the

Plate 55. Sheringham, Norfolk, crab boats launching off the beach with dipping lug ready to hoist when the boat is rowed clear of the surf. *Photo – Judges Ltd.*

hand, leaving it coiled in the stern. His mate stood between the second and third thwarts to take the pots as each came, untied them and grabbed the catch behind the claws before they grabbed him. Lobsters went forward and crabs in a pen under the amidship thwart. Undersized and soft shelled crabs went overboard. Bait of dogfish, sea toads and other 'offal' from trawling ports was fixed and down went the lid, the pot being placed between first and second thwarts, with the line pushed to one side for clear running. The pots beach to lie in her shore position with a stool under each bilge.

If possible, beaching at low water was preferred, landing on the sands below the shingle. During infrequent, settled weather the crab boats were left anchored off the beaches, the catch being put ashore in other boats. Prices for the catch varied with season and demand. Much of it was sold to local hotels and fishmongers and some was sent off by rail. James Pegg of the well known Sheringham family of beachmen and lifeboatmen was born about 1882 and remembered selling crabs for a penny each and lobsters for nine pence or one shilling a pound.

Crab boats were also used for whelking, particularly by Sheringham men. The whelks were found well offshore, often up to fifteen miles seawards and in calms the boats had to be rowed all the way out and after hauling, clearing, rebating and shooting the whelk pots, they rowed all the way home. There were thirty-six pots on a shank, separated by a tow of fifteen fathoms, and up to six shanks were worked by each boat. A nineteen foot boat might carry thirty-eight wash of whelks weighing about 1350 pounds.

Constant launching and hauling up Sheringham's stony beach kept boatbuilders busy repairing and building crabbers, which did not last long on that boisterous coast. Many were built there by Lown and later by John Johnson, also by Lewis and Robert Emery whose shop had been a Salvation Army citadel. There a whelker was often building on the ground floor and two smaller crab boats on the first floor, to be lowered out of the end doors to the ground on completion.

In 1912 Robert built a nineteen foot crabber, complete, for £19-2s-6d, which could not have given him any profit. Other crab boat and whelker builders included Howard Brett of Cley, William Starling of Blakeney, Tom Dack and Whittaker of Wells and Gaze of Mundesley.

In 1915 a single cylinder petrol engine was fitted in a crab boat and others quickly followed. When motors were introduced in the boats Robert Emery discussed improvements of the type with the fisherman 'Go farther' Pegg. They produced a new shape of hull with steeper rise of floor, a high, hard bilge and fuller quarters to provide adequate buoyancy under power. When the lugsail, which the boats still carried in case of engine breakdown, was set, they proved to be faster than the old pure sailing type, planing like a dinghy on a reach in a breeze and astonishing the builder; so much for traditional evolution!

One crab boat was bought by an amateur sailor who rerigged her as a sloop with a gaff and boom mainsail, a foresail set on a short bowsprit and a yard topsail for light airs. He sailed her around England, putting in each night at some port, or beaching where this was impossible.

Similar small luggers worked from Bacton, which about 1890 was a thriving village with a quay used by colliers, all now covered by the shifting beach. The Bacton boats dredged whelks off Happisburgh. They were used to bait long lines laid off Winterton in summer for skate. In winter they fished for cod and in spring and autumn drifted for inshore herring.

Many Norfolk beachmen moved to the then developing Lincolnshire fishing port of Grimsby and at one time seventeen Norfolk-style crabbers were moored at Grimsby fish dock and the south Yorkshire coastal villages of Hornsea, Withernsea and Spurn had half a dozen each. Other Sheringham fishermen worked during part of the winter from the Lincolnshire coast in the Mablethorpe district and a Cromer man named Harrison moved his boat and pots by rail to and from Yorkshire for the seasonal fishing. In the early 1920s Mr Little, a Sheringham fisherman, moved to Felixstowe in south east Suffolk and worked his crab boats *Rose* and *Star of Peace* off the beach. Another Sheringham 'colony' of whelkers was established at Whitstable the small harbour on the Kent coast of the Thames Estuary.

The Hovellers

Larger luggers known as 'hovellers' also worked from Cromer and Sheringham beaches. These were about fifteen feet keel length but the well raked ends made them longer overall. The name suggests use in salvaging and tending shipping, but the boats appear to have been principally used for herring and mackerel drifting and long lining for cod.

The hovellers were rigged with a dipping lug, like the crab boats, and resembled these in form and construction. When used for herring drifting a removable cuddy was shipped forward and the forward arruck holes of the four or five on each side were closed with fitted cork plugs, the use of a box-like removable cuddy to provide primitive accommodation, in common with many beaching craft of the Kentish coast, may have something to

do with the ill defined word 'hoveller', which usually signified a craft used primarily for giving pilotage or other assistance to shipping.

At Sheringham the cod liner's catch was laid out on the beach for auction by the boat owner who, when bidding had reached finality, banged two beach stones together to signify conclusion of the sale; a practice persisting at nearby Cley during the 1930s and which is believed to have existed in many places where cod was sold, giving rise to the term 'cod banger' for these fishermen.

Hovellers were also used for whelking, laying plaited pots for these small, snail-like shellfish which were much used for bait for long lining. Sheringham whelkers were known as 'shannocks' and their trade and boats spread to Wells Next The Sea; an old Norfolk port whose entrance was badly silted with a bar dangerous in onshore winds. Some crab boats and hovellers dredged mussels in or near the harbours of Wells and nearby Blakeney. For this work in confined waters, with much manoeuvring, the rig was changed to gaff and boom sloops or cutters.

Pinkers and Dandies

Until the mid-nineteenth century, larger half-decked luggers called 'pinkers' fished from Cromer for cod and are believed to have been similar to the Yarmouth luggers, but had a pink stern hence the name. This shape was once common in coasting and some fishing vessels and was later used in north eastern America where a type of small fishing schooner was known as a 'pinky'.

Cromer and Sheringham also had larger luggers known as 'great boats', built at Great

Yarmouth and similar to the three masted fishing luggers built and owned there. During the 1870s many were converted to dandy rig, with a boomless gaff mainsail and standing lug mizzen. These luggers followed the herring shoals off the Yorkshire coast, using Scarborough as a port, besides drifting in the autumn 'home' fishery for herring from Great Yarmouth. Part of the year was spent long lining for cod and from the last week of March until June or July, many were crabbing off the Yorkshire coast, carrying two crab boats on deck to work the strings of pots and getting them overside by masthead tackles. The catches were landed at Grimsby.

After the herring fishery some Cromer luggers sailed 'down the north', lining for cod, again landing at Grimsby and ports on the Yorkshire coast. Crab boats were again carried on deck for laying and recovering the lines which were baited with Dutch eels imported in tubs. The luggers returned to Cromer in spring to fit out for crabbing and on the voyage home brought quantities of crabs caught off the Yorkshire coast which were shot overboard off Cromer to help replenish the local resource. At Cromer a crab of light brown colour was called a 'Yorkshireman'.

During the 1860s about forty large luggers were owned at Cromer, Sheringham and nearby fishing villages but by 1880 the fleet had shrunk to thirty; two of them converted to dandy rig. By the 1890s only four luggers remained and seven dandies, including one original large lugger. In the heyday over thirty of the large luggers were owned at Sheringham and about twelve or so at Cromer, the others in Northrepps, Overstrand and Runton. Some were built at Cromer. Most were owned by families of fishermen, all having shares in the boat and her gear. A crew of ten was shipped for the herring voyage; probably four of them would be local fishermen, members of the owning family, and the remainder were capstan hands recruited from the surrounding countryside and paid on a rate related to the catch. Many of these men were farm workers at other seasons and these crews became known as 'half and halfers'. The large luggers returned home two or three times annually to land their nets and gear before laying up at Great Yarmouth or in Blakeney harbour, or to fit out with new gear which was ferried off in crab boats while the luggers anchored offshore. Life on board these luggers was hard; crews having occasionally been reduced to eating dogfish fried in tallow candles. Occasionally disaster struck the fleet; in 1858 the Cromer lugger *Brothers* was lost during the herring voyage and another was wrecked at Beeston, to the east of Sheringham, where the fleet was caught by a gale as they lay off shipping gear. She drove ashore, capsized and her crew of eleven drowned. A man was lowered down the cliff to identify the battered hull pounding in the surf of the inaccessible beach.

Now full powered crab boats lie on Sheringham and Cromer beaches. Though all, even those built of plastic resemble the form and appearance, of the sailing craft, not one sports a lugsail.

The Norfolk canoe
Further west along the north Norfolk coast at Cley and Blakeney the shore is indented with

marshes, intersected by winding creeks, and a type of simple flat bottomed boat, locally called a 'canoe', was developed to carry loads of mussels from the scaups, or banks, to these villages. Average dimensions are 13ft 6in to 16ft length overall, beam 4ft 10in to 5ft 9in. The bottom is not absolutely flat, being rockered about two inches in its length and cambered about half an inch in breadth; known locally as 'kammel', probably a corruption of the more correct term 'camber'. This feature is also found in the Somerset flatners (Chapter 7).

Side planking is laid with lapped seams and up to three or five strakes each side, meeting the bottom at a chine. Sawn frames are fitted, fairly straight forward and amidships but often shaped aft where the stern has some attempt at an 'S' shaped run, though the bottom is carried out to a flat at the transom, often eight or nine inches wide, the effect being like a tuck-sterned boat with the bottom cut off. This feature is believed to be unique in Britain but was used in many American and some Danish small craft. It was necessary to increase displacement without seriously increasing draught when carrying loads of mussels. Often the boats were loaded to within six inches of the gunwale.

The term canoe may derive from the canots which were nested for stowage on the decks of the French cod fishing schooners, several of which were wrecked on the Norfolk coast; the last, *La Gracieuse*, in 1912. The boats of these craft were much sought by locals and copied. It is difficult to avoid speculation on this term as for instance, the boarding boats carried by New York pilot schooners in the days of sail were referred to as 'canoes'.

The Norfolk canoes first appeared on a photograph taken in 1865 and probably originated much earlier than that, but few drawings or pictures of them exist. As these were built in several places, usually by their owners, design and construction varied At Wells, Whittaker built with broad, heart-shaped transoms which were practical and handsome. Others were built by 'Kammy' Brett at Cley. English elm was preferred for bottom planking and the side planking, on oak frames and knees. Fastenings were frequently galvanised steel nails, though earlier canoes were copper fastened. Traditionally Blakeney canoes were painted white.

Canoes were rowed or poled and set a boomless standing lugsail. Steering was an oar over the stern. To get them to windward they were trimmed down by the bow, using the crew's weight, and the steering oar was held over the lee quarter to act partially as a leeboard. When light they were heeled gently to leeward by the crew's weight but care was needed to prevent capsize. Canoes rowed badly when light but improved when deep loaded. The type is still in use and an occasional one is built in somebody's garden.

The East Anglian beachmen

The lug-rigged beach yawls of Norfolk and Suffolk were amongst the largest and fastest open seaboats and developed during the eighteenth and nineteenth centuries to attend shipping off the East Anglian coast. Beachmen have been active along that shore at least since the fourteenth century, when shipping first began to regularly carry coals from the north east coast to London. As the North Sea became an established route for a variety of shipping, there was increasing need for the services of small craft from the shore of East Anglia, where the roadsteads off Great Yarmouth, Lowestoft and Southwold offered some protection. These were often crowded with ships lying windbound for days, or awaiting improvement in the weather. Unhandy, square-rigged vessels and schooners and ketches swung at anchor, constantly threatened by collision, by being run down by other vessels which had a fair wind, or of foundering or driving from anchor in gales. If they anchored for a long time provisions might run short.

Sometimes there were hundreds. In April 1843 almost seven hundred ships lay windbound in Sole Bay, off Southwold, Suffolk. Onshore gales caused widespread loss and damage; in 1692 two hundred ships were driven ashore from Yarmouth Roads in one gale and a storm in 1836 stranded twenty-three ships on Great Yarmouth beach, with a score of others wrecked nearby.

Small boats launched from the beaches soon made the most of such opportunities and the Napoleonic wars provided a long period of prosperity for the Norfolk and Suffolk beachmen. Warships and merchant vessels frequently anchored in the roadsteads in numbers and required pilotage, stores and other attendance. Masters of seagoing merchantmen made much use of the beach boats as few could trust a boat's crew not to desert, once ashore. the beachmen

took off anchors to ships which had cut and run in a gale and sometimes cables and spare spars. Of the many badly found, leaky and ill manned ships stranded or wrecked, about half were colliers, usually brigs from the north east coast of England.

In the mid-nineteenth-century heyday there might be 50,000 passages past Great Yarmouth by vessels each year and in a gale there would be several hundreds lying in the Roads, so the scope of the work can be appreciated. Local conditions were similar to the Kentish Downs though usually smaller numbers of ships were involved.

The communities of the Suffolk and Norfolk coasts responded to this opportunity to seek salvage, provide assistance, take off stores, anchors and cables and, if necessary, extra hands for pumping and ship handling; all at a price. They also saved life and landed them from outward bound ships and boarded pilots to inward bounders. After institution of pilotage authorities the locals offered unlicensed pilotage. But salvage of vessels that had grounded or from the wrecks they became was the beachmen's principal business and they made hard bargains when by their skilled aid a vessel might be brought off a shoal or piloted to safety. Probably many a captain whose storm battered ship was at last safely anchored in Lowestoft or Yarmouth Roads, or moored in harbour, regretted the arrangement he had made with the crew of the lean yawl plunging alongside in the howling blackness a few hours previously in response to his burning tar barrel, but took comfort that had he not done so she might not still exist, and nor might he.

Salvage companies

The beachmen were organised into 'companies' which existed in East Anglia during the early eighteenth century. The Old Company was established at Lowestoft about 1800. Each company owned a shed with a waiting room or 'court' attached, on the beach. By it was a lookout tower. A company owned one or more yawls for salvage or other work in bad weather or for carrying off stores or pilots, two or three gigs, a smaller pulling boat for boarding and landing pilots or people from ships in fine weather, and perhaps other boats such as the burdensome type called 'ferry boats' which were used to land fish from luggers and smacks in Yarmouth Roads, or for taking off anchors or other weights.

There were beach companies along forty miles of the Norfolk and Suffolk coasts, from Winterton in the north to Aldeburgh in the south. They were sited at Winterton, Palling, Caister and California, north of Great Yarmouth, Norfolk's principal port, where during the early nineteenth century beach companies were often known by the surname of the principal and included Laytons and Dennys (later Denny and Brock). By the 1850s there were the Holkham, Standard, Young, Diamond, Roberts, Star and Dennys companies, most of which had nicknames such as the 'Young 'uns', 'Silver Spoons', 'Strong 'uns' and 'Wiggle Bums'. At Gorleston the Storm and Ranger companies launched off the beach and, further south at the Suffolk port of Lowestoft were the Old Company, the Young Company and the North Roads Company. The villages of Pakefield and Kessingland had one each and the old town

of Southwold had the Kilcock Cliff Company and two expressing local connections with America; the Long Island Company and the New York Cliff Company. Southold, Long Island, New York state was colonised by emigrants from Southwold who sailed from Great Yarmouth in the ship *Mary Anne* during 1637.

Further south there was a company at Thorpness and two at the ancient borough of Aldeburgh; the Upstreeters and the Downstreeters, whose brick lookout towers remain a feature of the sea front of this charming beach town.

A company might comprise twenty to a hundred or more members. Printed 'Rules and Regulations of the Caister Company of Beachmen' laid down that it was 'formed for the purpose of saving property and of rendering assistance to vessels or ships aground, stranded or wrecked on the sands or beach, or in any kind of difficulty, distress or disaster at sea, consists of forty shareholders, having an equal share, right and interest in certain boats, boat house or shed, tackling, etc . . .'

All profits were placed in common fund, to be regularly shared out. On joining, a member paid his share subscription entitling him to a place in the crew of the yawl or other company craft at launch, if there was room. However, as all members could not usually be employed at a call and to maintain keenness, most companies had a rule for attendance, as at Caister where it defined that 'Every man who shall touch any coble, gig, yawl or outrigger of the same, or any boat, belonging to or in the use of the company, as she

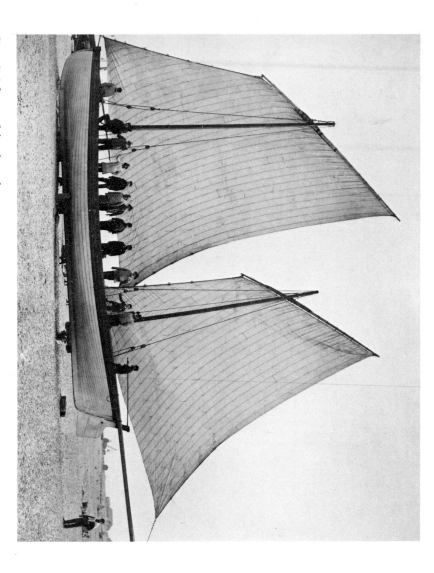

Plate 56. A Lowestoft beach yawl stretches her lugsails for the camera with the usual working crew on board. Photo – Ford Jenkins.

is going off to any vessel, shall be considered as belonging to that boat, and shall be entitled to an equal share of the earnings and emoluments of that boat, to which he shall thus be considered to belong'. There were other rules, including means to share salvage money when more than one boat took part.

Money earned for a job was divided in varying amounts. Each company member serving in or touching the boat or her setting pole at launch received a 'dole', as each share was termed. Each sailing yawl was allotted four doles for maintenance and each rowing gig two. A half dole was given to every aged or sick member, or to a widow. In the heyday there were substantial numbers of beachmen. Yarmouth companies had about a hundred and eighty members, Caister forty, California thirty, Newport fourteen and Winterton sixty, divided into two companies which specialised in pilot work. In 1882 at Lowestoft, there were a hundred and nineteen members of the Old Company, ninety of the Young Company and about seventy in the North Roads Company. The nearby Pakefield Company also had about seventy members.

Palling, Norfolk, had an active beach company with about forty members using several yawls and two pulling and sailing lifeboats. They had the world's second highest record for life saving a century ago and a beachman was always on lookout from their watch hut on the beach, the uneasy surf of the North Sea creaming alongshore, with the dreaded Haisborough Sands eight miles seawards: a graveyard of hundreds of ships. If something caught attention the lookout clambered up to a square box at the top of a fifty foot spar which stood upright in the beach. From this his telescope could scan miles of sea and shipping.

At the end of the nineteenth century the Palling beachmen's watch was reinforced by the naval coastguards whose station on the dunes was manned by a petty officer and four or five ratings who had a line throwing mortar and later a small lifeboat provided by a local resident. If coastguard or beachman spied a ship with distress signals, or heard the boom of the guns of light vessels off the sands warning of a ship ashore, the mortar was fired twice to summon the beachmen from their ordinary occupations of farm work, fishing and other things, to man the lifeboat, if a beach yawl had not already gone off or if it was bad weather. There, too, it was a rule that any man who failed to touch the boat before she went off could not share in any salvage money she might earn.

Despite the gradual growth in the numbers of lifeboats during the nineteenth century, much of the lifesaving was done by the yawls. The English term yawl is generally thought to be of norse origin, from the scandinavian 'yoll' or 'jolle', applied to many pointed stern small boats. However, I feel it more probably originated from a type of Phoenician trading vessel called a *gaulos*, as many British maritime words and traditions probably owe more to Mediterranean and French influence than is realised.

Form and construction of the yawls

Many beach yawls and gigs were built at Great Yarmouth by Hastings Brothers, Spence Brothers, James Beeching and later by J. and H. Beeching, with others by Jermyn and Mack. Several Lowestoft builders constructed them and at Southwold, James Critten built at least six beach yawls between 1846 and 1870: the *Reliance, John Bull, Swiftsure, Young Reliance, Bittern* and the fifty foot *Nil Desperandum* which he launched in 1856 for the Kilcock Cliff Company at a cost of £1-6s-6d per foot of length. Shares in her offered at £3 each were soon taken.

Some older yawls were about seventy feet long with twelve feet beam. Later ones averaged fifty feet long with ten feet beam and carried about one and a half or two tons of shingle shifting ballast in white painted canvas bags, besides some pig iron. The crew varied from fifteen to twenty-five men. The 69ft three masted yawl *Reindeer* of Great Yarmouth cost about £250 to build and needed thirty men to sail her. A ferry boat then cost about £40 and a gig £20.

Yawls usually had pointed sterns though some had finely shaped transoms. All had fine forward and after waterlines and a narrow but flat floored midship section with small bilge radius. The hull was clinker planked on small sectioned bent timbers. Despite having eight or nine thwarts and associated knees the hulls were flexible and twisted considerably in a seaway or during hauling out. Keel and centreline were oak with a pine keelson. Planking was often American white pine on oak timbers. Earlier yawls were planked in oak, which withstood wear better than pine. A bilge stringer was fitted for about two thirds of the length amidships and all fastenings were copper.

The following typical specification and scantlings are of the yawl *Band of Hope*, built by Beeching Brothers of Great Yarmouth in 1897:

Length 51ft 2in. Beam 10ft 11in. Depth 3ft 4in.
Plus 6in washstrakes.
Keel 7in × 3in. With 1½in thick keelband, tapered at ends.
Hog piece. 5in × 1in.
Keelson. 6in × 8in.
Stem. 3in × 5½in at head.
Sternpost. 3in × 5½in at head.
Timbers 1in × 1½in on 7 inch centres. Scored.
Gunwale. 2½in × 2½in.
Planking. ⅝in thick. 16 planks a side. Nail between each timber.
Three 2in floors in bow.
Four 2in floors in stern.
Thwarts. 7in × 1¼in.
Risings. 13in below rail at amidships.
Bilge piece. 3in × 1½in inside.
Four bilge splines outside.
Fastenings in planking, bolts through keel, etc. copper.
Foremast 7in diameter at rail. Square at heel.
Mizzen. 7in diameter at rail. Square at heel.
Outrigger. 6in diameter at sternpost.
Rudder blade. 2in. 12in below keel.
Fastenings in planking, etc. copper.
Bolts through keel, etc.

There were light gratings forward and aft for helmsman and bowman and bottom boards amidships. Beams were fitted forward and aft to support the gunwales, a washstrake was shipped above the gunwales and square oar ports were cut in this for rowing. When sailing these could be closed by sliding shutters. Yawls were rowed in calms or light head winds when their length allowed attainment of considerable speed. Oars were also frequently used to bring them round when tacking, as the long straight keel made them very slow in stays. The masts stepped between longitudinal timbers between two thwarts. These were called 'lears' and steadied the masts when being raised or lowered. Until the mid-nineteenth century most beach yawls were rigged as three masted luggers setting a total of 1,500 square feet, or more. The mainmast and its large lugsail was sometimes left ashore in winter or for a special job such as taking off a large anchor and cable. Three masters set a large main dipping lugsail, a slightly smaller dipping lug foresail and a much smaller standing lug mizzen, stepped just inside the sternpost and sheeted to a long outrigger. In fine weather a large jib was set on a running bowsprit.

Yawls had two suits of sails; one of light canvas for summer or fine weather use and the other of heavy canvas for winter, with three or four rows of reef points. By the 1860s the mainmast was more frequently discarded and the yawl *Mosquito*, built in 1853 for the Young Company of Lowestoft and named for the famous racing yacht, was the first built with the foresail and mizzen rig which quickly became usual.

The fore lug tack was hooked into a short bumkin projecting from the stemhead. It often had two hooks. The smaller winter foresail hooked inside the stemhead ringbolt. The forelug and the main, if carried, had two sheets which led through a ringbolt at the sheerstrake on each side. the lee sheet was brought in to the samson post forward of amidships and an experienced sheetman kept a couple of turns around this, surging it as felt necessary in the puffs and keeping an eye on the helmsman's intentions. When tacking, the fore lug and if carried, the main lug had to be lowered and the tack unhooked, the yard and sail were brought round abaft the mast the sheet was unhooked, the halyard shifted to windward, the tack hooked in again and the sail was re-hoisted. As she came round, perhaps helped by a pull on a bow oar, the ballast bags were flung up to the new weather bilge.

The mizzenmast had pronounced forward rake and the mizzen outrigger was termed the 'outligger' by the beachmen. In summer or light winds the mizzen tack was taken to a hook or a strop on the thwart just forward of the mast. In winter or strong winds it was set up to the mast heel.

A yawl fifty foot long with a beam of ten feet might have a twenty-nine foot foremast and a twenty-six foot mizzen, with the mizzen outrigger about nineteen foot outboard. Masts were made from young fir trees and the fore lug yard was twenty-nine feet long and the mizzen twenty-four feet.

Fore and main halyards were burtons, set up to windward. The mizzen was stayed with a burton on each side and another set up to windward. The narrow beam aft made this additional staying necessary. The mizzen forward stay was termed the 'Tommy Hunter' and set up to a ringbolt in the keelson amidships. All running gear was best

285

Plate 57. The yawl *Bittern* on the beach at Southwold, Suffolk, shows her fine ends and shapely bilge. *Photo – Suffolk Photo Survey.*

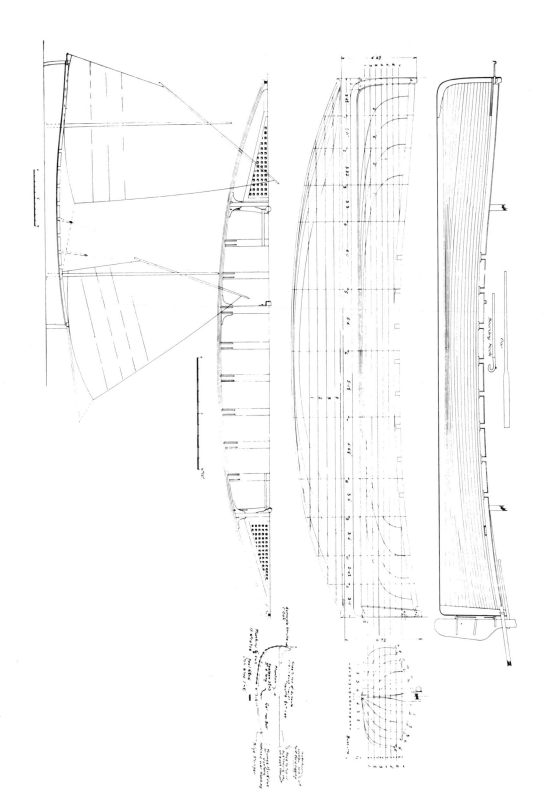

Figure 89. Lines, arrangement and sail plan of the 48ft 2in beach yawl *Bittern* of Southwold, Suffolk, built in 1892. One of the smaller yawls built at the end of the usefulness of the type. *Science Museum, London.*

manilla rope. Boat gear included an anchor and cable, box compass, fenders, boathook, several long warps, axes, handspikes, a lantern, buckets, bailers, a flag for signalling and a couple of buoys.

The helmsman stood to an iron tiller shipped over the iron-shod rudder head. The names of many yawls had a romantic streak, suggestive of the crews' pride in their speed and seamanship: *Redjacket, Nil Desperandum, Reindeer, Gloriana, Young Prince, John Bull, Swiftsure* and others. Under sail they were the pride of the coast, expressing the hope of gain and adventure of small communities. Yawl names were perpetuated for many years. There were for instance, four yawls named *Happy New Year* and there were examples of three yawls having the same name at work at once.

The work of the yawls

A day and night watch was kept from each beach company's lookout, sometimes an elaborate wooden tower or perhaps an old mast with a crows nest at the top, reached by wooden steps. The lookout scanned for a pilot flag, flare or other signal, for ships in difficulty or likely to be. Yawls and gigs were kept ready for instant launching and in bad weather there were several company men about the tarred and weatherbeaten sheds which were ornamented with nameboards and figureheads from wrecks. The beachmen passed the time in the court braiding nets, making and mending ballast bags, cutting linen pegs and smoking, yarning and playing their favourite game of draughts. Beachmen would never enter the court of another company, even for religious or benevolent purposes and to become a member of a company was not easy. The yawlmen were independent and hard. They needed to be in winter, crouching on the bottomboards while freezing spray drove over them in sheets. All could row and sail small craft well and most were experienced and adept at pilotage and salvage work. Many had served at some time in square-rigged, foreign-going ships and knew how these were handled.

The beachmen's skills descended through generations into the early twentieth century. The old families included the Hayletts and Woods of Caister and the Gilbert, Leach, Green, Symonds, Temple, Nickolds, Hollingsworth, Harper, Beckett and Knights families of Great Yarmouth. The Lowestoft Swan, Burwood, Sterry, Hook, and Barber families rivalled the Peeks of Pakefield and Strowgers of Kessingland. Herringtons, Cragies, Mays and Smiths were redoubtable Southwold men and the Cables and Charls were Aldeburgh champions.

During the mid-nineteenth century yawls were launched frequently in winter and half a dozen rival beach companies might be at work at once. The launching cry of 'Running Down!' echoing along the beach and streets brought people flocking in excitement. Skids were placed under the bow and with cries of 'Hold her up!', the bilge stools were removed and the yawl started down the beach. The ballast bags were put on board at the waters edge where all hands tumbled on board. Launching from East Anglia's beaches was not so spectacular as at Deal and Walmer as these shelved more gradually, so a launching boat could not carry her way through shallow water and surf before she could sail clear. A yawl was given added impetus to get off by a push from men with a long setting pole applied to the roller at the head of the sternpost. The mizzen was often set in onshore winds, when she would be got off under oars until the fore lug could be hoisted and she filled on the best tack. Then most of the crew settled down on the bottom boards amidships and kept a sharp lookout for any visible competitors.

The plank lands of a yawl sailing hard in a seaway created considerable noise. Going to windward the helmsman had to be alert to avoid the forelug being taken aback. If this happened in strong winds the yawl almost certainly capsized. The foresheetman kept a turn of the sheet round the amidship samson post and surged it in the puffs, which put the lee gunwale under like a racing dinghy. The bows of some yawls had flare or flam to throw the bow wave and spray clear and reduce the frequent need for bailing which kept many men busy in strong winds.

A yawl was sailed to avoid a heavy sea striking her broadside, the helmsman always attempting to meet a big sea bow on, with plenty of way: the greatest danger was turning a yawl in rough seas, when he waited for a smooth and hustled her round with help from oars on both sides. If the ship they were seeking was on the other side of a sand and the tide was suitable, with little sea, and the wind afforded a fetch, the yawl might stand over the sand through broken water to save time as she might have to sail ten or fifteen miles to a job and then probably face a vicious sea when boarding her in a flurry of fenders, lowering

lugsails, boathooks and leaping; shouting men, often in darkness. Then the real work had to commence: perhaps letting go an anchor, manning pumps, cutting away a mast, lightening ship, making sail, salving cargo, getting survivors into the yawl and many other tasks for skilled men.

Unwritten beach lore held that the first yawl to board a casualty got the salvage, resulting in fierce rivalry when several yawls were launched to the same ship, sometimes tempered by the first agreeing to share with others for assistance. Naturally there were abuses of tempting situations by beachmen earning a meagre and uncertain living. Boatmen sometimes exaggerated dangers to anxious shipmasters and high charges were made for supplying anchors which cost little to sweep up from the anchorages in fine weather.

However, yawls were often launched into a severe gale when there was no chance of salvage but hope of saving life. Occasionally they were lost in the attempt. In 1853 the three masted yawl *Increase* owned by Laytons Company of Great Yarmouth, capsized when her lugs were taken aback shortly after putting three men on board a Spanish brig to assist her into the Roads. Seven beachmen and a sick man they had taken off the Newarp light vessel were drowned, but the mainsheetman, Sam Brock, swam for about eight hours and was picked up by a brig in Yarmouth Roads, 14 miles from the scene of capsize.

The Yarmouth yawl *Phoenix* was lost during a severe gale in 1845. She had launched to assist a brig driven on the Scroby Sand, with sails and rudder gone. The *Phoenix* made several attempts to board and rescue the crew who were lashed to the shrouds, but successive seas flung her clear and she was afterwards overwhelmed.

Three Lowestoft yawls were lost during the nineteenth century; a good record considering the thousands of launchings in all weathers.

A rescue by the Lowestoft yawl *Happy New Year* in October 1854 had a happier ending. At dawn the beachmen saw a ship ashore on the Holm Sand, with survivors in the rigging. She was smothered in breakers from the strong, south west gale. The yawl launched with a crew of twelve but the broken water round the wreck was so violent that some thought she should return for the lifeboat. The coxswain guessed the ship would sink before they could return, so he put the yawl into the surf and reached the ship's side. Two of her crew jumped into the yawl, one first throwing the beachmen a leg of mutton! The captain fell into the sea but was dragged into the yawl, which set sail and just cleared the ship as her mainmast fell. Before the *Happy New Year* was beached the ship had broken up and disappeared. On landing the captain asked the beachmen if they would receive any payment for their efforts. When he knew they would get nothing he took their names, including James Saunders, a humpback; a deformity he jokingly referred to as 'the boy'. A few weeks later a cheque for £13 arrived; a pound each for eleven men and two pounds for James Saunders and 'the boy'.

Robert Hook was one of Lowestoft's beach heroes. A six foot three hercules, born there in 1828, he was in the crew of a beach yawl at sixteen. Christmas time 1847 was typical of his experience. On December 21st he was in the company yawl *Princess Royal*, beating out to assist a ship driving over the Holm Sand in a strong easterly gale. Having got her over and anchored, the yawl fell in with a Dutch galliot sunk on the Holm Sand with her crew in the rigging. The yawl's sails were lowered and she was rowed through the surf over the sand to rescue the whole crew. Three nights later the yawl rescued six men from the brig *Heart of Oak*, aground on the Newcome Sand and filling with water. It was a bitter, blowing Christmas Eve as they landed the shipwrecked sailors and hauled up by the shed. Bob Hook became a noted salvager, fisherman and lifeboat coxswain.

Ill-found ships and incompetent captains provided much work for the beachmen, but many well found vessels also went ashore or were in difficulties off that treacherous coast. Some shipmasters were truly grateful for the beachmen's assistance and records preserved at Caister, Norfolk, include a certificate dated February 26th 1862. It states 'I hereby certify that I give the Caister Beach Company to take charge of all the stores, sails and rigging belonging to my ship the *Sisters* of Whitby as I consider they saved me and ships crew from a watery grave. Phatuel Granger, Master, Brig *Sisters of Whitby*'.

The beachmen were ever ready to help their own kind. In 1859 a Yarmouth fishing boat struck a sunken wreck and filled off Pakefield, just south of Lowestoft, where beachmen promptly put off, picked up her crew and salved her nets and gear 'for which service they made no charge, the property belonging to a poor fisherman'.

A yawl once followed a Greek barque which

she thought needed assistance. The Greek captain thought the rakish lugger was a pirate and armed his crew to repel boarding. Fortunately he realised the error before someone was killed. A tug had also followed and when the yawl turned for home, times were taken and she raced the tug, sailing at just over thirteen miles per hour, to beat her easily.

When beaching, the mouths of the ballast bags were untied and the shingle was shot overboard, leaving the yawl light and buoyant. When she touched, the crew jumped overboard and with helpers, hauled her up clear of the water and turned her round ready for the next launch. The length and light construction of these boats made careful shore handling vital.

Development of the yawls

The beach yawls reached a peak of development between about 1840–95 and became of two principal sizes; one of narrow beam with fine ends, designed and built for speed in boarding and landing pilots and others, for carrying light goods and messages and to board ships. The speed of this type constantly increased during the early and mid-nineteenth century when some yawls were seventy feet long. The sixty-nine foot Yarmouth yawl *Reindeer* sailed at sixteen knots on a reach and in 1861 the forty-six foot *Happy New Year* sailed one and three quarter miles in seven and a half minutes and the fifty foot *Thought* once sailed eight miles in thirty-four minutes. The other type of yawl had more beam and a flatter floor, with fuller ends to improve the carriage of weights for salvaging or taking off an anchor or

cable. But the beachmen's life was not all gales and hazard. From May to September they ferried mackerel ashore from drifters lying in the roads off Great Yarmouth at one shilling per hundred or, if they were lying further off, two shillings. From September to December they found similar work with herrings and sometimes landed trawl fish from the fast cutters sent daily from the North Sea fleets of trawling smacks. Throughout the year the work of pilotage and assistance to ships continued and when things were slack the beachmen went long lining and drift netting alongshore and yawls might sweep for lost anchors in the roadsteads and sometimes salved coal from colliers wrecked in winter gales.

Establishment of lifeboats early in the nineteenth century brought some competition for the yawls, though to be a member of the Yarmouth lifeboat crew it was then necessary to also be a member of a beach company. The first sailing lifeboat was built at Great Yarmouth by Beeching and was of similar form to a beach yawl. She was stationed at Lowestoft in 1809.

Lifeboat competition in life saving and salvage did not intrude too much on the beachmen's income but when steam tugs were introduced at Great Yarmouth and Lowestoft, competition for salvage became keen as speed and seamanship no longer guaranteed salvage money. The Lowestoft tugs were operated by the railway company which owned the harbour. The tugs first attempt to refloat a stranded ship was met with a hail of stones when angry yawl crews surrounded the tug. At Great Yarmouth the beachmen soon realised the tugs were salvors of the future and

Plate 58. A beach yawl leaving Lowestoft harbour under racing canvas, about 1895.

560 in the mizzen. Ballast was from one and a half or two tons of pig iron and shingle bags. She rowed six to eight oars and a crew of ten to twenty handled her, twenty or more when racing. Although the beachmen's work diminished, they continued to gather at their sheds to while away the time yarning, smoking and playing draughts when they were not fishing alongshore or doing other odd jobs.

Racing

The old rivalry between companies remained and became explosive at the coast regattas of Great Yarmouth, Lowestoft, Southwold and Aldeburgh, which besides races for yachts large and small, usually included races for local yawls, gigs and sometimes for pilot cutters, lifeboats, shrimpers and beach punts.

The yawl race was locally regarded as the greatest event of the regatta. Most beach companies were represented by at least one yawl, sometimes more, and crowds of spectator beachmen followed the racing ashore and waged wordy and often physical battles, particularly with those from other places. The course was, if possible, triangular and about ten or fifteen miles long. Start was from anchor with sails lowered. At the gun the big lugs rose as though by magic as each yawl attempted to cast off on the best tack, some being manoeuvred into irons by competitors and in danger of capsize unless skilfully handled. Then they were away, perhaps in a fresh breeze with 4–6 men constantly bailing and the remainder, perhaps 15 or so, crouched on the bottom boards to weather, waiting to tack.

some later acquired shares in one. The beachmen's principal complaint against the tugs was that when valuable cargo was at risk a tug would get to the ship before the yawls, but at wrecks where life was at risk with little payment of reward, the tugs generally stayed in harbour and yawls did the job.

As steamships steadily replaced sailing vessels, yawls were reduced in numbers and size until by the late 1880s a typical beach yawl was forty-five or fifty feet long with eight to eleven foot beam and might set 840 square feet in the fore lug and

Sometimes two main and forelugs were carried, one on each side to save time when tacking. As soon as one was lowered the halyard was made fast to the other, which was hoisted and sheeted in minutes. Some regatta committees ruled that only one lug should be carried for each mast, probably to enable the more workaday yawls to compete. Off the wind a jib was set on a temporary bowsprit and on a reach the racers might attain fourteen knots or more.

During the mid-nineteenth century, handicaps of half a minute per foot of length were allowed in yawl races and sometimes the closeness of finishes allowed smaller yawls to win; always an unpopular result in any class. In an 1849 race the Lowestoft yawl *Greyhound* finished six minutes astern of the much larger *Royal Sovereign* but beat her for third place on time allowance. During the early nineteenth century many fishing and coastal craft made considerable passages to compete in east coast regattas. In 1833 the yawl *Royal Sovereign*, owned by Laytons Company and built by Jermyn and Mack, won a silver cup in a race for all comers at Walton on Naze regatta, fifty-six miles south of Great Yarmouth.

In 1838 Jermyn of Great Yarmouth built the large yawl *Reindeer*, sixty-nine foot long and twelve foot beam. She carried eighty-five people when launched and was the fastest beach yawl, sailing at a reputed sixteen knots on a broad reach. In 1851 the schooner yacht *America* visited England and won a Cup given for a race round the Isle of Wight; a trophy which became the America's Cup, still in international competition. Her success and the events surrounding the race

aroused considerable publicity and misconceptions regarding the ability of British yachts, which annoyed British yachtsmen. The owners of the *America* yawl *Reindeer* challenged the owners of the *America* to a race for a £200 stake and a representative of the Americans travelled to Great Yarmouth to check the remarkable claims of the yawl's potential speed. He advised declining the challenge on grounds that she was an open boat, not a yacht. However, the *America*'s owners stated they were willing to race for £1000 per side, a sum the beach community could not raise, so the match never occurred.

The yawl's challenge was a spirited piece of bravado, probably aimed as much at British yachtsmen and their craft as at the American visitor. It was well for the beachmen that the *America* refused as although the *Reindeer* might have held the schooner on a reach in light winds, the *America* would have tramped away from her in all other conditions. Local pride, probably backed by enterprising shopkeepers and hoteliers, put steam into the challenge.

Despite their apparent dislike of yachts, the beachmen were fond of protesting each other. In the 1848 North Roads Regatta, Great Yarmouth men objected to entry of the Lowestoft yawl *Greyhound* and the *Swiftsure* of Southwold on grounds that these were not 'registered'. This was overruled. During the race, three yawls broke their foremasts. Later that year the Lowestoft beachmen objected to a Southwold entry in the gig race, stating she was not a sea boat, but this was not allowed.

In 1887 thirteen yawls started in one race and

the following year sixteen starters carried over four hundred beachmen in their crews and the Lowestoft yawl *Success*, sailed by Jack Swan, was a noted competitor.

During 1892 a group of wealthy men who admired the beachmen of the Young Company of Lowestoft combined to present them with a new yawl to replace the worn out *Young Prince*. The 48ft 6in *Georgiana* was built there by Allerton for £150 to a design by a local man named Capps. The day after launch she won the yawl race at Lowestoft regatta with Jack Swan at the helm, beating the *Bittern* and *Young Reliance* of Southwold, the *Sophia* of Kessingland and the *Sir Savill Crossley* of Pakefield, besides others from Winterton and Caister.

With a rare flourish of pride the Old Company commissioned George Watson, the internationally famous yacht designer then at the peak of his career and turning out large racing yachts such as *Britannia*, *Valkyrie II* and *Valkyrie III* and *Meteor*, to design them a new yawl. She was built by Henry Reynolds of Lowestoft and was launched in 1894 as the *Happy New Year*. She was 50ft 2in × 10ft 5in × 3ft 6in depth, compared to the *Georgiana's* 48ft 6in × 9ft × 3ft, but could not beat her. The *Georgiana* with Jack Swan at the helm, remained cock of the yawls until racing ended about 1908, winning fifteen first prizes.

The end of the yawls

In 1898 companies owning one yawl and one gig remained at Winterton, Palling, Caister and Southwold. There were at Lowestoft; the Young Company, the North Roads Company and the Old

Plate 59. The Lowestoft beach yawl *Georgiana* wears her prize flags, including five first prizes, as her racing crew pose for the photographer. Bags of shingle ballast lie on the staging and a lug-rigged pulling and sailing lifeboat is in the background. *Photo – Ford Jenkins.*

or South End Company which owned the yawls *Happy New Year*, *Success* and *Salem*.

By 1900 the beach companies were beginning to dissolve and for forty years previously their prospects of salvage had been increasingly diminished by steam tugs and steam ships. The last yawls were built in the 1890s almost as a defiant gesture as there was little work for those existing. Early in the twentieth century many beach yawls were sold away, some to the Essex seaside resorts of Clacton and Southend, where they were rerigged as gaff ketches and worked from the beaches, taking trippers for a sail. At Southend these became known as 'lifeboats' and were so popular with Edwardian holidaymakers that general design was copied by local builders in new pleasure boats.

Some yawls were sold to become houseboats on the Broads of Norfolk and Suffolk, others were sawn up for firewood or rotted away in odd corners, the sweeping power of their lines beautiful even in decay. The *Bittern* disintegrated at Southwold about 1829. The *Georgiana* was laid up at Lowestoft throughout the First World War and was afterwards converted to a houseboat. The *Happy New Year* foundered under tow at sea about the same time. Not one remains and only an occasional coaster or fishing vessel breaks the seascape of once crowded roadsteads.

The beachmen's punt
From Happisburgh on the north east shoulder of Norfolk, south to Aldeburgh in Suffolk, beachmen used small, clinker-planked open luggers, generally known as punts, for alongshore fishing.

Usually the rig was two masts, setting a dipping lug forward and a standing lug mizzen sheeted to an outrigger. Some Norfolk punts eighteen to twenty feet long set a single dipping lug. Larger ones about twenty-five feet long had the two sail rig and when trawling for bottom fish some of these set a boomless gaff sail, temporary bowsprit and a jib.

Punts were often owned by beachmen who, until the 1940s, usually shipped in larger craft for the East Anglian herring season and for other voyages, using the punt as a secondary means of earning, particularly for sprating and shrimping. Many were owned at Kessingland, Southwold and Aldeburgh and at the large ports of Great Yarmouth and Lowestoft. Small coastal communities at Thorpness, Dunwich, Pakefield, Caister, California, Palling, Winterton, Hemsby and Happisburgh had several chocked up with stools on the beach. Rowing skiffs twelve to fourteen feet long were also used for alongshore drifting in fine weather.

Many Norfolk beach punts had pointed sterns but transoms were preferred in Suffolk. Length was usually between fifteen and twenty feet with some fishermen favouring a twenty-two foot boat. Like the yawls, most punts relied on fine waterline endings to get them to windward, though around 1900 some were built with a centreplate to improve performance. Spence of Great Yarmouth built many planked in oak. In 1913 he completed a twenty footer complete with sails and gear for £27. Others were built at Lowestoft by Reynolds, and earlier by Sparham, while most of the many working from Southwold trawling smacks. Its deep water harbour encouraged alongshore fishermen to evolve much larger 'punts' than elsewhere, ranging up to 37ft × 12ft × 5ft but remaining undecked because this enabled them to be worked with a crew of four men and a boy; two men less than a comparable decked boat.

The Yarmouth alongshore men also developed gaff sloops for local shrimping but Lowestoft men preferred lug-rigged punts, often twenty footers. As these were moored in a harbour, without need to beach, they developed with deeper and beamier hulls, greater displacement and with permanent iron ballast. A twenty footer might have eight feet beam and four feet moulded depth, allowing a decked cuddy cabin forward where two or three could sleep. Harbour use also resulted in the tack of the dipping lug foresail being taken to the stem head instead of the usual short bumkin. The mizzen in some boats was an almost triangular 'jigger', spread by a boom secured to the sharply steeved mizzen mast with a rope snotter and sheeted to a short outrigger. In summer these boats worked a shrimp trawl in three or four fathoms around the Newcombe Sands or in the South Roads off Lowestoft, and drifted for herring and sprats in season.

Pakefield, a village south of Lowestoft but now swallowed by its suburbs, had many punts. It was notorious for its nineteenth-century beachmen who often turned smugglers. They were known as 'The roaring boys of Pakefield' from an encounter with the village parson one night as a cargo was being run on the beach. Before the parson could bolt to tell the preventitive officers he was gently

Plate 60. Model of an 18ft × 6ft 3in Yarmouth mackerel boat with a dipping lugsail.

and Aldeburgh, Thorpness and Dunwich were by Critten or Ladd of Southwold.

Construction entirely of oak was favoured until the late nineteenth century when larch began to be used for planking. Timbers were bent in, but joggled over the plank lands to provide maximum bearing to the planking and minimise working of the hull when being handled ashore. Bilge doublings were added to take chafe and the boats well withstood the hundreds of launchings they experienced in all weathers. Great Yarmouth was then the home of fleets of herring luggers and

Plate 51. A Suffolk beach punt coming ashore at Thorpe. A visitor drags the haul up rope down as she lays at the tideline with lugsails drawing. The trawl beam protrudes well beyond her stern.
Photo – Suffolk Photo Survey.

seized and buried up to his armpits in the shingle until the goods were ashore and he could be safely released. East Anglia's love of a robust joke against the authorities resulted in the rhyme commencing 'The roaring boys of Pakefield, oh Lord how they do thrive! They had but one poor parson and him they buried alive'.

The little town of Southwold clusters around its lighthouse on a low cliff and was a home of fishermen when the Domesday Book was compiled. Besides deep sea fishing through the centuries, its beachmen owned many punts (Plate 61) and various generations of the Critten family built them up to twenty-one feet long, besides larger craft. Sprat shoals appeared off Southwold and Aldeburgh in October and the beach punts might glean a profitable early harvest of prime fish before markets became glutted by the bulk catches of the Essex smacks with their huge stowboat nets a few weeks later. (See the author's *Gaff Rig*.)

The little Suffolk beach punts could not work stowboat gear and as it was not worth larger local craft participating in this short fishery, drift nets were used, often thirty yards long and six yards deep, a punt perhaps working twenty in a fleet, riding to them with a lantern and the beachmen huddled, dozing under the lowered fore lug, with one on watch occasionally 'looking on' at the first net to see if the fish were swimming.

It is wet work hauling drift nets in an open boat and attempting to clear some of the catch from the nets while getting them inboard as quickly as possible. Then it was a sail or perhaps a long row to windward back to the beach and

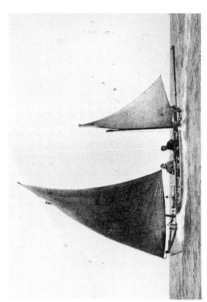

Plate 63. An Aldeburgh beach boat reaching fast under dipping lug foresail and standing lug mizzen. Circa 1901. *Photo – R. Welford.*

haul up, when the nets could be properly cleaned (Plate 62). The catch was either packed in ped baskets and sold to a merchant or sent off by train, or was perhaps hawked round the locality. A punt might catch forty bushels in eight hours work or she might get little or nothing; spratting is mostly chance and hard work

Plate 61 shows a punt beaching under sail in fine weather at Thorpness, just north of Aldeburgh, with another sailing alongshore and more hauled up. This boat was working a beam trawl about six feet longer than her overall length.

Aldeburgh is a clean, windswept and ancient borough which has a proud history of seafaring and was the home of many beachmen owning punts. (Plate 63). These chubby twenty footers

Plate 62. Beachmen shaking out sprat nets at Southwold, Suffolk, circa 1905. *Photo – Suffolk Photo Survey.*

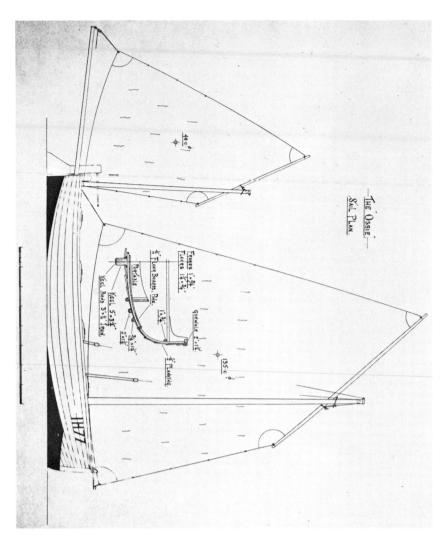

Figure 90. Sail plan of the 15ft 2in
Aldeburgh, Suffolk beach boat *Ossie*, built
by Critten at Southwold in 1893. *Science
Museum, London.*

were worked by three men for longshore herring.
Smaller punts fifteen to eighteen feet long gave a
better share for two and were more popular for
earning something of a living for a family; drift
netting for herring and sprats in winter and beam
trawling for soles, plaice, dabs and roker (skate)
in spring and summer, perhaps with a bit of
shrimping and wood gathering at odd times. Such
boats asked little more than regular painting and
good sails and rope, to last for many years at
minimum cost, unless damaged during beaching.
Average length was sixteen feet and they had
broad transoms. In 1893 Critten of Southwold
built the beach punt *Ossie* for an Aldeburgh
owner. She was 15ft 2in long × 6ft 3in beam × 2ft
4in depth and cost about £30. Clencher planking
was oak on oak bent timbers and a straight oak
keel. The full bodied hull had fine ends and
pleasing shape. Three thwarts gave her transverse
stiffness and enabled three men to row. Unlike the
Norfolk crabbers these beach boats of the eastern
shore worked oars between wooden thole pins at
the gunwale.

Tradition entered into the arrangement of even
these small craft and the bottom was divided by
shallow shifting boards into 'rooms' for soles,
plaice and roker, with a 'net room' between the
after thwart and the helmsman's space.

The dipping lug foresail spread 135 square feet
and had four rows of reef points. Its tack hooked
to a twelve inch iron bumkin at the stemhead.
The 48 square feet mizzen set on a mast stepped
inside the transom and sheeted to a relatively long
outrigger (Fig. 90). This also had three rows of
reef points and these little boats would stand

much wind in skilled hands, and the reefs enabled speed over the ground to be controlled when trawling.

Like many small fishing luggers the *Ossie* had a ridiculously short tiller and even so, the mizzen mast had to be stepped well of centreline to starboard to clear it. However, such niceties did not worry the beachmen as long spells at the tiller were rare in their work within three miles seaward of Aldeburgh beach and south into Hollesley Bay, by the long shingle spit dividing the lonely River Alde from the sea.

Motor boats resembling the old punts still launch off Aldeburgh's steep shingle beach, dominated by the brightly painted lifeboat lying with her bows pointed challengingly at the growling, grey North Sea. The lugsails have gone but the spirit remains.

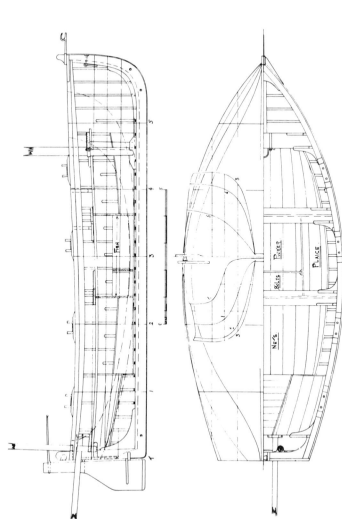

Figure 91. Lines and arrangement of the Aldeburgh beach boat *Ossie.* Dimensions 6ft 3in × 2ft 4in moulded depth. *Science Museum, London.*

10

Essex, the Thames and Medway

The River Thames and the coasts of Essex and Kent bordering its estuary was a stronghold of spritsail rig in England. Besides the well known cargo carrying spritsail barges which are described in the third volume of this series of books, there were many smaller craft used by fishermen and watermen who preferred the spritsail for its handiness in adjusting sail for fishing or its convenience in rowing and sailing boats, encouraged by a long tradition of its use. But the Essex and Kentish men preferred lugsails for some purposes and although the Essex Rivers Colne and Blackwater were strongholds of cutter rig, several luggers were owned and built there during the eighteenth and early ninteenth centuries. Many were general purpose craft, used for fishing on the east and south coasts, also for occasional salvaging, as assisting and dismantling wrecks on the Essex and Suffolk coasts was termed, sometimes for smuggling (see Plate 1).

Smugglers
In 1808 the lugger *Hawke* was offered for sale at Colchester, and the lugger *Aid* of the same port was giving assistance to a brig on the Gunfleet Sand in 1831.

Daniel Sutton of Wivenhoe, town clerk of Colchester from 1813 until 1818, was a lugger owner and reputedly also a smuggler. His lugger was engaged in salvaging off the coast and in 1815 is reputed to have brought first news of the victory of Waterloo to the Colne and possibly to England.

Philip Sainty, the legendary Colneside builder of fast ships, yachts and other craft, was involved with the large smuggling lugger *Wolverine*, commissioned about 1825 by his brother Robert to be built from Philip's lines by an Old Shoreham boatbuilder named Grinyer, ostensibly for the south coast herring and mackerel fisheries. For seven years the *Wolverine* landed contraband cargoes at a cave on the shore between Beachy Head and Newhaven, Sussex. She was eventually caught between two revenue cutters which came out from Newhaven and Beachy Head and although the swift *Wolverine* outsailed one, the cutter from Beachy Head overhauled her. Ironically she was made out to be the *Wasp*, built at Wivenhoe by Philip Sainty for the revenue service.

The *Wolverine* was run ashore in desperation on Worthing Flats and set on fire, her crew escaping. Robert Sainty managed to blow up the cave with a charge of gunpowder before escaping to further adventurous smuggling in other craft.

The *Wolverine* and the Essex luggers would be two or three masted, clench planked and of fine form with deep draught, but Essex smugglers generally preferred the less conspicuous and more efficient cutter rig and an anti-smuggling law of 1816 had prohibited the construction of luggers of more than fifty tons, which indicated the size of some smuggling craft, many of which were well above sixty feet long.

In 1815 the Colchester revenue cutter *Fox* encountered a large, open smuggling lugger in the English Channel and, seeing she was well armed and had a crew of thirteen, decided not to attack but followed astern. Sensing their superiority, the smugglers bore down and rammed the *Fox*, which was stove in and sinking. During the ensuing fight several were killed and injured on both sides, fighting continuing after the craft drifted apart, until a brig was sighted and the lugger made sail. The captain of the *Fox* and one seaman were killed and three seamen were injured, leaving only one man unscathed. A Deal pilot lugger picked them up and eventually two of the smugglers were caught and hanged.

In March 1817 the Yarmouth revenue cutter *Ranger* lost three men in action against a heavily armed lugger with a crew of thirty-six and mounting twelve nine-pounders. The *Ranger* came up with the lugger off Robin Hood's Bay, Yorkshire, and the fight lasted one and a half

hours before half of the smugglers crew abandoned the lugger and escaped ashore, leaving the remainder, with two dead, on board. The captured lugger was towed to Great Yarmouth under sail, then a common occurrence.

Smugglers' cargoes were often spirits and tobacco but many other items became desirable contraband; snuff, playing cards, laces, pictures and loaf sugar, rendered valuable by the usual unenlightened taxation laws and by the poverty of many fishermen and other seafarers.

By the 1820s French luggers were increasingly used for smuggling into England, with crews half French, half English, as an alien could not be charged with an offence committed beyond his territorial waters. In 1819 the revenue cutter *Eagle* brought the Boulogne lugger *Huzza* into Harwich with a crew of eleven French and twelve English, loaded with smuggled tobacco and spirits. The cutter *Scout* captured the luggers *William* of Flushing, the fifty-seven ton *Le Chasseur* of Boulogne and the *Maria* of Folkestone, which had a crew of six foreigners and four English who were promptly pressed into the navy while the foreigners were discharged!

Lobster boats and bumkins

The big Essex luggers died out by the 1850s, but the rig survived in small boats, such as the lugsail- and spritsail-rigged lobster boats which fished from the Essex coast resort of Walton-on-the-Naze, which developed during the late nineteenth century when a Great Eastern Railway branch line arrived there. As elsewhere, the summer visitors demanded sea food and with a rocky

Plate 64. Sprit- and lugsail-rigged lobsterboats at Walton-on-the-Naze, Essex, about 1895.

bottom conveniently near the promentary of the Naze, the few local watermen were quick to fish there, using small open boats from fourteen to eighteen feet long, transom sterned and clinker planked and rigged with a single dipping lugsail (Plate 64). A few were larger, perhaps twenty-two feet, rigged with a high peaked spritsail, with a boom, and a staysail tacked down to the stemhead. Lobsters and whelks were taken in circular hoop nets, baited with the meat of shore crabs, or fish offal and hauled up rapidly at intervals to surface the feeding lobster. These boats were also used to carry trippers off the beach during summer afternoons, well scrubbed out and with the owner in clean guernsey and trousers at the oars or tiller.

When not fishing their bold, cutter-rigged smacks, some Colne and Blackwater fishermen set a lugsail in small boats to do odd jobs.

The age old rowing and sailing ferry between East Mersea Stone and Brightlingsea, across the River Colne, was worked for over fifty years by Mr Mole with his lugsail boat, typical of thousands of similar craft all round the British coast with a standing lugsail, useful on a reach or run but not intended for much windward work in a boat without a centreboard.

Winkle Brigs

West Mersea winklers and oystermen used lugsails in their small open boats known as bumkins, often now called 'winkle brigs'. These little craft were inexpensive to build and maintain and worked principally in the River Blackwater

Plate 65. The West Mersea winkle brig *Black Duck* was probably a discarded yacht's boat rigged with a standing lugsail for work in the river Blackwater and on the Dengie Flats.

and its creeks, oystering, winkling, fetching and carrying, besides being occasionally sailed for pleasure, particularly in the fishermen's boat race at West Mersea Town regatta. Many older bumkins were cast off, transom sterned ships boats, finely formed in the days before the Board of Trade reduced them to stable hulks, incapable of propulsion by sail or oar. Some bumkins set a single standing lugsail on a mast stepped through a thwart. Others ventured to a gunter-lug main and a foresail set to a short bowsprit, but most later ones were rigged as gaff sloops.

The winklers boats at first had no centreboards and steered with an oar in the transom sculling notch. Such boats were suitable for the river, but for working 'down the main', along the Dengie Flats to the south of the Blackwater, a larger craft was desirable, yet winklers rarely required use of a small smack, which had to lay in the deep rills of outfalls draining the extensive marshes behind the sea walls. So the bumkin type was adopted by winklers who wished to get home at night.

William Wyatt, the tall, white bearded West Mersea boatbuilder who became a legend amongst east coast yachtsmen and from whom I bought the first boat I ever owned, used to recall with enthusiasm his own brig; a sixteen footer he built and named *Mersea Hard* – 'Cos she spent so much time a 'lying on ut' he explained with a twinkle. William used her for a variety of jobs connected with his business, and for pleasure sailing. Her most profitable days were during the First World War, when Gowen's sail loft at Tollesbury was busy making tents, and many bales of canvas needed taking from West Mersea to Tollesbury. The quickest and most logical way was by water and, as times were slack for William, with all the little yachts laid up and only an odd smack or gun punt to repair, he got the job and loaded the *Mersea Hard* with bolts of canvas, a ton at a time worth £200, and sailed it round, blow high or low, without wetting a thread. Bumkins could also mount a big duck gun for winter fowling; perhaps a four bore with muzzle lashed down to the ringbolt inside the stemhead and the breech made fast to a timber placed across the gunwales, abaft the mast. Sighting was achieved by manoeuvring the boat to line up with the feeding fowl. It was surprising how close a sailing craft could approach in open water with a light wind, the crew keeping quiet and moving stealthily. The shattering shot recoiled the boat but usually left a dozen widgeon floating dead, with cripples vainly trying to escape and the rest of the flight winging low over the estuary.

Winkle brigs have also had their moments of drama. When 'Swan' Mussett's Mersea smack went ashore and filled in the Blackwater during a blow, he climbed up the mast as the tide rose. But help was on its way in the person of his nephew in a brig which rounded up by the few feet of mast remaining above the water. With feigned surprise he shouted 'Why, uncle, whatever yew doing up there?' Swan replied with spluttering anger and refused all offers of being taken off. 'Salvage' he shouted. 'That's what you're after, I know.' Stung by the insinuation his nephew grabbed a long handled eel spear from the brig's armoury and prodded the bulging bottom near

the masthead. Swan fell down the mast 'A' roarin like a bull', to tumble aboard the brig and be unwillingly salvaged.

Brigs merit the description of one owner as 'Werry versatile little craft'.

Like the annual regatta struggle between the West Mersea and Maldon smacks, the race for fishermen's boats at Mersea for the Oswald Lewis Cup was lively, informal east coast racing, causing furious bottom scrubbing and much borrowing of big jibs, to be set with billowing efficiency in light airs and sometimes with a knot in the head if they were a bad fit; no sailmakers benefits here.

Perhaps the 1947 regatta was best of all. They came bursting up the Quarters in the sun sparkle of that hottest summer; mellow tan canvas set smart, leaning in light and shadow, foaming bow waves creaming away along newly painted sides and bottoms shining with black varnish. Mr Stoker's *Winnie* leading Leslie French's *Oyster*; Jim Mussett's *Jack* and *Gunner's Pride* battling it out, a Mussett at the helm of each; and *Stella* bow to bow with the lugsail-rigged *Wheezy Anna*, sailed by Jack Mole. Sheets in, heeling in the puffs, to finish at the crack of a twelve bore from the committee launch. Winkle brigs are still raced each West Mersea regatta, as pleasure craft, while others have been built and refitted recently and turn out for a tussle with the old timers. Such simple craft give years of pleasure and joyful expectation in pride of ownership. They satisfy a desire for a return to simplicity in sailing and maintaining a boat; the natural feeling of applying paint to the hull and splicing rope for the elementary rigging.

Gun punts

The Blackwater gun punts are the simplest of the many varieties of gun punt in the British Isles; open or decked, beamy or narrow, to suit the needs of different areas. The broad, tidal Blackwater was undoubtedly the finest wildfowling river in Britain, attracting a wide variety of fowl from large geese to tiny oxbirds, besides occassional exotic species. Locals took full advantage of this, particularly when rail transport enabled large bags to be sent quickly to the London game market.

The sheer numbers of birds now seem unbelievable. Squire Thomas Kemble of Runwell Hall recalled in 1894 'I have seen the sky darkened with wild geese covering a space of half a mile by a quarter of a mile, as thick as manure spread upon the ground and making a noise which I could only compare with fifty packs of hounds in full cry. I have seen seven acres at low water covered with widgeon, curlew and ducks, making such a noise that I could not hear my brother talking to me a few yards off. Colonel Russell was off the coast in his yacht. He told me that he had sent off from Maldon to London upwards of two tons of geese'.

Form and construction

Essex gun punts can be sailed and are traditionally rigged with a low spritsail, some with a standing lug or a leg of mutton (triangular) sail. Some punts carried a foresail when racing at regattas. The punts were principally used for shooting wildfowl in the rivers, creeks and marsh rills. Very rarely as a principal means of earning

a living, but frequently to supplement meagre incomes of fishermen and waterside dwellers.

John Howard, the Maldon yacht, barge and boat builder was acknowledged to build the best gun punts, which were preferred by the professional gunners of the Blackwater in the late nineteenth and early twentieth century. William Wyatt, the West Mersea boatbuilder, continued the tradition and built his last in 1949 at the age of eighty-five. Some were built by their owners. The Blackwater and Colne one-man gun punts are pointed sterned and between sixteen and seventeen feet long, from 2ft 8in–2ft 10in beam and are deep sided, almost hiding the gun and gunner. These are comparatively light and handy for getting on deck of a smack or launching over mud. As punts go these are seaworthy and locals claim they can drown any decked punt yet designed. Certainly they are used successfully in rough and severe weather. The English elm bottom is flat and the almost vertical sides are formed by two broad strakes of pine planking on oak grown frames and floors. The gunwales are stiffened aft with two reinforcements for a row of thole pin holes, so the punter may row in whatever position best suits the punt's trim. The oar leathers are greased and work in a wad of oakum or old cloth, to minimise noise. Seventy years ago a similar punt cost only £2; by 1908 fowlers were grumbling that the price had risen to £3, and it has never fallen since.

The fittings are simple; the wedge shaped breasthook at the stemhead is grooved about a quarter of an inch deep to take the gun barrel. Its stock rests on the thwart and is so balanced that

Figure 92. Typical undecked gun punt of West Mersea, Essex, with muzzle loading wildfowl gun mounted forward. The full lines show the usual spritsail rig. The light weather regatta day racing rig is shown dotted. Steering was by a short oar over the quarter. A 'hick', shown dotted, was used when setting to fowl.

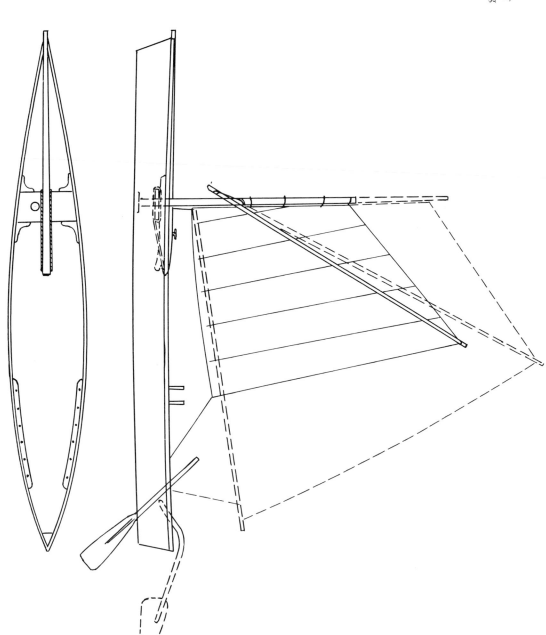

the gun is readily tipped. The gun is aimed by manoeuvring the punt and the elevation is adjusted for ordinary range by a chock on the thwart, if necessary. Some variations in range can be achieved by the gunner moving forward or aft and for a long shot the muzzle is lifted out of the groove and is allowed to rest on the gunwale. The rope breeching is short and fastened around the thwart to prevent the recoiling gun damaging the gunner's face.

A typical punt gun might be six or seven feet long and fire from six to eight ounces of shot. It may be breech or muzzle loading and many muzzle loaders are still in use. The hitting power of breech loaders was regarded with profound scepticism by Essex gunners, one of whom described them a 'wonnerful cowards'. Muzzle loaders were usually reloaded with the punt brought to the shore or lashed alongside another vessel.

The end of the gun barrel is kept about half an inch from the face of the stem to allow it to clear when the punt's bow is run into the cant of the saltings, when it might become choked with clay or mud and burst on firing.

A punt gun was the fowler's pride and its cost was a major item to the professional gunner. A second hand punt gun cost anything between £1 to £20 seventy years ago; now they may fetch £300. some punt guns achieved considerable age and the muzzles of some were rusted as thin as paper. Occasionally a section left the muzzle with the charge, but often the gunner reckoned the gun shot better without the missing piece! If not, a piece of steel pipe was shrunk on the end and

the gun was considered as good as new again.

Size was important in choosing a punt gun and most were classed by the weight of shot discharged. The Mersea guns were classed by the number of clay pipefuls of powder and shot they carried. Gunners spooned the charges into the gun with a pipe and might describe a weapon as a 'six pipe gun'.

Light grey was the favourite colour for Blackwater punts and for punt guns: applied as a flat paint, without gloss, it is most effective camouflage in moonlight or mist. Punts were usually rowed to or from a shoot with short oars known as paddles, working in wooden thole pins. When 'setting to fowl' the punt may be propelled with small boards known as 'hand paddles', or with 'push sticks' in shallow water. The Mersea gunners used what was locally termed a 'hick'; a form of rudder made from a bent tree branch with a piece of board nailed to the outer end. A pivot bolt was driven through the branch and shipped into a hole drilled through the after breasthook. The forward end was held between the punter's heels and so he steered the punt when setting to birds, leaving his hands free to propel her with hand paddles. If his luck holds the punter aims punt and gun at the birds, which are perhaps feeding in a creek. When ready he gives a smart rap on the bottom of the punt with the toe of his boot, to put up the birds. As they rise he fires and with luck may kill a dozen duck or geese, but more likely five or six. There are recorded bags of fifty or more with one shot, but this is now rare. Charles Hipsey of Maldon once shot seventy-five widgeon with one discharge and over a dozen more were picked up by other punters, for in those days punts sometimes worked in fleets along the tidelines. His neighbour John Basham once shot 288 little oxbirds with a single shot as they settled on the icy Blackwater.

Handling

Most Blackwater gunners set a spritsail, though this has become uncommon since 1939. The slender four or five foot mast was stepped through the gun thwart to one side of the gun stock. It had no shrouds and bent in a breeze. It is amazing how these narrow punts sail, especially to windward. The secret is to keep them heeled so the almost square chine acts as a keel. When sailing they are steered by an oar over the lee quarter, the punter lying along the punt and using his foot as a rest for the oar, which also acts as a leeboard. Punts can be sailed up to fowl in daylight or at dusk or dawn, as wildfowl seem to have little fear of a craft under sail and apparently do not associate it with danger.

Two-man punts were common in the mid-nineteenth century but became rarer later. These carried a larger gun, sometimes a full rigged stanchion gun firing one and a half or two pounds of shot in one charge and capable of fearful destruction. These could sweep from sixty to a hundred and twenty yards with shot. A few have been built since and were sometimes rigged with two spritsails and a small foresail. A large, two masted, two man punt was built by Wyatts at West Mersea in 1948 for use on the Dengie Flats from Tillingham.

Gun punts are still used from the Essex village of Manningtree, on the River Stour, which joins with the Suffolk Orwell at Harwich. Manningtree puntsmen use them for eel fishing, netting flatfish, for setting small seine nets, and in the winter twilight and dawns for flight shooting in the winding shallows of the Stour and the shallow bays bordering its peaceful shores.

Manningtree punt proportions and building methods have been handed down through the generations and most were built by the owners, many by the Porter and Lucas families. The type is three quarter decked and has slight sheer. Typical dimensions are 17ft length by 3ft 4in beam with eleven inch freeboard and some longitudinal rocker in the bottom and slight transverse round of bottom or 'kammel'. The bottom is often of three pine planks laid longitudinally. The sides are two planks deep, lapped, clinker fashion of English elm. Oak knees form the stem and sternpost, fastened to the ends of the centreline plank. Oak or English elm knees form the side frames and the straight floors are fastened to the bottom between these. These punts row well, as a result of the pointed stern hull form but are not as handy as the Blackwater type for taking on board a smack, or so roomy inside, because of the decking.

Until the 1930s there were twenty or thirty punts in use from Manningtree, with six or so families earning something of a living from fishing and shooting wildfowl on the river. Most of the dozen remaining gunners build their own punts for sport and still prefer muzzle loading guns. One of them, Peter Ainger, recently built his own punt gun. A muzzle loading gun can be reloaded in three minutes, with the punt run ashore, but has little disadvantage compared with a breech loader as a shot will raise fowl over a wide area and probably leave little chance for a second attempt for some time.

Racing

Most of the Manningtree punts enter for the annual sailing and rowing races at the village regatta, where the old local families of Lucas, Porter and Ainger figure prominently in the prize list. This is a tradition well over a century old, which was also featured in other Essex regattas at West Mersea, Maldon and elsewhere. The Manningtree punts are sailed by one man and have no centreboard or leeboards.

Steering is with a short oar over the lee quarter and a single spritsail of generous area is set on an unstayed mast (Fig. 92). A punt's large spritsail is typically 15ft on the luff, 19ft on the leach and 13ft 9in on the boom, but smaller sails are set in strong winds. The regatta is a brave sight; the lapping high water, blue against the green woods and cornfields of the Suffolk shore, criss-crossed by the tacking white spritsails which are now set only for pleasure.

Methods of Essex wildfowl shooting have changed little over the years and great skill is needed to secure a good punt shot. Ownership of a punt and big gun is still within reach of almost anyone who chooses to follow this physically exacting winter sport and the wildfowling grounds of the salt water rivers and the great estuaries are free; the punt gunner has no keepers to maintain his game and can move wherever the tide flows.

Spritsails on the Thames

The River Thames has developed its own types of craft for many centuries and was a home of the spritsail rig.

Rowing and sailing skiffs, wherries, fishermen's peter boats and the larger hatch boats and pinks all evolved with light, clinker planked hulls and fine lines, which enabled them to achieve speed under oars or sail.

Skiffs and wherries were used principally for river transport and for pleasure. Some wherries were worked by fishermen in the tideway and had flaring bows with a well rounded deckline forward and along run aft to a narrow transom stern. The sheerstrake had no gunwale and was pierced for rowlock holes. The hulls were planked on sawn frames, fitted over the planking in short lengths, well clear of each other so that straight grained oak could be used. This method allowed a flexibility of structure which many thought improved speed under oars. Wherries could set a spritsail for a fair or reaching wind and possibly also a foresail. There were various sizes and forms to suit uses from passenger carrying to fishing in the lower reaches. One was fishing from Holehaven, at Canvey Island in Sea Reach until about 1900, worked by 'Old Hoskins', a London fisherman who kept his catch in her well.

A wherry adventure

The words 'yacht' and 'yachting' were not introduced into England from Holland until the reign of Charles II, but coastal cruising in small craft is a much older pastime. A log survives of *The most dangerous and memorable adventure of Richard*

310

Ferris, published in 1590 'at the sign of the gun, at the little north door of St. Pauls', in the City of London.

Richard Ferris was one of the five ordinary messengers of Her Majesty's Chamber; a civil servant, he admitted he was no sailor, yet in a spritsail-rigged Thames wherry he voyaged in 'The late dangerous attempt rashly by me undertaken, to row in a small boat to the city of Bristow (Bristol) along the perils rocks, breakers, races, shoals, quicksands and very unlikely places for such small boats along the coast of England.' His seafaring appears to have been inspired to seek publicity, but he had sense to seek an experienced coastal seaman to accompany him and his equally inexperienced friend. They embarked at Tower Wharf on midsummer day, before a large crowd. The boat was an ordinary Thames passenger wherry, clench planked with a green hull, oars and spritsail. Calling at Greenwich, where the court was residing, they carried on to Margate; then to Dover 'where we stayed about six hours and were greatly entertained'. The wherry coasted uneventfully to the Solent where a 'great storm' caught them near the Needles, forcing them to shelter under the lee of Hurst castle. Afterwards the wherry made Swanage, in Dorset.

Westward was an inhospitable coast for a small boat and the wherry had a rough time passing through the races at St Albans and Portland and coasting around West Bay. Ferris and his companions were well entertained wherever they landed and were given 'great entertainment' by the Navy on reaching Plymouth.

The wherry was almost lost in the race off the Lizard and next day they were chased by pirates off Lands End. Ferris described the encounter; 'Setting out from Penzance with out half tide, to recover the first of the tide at Lands End, we being in our boat a great way from the shore; our master descried a pirate, having a vessel of four tons; who made towards us amain, meaning doubtless to have robbed us. But doubting such a matter, we rowed so near the shore as we might. And by that time, as he was almost come at us, we were near to a rock standing in the sea; where this pirate thought to have taken us at an advantage. For being come close to the outside of the said rock, called Raynalde Stones (the Runnelstone) he was becalmed and could make no way, and so were we. But God (who never faileth those that put their trust in him) sent us a comfort unlooked for. For as we rowed to come about by this rock, suddenly we spied a plain and very easy way to pass on the inner side of the said rock; where we went through very pleasantly; and by reason thereof he could not follow us. Thus we escaped safely; but he was soon after taken and brought in at Bristow.'

The Bristol Channel and bad weather delayed the voyage and they did not arrive at Ilford Coume (Ilfracombe) until August 1st. Ferris urged his companions to hurry on to Bristol. They sailed that night in a fresh breeze, sailing, rowing and bailing; past Minehead and between the islands of Steepholme and Flatholm. The wherry made one tide of it to Bristol where Ferris enjoyed the welcome by the Lord Mayor and aldermen; the crowds of sightseers and procession 'with trumpets,

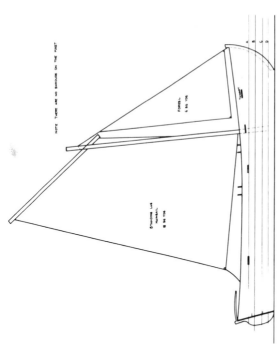

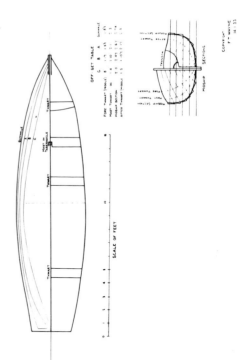

Figure 93. Lines and sail plan of a 20ft 6in × 5ft 3in Gravesend waterman's wherry built in 1932 by W. Warner of Gravesend. *Science Museum, London.*

drums, fifes and ensigns to go before the boat; which was carried on men's shoulders round about the city … then a feast at the Mayor's house'.

Thames watermen

The Thames was alive with small working boats until the end of the nineteenth century. Towards the end of the seventeenth there were about 10,000 licensed watermen plying for passenger hire across the then unembanked river which had few bridges. Their work took them up and down stream between Gravesend and Windsor. With the decline in passenger traffic by the early nineteenth century, the watermen increasingly became employed to assist in mooring and unmooring the growing number of ships which were then making London the world's largest port. They also tended the ships' needs in the tideway, taking off stores and crews. Much of this was carried out with small open boats which retained the name wherry.

Gravesend watermen used sprit sail or lug-rigged transom sterned open wherries which were often about twenty feet long. These assisted shipping in the river to berth or moor, ranging well down Sea Reach in search of a ship and frequently 'hooking on' in the manner of their contemporaries of the Downs and elsewhere. Although these clinker-planked wherries were narrow for rowing and had no centreboards, many carried a boomless standing lugsail and a foresail tacked to the stemhead for a reach or a run. Some also set a lug mizzen. A 20ft 6in by 5ft 3in wherry of this type was built by W. Warner of

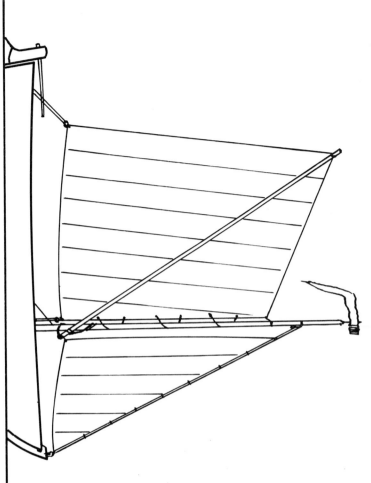

312

Figure 94. A spritsail-rigged passenger wherry of the Norfolk and Suffolk Broads, circa 1808. Forerunners of the later gaff-sailed cargo wherries.

Gravesend as late as 1932, but the few remaining have long been unrigged.

Wherries of the older, Thames passenger type were also used on the Broads of Norfolk and Suffolk. The first recorded was the *Spread Eagle* of Great Yarmouth, in 1610. Chunky, swim ended sailing barges and round bilged, pointed sterned keels then carried cargo through the miles of shallow, reed bordered waterways spreading out from the busy port of Great Yarmouth and especially connecting with the inland city of Norwich, centre of the vast agricultural lands of East Anglia.

Broads passenger wherries were sailing craft up to thirty-five feet long and had the same raking stem and apple-bowed hull form above water as the Thames craft, with similar fine lines underwater and a small transom stern. When Crome painted wherries in 1808 many set a foresail as well as the spritsail (**Fig. 94**) and it is possible that as the size and swiftness of the Broads wherry increased to enable her to carry light cargo as well as passengers, someone quickly decided to build a larger version for increased speed and profits from quick freights.

These new cargo wherries retained the small transom stern but gradually larger ones, still clinker planked, adopted the pointed stern of the keels to produce the Broads wherry hull as it survives in the few that remain. The sprit mainsail was replaced by a gaff sail, which set flatter and was more efficient in the frequent turning to windward on these narrow waterways, besides stowing more easily out of the way for loading or discharge and when shooting bridges.

However, the square-headed shape of the spritsail was retained in the new, near horizontal, gaff-headed sail, and the sheeve at the masthead of a wherry is still referred to as the 'eering hole', from the throat cringle of a spritsail which is called the eering. These larger, faster and more elegant cargo carrying wherries gradually replaced the barges and keels, and a few remain sailed for pleasure on the Broads.

The peter boat

The spritsail-rigged peter boat was the oldest type of craft fishing the tidal Thames and varied from twelve to about thirty feet long. The smallest sizes were used as far upstream as Chiswick and the largest boats worked from Leigh and other estuary ports, with some fishing coastwise to the Rivers Blackwater, Colne and the Suffolk Stour and Orwell, or along the Kentish shore to Margate.

In basic form the peter boat was a twelve to fourteen foot pointed stern boat of good depth, which could be rowed well and, when necessary in fishing, could be rowed stern first. She carried two men and had a small wet well built into the hull to contain the catch. There were side decks set about four inches below the almost horizontal sheerstrake, which had no gunwale so that nets and corklines slid over unhindered when setting the net. Numbers of these small, unrigged peter boats were used on the Thames and in the rivers and creeks of north Kent and Essex. Favoured dimensions were 14ft by 5ft by 2ft depth.

The peter net was a small seine about twenty or twenty-five fathoms long but t did not have a

PETER BOATS AT GREENWICH

Plate 66. Thames peter boats at Greenwich, drawn by E. W. Cooke in 1828. The small boat in foreground shows the wet well amidships, the forward, after and side decks, rowlock openings in the sheer and the unshipped rudder. The larger peter boat has a tilt over the forward part of the well. A keep chest or 'koff' for keeping fish live in water lies on the shore.

pocket to collect the catch. It was set in various ways by fishermen from different localities in the area. Small peter boats used it principally as a seine of fine thread which was set around a shoal of fish with a buoy at one end, which was retrieved after encirclement was completed and the ends of the net hauled together. Besides surrounding shoals of fish, peter nets were much used for stopping creeks, set across with stakes at low water and left until the next ebb, when the fishermen came downstream flailing oars on the surface to frighten fish into the net. Stop netting was made illegal but it did not stop the peter boat men.

Peter boats had considerable rise of floor and although fairly fine at the waterline endings, were full in the bow and stern above water, with a rounded stem profile and less rounded, raked sternpost. The rockered keel protruded only slightly below the garboard strakes to assist in turning the boat under oars, which was also why the hull was kept as short as possible, consistent with seaworthiness and range of use. The clinker planking was laid on sawn oak frames, notched over the lands. There were short forward and after decks set four to six inches below the top of the sheerstrake and drained through it by small scupper holes. A coaming of about that height was set across from sheer to sheer at the forward end of the cockpit and side deck coamings were carried as far as the after coaming, which might be square across the boat, or was sometimes rounded. In small peter boats the rower sat on the enclosed, wooden watertight well which was connected to the water by small holes through the hull planking. Fish were put into this through a small hatch in its top and while the boat floated were kept alive until needed for landing. Peter boats were probably the earliest wet well fishing boats in western countries, though wells were earlier used in China and possibly elsewhere.

The oars were of heavy, rectangular section inboard of the rowlocks to help balance and allow the rower to let go of them suddenly when fishing, without them slipping out of the wooden rowlocks mounted on the sheerstrake.

Peter boats of all sizes were rigged for sailing, the smallest with a boomless spritsail lashed at the throat to an unstayed mast and a foresail hanked to the forestay or set flying, tacked to the stemhead. Centreboards were not used and peter boats relied on the fine ends to work to windward. The spritsail had a single brail from the throat to the middle of the leach and the sprit had a yard tackle to set it up and support it, leading to the masthead. The rudder shipped on pintles.

Sailing and rowing peter boats were drawn by E. W. Cooke in his etching of the foreshore at Greenwich (Plate 66) and similar, small peter boats remained at Putney foreshore in 1927.

Many peter boat fishermen lived in the now demolished Crooked Lane district of the City of London and a shop sign of 1668 still hangs on Fish Street Hill. It shows a small, unrigged peter boat shooting her net. The rower is forward and his mate aft, flinging the net over. The hull form and its clinker planking are well shown and the figures are very lifelike.

These London fishermen worked the then fairly

clean waters of the river reaches below the city, down to Gravesend, fishing with peter nets, whitebait drag nets, seines, primitive trawls called trim trams for flat fish and shrimps, and with stake nets on the foreshores, called keddles, hence the old term 'A fine keddle of fish'.

Peter boats also laid in the tideway of the Thames with a small, conical shaped stowboat net lowered over the bow and streaming under the boat and astern in a bag of fine mesh with its mouth held open by two wooden baulks, in the manner of the huge stow nets worked by the Essex smacks (see *Gaff Rig* chapter 11).

Larger, open, sailing peter boats, perhaps eighteen to twenty feet long, rigged a canvas tilt for shelter at anchor on three half round hoops, with the mast and sprit lowered and lashed down from the forward to after decks, on the centreline. This allowed the crew to work away from home for a few days and little groups of tilted peter boats gathered in the lee of Thames foreshores for shelter overnight or during bad weather, smoke curling from a stovepipe poked through the tilt. A typical sailing peter boat used below London might be 19ft by 7ft by 3ft depth.

Larger peter boats existed at least by the end of the eighteenth century when there is record of the 25ft 4in *Friends Goodwill*, built in 1790 and the 26ft 7in *Good Intent*, a 'round sterned peter boat' built in 1797, indicating that she had a pointed stern and that transom sterned ones were then known.

A large, pointed sterned, spritsail-rigged peter boat, probably used for pleasure sailing is shown on a watercolour of 1814 in the possession of

Frank Hussey, the maritime historian of the Orwell. She carries an extended pole masthead as provision for setting a topsail and a brail is clearly visible across her mainsail, which appears to be boomless. Her hull is clinker planked and she has a jaunty sheer.

When peter boats became too large to be easily manoeuvred under oars to work a net, the usefulness of the pointed stern was gone and the less expensive transom stern began to be used as it increased working space aft and improved stability under sail. Some set a sprit mizzen and many had a portable wooden cabin top over the space between the foredeck and the wet well.

Latter day, transom sterned peter boats might be up to thirty feet long and worked anywhere about the Thames Estuary. Peter boats from Barking creek and Gravesend were regularly fishing at West Mersea during the 1870s but by then the type had become transom sterned gaff cutters. Their crews stopped the creeks for flounders and drove them into the net by jingling a few metal curtain rings on a line. Thornfleet was their usual anchorage, where they consumed their favourite delicacy of boiled sheeps heads, giving it the local nickname of 'Sheeps Head Bay'.

Many peter boats were owned at Leigh, the ancient fishing village on a creek to the west of the modern pleasure resort of Southend on Sea. Here, as elsewhere on the lower Thames, the larger peter boats retained the spritsail rig and with increasing size became known as 'pinks', from the pointed stern.

Leigh peter nets averaged twenty fathoms

length, forty-two to forty-five meshes deep and with mesh sizes varying from three and a quarter to three and three quarter inches, with a few preferring four inches to catch larger flatfish. 'Petering' as such netting was called at Leigh, usually meant setting the net across a creek or a 'swim' across the sands. The commencement of the flood tide outside was a preferred time as there was then little current in the swim. A buoyed anchor was let go near one edge of the channel and the peter boat was rowed to the other side, paying out the anchor ropes which fastened to the ends of the top and bottom ropes of the net, which was then payed out. Its other end was similarly bridled and anchored near the other shore so it formed a wall of mesh across the channel, into which the fish would swim. Sometimes other nets were set some distance above and below the first.

The fishermen then rowed back parallel to and a short distance from the lines of the headropes, beating the water with an ash pole to drive fish into the net. On reaching the other side one lifted the net buoy and anchor while the other rowed the boat ahead slowly as the net was hauled into the boat, its top and bottom brought together to form a bag and prevent fish escaping.

When there was no flow of tide the fishermen 'tinkled' the fish by jingling eight or so three inch diameter iron rings strung loosely on a bight at the end of a piece of line, lowered to the bottom and bounced up and down as the boat was rowed across the nets. This forced the fish from the bottom, where they bury themselves at low water. Besides the usual net fisheries, some pinks sailed

down to the Maplin Sands off the flat shore of Foulness Island and set trot lines for flatfish, with hooks made from thorns, pegged down to the sands at low water. This was called banding.

Flatfish were also taken alongshore from Leigh to the Maplins with peter nets. The catches were transferred from the wet wells to store pits at Leigh from which, every two weeks, they were hauled by drag net and loaded into the wells of carrying peter boats which sailed them upriver to be sold at Billingsgate, London's fish market.

Pinks

Pinks were fully decked and had a small, low cabin top and usually set a sprit mainsail with a topsail over, set on a topmast, staysail, and a jib set on a bowsprit of modest length. There was no windlass for the anchor.

These boats worked mainly between the Nore Sand and Holehaven, at the upper end of Sea Reach, at Canvey Island.

Pinks had small wet wells amidships, bulkheaded off from the small cabin and the hold. Like all such wells these were the full breadth of the hull up to around the waterline, then rose in a tapering trunk to reduce the free surface effect of the water in them adversely affecting stability.

A coloured aquatint by W. H. Timms entitled *Off Miffin Land* (Plate 67) illustrates mid-nineteenth century shipping in the Thames Estuary and shows a sprit-rigged pink or large peter boat in the right foreground. She has what appears to be a carved-planked hull and is rigged with a boomed-sprit mainsail with a loose foot, a staysail, jib and topsail set on the pole masthead.

Plate 67. This mid-nineteenth century picture of shipping in the Thames Estuary includes a 'pink' or large spritsail-rigged peter boat in the foreground. The cutter at right, sets a topsail with a studding sail and a topgallant over. The title *Off Miffn Land* is a mystery. *Coloured aquatint by W. H. Timms.*

317

318

The detail and feeling of the craft drawn suggests they were accurately observed rather than drawn from fancy and the peter boat represents a size and rig well suited to the estuary and capable of coastal fishing in fine weather.

About 1830 the *King William IV* was launched as the first Leigh peter boat with a transom stern. Only half a dozen were built during the next ten years, but gradually the pinks and peter boats were replaced by these transom sterned peter boats which developed into the powerful, gaff-rigged bawleys. (See Chapter 6 of *Gaff Rig*.) The last Leigh peter boat was fishing eels in 1902 and the type is now remembered there only by the well known pub.

Hatch boats

The rough, tidal waters of the lower Thames developed another type of pointed sterned, clinker-planked, beamy and decked spritsail-rigged fishing craft known as 'hatch boats', possibly from the long, narrow cockpit ending in a small cabin top over the forward accommodation. Hatch boats were often thirty feet long and had a wet well like the peter boats, whose rig of spritsail and foresail they at first carried, later developing a topmast and topsail set above the sprit mainsail, and a jib set on a running bowsprit. The mainsheet worked on a horse above the tiller and the mainsail had a single brail to its throat. Many of the largest stepped a spritsail mizzen with the boom sheeting to the top of the sternpost; a rig of yawl proportions. These boats were steered with a rudder head yoke and tiller lines. Many were fast and certainly the lines appear well formed and fine in all contemporary prints such as E. W. Cooke's *Hatch boat off Gravesend*. The type seems to have evolved from the wherry rather than the peter boat and had the wherry's buoyant bow and flared sides above water.

During the early nineteenth century many hatch boats adopted the standing gaff mainsail with the gaff controlled by vangs, though the sprit mizzen was retained.

Some hatch boats with wet wells carried cod from floating keep chests moored off Gravesend, into which North Sea smacks discharged their live catches, and sailed them upriver to Billingsgate market. Others fished the Kentish and Essex shores from the North Foreland to the River Blackwater, usually with peter nets and dredges.

A few migrated to fish out of Maldon and possibly West Mersea. Six hundred and thirty-five hatch boats were sailing in 1854 but only ninety-seven were recorded by 1863, when the cutter-rigged smacks and bawleys more suited to trawling for the quickly growing city markets were multiplying fast.

Dobles

Small, spritsail- and foresail-rigged pointed-sterned, clinker-planked fishing boats worked from the River Medway and the Swale, on the Kentish shore of the Thames Estuary and were known as 'Dobles'; a term which in Essex and Suffolk described a transom-sterned, flat-bottomed rowing skiff often used for light, river fishing. The Medway dobles were almost indistinguishable from peter boats and most were owned at Rochester, Strood, Chatham and Queenborough,

Figure 95. A Medway fishing doble, circa 1900. Note fish well and daggerboard. Dimensions 18ft 6in × 6ft 6in × 2ft 3in internal depth. *Science Museum, London.*

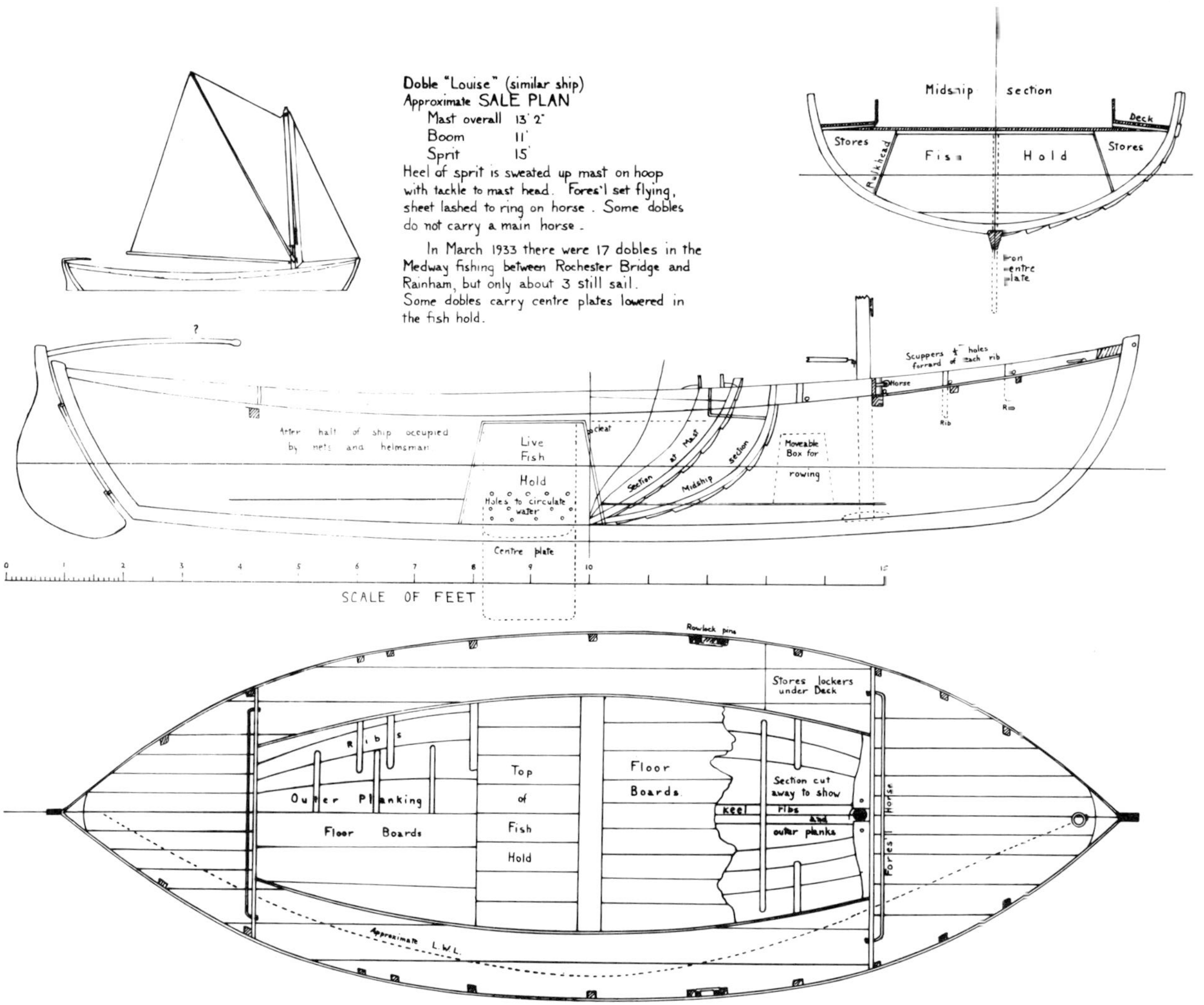

Doble "Louise" (similar ship)
Approximate SALE PLAN
Mast overall 13' 2"
Boom 11'
Sprit 15'
Heel of sprit is sweated up mast on hoop with tackle to mast head. Fores'l set flying, sheet lashed to ring on horse. Some dobles do not carry a main horse.
In March 1933 there were 17 dobles in the Medway fishing between Rochester Bridge and Rainham, but only about 3 still sail.
Some dobles carry centre plates lowered in the fish hold.
Midship section
Stores
Fish
Hold
Stores
Deck
Bulkhead
Iron centre plate
Scuppers 1" holes forrard of each rib
Horse
Rib
After half of ship occupied by nets and helmsman
Live Fish Hold
Holes to circulate water
Centre plate
cleat
Section at Mast
Midship section
Moveable Box for rowing
SCALE OF FEET
Rowlock pins
Stores lockers under Deck
Ribs
Outer Planking
Floor Boards
Top of Fish Hold
Floor Boards
Section cut away to show ribs and outer planks
Keel
Fores'l Horse
Approximate L.W.L.

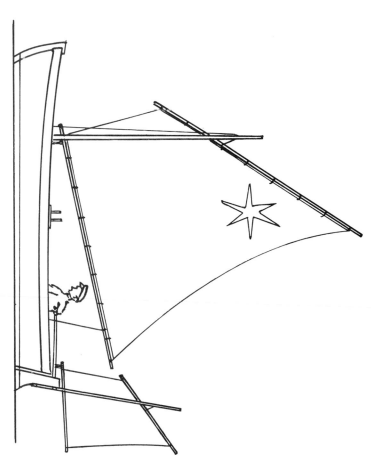

Figure 96. Medway huffler's boat, circa 1890. Note mizzen tacked to tiller to assist turning and steering and distinguishing emblem on sail.

with others elsewhere. Seventeen were still working from Strood in 1933. The doblemen's spritsail often had a boom and the foresail was set flying to the masthead. Many had centreboards fitted and in later years some were converted to a standing lug and a foresail. A few carried a jib on a bowsprit. The smallest dobles were about 12ft by 4ft 6in by 1ft 6in depth and the largest perhaps twenty-two feet long, with similar proportions. Besides peter nets, these boats worked small beam trawls and drift nets. Many small dobles were owned by fishermen who also had larger, gaff-rigged bawleys from which they worked when peter netting for smelts on the foreshores and sands. The fishermen lived on board the bawley, which sailed the catch home with the doble in tow astern.

Hufflers

The 'hufflers' of the river Medway assisted spritsail barges through Rochester Bridge, and cruised off Chatham and Rochester in open, lugsail boats on the lookout for a huffle, as this work was termed. These smart little clinker-planked boats averaged fourteen foot in length and were rigged with two lugsails (Fig. 96). The standing lug mainsail was set on a short mast stepped through the forward rowing thwart. It was a relatively short luffed sail with a single reef and set on a long yard and boom, controlled by a single part mainsheet nipped under a pin on each gunwale. The mizzen was a balance lug set on a light mast stepped on the after side on the rudder head. The forward end of the mizzen boom was lashed to the tiller, turning the sail as the helm

321

was moved, aiding steering and turning the boat in a similar way to the spritsail mizzen of a sailing barge, though this sheets to the rudder. This useful arrangement does not appear to have been used elsewhere.

The hufflers' boats were usually painted black, with a white sheerstrake, which was well fendered. They could be rowed from the amidship and forward thwarts, the oars working between thole pins.

Although none of the boats seem to have had centreboards, they sailed well and always provided good sport at Rochester regatta, where the hufflers race was a fine display of boat handling.

Hufflers had distinctive emblems painted on their main lug; stars, diamonds, etc., as recognition marks for barges they regularly assisted. The huffler luffed alongside, lowering his sails, and his boat was towed astern while he helped the bargemen prepare to lower the mast, sails and gear for shooting the bridge, sometimes also steering the barge if her skipper were strange to the passage. The barge approached the bridge with the tide under her and all sail set. When her topmast was within a few yards of the roadway the stay fall tackle of the forestay was quickly eased away and everything lowered to clear as she carried her way through. Then came the greater labour of heaving it up again on the windlass, before the huffler stepped back on board his little lugger with a shilling or two jingling in his pocket.

After about 1933 barges anchored or secured to a buoy to lower their gear before being towed through the bridge by a tug, but the Medway hufflers worked into the mid-twentieth century, when sailing barges still traded above Rochester bridge, though the hufflers characterful lugsails had disappeared by the 1920s.

Part III

Spritsails and Lugsails
in North America

11

Spritsails in New England

Martha's Vineyard and Noman's Land

There were many sizes and styles of small spritsail-rigged boats fishing and working from the north east coast of America and these various similar boat types had to be small and light to be rowed, which dictated easy lines, shallow draught and light displacement, qualities inconsistent with a powerfully-rigged sailing craft. They were used from coast villages, small towns, isolated coves and beaches, where lifting and small slipway facilities were unusual and as the boats had to be maintained from the subsistence economy of the coast, each owner had to be able to haul out and maintain his own boat. Above all, they had to be seaworthy, inexpensive and suitable for the fisheries.

A two masted rig enabled sails to be adjusted in sheeting to ease the helm and to suit weather and sea conditions; important in boats where the tending of gear and catching of fish was more vital than pure sailing performance.

The origin of these boats is obscure but is usually ascribed to the shallop style boats of colonial America. A personal view is that they were developed from fishing boats brought and

built on the Massachusetts and Maine coasts by Portuguese fishermen working the shore fisheries, probably a century before the revolutionary war, as very similar pointed sterned craft with the same spritsail rig were built and used in the coast fisheries of Portugal for many years.

It is difficult to define the olcest of these types, which continued in use until su-passed by powered craft early in the twentieth century, but the harsh simplicity of life of those who evolved and fished the spritsail boats used in the Vineyard Sound area, south of Cape Cod. and their interdependent fishing–farming existence, makes these boats most representative of the alongshore venturing of early American settlers.

Small sailing and rowing fishing boats usually capable of being beached, developed in a distinct form south of Cape Cod, Massachusetts, being principally used from the Islands of Martha's Vineyard and Noman's Land, but also being used and built at Nantucket Island and along the nearby southern shore of Cape God. Many were built by James Beetle at his new Bedford boatyard.

Possibly the boats were first used at Martha's

325

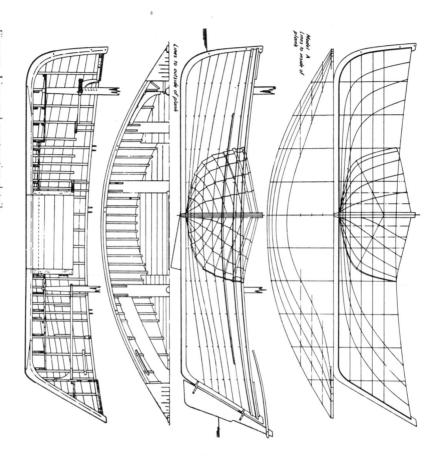

Model A
Lines to inside of plank

Lines to outside of plank

Figure 97. Lines and construction details of a Noman's Land fishing boat, showing fine stern, lapstrake (clinker) planking and rectangular centreboard case. *Courtesy John Leavens.*

Vineyard where the island's fishermen-farmers needed fish to salt down as winter food, and the original Indian inhabitants had passed on their custom of fertilising the ground with fish, particularly for corn, enriching the islands sandy soil; so a fishing boat was a desirable possession.

They needed able boats which could carry sail in a breeze, could be rowed by one man in a calm and would carry perhaps a ton of fish. As their homes were scattered along the shores the boats had to be light enough to haul out up the beaches and early ones were about sixteen or eighteen feet long on the keel, had a sharp flaring bow and a sharper and more flaring pointed stern. The sheer was well curved and rose sharply aft. The hull was full bodied and had three thwarts. Rig was two spritsails of almost equal height which were readily unshipped. Steering was by a rudder hung on the sternpost.

Construction was strong and light, generally with clinker (lapstrake) planking of north eastern cedar on oak frames, though some boats were carvel planked. Most were built by the owners and were weatherly enough to beat home-against a strong wind when loaded, but could be sailed by one man, who could also row the boat off through surf stern first. Centreboards were not used in the early boats which had a narrow keel. Inside there was a few feet of level flooring at the stern and a lining of bottom boards elsewhere. There was an absence of non-essential gear and ironwork but the boats were usually of good appearance and many were well finished. All had a hole bored transversely through the stem near the waterline, in which an iron or oak peg was thrust on beaching to form a hauling up attachment.

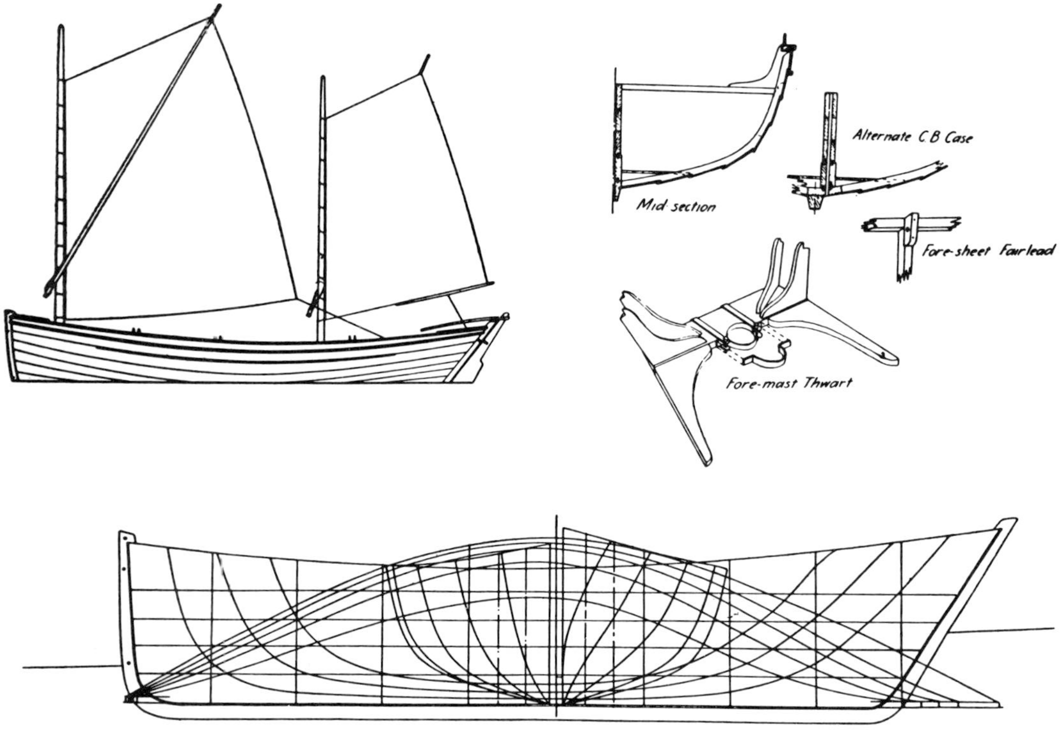

About 1875 Perez Horten of Vineyard Haven is reputed to have improved the boats by fitting a coaming, locally termed a wash strake, inside the gunwales, which were covered by side decks, ending in short forward and after decks.

Later, the foresail was increased in area and the 'mainsail', as the after spritsail was called, was reduced, giving the rig ketch proportions.

During the 1890s some Martha's Vineyard fishermen owned boats of the same rig and arrangement but built with deeper hulls for weatherliness without need of a centreboard.

The craft were kept and launched off the north and south shores of the island, being locally known as Vineyard or Chilmark boats, respectively. Many were beached along the north shore from West Chop to Gay Head and places such as Lamberts Cove were probably named for landings of early settlers.

The method of hauling up seems to have remained into the twentieth century. A 'ladder' of oak saplings was nailed or bolted together and a rectangular groove, in which the keel slid, was cut in the centre of each rung. Several lengths of 'ladder' were laid before a beaching boat, the grooves were smeared with grease and one or two oxen were hitched to the haul-up rope fast on the bow pin. Then she was hove up the beach, steadied by the crew and any helpers nearby. In later years, stunted oxen for hauling up were owned by Israel Luce, who charged each boat five dollars for the season, no matter how often she was beached. Wooden beach capstans were used by isolated boats, with purchase increased by

327

Figure 98. Sail plan and lines of another Noman's Land fishing boat showing typical spritsail rig proportions and construction arrangements. *Courtesy John Leavens.*

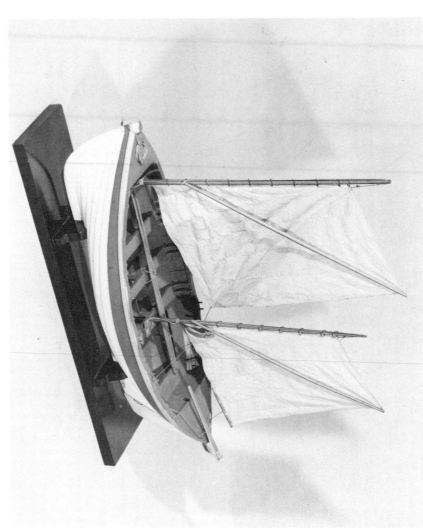

Plate 68. Model of a Nomans Land boat used in the fisheries around that island and from Marthas Vineyard, off the Massachusetts coast during the late nineteenth century. The 'mainsail', as the after spritsail was termed, had a club to spread strain of the sheet on the clew.

Photo – Smithsonian Institution.

a tackle to a 'deadman' anchor.

The boats worked long lines, which American fishermen termed 'trawls'. These were shot from wooden tubs, in which they were baited and coiled ashore, before sailing, in the manner of British and European beach fishermen. A typical long line worked by the Noman's Land boats was four miles in length, set from six tubs with ten 'skates' or parts, each of sixty fathoms, in each tub; a total 3600 fathoms of gear, all set and hauled by hand, often in strong tideways. Each end of the trawl was anchored by a killick, simply made from a three-pronged crutch cut from an upper branch of an oak tree, with a twenty pound beach stone jammed and lashed in its fork. The killick was made fast to about twenty fathoms of light buoy rope attached to a waterlight, ballasted keg to which was lashed a long spruce sapling with a marker flag at its head. The trawl ground rope had three foot long 'gangings' of cod line bent to it at six foot intervals and each had a soft iron hook seized to its end.

One of the tarpaulin-aproned crew hauled the ground rope in over an iron roller which shipped into a socket on the starboard coaming. As each cod appeared he stunned it with a 'muckle' or heavy oak club before heaving it aboard. The other man coiled the ground line in the tubs which were stowed aft, and helped to gaff awkward fish. Fish other than cod were termed 'scrubs' and were usually thrown back. If fishing was good and the weather reasonable the trawl might be 'underrun' or brought aboard over the roller, cleared of its catch, rebaited and reshot as the boat moved along its anchored length. Often this would be carried out by one fisherman. The catch was stowed amidships and might be covered by a light tarpaulin in hot weather.

Although fishing was confined to a comparatively small radius these boats had other uses. Everything needed or produced on the Vineyard or Noman's Land was carried to and from in them. Almost every day, at least one made a passage to New Bedford, on the nearby mainland, twenty miles distant, and sometimes they were sailed to the island of Nantucket or to eastern ports of Long Island, across forty miles of open water. A few of the larger boats carried white clay, dug at the Vineyard, to New York, where it was used in the manufacture of chocolates.

One boat twenty-two feet on the keel, was reputedly specially built to carry cargo to and from the mainland. At the end of the season some owners carried their last fish catch to New York market as a traditional outing to the big city rather than of economic necessity. The crew slept wrapped in the sails.

Six miles south of Gay Head, on the Vineyard, lies the small island of Noman's Land, about two miles in diameter. In spring and autumn, cod schooled on the ledges around it and from at least the mid-nineteenth century and probably earlier, this opportunity for good fishing attracted Vineyard islanders who ferried their fishing gear, families and basic furniture and effects there to live for the fishing season in a string of dwellings along the north shore. Between fifty and a hundred fishermen worked there during the

seasons which lasted from about April 1st to the end of May and from early October to mid December; but some men fished all winter, when weather permitted. The island had no harbour and, except in fine weather, the boats had to be hauled out at night. This was achieved by cooperation of the whole settlement, as was usual in most beach communities.

The men were about at dawn, loading gear into the boats and, if a breeze was anticipated, ballasting them with stone to augment the permanent iron pigs in the bilge. If sufficient fish was caught the stone was thrown overboard. One after another the boats slid down the beach on ladders or skids and launched off. The one or two man crews had to row hard, stern first through the alongshore breakers until there was sufficient offing to step the foremast. With the spritsail set and sheeted, and the boat drawing clear, the mainmast was stepped and its spritsail set. In light winds or calms they might row twenty or thirty miles during a day's fishing which, with the backbreaking labour of setting and hauling the long lines, was extremely hard work.

In the evening the boats sailed close to the breakers, crews furled the sails, unstepped the masts and rowed for the shore, where others brought down ladders or skids and laid them where the boat was expected to beach. Sometimes she might strike fairly and slide up, half out of the water. Misjudgement in beaching could mean a slew broadside and a capsize, with boat, crew, catch and gear all rolling in the surf. As the bow slid up, one of the shore party slipped an iron or wood pin through the hole in the stem and turned a strop round it in which the haul up rope was hooked and with shouting and whip cracking the oxen drew the beached boat above high watermark.

Then the crew had to dress and salt the catch in a fishhouse or on the beach; splitting the cod and putting livers and tongues in separate barrels. Coarse salt was rubbed into the interiors and the fish were finally plunged into a barrel of brine pickle. Still work was unfinished, as the trawl had to be overhauled and rebaited, with perhaps some of the hooks to be reshaped before carefully coiling it in the tubs to run freely during the set next morning. Hard, backbreaking labour for subsistence living by a community who were strongly independent.

Gradually, a few Vineyarders lived the year round on Noman's Land in a settlement of weatherbeaten cottages and a few small farms, with a church which also served as meeting house and school. It must have been a striking but harsh home, the gravelly beaches creaming with clean Atlantic surf in the shimmering blue haze of summer but roaring white in autumn gales.

Lewellyn Howland captured the fascinating spirit of Noman's Land in its last days as a fishing colony in his *South West and by West of Cape Cod*, which is one of the most beautifully written American books. He described the *Islander*, a typical Noman's Land boat in which he had fished, though the fishermen appear to have called them 'island boats'. In their life of comparative isolation and hard work these fishermen—boatbuilders often constructed beautiful craft in which the best timber and only copper

fastenings were used. The *Islander* was carvel planked and double ended, about eighteen feet long by almost seven feet beam and 2ft 6in hull draught. Lightly built, flat floored and hard bilged she had short decks forward and aft with narrow side decks and coamings fitted around an open well and rowlock chocks clenched to them.

A locker was fitted under the after deck and the tiller worked through a wrought iron sheet horse fastened to the head of the sternpost. The after spritsail sheeted to this. The foremast stepped through the forward thwart. There was an amidship thwart and another three feet abaft it, through which the mainmast stepped. The foresail was considerably larger than the mainsail and both were spritsails. The boomless foresail overlapped the mainmast when close hauled but the mainsail had a light club at the after end of the foot. The foresail had double sheets rendering round strong oak pins fitted vertically under the gunwales, which were tended at each tack. The mainsheet worked through a block on the sheet horse and led through a bullseye on the club, then down to the helmsman. Sails were stowed by lifting the heels of sprits out of the snotters and furling the sails by frapping them to the masts with the sheets. A staysail was not carried and the masts were unstayed for ease of lowering and beaching. These were not fast craft but were good seaboats which could work to windward through strong winds, and a sea. They do not seem to have been quick in stays due to the long keel, but probably improved when centreboards were adopted; the first was believed to have been fitted by George Butler of Noman's Land in the 1870s, and others soon followed. The centreboard case was often offset to the side of the keel, with the slot through the garboard strake to minimise jamming with clay and stones when beaching. On a long tack to windward it was customary to place the 200 pounds or so of the iron pigs along the weather side.

It was said that only two boats were lost when fishing around Noman's Land or in making passages to the mainland or nearby islands. Sometimes the owner of a new boat, enthusiastically boastful of her qualities, was challenged to a race, when three men sailed each boat; helmsman, foresheetman and bailer. Some races were regarded as feats of endurance rather than speed, reflecting working conditions, with the racers carrying full sail in strong winds and heavy seas.

larger than usual and had the cat rig. These were generally used for hand lining and were fast, seaworthy and generally easier on the helm than transom sterned catboats.

When the Noman's Land fishing season ended some boats were hauled out and laid up on beaches at the Vineyard, where owners returned to their farms. Others, worked by full time fishermen, were kept on moorings of the now deserted settlement of Lobsterville, between Gay Head and the inlet to Menemsha Pond, with canvas covers laced over them. There the boats were protected from north and west gales by a submerged bank which ran parallel with the beach. This anchorage was disused after the inlet to the pond was dug to form a harbour. Later boats were often larger; about 20ft by 6ft 6in by about 1ft 8in hull draught and were usually carvel planked.

Soon after gaff-rigged catboats were owned at the Vineyard, some island type boats were built

In the late 1870s William Mayhew of Vineyard Haven rigged his island boat with two gaff sails and started a controversy on rig efficiency which divided the fishermen for some time. Many accused him of being too lazy to furl a spritsail! However the gaff sails with the same proportions of shape as the sprit rig became generally used, as did another innovation by Mayhew, who rounded off the heel of the sternpost, enabling the boat to be launched or hauled up stern first and afforded improved manoeuvrability when rowing off stern first through surf.

Many island and Noman's Land boats had these amendments until petrol engines were installed about 1903. The mizzen was soon discarded and a larger mainsail was fitted but inevitably was used less and less. Booms were put ashore and finally sail was abandoned. The Gay Head Indians purchased some of the old boats for scalloping and lobstering and two boats remained in use with auxiliary engines until the early 1930s, when Noman's Land had become a game reserve with a solitary keeper. Some of the men who had fished there under sail still came off from the Vineyard and mainland ports in motor fishing launches to haul cod from the ledges, crewed by their sons and grandsons.

Plymouth Bay

The shallow area of water enclosed landward of Manomet Point and Gurnet Lights at the tip of

Plate 69. The Kingston lobster boat *Annie Fuller* under sail in Plymouth Bay, Massachusetts, circa 1900. Note mast hoops instead of luff lacings or robands.

Photo – Mystic Seaport.

Duxbury Beach, on the Massachusetts coast, generally known as Plymouth Bay, has the towns of Plymouth, Duxbury and Kingston on its shores. Here, small spritsail-rigged boats fished for lobsters and were generally known as Plymouth lobster boats, after the larger town, though most were built in Duxbury or Kingston. They also fished from Hull and other places and were also variously known as Kingston lobster boats, Hull lobster boats or north shore lobster boats.

The Bay is a wide, shallow expanse of mud flats intersected by narrow deeper channels and having a ten foot range of tide filling and draining it twice daily. The entrance was only a mile wide with a four knot current in the main channel, which caused a breaking sea when a strong wind opposed tide. In contrast to these shallow home waters the lobster fishermen laid their pots alongshore in water up to twenty-seven fathoms deep, where the seas were long but had great force; from Rocky Point to Manomet Point, around Gurnet Point and towards and beyond High Pine Ledge and well seaward. Sixty pots was a normal string for one man to tend under sail and oar and each man had a marker of distinctive colour or shape.

So the lobster boats had to be shoal draught, weatherly and seaworthy. Originally these were about sixteen or seventeen feet long by five feet beam, with plumb stem and stern, deep hulled with considerable rise of floor and bluff bows. Reputedly these had used a two-masted spritsail rig since the beginning of the nineteenth century, the foresail being larger, and hoisted the sails on single-part halyards leading over sheeves at the mastheads. The fore halyard led down to belay on a pin in the stemhead, the main to a cleat on the mast or on the thwart through which it was stepped. Each sail luff was attached to the mast by a lacing or hoops and both had considerable peak from the long, light sprits which slipped into spliced rope beckets or snotters. There were no shrouds, the foresail sheets were arranged in two single parts and the mainsheet was rigged as in (Fig. 99). Early boats had the reputation of sometimes running under in a strong wind and were so slow to windward that many owners shipped a boy at fifty cents a day to help row them home against a foul wind. Many were built with an outside deadwood and transom stern, with much less rise of floor than later boats and a small bilge radius. Planking was clinker or carvel and most had centreboards with small wet wells on each side.

Local tradition held that the first of an 'improved' type of lobster boat was built at Duxbury by Samuel Alden during the 1820s and continued to be built by him in numbers, with only slight improvement, for fifty years. Many of his apprentices subsequently commenced business in the area, building and developing the type, which by 1870 was undergoing change, being particularly influenced by yachts.

During 1871 Nathan Watson commenced building lobster boats at Kingston, reputedly constructing the first clinker planked one there three years later.

Edward A. Ransom opened a boatbuilding business at Kingston in 1879, on the site of once flourishing shipyards which had built ships and

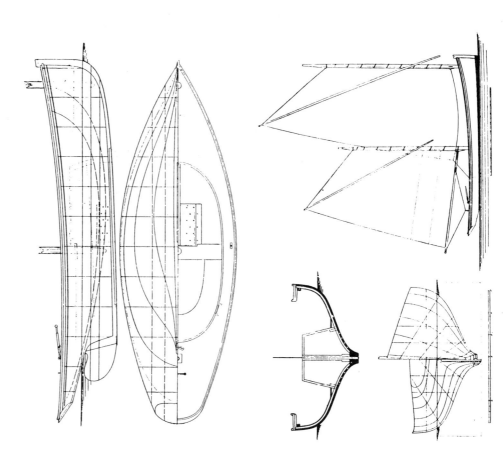

Figure 99. The Plymouth lobsterboat *Vixen,* designed and built by James Watson, Clarks Island, Duxbury Bay, Massachusetts, 1893. Note fine sections and fish well. Dimensions 19ft 8½in overall. 16ft 5½in waterline × 6ft 9in beam × 2ft hull draught.

schooners up to 700 tons, which were launched into the head of the James River and were towed down to the bay by teams of oxen.

By the 1870s lobster boats were occasionally raced during summer in typically informal, fisherman fashion. Gradually summer visitors and local yachtsmen sought refined lobster boats for pleasure sailing and racing developed into two classes with cups for working lobster boats and those built for pleasure sailing, the culminating event of the season being a regatta between the towns of Kingston, Plymouth and Duxbury.

In summer, Ransom was skipper of a Boston-owned schooner yacht, which viewed the 1885 races for the America cup between the American sloop *Puritan* and the British cutter *Genesta*. When the *Puritan* was hauled up that autumn, Edward Ransom studied her hull shape, mentally photographing Edward Burgess' lines, which he was determined to apply to a fast racing lobster boat he would build that winter to beat all comers on the Bay. He was well qualified to produce her, having started as a boy of nine pulling an oar in a lobster boat, being allowed to haul pots alone three years later and eventually becoming thoroughly familiar with the type and its work. Subsequently he worked in Samuel Alden's boatbuilding yard before setting up independently, building a boat each winter and sailing her through the season, then selling her, to start again.

His new style lobster boat was named *Solitaire* and had a counter, a fine hollow bow entrance and hollow curve to the hull bottom sections. She was conceived and built to race and won almost

every one entered, so her proportions and form were quickly imitated locally. These new boats had reserve buoyancy in the flaring forward sections and tended to lift when running hard and although they influenced the working lobster boats, they remained pleasure boats, with the *Solitaire* dominating the fleet of thirty racers until Ransom launched the *Aphrodite* in 1892 for Addison G. Fay, then a schoolboy of 17, who drove her so hard that Ransom in *Solitaire* was usually pressed to beat him.

Like most of his contemporaries, Ransom designed by half model, lifting the lines from it for lofting and mould making. He preferred carvel planked hulls with oak planking and galvanised fastenings, but many working lobster boats were planked in three quarter inch thick white pine or eastern white cedar, which was also used for ceiling. Keel, frames and coamings were often white oak and decking white pine, with a white oak toerail.

Ransom's rival, James Watson of Clarks Island in Duxbury Bay, often used clinker planking. He had similar background to Ransom, but while Ransom turned increasingly to boatbuilding, Watson spent most of his time skippering yachts, many of them designed by Edward Burgess, and he also applied their basic hull form to his lobster boat construction, the *Vixen* (Fig. 99) being typical of his best. She was 19ft 8½in overall, 16ft 5½ins waterline length by 6ft 9ins beam with 2ft draught with centreboard raised and up to 4ft 6in with it lowered. The yacht-like counter was flat sectioned but the hull had considerable rise of floor with a high, slack bilge and was typical of the peak of development in 1893. The elliptical cockpit had one thwart, with the mainmast stepped through it, the foremost being in the eyes of the boat. A small wet well was built on each side of the centreboard case and a wooden cover could be shipped over the cockpit forward of the mainmast, but generally these boats were dry in a sea. Most working boats had all inside ballast of bags of shingle, rock or iron ore. Some, particularly pleasure boats, had a small external iron keel shoe. Hull colours were often dark green sides, pale buff deck, white ceiling and bulkheads and varnished spars, thwarts, coamings and trim.

The boats sailed to and from the grounds under foresail and mainsail in normal weather but when hauling or shooting pots the mainsail was furled with sprit and boom against the mast. In stronger winds, it was usual to unship the mainmast and stow the sail away to increase working room in the cockpit and under the loose footed foresail the lobsterman worked up the string to windward, tacking, hauling, emptying, re-baiting and setting the pots as he went from buoy to buoy. Some lobstermen took the string before the wind, letting the foresail flow forward while busy with the pot, then running on to the next without losing time. However, this was more difficult than beating along the string, as the boats drifted fast to leeward, even under bare poles, and the pots might be dragged through the water, needing considerable exertion to recover them while the boat was laid-to with the foresail sheet eased and helm down. Some eager fishermen even took the string before the wind under foresail and mainsail, which needed great effort.

The foresail had no reef points and in a fresh wind either the whole sail was carried or, when this became overpowering, the foremast and sail were struck and the smaller mainsail was shifted forward in its place. If the wind increased further two reefs could then be tied down, reducing the sail area from the total of perhaps 400 to 70 square feet. Under this snug area lobster boats could sail home under the most adverse weather, beating in against tide and wind of gale strength or come roaring in over the ebb before a fresh easterly. Often, at the first sign of strong wind, the foresail sprit was unshipped and the sail was lowered. Then the foremast was unstepped and its heel was placed under the foredeck, with the truck projecting beyond the stern. Then the mainmast and sail were shifted forward in its place. As an average foremast was twenty feet long and had a maximum diameter of four and a half inches and the sprit might be twenty-two or three feet long and three inches diameter, this was hard work in smooth water, but to do it in a seaway, standing on the narrow foredeck, took considerable nerve and seamanship. However, a fisherman dare not delay and if necessary he sat with legs astride the stem to grip the mast and lift it out of its step and deck hole and quickly lower it behind him on his shoulder. Stepping the mainmast forward, he thrust its heel against the stemhead and raised the mast well up, then dropped it through the deck hole and hopefully into the step on the keel before the swing of the seas sent it through the bottom planking. When used as a substitute foresail, the mainsail boom aided the desirable flat set of the

335

sail. However, in squally weather the mainmast had to be struck and bundled out of the way, leaving the larger foresail to contend with the wind until the boat could bear away before the wind or the foresail could be lowered.

The lobstermen were always conscious of the rig's failings in strong winds and a sharp bait knife was kept handy to cut sheet or halyard, if necessary. Essentially the two masted rig was an evolution from small open boats carried into larger boats which in some conditions would have been better rigged in other ways. The need for mast shifting was its greatest weakness and in many parts of the coast from Rhode Island to Eastern Maine, it was superseded for lobstering by the handier sloop with one or two headsails, which could be reefed down in a breeze. Many boats unshipped the foremast and foresail in late autumn and left them ashore, stepping the smaller mainmast and mainsail forward as a snug winter rig. However, lobster boats became dull sailers when rigged as sloops or catboats, to which some were converted.

The unstayed masts had round tenons into the steps, rather than the more usual square ones to enable them to rotate completely when the forehalyard was made fast to a cleat on the mast. This was useful too when hauling pots with the foresail flogging out before the bow like a flag.

Originally the mainsheet was a single part, so it was not necessary to unreeve it when shifting masts and sails. Ransom-built boats had a deep hook instead of a mainsheet block. This was mounted on a deck traveller and the mainsheet led from the boom end, under the hook and to a cleat on the forward end of the boom. It was always in reach of the helmsman, even when before the wind.

These lobster boats were fast and handy in their own waters, capable of going to windward with the board up providing the sea was not too big. They were reasonably dry and easy on the helm. Ransom experimented with hull shape, building many boats with 'S' shaped after end sections and some with a simple outside deadwood and no reverse turn, which were usually difficult to steer. However, the shapely, counter sterned boats were expensive to build and the advantages of the simple-shaped, earlier boats were soon lost. During the 1880s a typical boat cost $250; by the late 1890s this was doubled.

Lobster boats of this type were built along the southern Massachusetts coast from Hingham to Plymouth but were different from the strip planked and reputedly inferior craft working from Cohasset, Scituate, Green Harbour and Hull, whose boats were distinctive by a taller rig.

Around 1900 some boats were rigged with a long gaff on the foresail, which remained boomless but set flatter and was reckoned more efficient than the spritsail. Many of Ransom and Watson's boats were sold for fishing or pleasure use to owners at Boston, Northern Massachusetts, Maine and occasionally South of Cape Cod.

The lobster boats worked throughout the year and inspired their owners with confidence until petrol engines were installed around the years 1900–10, after which the sails were soon laid ashore. Ransom ceased boatbuilding in 1922 but his workshop still stood by the James river in 1969.

Hampton boats

Further north, on the coasts of New Hampshire and Maine, the two-masted Hampton boat was much used alongshore until the early twentieth century. Tradition maintains that a boat built in 1805 by Enoch Chase of Seabrook, New Hampshire was the prototype Hampton boat. She is recorded as having a moderately sharp bow and a 'pinkie' (or pointed) stern. A wooden false keel about twelve inches deep was carried the full length of the hull to give lateral area and ballast was iron or sand. She was rigged with two masts setting a large foresail and a smaller mainsail, and had a 'jib' tacked down to a removeable bowsprit, which was used when making passages to and from the fishing grounds. Except for a centreboard, this boat had the principal characteristics of the later Hampton boat type as it existed for many years, and many were built by Chase and later by Locke, both in the Hampton-Seabrook area of New Hampshire.

First known literary mention of the term 'Hampton boat' occurs in John J. Audubon's *Delineations of American Scenery*. During a trip to Labrador in 1833, the noted ornithologist saw the boats in use from fishing vessels hailing from Maine and Massachusetts, in the manner of the later dories, and wrote ... 'A vessel of one hundred tons or so is provided with a crew of twelve men, who are equally expert sailors and fishers and for every couple of these hardy tars a Hampton boat is provided ... at three in the morning the crew are prepared for their day's labour and ready to betake themselves to their boats, each of which has two oars and lugsails.'

The reference to lugsails probably meant the lug sheet foresails overlap of the mainsail. A short club was usually sewn across the clew of this sail to support the strain of sheeting.

The length of sprits differed in the boats; sometimes these were long, with the heel near the sail tack and others, particularly in earlier boats, were short, with the heel set about half way up the sail luff. These points were chosen to avoid chafe of the sprit heel on the clew of the overlapping foresail. When running, the foresail foot was often boomed out by an oar or similar spar. Hampton boats were carried on board New England vessels fishing for cod off Newfoundland and in the Gulf of St Lawrence until the late 1880s, some carrying four boats on deck and one in stern davits. With a full load of fish in the hold, the boats were often sold in Nova Scotia, Newfoundland or Labrador and new ones were purchased for the next trip. However, in Maine similar boats were built around Casco Bay and alongshore to Muscongus Bay and developed separately from the Hampton type built in New Hampshire and Massachusetts. Usually these had a well tucked up transom stern, fine bow and bottom shape, with hollow bottom sections and some tumble home in the quarters. Twenty-two feet appears to have been a usual length with the rig and other arrangements resembling the Hampton boats.

About 1864 Elijah Kellog, Minister of a Church at Harpswell, Maine, mentioned the Hampton boats' qualities in one of his books:
'A fisherman wants a boat too, that is smart, stiff to bear a hard blow, buoyant, will mind her

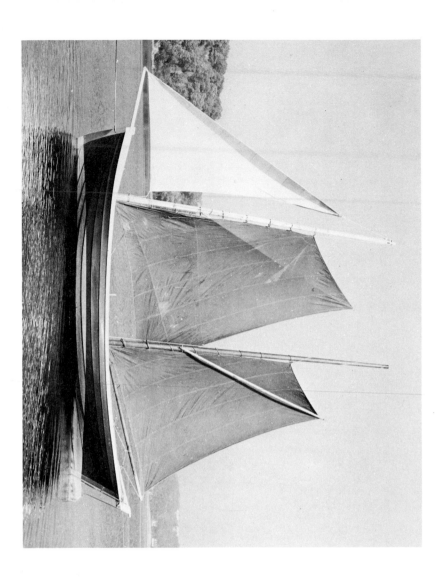

Plate 70. This 23ft 6in 'Hampton' or 'New England' boat was built before 1850 at Birch Island, Maine, and sets the two masted spritsail rig of the type. She does not have a centreboard and is preserved at Mystic Seaport, Connecticut.

Photo – Mystic Seaport.

helm and work quick to clear an ugly sea, and sail well on a wind ... There are boats now built at Hampton or Seabrook that would beat into Boston Bay with a man in them that knew how to handle them in a gale of wind, when a ship couldn't do it.'

Young Elijah Kellog became Minister at Harpswell in 1844 and, always fascinated by maritime things, soon afterwards had a pointed stern 'Hampton boat' built for him by Durgin, the boatbuilder of Birch Island, near Harpswell, Maine, sometime before 1850. She was 23ft 6in long by 6ft 9in beam and drew 2ft 5in. A centreboard was not fitted but she had very fine lower waterlines at each end, providing lateral plane for windward sailing.

Kellog sometimes sailed her from Harpswell to Boston, where he was chaplain to the sailors' home and kept her until his death in 1901, after which she remained stored in his barn until 1955, when the boat was presented to Mystic Seaport, Massachusetts, where she was restored and is exhibited afloat, fully rigged. The Maine boats were often good sailers, particularly to windward, which reflected their work in estuaries, rivers and bays. Many were clinker (lapstrake) planked but by the 1890s carvel planking was more usual.

Some had a short 'plank' bowsprit which was shipped in light weather to set a jib. Many were built by John Pettingill who lived and worked on Crotch (later renamed Cliff) Island, Maine; and five of his half-models survive. Ward Bickford was another Crotch Island boatbuilder, and John Walker another, who later moved to Yarmouth, where he continued to build pointed and transom sterned Hampton boats into the 1890s.

In 1868, David Doughty of Great Island, Maine installed the 'first' centreboard in a Hampton boat and is also believed to have first locally fitted the narrow side decks known in New England as 'washboards'. About 1875 strip planking was used; an innovation locally credited to David Sinnett of Baileys Island, Maine.

Many had pointed sterns which were thought to make them good sea boats. The transom sterns provided more space aft but generally the transom was small and narrow, leaving the after form effectively pointed-sterned. The exaggeratedly lean bow was a weakness, allowing the hulls to pitch and generally the hull shape seems to have tended to become extreme by the 1890s, when use of the boats had become widespread.

Fig. 100 illustrates a typical Maine Hampton boat of this period. Note the raised straight keel, comparatively small centreboard, fine tuck and quick sheer at the stern and thole pins for the oars. The low feet of the spritsails were inevitable as part of a low sail plan but they hampered the crew, particularly the mizzen boom, which, with the cramped seating arrangement and awkward mainsheet, demanded a patient helmsman.

Both sails were usually attached to the masts by wooden hoops and were hoisted by a single part halyard. The sail was usually hoisted and then the head of the sprit was slipped into the eye at the peak, set up and then the heel was slipped into the snotter.

In fine weather, many Maine fishermen preferred to furl the foresail by lowering the sprit

Plate 71. A 'Hampton boat' spreads her spritsails to a light air in a Maine harbour, about 1890. The helmsman keeps an oar shipped to help her round in stays. His mate prepares fishing gear forward. *Photo – The Mariners Museum.*

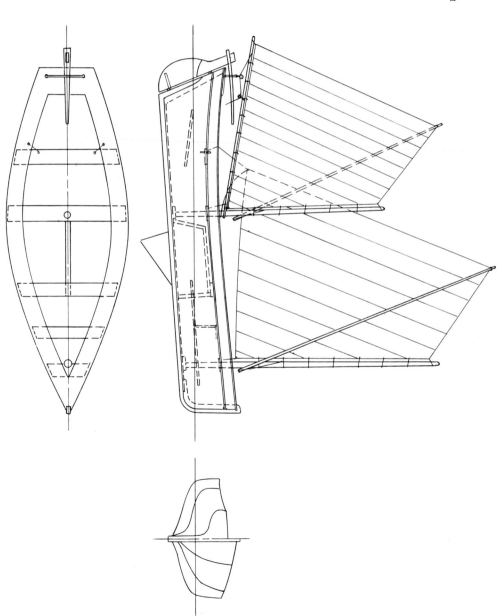

Figure 100. Sail plan and arrangement of a typical centreboard 'Hampton boat' of the 1890s having a fine bow and tucked up transom. Dimensions 20ft × 7ft × 2ft 6in hull draught.

heel down and with the sprit against the mast, frapped the sail around both, making fast with the sheet.

The bilges were easy and the bow was slightly fuller in shape than the stern. Apart from being tender they appear to be reasonably balanced hulls. The inevitable search for speed developed sharper bows and exaggeratedly fine sterns with badly distorted waterlines, harder bilges and hollow bottom sections extending from the stern to forward of amidships.

Similar boats, rigged with a low sprit mainsail, without a boom, and with the clew spread by a club for sheeting and a foresail set on a bowsprit, were built for use from Matinicus Island, off the Maine Coast, and from some places alongshore from Boothbay to Rockland. These sprit-rigged sloops had centreboards and were probably the forerunners of the gaff sloops known as the

'Muscongus Bay type', where many were built as predecessors and contemporaries of the better known Maine fishing sloop often called the 'Friendship' sloop.

The first petrol engines were installed in Hampton boats between 1900–05, and as the hull form adapted well to low powered engines, sail was quickly discarded.

During the 1870s similar pointed stern boats under thirty feet in length were used in the Labrador and Nova Scotia fisheries. These were open except for short decks forward and aft, set a sprit foresail and a gaff or triangular mizzen, were fitted for rowing and later had an iron centreplate. This may have been the origin of the larger 'Tancook whaler' type of fishing and working boats developed and built in Mahone Bay, Nova Scotia, but rigged as gaff schooners.

12

New Jersey to
the Mexican Gulf

Some of the most unusual and interesting small sailing craft in America were evolved and used by fishermen and watermen between New Jersey to the Gulf of Florida.

The Sea Bright Skiff

The spritsail-rigged, New Jersey beach skiff, later generally known as the Sea Bright skiff, originated for fishing and other work off the exposed beaches of northern Monmouth county, to the south of Sandy Hook, at the southern entrance to the approaches to New York.

Local weather conditions affected the hull and rig development of these beach boats; in summer the sea alongshore was usually calm under the westerly, offshore wind of the morning, which often veered to the southeast by afternoon, raising a short, steep sea and a surf alongshore through which craft had to launch and beach. Autumn and spring storms rise sharply and are often accompanied by sleet and snow, while fog is frequent.

The coast had few harbours of refuge. The first, Shark River, is twenty miles south of Sandy Hook; Manasquan Inlet a further six miles, and

Barnegat Inlet twenty-four miles below it. These narrow inlets are difficult to enter in bad weather and almost impossible in hard north easterly winds. So, once launched, the beach boats had to be capable of beaching through surf.

Probably small boats had launched from this coast for many years before the growth of immigrant population in the New York area during the period 1830–50, many of them of catholic religion, created a considerable demand for fish which immediately adjacent fisheries could not satisfy, and New Jersey's shore fisheries boomed as a result.

Nauvoo, near the present Sea Bright, was amongst the first of these communities to flourish, about 1845. Later, another named Galilee, grew up close to the site of the present Monmouth Beach coast guard station and another developed at Long Branch. The first two were the usual cluster of fishermen's sheds, fishing gear, boats and beaching equipment internationally typical of such places; with the addition of ice houses, necessary to hold stock for icing the catches for transport.

From fifty to seventy-five beach skiffs worked

from each landing and at that time catches were heavy; mainly bluefish, mackerel and sea bass, caught by 'jigging' with hand lines which had painted or bright metal 'squids' to attract the fish. Sometimes fish were attracted by 'chum' as ground or chopped fish thrown overside as a lure was termed, the fishing hooks being baited with the same type of fish. Shrewsbury Rocks were the favourite fishing ground but areas north and south of this were often worked, the season being from May to November.

The catch was landed at the end of each day's fishing was cleaned, packed in ice and despatched as fast as possible to New York by carrier sloops or by steamers. Beach seines were also used and in winter some went cod fishing.

The principal families then working these fisheries included Wooley, West, Lippincott, Warner, Ridley, White and Tallman, of which the first three probably originated from English South Devon beach families, possibly from Sidmouth. Many boat owners employed men outside their own families and typically a fisherman worked in a team of four men, whose annual income might then be $500–$1000.

Contemporary beach skiffs averaged fifteen feet in length by five feet beam and had a flat plank keel, rockered in profile, rounded sides with lapstrake (clinker) planking of white cedar on sawn or a combination of sawn and bent, frames, a strong sheer and well raked transom – all basic features of the New Jersey skiff type which have survived to the present.

The garboard planks were fastened to the sternpost below the transom and met the

343

Plate 72. William, Isaac and Walter Seaman of the noted skiff building family in the spritsail-rigged beach skiff *Lizzie* built at Nauvoo, New Jersey, 1872. Note the balanced boom spreading the foot of the foresail. The helmsman steered with an oar. *Photo – Harold A. Seaman.*

next plank above at an angle forming a 'box' deadwood, giving buoyancy when beaching, with light construction; a feature later developed in the power skiffs to achieve an acceptable angle of propeller shaft.

The bottom plank varied in width up to about a third of the beam amidships, tapering at the ends. It allowed the boat to slide over the beach, which a conventional keel would not, and was a natural feature of a hull form which gave quick buoyancy when launched. Its longitudinal rocker aided quick turning afloat or ashore; valuable in a bench boat.

The beach skiffs had to be good rowing boats and were also rigged with a boomless, rather low, square headed spritsail and foresail. Sometimes the foot of the foresail was spread by a boom which was made fast to the stem head. A small daggerboard or a centreboard was fitted and steering was by an oar held in the sculling notch in the top of the transom, or in wooden thole pins on the quarter or in a rope strop. There were two rowing thwarts and tholes to suit at the gunwales. The mast, spars and sails were usually stowed in the boat when rowing any distance, protruding over the stern while the bewhiskered and often bowler hatted crew pulled a steady stroke.

William Manson and Edgar Dennis were building such skiffs at Long Branch by 1850 and during the following twenty years others were built in that area by Lane, Laber and Emery, the last possibly originating from the English boatbuilding family at Cromer, Norfolk, who were noted for their beach boats and some of whom reputedly went to America. These men might construct up to four skiffs annually, sometimes also building dinghies and other small boats. Other skiffs were built by fishermen, for themselves or others.

Some skiffs were used for alongshore lobstering from Sea Bright and Long Branch in the 1860s, for local sale. By 1880 fourteen boats were working, each with a crew of two, setting thirty or forty pots and then filling in the day hand lining, before lifting the pots. Thirty miles were often covered in a working day under sail and oars. The skiffs had then increased to about seventeen feet length and fishing by pound nets was swelling landings. These were a form of huge netted trap, supported by wooden posts driven into the sea bed alongshore and usually equipped with elaborate leading nets to the mouths.

Between August and November some fishermen worked gill nets (drift nets) for bluefish and weakfish. These were often one hundred fathoms long, set in a line at first (a method which caught many bluefish), but later two nets set in a 'T' were used for mackerel.

There was also seine netting in bays and rivers, occasionally alongshore and even under the winter ice.

Many sailing ships were wrecked on the New Jersey beaches in onshore gales each winter; mostly coasters and deep watermen. The beachmen achieved a reputation for bravery and fortitude in saving life and the inevitable occasional branding as sharks and pillagers of wrecks. They were skilful salvagers and developed a larger and lighter type of skiff for this work capable of launching and beaching through the heavy surf. These specialist surf boats existed in 1846 and apart from their original purpose were often used in fishing but were not sailing boats. The shore was divided into districts, each in charge of a wreckmaster who was also usually owner or part owner of the four- or six-oared surf boat. This could be transported overland or along the dunes and sands by waggon and about ten were stationed alongshore ready to launch to the assistance of the average of eighteen strandings occurring annually on that coast.

Typical dimensions were twenty-three to twenty-seven feet long and 5ft 6in to 7ft beam. All clinker built of cedar with flat bottoms and transom sterns. They lasted about fifteen years in service.

Some skiffs were built from plans, occasionally of excellent draughtsmanship; others from half models, which were also frequently made to prove the draughted lines.

The Seaman family were amongst the most noted builders of skiffs. Isaac Seaman of Pamrapo, now named Bayonne, migrated to Nauvoo for the fishing each spring until about 1861, returning in autumn. During the winter he built skiffs and became a full time boatbuilder. His son Walter joined him in the business followed by grandson William and great grandson Harold who was still building boats in 1965, aged 83. This family introduced many innovations and improvements in the design and construction of skiffs and about 1875 their advertising made first use of the now well known term 'sea skiff', while Harold Seaman is credited with developing the New Jersey speed skiff which achieved remarkable speeds under power.

About 1890 some gill net fishermen commenced journeying to Florida each winter, exploring its fisheries and establishing a small seasonal colony. Fort Pierce was the favourite rendezvous. Their gear was carefully prepared before leaving New Jersey and a rapidly established tradition was the ordering of a new skiff for next season's New Jersey fishing, before leaving for Florida. The fishermen their skiffs and gear, usually shipped aboard a coastal passenger line ship to Miami, but some went by train to Fort Pierce, from where they sailed and rowed to Miami for the winter fishing which lasted until April, when the skiff and gear were sold to a 'Florida Cracker'. This cycle lasted at least until 1917. Another, shorter migration was to the rivers of New Jersey, Maryland and Virginia, particularly to the Hudson and the Delaware, for the shad fishing.

By 1908 low powered petrol engines were being installed in New Jersey beach skiffs and two bladed propellers were poking cut from the skegs. Sails were soon obsolete but oars remained in use for launching and beaching until the skiff developed into full powered craft which have no place in this book but have been accurately described by Peter J. Guthorn in his splendid study *The Sea Bright Skiff*.

With more powerful engines, owners increasingly kept skiffs moored in the inlets, so size increased and beach work diminished. Power quickly doubled the operating radius and diminished the labour of handling the boats, intensifying fishing.

The sneak box

Barnegat Bay proper starts at Bay Head, New Jersey, but the influence of Bay tradition spreads northwards a few miles, to the waters of the Mannesquan River. The baymen were typical of amphibious working populations everywhere; resourceful, shoal water sailors, shore gunners, fishermen and boatbuilders; a breed distinct from the nearby Hinterland population. Their love of wildfowling, fishing and competitive sailing produced a unique type of small boat known as the 'sneak box'. Traditionally the sneak box was originated about 1836 by Hazleton Seaman of West Creek; a boatbuilder and keen wildfowler. He conceived a low, fully decked gunning boat and named her 'the Devil's Coffin'. Locals termed her as a 'sneak box' from its use in stalking duck. The type was copied and spread rapidly, being developed by the fitting of a single, boomless spritsail and a single leeboard shifted from side to side at the change of tack, enabling the surprisingly stable sneak box to sail to windward; further improved by the adoption of a daggerboard fitted in a trunk just forward of the small rectangular cockpit. The rudder was hung on the shallow transom and usually a yoke and tiller lines were used, but some steered with a tiller. They sailed well to windward and handled like a small catboat under the low, spritsail set on a mast stepped through the foredeck. Usually the sneak box was used by one gunner who sailed, rowed or poled the boat to an area where duck were expected. Often accurately made wooden decoy ducks were set floating nearby to tempt live ones to alight and be shot. Market gunners who

shot for a living and many sportsmen, carved and painted remarkable lifelike decoy ducks which have become treasured works of art.

A typical sneak box is illustrated in Fig. 101. Her principal dimensions were: Length overall 12ft, Beam 4ft, Breadth at stern 2ft 9in, Depth at Transom 7in, Depth from underside of coaming to top of ceiling 13in, Cockpit 3ft 4in long by 19in wide, Coaming $2\frac{3}{4}$in high forward and aft, 2in amidships.

The daggerboard trunk was on the starboard side alongside the coaming, raked in profile and accepting a 15in wide board.

The spoon shaped bottom enabled boxes to be dragged over marsh or beaches, or amongst ice, without serious damage.

The hulls were carvel planked in $\frac{5}{8}$in cedar or pine on light sawn frames and the $\frac{5}{8}$in deck planking was tongued and grooved. At the forward end the planks were fastened to a horizontal harpin at the sheer.

The heavily cambered deck traditionally built into sneak boxes arose from the need, in a twelve foot boat, for the gunner to place his feet under the deck and as two pairs of socks were necessary in the winter cold, ordinary feet soon increased to twelve inches long, and this depth had to be provided inside the hull.

Sneak boxes were stiff enough for one or two men to stand in when shooting or working fishing lines and the loaded draught of four to six inches with daggerboard raised, was ideal for local waters.

In some sneak boxes the centreboard or daggerboard was placed off centre, in line with the side of the cockpit. Both centreline and offset installations were used with varying success, the position depending on the gunner's choice; some preferring length gained with it offset; others the width when it was forward.

Daggerboards were often of 'dagger' shape to reduce wetted surface (Fig. 1C1) rather than a simple rectangular board.

Some professional gunners discarded both rudder and centreboard and used a single leeboard and steered with an oar held skilfully against the quarter; a method much used in sailing the very different gun punts of Essex, England. (See Chapter 10) A triangular 'leg of mutton' sail was often set for gunning.

The wooden rowlocks were six inches high and set nine inches outboard of the coamings. Positioned 7ft 5in aft of the bow in a twelve footer they were designed to fold down to the deck, being maintained erected by an iron hook engaging with an eye. A 'stool 'ack' of three wooden boards set around the deck abaft the rowlocks was used to retain the wooden decoy ducks when on passage under oars. The rack boards were notched and were stayed to the deck and to each other with hooks and wood cleats.

Sailing sneak boxes of the Deware were commonly fitted with a vertical washboard around the deck edge, which increased the sailing freeboard without making the hulls too deep and heavy.

For rowing in a chop the gunners developed a canvas 'apron', held up by a vertical stick from the forward coaming and flaring out its aft ends to the rowlock chocks. In some boats the apron

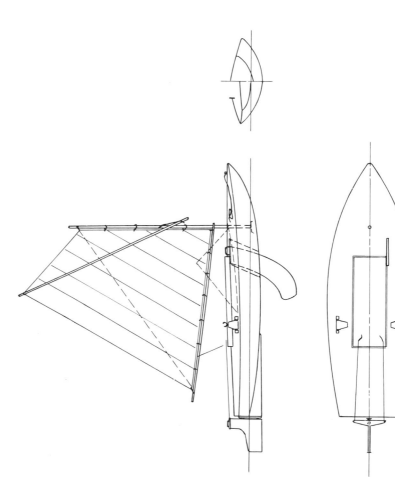

Figure 101. Barnegat Bay, New Jersey, sneakbox evolved for duck shooting and, later, pleasure sailing. Dimensions 12ft × 4ft. Note curved daggerboard offset from centreline. Jib headed sail and weathercloth shown dotted.

347

was tacked to the deck. Later the apron was often spread by a wood or iron hoop. With this rigged the baymen reckoned a sneak box would live through anything a man could row against.

In many boats the cockpit could be covered by a hatch which could be locked by a hasp and staple, enabling the gunner to leave his gear safely stowed in the hull. Hardy baymen also slept aboard their sneak boxes under the hatch, rolled in a blanket on the floorboards, the precious fowling gun laid handy for the first sound of duck whistling overhead in the dawn.

When gunning the boats were often disguised by thatching the deck with sedge and bushes, when they could be used as a static shooting station in marsh or reeds, or be anchored in creeks and sounds as a camouflaged 'island'. This practice probably originated the name sneak box, instead of sneak boat.

As early as 1885 some sneak boxes were built as miniature cruisers, equipped with a small oil stove in a compartment set in the after deck and some owners rigged a canvas awning over the cockpit, converting it into a small cabin. The sneak boxes would have remained unknown outside Barnegat Bay and adjacent waters but for the publicity given to the type by Nathaniel Bishop who had moved to Toms River, New Jersey by 1864 as a horticulturist who also speculated in property and land. He was a keen sailing and boating personality who initiated the American Canoe Association in 1878 and became its first Secretary. He owned five sneak boxes in succession and in 1875 ordered a new twelve footer named *Centennial Republic*, to be used in a voyage from

Pittsburgh to Florida by the rivers Ohio and Mississippi. Accomplishing this successfully, mainly under oars, Bishop published a book *Four Months in a Sneak Box*, during 1879, describing the *Centennial Republic* as ideal for the voyage, particularly praising the type's stability and sailing qualities.

The publication of Bishop's book brought wider interest in the sneak box which began to be produced by builders in other states, usually for pleasure use as sailing boats, but occasionally for gunning. Some were designed with broader scow-like bows and increasing sail areas of gaff, lug and later Bermudian rig. Sailing sneak boxes were certainly raced before any were specially built for competition. The design of a sixteen footer was published in Forest and Stream magazine during 1885, rigged with an effective but untypical balanced lug sail. A class of gaff-rigged sneak boxes was introduced in the early 1890s and rapidly grew to about thirty boats.

Racing

Soon after the yacht designers were designing classes of racing sneak boxes, some with bows resembling the later popular and exciting fast sailing scows. During the next forty years new classes of racing sneak boxes appeared at intervals but most were gaff or Bermudian rigged, the sprit sail proving inferior for competitive racing in summer conditions. A fifteen foot sneak box class designed and built by J. H. Perrine of Barnegat, in about 1918, flourished and around 3000 boats were built, making it one of the largest racing classes of its time. Racing sneak boxes were still car's roof rack. This is a production sailing or rowing boat for one or two people with dimensions of 12ft by 4ft beam by 6ins hull draught and boomless spritsail rig set on a spruce mast and sprit. A light alloy caggerboard lowers to a sailing draught of three foot. The moulded hull and terylene sail mean minimum maintenance, maximum use potential and lightness for lifting, beaching and carrying. With yellow hull and blue sail the Melon Seed is a colourful class which offers sailing and rowing to everyone, with the bonus of the character of long tradition to the discerning owner.

Other wildfowl skiffs

Rail gunning skiffs were another Barnegat and Delaware Bay type used for wildfowling in these and adjoining waters. They were sometimes known as reed bird skiffs or pole boats and were pointed stern craft of fine form, mostly but not always rigged and used for wildfowling. Many were owned on the Delaware and at Egg Harbour, but the type was used in a wide area of the eastern states. The skiffs were generally well built and finished examples of the boatbuilders art and are known to have been constructed before 1850. John B. Gray of Bridgeport on Racoon Creek, was typical in building nine skiffs during a year (1870) worth $288, besides building other craft.

16ft by 4ft were typical dimensions of the lapstrake planked hulls which had a very easy bilge and lacked initial stability in the manner of a dory which, with a narrow flat bottom, they resembled. The cedar planking was copper

Plate 73. A sprit-rigged Barnegat Bay sneak box built by Bartine Clayton in 1930. Note raised wooden rowlocks and the quarter boards. *Photo – Peter J. Guthorn.*

being constructed in 1960.

American wildfowling has declined with the reclamation and pollution of the marshlands and tidal waters, but gunning boxes are still built in glass reinforced plastics following traditional form and arrangement, while in Britain David Leather has designed the 'Melon Seed', a sneak box of moulded wood construction, designed for pleasure sailing and rowing and which can be carried on a

Plate 74. Spritsail-rigged gunning skiffs dot a New Jersey waterway in Thomas Eakins painting *Setting out after rail,* 1874. *Museum of Fine Arts, Boston.*

fastened to bent frames and construction aimed at lightness with strength. Each end of the hull was symmetrical and had short decks. Centreboards or daggerboards were fitted, the former being preferred, fitted about a quarter the length from forward. The heels of stem and sternpost were well rounded to facilitate turning and poling in either direction. The small rudder was of almost circular profile and hung on pintles and gudgeons on the end permanently regarded as the stern. Other skiffs may have used leeboards and some had a small false keel.

Noted wildlife artist Thomas Eakins was a keen amateur wildfowler from Fantom who painted the skiffs in detail. Plate 74 is his *Setting off after rail* (1874) which well illustrates the craft. The single spritsail was rather square headed, broad and low to keep the heeling effect within the capabilities of the fine hull. It had a relatively short sprit and proportionately long boom which had jaws to the mast. The mast stepped through a forward thwart and another was fitted immediately aft of it, connecting with the top of the centreboard case. A main thwart was arranged just abaft amidships but the helmsman sat in the bottom or on the gunwale.

Occasionally they were rigged with a well raked mast on which a triangular sail was set, Chesapeake fashion.

Gunning for rail

Gunning for rail was restricted to two or three hours each high water and the skiffs were sailed to distant gunning areas in the fresh water marshes. They were also often rowed, sometimes with two pairs of oars. In reeds or very shallow water they were poled with saplings about twelve to fifteen feet long with wooden 'toes' fastened at the lower ends to find a grip. The poler stood on the after deck or after end of the cockpit with the gunner ready forward.

There were variants of the rail skiffs, many without sails and some having flat bottomed, single chine construction. The typical skiffs resembled the hull form and construction of the punts used for wildfowling, eel fishing and pleasure sailing on the English Norfolk Broads.

Joseph Myers of Fairburn reputedly built the last of them in 1940.

The North Carolina fishermen

The shoal waters between the North Carolina alongshore banks forming Cape Hatteras and the hinterland were fished by men netting fish and tonging oysters. They evolved two types of small centreboard boats rigged with spritsail and foresail, one type round bilged and the other of chine form.

These were the only American spritsail rigged craft to set a topsail above the mainsail. They were principally developed for the shad fishery in the sounds and creeks which line the North Carolina coast and were locally known from their place of origin and use as Pamlico, Currituck, Albemarle or Croation boats.

The round bilge boats probably appeared about 1870. Length ranged from about nineteen feet to thirty feet and a typical boat was 25 feet long by 7ft 8in beam by about 2ft 4in depth. Maximum beam was just forward of amidships as

was the rectangular centreboard which increased draught to four or five feet.

The straight and raking keel was often cut from a plank and the straight stem was well raked. Sometimes the sternpost was fitted outside the heart shaped transom. The midship section had a moderately rounded bilge and considerable rise of floor which was carried through the hull which had flared sides forward and much sheer (Fig. 102). Sometimes the garboard rebate was swept up to the waterline at the transom, exposing the deadwood and making planking easier, but many boats had fully planked, tuck sterns and all had a fine entrance and run, enabling them to sail and row well.

Many were built on the west shores of Pamlico Sound and on Roanoke Island, where Washington Creef was a noted builder. Plate 75 shows him outside his simple boatbuilding shed with two shad boats completing in rural surroundings. Construction was usually entirely of juniper; the frames being cut from juniper roots to obtain natural crooks, and these were fitted about twelve inches apart in a peculiar manner; stopping short of the keel with the heels ending in the middle of the garboard strakes. Floors were fitted between them to preserve transverse strength. The boats were often planked over moulds before the sawn frames were fitted; suggesting they might originally have been lapstrake (clinker) planked.

A broad, plank sidedeck or washboard with low coamings aided dryness and some had a short after deck. Rowlocks were arranged for four or six oars and four or five thwarts were often fitted,

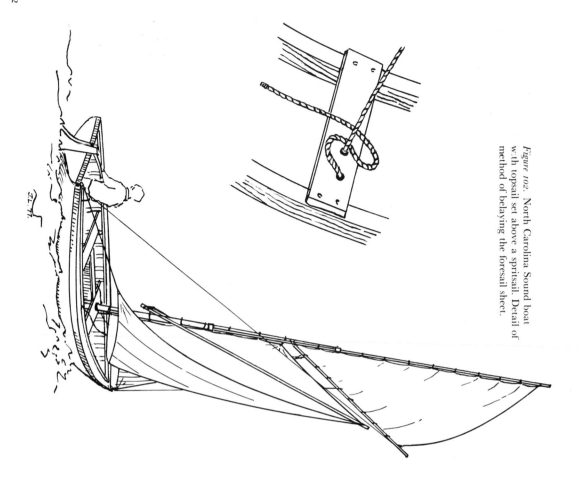

Figure 102. North Carolina Sound boat with topsail set above a spritsail. Detail of method of belaying the foresail sheet.

353

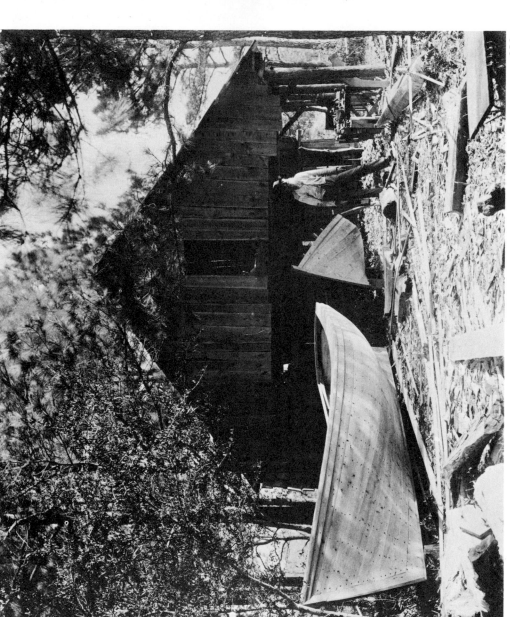

Plate 75. Albermarle Sound shad skiffs being built at Roanoake Island, North Carolina, at the end of the nineteenth century. Washington Creef stands before his simple boatbuilding shed where he constructed many skiffs from local timbers. *Photo – Smithsonian Institution.*

354

besides the heavy thwart through which the mast stepped.

The rudder was shaped like that of a ship's boat and did not project below the keel. The topsides were usually white, sometimes with black or red sheerstrakes.

The boats were ballasted with up to thirty sailcloth sandbags, each weighing about seventy-five pounds, which were shifted to windward at each tack in a breeze. They were weatherly and fast when handled by their experienced owners, who were excellent small boat sailers; and had to be capable of carrying two or three fishermen, a pile of net and perhaps half a ton of fish in choppy and often restricted waters.

The spritsail rig was low and of moderate area, averaging sixty square yards of canvas in mainsail and foresail. In a thirty foot boat the mast was fourteen feet long and seven inches in diameter at the thwart. The sprit was eighteen feet and the mainsail was boomless. The mainsheet had two single parts, worked hitched under a thole pin in each quarter knee, and belayed to a pin in the after thwart.

The mainsail luff was laced to the mast and the lacing line was sometimes used as a halyard rove through a masthead block or sheeve before being laced down the luff and round the mast to belay on a cleat below the tack. In some boats the mainsail was furled by partially releasing this lacing and making up the mainsail as it hung from the sprit which was then topped up by the lacing line through the masthead block. More usually the sprit was topped up and the sail furled around it and the mast. Small boats unshipped

the sprit before furling the sail around the mast.

An unusual topsail was sometimes set above the spritsail and could be used when this was not set. It provided effective sail area when the mainsail and foresail were frequently blanketed by the then wooded shores of the area.

The luff was laced to a long yard which had a spectacle or topmast iron fitted on its aft side just above the topsail sprit or yard heel which extended the topsail foot and was set up by a snotter to the topmast, arranged to be above the lower masthead. The sprit was controlled by a single or double sheet led from its outer end down to each quarter, allowing it to be trimmed independently of the spritsail below it.

Typically the topsail was fitted with two brails which led around the sprit or yard and on each side of the sail, passing through lead eyes on each side of the topmast after which the parts were spliced together to lead down as a single rope to belay on a pin in the mast thwart.

The topmast, with brailed sail and sprit rigged on it, was shipped aloft by two men who dropped the spectacle iron over the shouldered down masthead. The lower end of the topmast was lashed to the mast above the thwart to make it stand smartly. After this the brails were let go, the sheets were trimmed and belayed to pins in the washboards or after thwart.

A light headstay aided setting up the topmast and set up to the stemhead, held it taut when sailing to windward.

Some owners laced the foot of the topsail to a jackyard which swivelled on the topmast by a hook and eye gooseneck. Others cut the foot of the topsail well below the heel of sprit or yard, setting it taut with tacklines to a pin on the mast thwart. If the topmast was unshipped in a breeze it was often let fall in the water and then recovered. Larger boats set up and lowered the topmast with a heelrope, made fast at the lower masthead, passing under a score in the topmast heel, then up to a masthead sheeve and down to belay on a mast thwart pin. This was useful when it became necessary to lower the topmast in a breeze and seaway without completely releasing the heel lashing.

The foresail hoisted by a single halyard and was usually set flying, tacked down to the stemhead; but some larger boats had forestays to which the foresail hanked. It sheeted through fairleads and the lee sheet was led across the boat to belay to windward in a peculiar way (Fig. 102). A wood cleat fitted across two frames had two holes bored through it. The sheet rove through these and was secured by jamming the loose end under the taut part and could be released by a jerk on the loose end, though it would not render very well.

Besides their better known work in the seine net fisheries for shad and mullet, the round bilged boats were much used in oystering until the 1880s when single chine, flat bottomed centreboard skiffs about twenty feet long, rigged with a spritsail and foresail and worked by a crew of three were introduced. These had similar characteristics to the older boats: ease and convenience of rig were important as they were frequently rowed, and good manoeuvring under oars was essential in the fisheries. The bow was

straight and raked, the fore body was fine, with pronounced outward rake of the sides which diminished as the maximum beam was reached about amidships, but again increased towards the transom stern. The bottom forward was horizontal as far aft as the centreboard case, abaft which it rose in a gentle curve to the transom. Without crew or fishing gear the skiffs floated with forefoot just clear of the water, the chines amidships level with the surface and the transom about three inches above. Working draught of hull was approximately four inches. The lowered centreboard increased this to 28–30in.

The skiffs were undecked except for a 'bow cap' or small foredeck about eighteen inches long, allowing maximum space for crew and gear. Framing and centreline materials were of yellow pine (pitch pine); planking was usually of juniper, close seamed without caulking. An external keel was not fitted. The transom hung rudder was fitted with a yoke, not a tiller, and was controlled by lines led forward to the helmsman.

The mast was often a pine sapling, twelve to fifteen feet long for a twenty foot boat. It was unsupported by shrouds and readily unshipped.

The well peaked sprit was held by a snotter (locally termed the 'muzzle') at the heel and the sail had no boom. It was not possible to fit a mainsheet traveller, which would have interfered with fishing gear, and two mainsheets were made fast by a single wooden toggle passed through a loop of bolt rope at the clew. These led through deadeyes on each quarter and then forward to cleats, making it necessary to handle and trim the mainsheet at each tack.

After unshipping the sprit from the snotter, the mainsail of these boats was furled by rolling the leach towards the mast, gathering in the peak. The foresail was furled from leach to bolt rope as it was set flying, without a forestay, the tack making fast with a toggle to the stemhead. When furling, the tack was cast off and the foresail was enveloped in the last folds of the mainsail. Then the mast was unshipped from its step and was carried ashore with the furled sails remaining bent on. Stepping the mast and making sail was equally a matter of ten minutes' work. Many skiffs had exaggerated peak to the spritsail but others set a topsail as described for the round bilged boats. Occasionally these also set a jib topsail on the topmast forestay. The skiffs were a common sight in the deep creeks winding amongst the sedge grass of the Roanoke marshes and alongside the fishing shanties built on piles above the tides.

The skiffs were sailed commercially until about 1925 and a few of the old hulls were still working under power in Pamlico Sound thirty years later. The spritsail rig is still used in the few which are preserved and sailed for pleasure.

Pilot gigs

Three masted, spritsail-rigged boats were used by pilots, stevedores and fishermen at Warrington and Pensacola on the Gulf of Mexico coast of Florida. These were reputedly the only three masted open boats used in American fisheries and ranged generally between sixteen and twenty-one feet, but some were probably larger. These appear to have developed from the basic American fast rowing boat type generally referred to as a 'Whitehall' boat, after the district in New York where these were used by watermen. Called 'pilot gigs' they originated for pilot work, leaving the shore at two or three o'clock in the morning to sail seaward until sunrise, sometimes twenty miles or so, seeking inward-bound ships. If none were sighted the boats returned, but shore lookouts were posted in elevated positions all day and if a vessel was sighted there was a general race to get the pilot job. The boats encountered big seas and strong winds and were able craft. The pilots and stevedores used them to board and tend ships in winter but hired them out in summer for fishing, usually to negroes who used them lining for red snapper, each taking one share of the catch in payment.

A typical 18ft boat had 5ft 2in beam, a fine bow and plumb stem, well shaped, upright transom and clean quarters. The centreplate was iron and three thwarts were fitted. A short afterdeck enclosed a locker for food and water. The oak keel was shaped to accommodate the centreplate slot, just forward of amidships. Stem, sternpost and transom were oak, timbers of mulberry, and carvel planking of white cedar, with garboards and thwarts of yellow pine. Fastenings were copper and brass.

Usually the boats worked under the foresail and mizzen, and sailed well to windward under this combination. In light winds or when driven hard, the amidship mast and sail were rigged. Under all three sails the boats had considerable area and needed sitting-out by the crew of from three to seven men. The fore and mainsails had no boom but the mizzen had a boom, sheeted to the top of the transom. Reef points were not used and when working, the sails were shifted. In strong winds and a seaway they sailed within three and a half points (40°) of the wind and could face bad weather if properly handled. The helmsman steered with tiller lines to a wooden yoke on the rudder head and sat before the mizzen.

Most were built by Robert Longford who for ten years turned them out full time; also employing other boatbuilders in his shop. Some Pensacola men had copies built in New Orleans, but these failed to outsail Longford's boats, which were well built and intelligently designed.

By 1875 trade led to stevedores competing for discharge of shipping and it became customary for them to sail seaward to solicit the job of unloading. They tried various odd types of boats for this but found the pilot gigs best and whenever a ship appeared on the horizon, a dozen stevedores and as many pilots might put off in a race to the vessel under sail and oars. As securing the job meant considerable gain, the perfection of the gigs became very desirable and expensive. By 1878–9 there was great interest in 'pilot rig' as it was called, in Pensacola Bay and many regattas were held for the boats, with up to thirty entries. Only experienced men were shipped when racing and in their hands these boats sailed remarkably well to windward. In the early 1880s the pilots obtained schooners in which to cruise seaward seeking ships and the stevedores abandoned boarding ships at sea. By 1885 there were a dozen or more ex-pilot gigs owned by the fishermen of Warrington, fishing eight months of

357

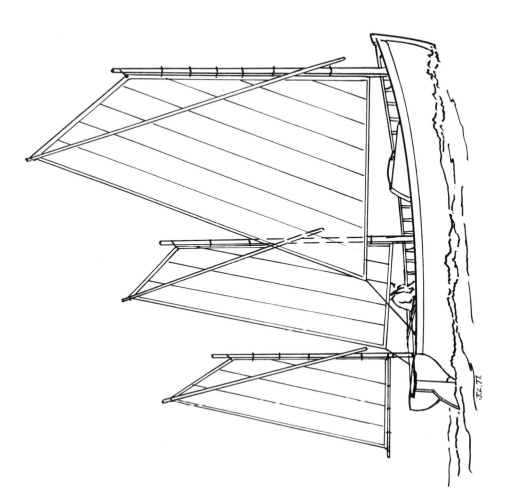

Figure 103. Three masted pilot gig of Pensacola, Florida, circa 1878.

the year with from four to seven men in each boat, working for a share each. They sailed at dawn and rowed and sailed to an area between five and fifteen miles from the bar to patches of good fishing ground to work their lines.

A day's catch might be anything from a hundred to a thousand pounds of fish per boat and as ice was not used they sailed for Pensacola and arrived, if possible, before the fish houses closed. In cool weather they stayed longer and sent the catch in by one boat the next morning. The fishing boats might regularly sail forty miles in a day's work but were later replaced by fishing schooners.

Henry Connett skiffs

Further west, spritsails were used by fishermen from Biloxi, Mississippi, in a type of flat bottomed, wedge shaped open boat known as a Henry Connett skiff, probably after a local builder. These were first built as rowing boats but were soon fitted with leeboards and a spritsail and foresail, to use the prevailing south-easterly winds on the run home from the alongshore fishing grounds.

Length was about sixteen to twenty feet and the use of a centreboard and then a gaff sail followed, the type evolving into a chine catboat, a type which remained in use for pleasure sailing into the 1940s. These Mississippi spritsail skiffs were also used at various places from Bay St Louis to Pascagoula, and occasionally as far west as New Orleans, and as far east as Mobile and Pensacola.

New Orleans luggers

The only dipping lugsail known to have been used in American vessels after the mid-nineteenth century was carried by shallow draught craft now generally termed New Orleans luggers, but which were owned in numbers from Texas to the west coast of Florida. Their principal use was in the oyster and shrimp fisheries of the Mississippi delta, but they also carried cargoes of goods and farm or market garden produce.

These luggers had to be capable of sailing in deep, tide ridden and often rough waters; yet be able to turn to windward through the narrow and shallow Louisiana coastal inlets and marsh waterways, possibly for fifty miles at a time, or manoeuvre through the lakes and bayous then lying in a watery network around New Orleans. From the city to the walled dyke at the South Pass approach channel on the Gulf of Mexico was 107 miles and in between the Mississippi flowed yellow through the wide bottom lands beyond the levees, with the luggers working patiently upstream.

They had to be of light draught to work over bars, oyster beds and sand spits, or be capable of sailing the marsh creeks, fishing for shrimp and flatfish. Sometimes the luggermen went wildfowling for, like most shallow water sailors, they were alive to any opportunity.

The oyster season opened in November and closed at the end of April. Shrimping commenced in mid February and lasted until mid April, but reopened in mid August until mid November. From early May to mid August things were quiet in the fisheries and many lugger owners

Plate 76. Model of a Mississippi lugger, used for fishing and to carry light cargoes in the river delta and adjacent coastal waters. The large dipping lug was the only such sail set by North American working craft. The shapely, shallow-draught centreboard luggers were swift sailers. *Photo – Smithsonian Institution.*

carried light cargo or refitted their craft, living on the fishing season's earnings.

Origins of the New Orleans lugger are obscure but the type must have been introduced by the French Louisiana colonists and until the end of sail, the dipping lugsail they set resembled those of the north French ports.

Reference is made to the luggers by 1830 when they were deep keeled craft, without centreboards which were introduced by the 1880s, when some deep-draught luggers were still sailing.

By the 1890s the luggers were used in the waters of the Mississippi Delta by fishermen, oystermen and shippers of fruit and vegetables of principally Italian extraction. The New Orleans lugger landing was a centre of activity and one of the city's characterful sights on the bank of the river. Scores of luggers lay in a long row loading and unloading cargo from wagons, and still more arrived in characteristic fashion, shooting up with the huge red lug flapping, to glide in with forefoot almost grazing the sloping hard of the waterside where the broad, slatted gangplanks reached up to the bustling decks. Luggers unloaded fish or took on ice for tomorrow's catch. Cargo luggers were loading general goods and equipment for the farms and plantations along the lower river and coast, returning by way of the bayous of southern Louisiana and the canals, with holds full of oranges or vegetables.

Although the rig was of European origin, the hulls of the late nineteenth-century luggers were pure North American; very similar to the shallow centreboard sloops of the New York area and similar semi-sheltered waters. Length ranged

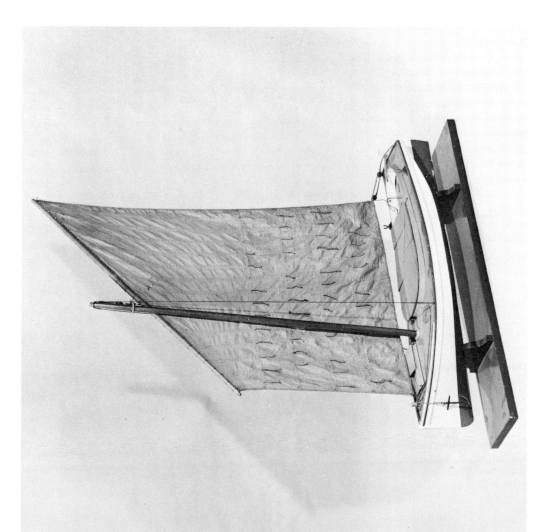

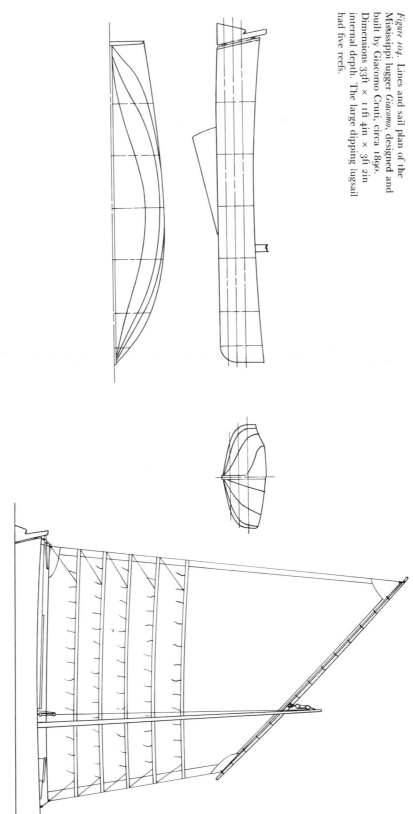

Figure 104. Lines and sail plan of the Mississippi lugger *Giacomo*, designed and built by Giacomo Cruti, circa 1890. Dimensions 33ft × 11ft 4in × 3ft 2in internal depth. The large dipping lugsail had five reefs.

New Orleans owners preferred luggers built in Louisiana, as there was an old Law exempting them from tolls and wharfage dues.

Henry Frentz of Biloxi, Mississippi, was a well known lugger builder. Typical dimensions of his luggers were 33ft 3in overall length, 11ft 4in beam, 3ft 2in depth moulded and 2ft 3in draught aft.

between twenty and fifty feet on the keel, but an average lugger was 37ft overall length by 12ft beam.

Large numbers were built at yards on the Calcasieu, Pascagoula and other rivers of that region, on Lake Pontchartrain and at Shieldsboro', Mississippi.

Many were built by their owners who usually launched shapely and efficient craft with hulls painted in bright green, yellow, red and blue stripes, to suit the owners' exuberant tastes.

The lugger *Giacomo* (Fig. 104) was designed and built by Giacomo Cruti, a noted craftsman who built most of his luggers from her model, which proved a good, average craft. His sons followed with the firm of Cruti Brothers which built some of the best and fastest luggers into the twentieth century. The stem was plumb with small radius of forefoot. The delicately shaped shallow transom was slightly raked and the midship sections had straight, rising floors with a firm bilge and almost plumb sides. The after waterlines were fine and the forward waterlines hollow to help the lugger keep up to windward when the centreboard was raised in shoal water; but there was power in the amidship sections when heeled. The centreboard was 13ft long and its trunk case cut the hold in two.

The lines were that of a swift sailer with the flaring sections at the ends increasing carrying capacity when loaded beyond her normal waterline. Luggers had to be seaworthy for sailing in the Gulf and fast, as many cargoes were perishable and had to be brought quickly to market in the warm climate. Hull shape varied; some were flatter floored, others carried the maximum beam well forward and some were bluff bowed. All had ample beam, a large centreboard, were carvel planked in cypress and later yellow pine, on sawn frames of red cypress or live oak, and had a shallow, broad keel to accept the centreboard slot. This tapered at the ends to suit

the stem and sternpost siding.

The deck was flush, with a low toerail. A long cockpit aft of the mast had rounded forward coamings which extended almost to the transom. The amidships space was bulkheaded off at the after end of the centreboard case to form a hold; divided longitudinally by the case, which acted as a shifting division for a large cargo. Loose hatch boards were shipped, principally as protection against sun rather than seas. The after end was an open cockpit with a 'U' shaped stern bench for helmsman and crew.

When away for more than a day the crew lived forward in a small, wedge shaped fo'c'sle, entered by a sliding hatch between the mast and the stem.

The rig was considered simple and of reasonable area by the luggermen Usually it did not exceed the square of the waterline length, though this characteristic was not arrived at mathematically. The mainmast was stayed by a single shroud on each side, set up by lanyards. The lugsail was an excellent, flat cut sail showing good workmanship. It was well cared for, being coated when not in use. The head was laced to the yard which was hoisted by a single halyard with a purchase having double blocks at masthead and at the yard, and worked on a metal mast traveller. The lugsail tack was set down with a purchase to a traveller on a short horse across the foredeck. The tack was hauled over when going about by a line through blocks on the forward rail. The mainsheet shackled to a traveller on a horse across the transom.

When on a tack which would bring the forward part of the lugsail back against the mast, the tack was hauled to windward on the horse and was held there by the bowline. Some owners led the tack tackle fall to a cleat on the footrail and set this up as a bowline. The mainsheet was got in and the sail flattened to stand clear of the mast, if possible. To set the boat up for a long tack, the tack was cast off and the sail lowered and dipped around the mast, to be reset and obtain an efficiently setting sail.

The lugsails were often tanned to a red ochre colour for preservation and when cut, had a deep roach to the foot and leach to allow for stretching due to lack of a boom. This occurred in the after part where a sail similar to that in (Fig. 104) might stretch two feet on the foot. The roach prevented the foot from becoming concave. A sail in this state was called 'nigger heeled' by sailmakers.

Five rows of reef points were usually fitted and in a heavy squall the sail was lowered in a few minutes, the long heavy yard bringing it down quickly. This was infrequent in the congenial climate, with few storms. The usual crew of two could handle the largest lugger, yet they were rarely in difficulties despite usually sailing without ballast, other than the cargo. When light, they were tender and liable to capsize if caught aback in a strong wind.

Many southern yachtsmen were surprised at the luggers' speed when their yacht had an impromptu race with one. In particular, they pointed exceptionally high to windward. The lugger *Greyhound* was crack of the fleet and had a shallow, flat-floored hull with hard bilges. She drew only a foot when light and handled like a

large racing dinghy.

Lugger rudders were hung on pintles and gudgeons, like a dinghy and could be unshipped when necessary by a purchase rigged to a short, stout pole like an ensign staff, which was stepped on the transom, by the tiller. Ropes led from the top of the rudder blade to either quarter. These were set up as kicking straps when at anchor or moored and could also be used for emergency steering should the tiller carry away. At anchor in a hard breeze and exposed position, the rudder was often unshipped and hauled aboard or sometimes was allowed to float astern on the two ropes.

The rudder lift pole also served, infrequently, as an ensign staff but more usually to sling a meat basket, an orange branch of ripe fruit, or perhaps a bunch of bananas, game, fish or any other perishables for the crew. The pole could also be unshipped and used as a mooring post pushed into a shallow, muddy bottom.

Two long setting booms or pushing poles for use in shoal water and a pair of long sweeps for rowing from thole pins on each quarter in a calm, were carried forward when sailing, or were stowed at moorings, raked with blades to the deck, between mast and the horizontally stowed lugsail, which was supported by the halyard and a scissors crutch at the transom.

Introduction of the petrol engine brought the decline of the New Orleans luggers and contributed to the development of Lousiana fishing activity at the Mississippi Gulf port of Biloxi which, though further from many fishing grounds than New Orleans, seized the opportunity which power craft offered and quickly became the fishing capital of the area from Ocean Springs to Pascagoula; one of the world's busiest fishing centres. Catches were prepared and packed to be shipped all over the Americas. Packing plants stood on marshy promontories and on mounds of oyster shell of their own creation. Biloxi became the world's second largest oyster port and Houma, Louisiana, the third. By 1920 these fisheries supported about 70,000 people, making their living from a coastal strip varying from ten to fifty miles wide, stretching from Mississippi Sound, across the Mississippi River, westward to the Sabine river in Texas.

New Orleans rapidly declined. In 1901 fifty or more luggers berthed at the landing. Eleven years later only a handful remained, supplanted by petrol driven sternwheel and screw launches, which in turn came to be called 'luggers'. Some sailing luggers were converted to sloop rig and worked from Bayou St John; a waterway which penetrated the heart of New Orleans and was

much used by fishing sloops and schooners seeking a direct market.

Louisiana Pirogues

The Louisiana Pirogue was another southern working craft; usually dug out from a single log or red cypress with hand tools. Pirogues were used in the bayous, rivers and sheltered waters of Louisiana and neighbouring states for fishing, fowling and carriage of light goods. They were rowed, poled and paddled. Many were rigged with a small spritsail and had a deep wood keel bolted to the bottom amidships. They were usually owner-built and ranged from 12ft by 2ft beam by 10in depth to 17ft by 3ft beam by 16in depth. The bow was fine, the midship section flat floored, with well rounded bilges and flaring sides. The transom stern and stem were plumb and the sheer and keel almost straight. The skill of building pirogues lasted into the 1940s and a few are still in use as reminders of America's earliest traditional craft.

13

East and West Coasts

Smack Boats

Early in the eighteenth century sloops and small schooners from Cape Cod ports fished offshore for mackerel and were making cod fishing trips to banks, where the catch was salted on board for preservation. These vessels were known as 'smacks'; a British and European term for a vessel having a watertight well with circulating access to sea water, in which a catch of fish was kept until the return to port. Probably these Cape Cod craft were originally so equipped, though many were merchant vessels which fished occasionally, during the appropriate seasons. Men from the Massachusetts islands were amongst the crews, though only one fishing schooner was reputedly built on the Vineyard, a hundred tonner later converted for whaling.

The smacks' crews worked hand lines from the deck and also from small, round bilged, heavily built, transom sterned boats whose form and construction was patterned after contemporary tuck sterned ship's boats. These were carried on deck during passage making and were hoisted overside by a tackle and bridle hooked to ringbolts in stem and sternpost. These were the

forerunners of the dory, known on the Cape as a 'Newbury Chaise', which later displaced them because of convenience of stowage, lightness and cheaper construction. However, the smack boats remained in use amongst the men of the Cape and the Vineyard as an inshore fishing boat which could be rowed or sailed by one man when rigged with a single spritsail; fishing for cod, bluefish, lobsters or scallops. Despite development of the larger, pointed sterned Vineyard or Noman's Land boats and rapid increase in use for inshore fishing, a few smack boats were in use by Cape communities until after 1900.

A typical example was 18ft overall length by 6ft 6in beam, with a delicately shaped tuck to the transom, low freeboard for fishing, moderate sheer and was open except for narrow side decks with coamings.

A live fish well was often fitted aft of the centreboard case. The boomless, usually tanned, spritsail was well peaked and fairly large as the boats were much used for bluefishing in summer and needed speed and manoeuvrability to work the lines which were trolled with imitation sand eel lures to attract the schooling fish.

There is the possibility that the name 'smack boat' originated independently from bank fishing, because of the wet well fitted in these inshore boats and the author conclude; that the craft now remembered as 'Woods Hole boats' were what were earlier, or perhaps simultaneously in other places, termed smack boats.

The 'Woods Hole boat' became known as a type during the 1880s, used by inshore fishermen of Cape Cod and Falmouth in the boisterous conditions around Woods Hole and Vineyard Sound; notorious for tide rips and rough water quickly raised by a breeze. Usual rig was a single large spritsail but some were cat rigged with a gaff and boom mainsail. Length varied between thirteen and eighteen feet and the transom sterns were finely shaped. Planking was carvel or clinker (lapstrake).

Typical dimensions of a boat built about 1885 were 14ft length by 5ft 9in beam. She had a centreboard and was rigged with a single spritsail, the mast stepping just aft of the stem in a chock on the apron. It was supported at the sheer by a metal clamp to a strong thwart, enabling the rig to be struck when the boat was rowed or left for long periods at moorings. The mast and sprit were about the same length and could generally be stowed in the boat.

Many Woods Hole boats used for fishing stepped a jigger, a triangular 'leg of mutton' sail about five feet on the hoist and the foot, set from a mast stepped through a thwart immediately aft of the centreboard case. The boom sometimes reached beyond the transom and the jigger was carried on all points of sailing.

Plate 77. Winslow Homer, perhaps America's greatest marine artist, painted this spritsail smack boat reaching along the New England coast, in 1876. His title *Breezing up* expresses the lively feeling of this picture. *National gallery of Art, Washington.*

Plate 78. A replica of a 12ft 7in Woods Hole boat of 1885, under sail, combining features of the Crosby catboat hull with the New England two masted spritsail rig; a useful type of small boat. *Photo – Mystic Seaport.*

Besides fishing for profit or pleasure, the Woods Hole boats were used to carry passengers, goods and mail between the islands and the mainland and for day sailing by summer visitors. Some were raced, being lightly built and kept hauled out to be as dry as possible when not in use. Several were owned on Martha's Vineyard, but the transom stern was not ideal for beaching, which was part of these islanders work.

John Gardner of Mystic Seaport recently redraughted the lines and construction of the Woods Hole boat *T.C.* built by Crosby at Osterville, Cape Cod, about 1890. Her bold, catboat-like hull, with typical Crosby transom which had no tuck, is 13ft 4in long by 6ft beam and has narrow side decks and coamings.

The Woods Hole boat type is one of the most attractive American small craft, with the special appeal that it is possible for an amateur to build, own and sail one of these practical and useful knockabout boats, which is small enough to be hauled out, trailed or be kept at home in the garden when not in use; yet has a pedigree as long as any of the larger traditional types. A replica of the *T.C.* has been built by students at Mystic Seaport boatbuilding workshop as part of the educational programme.

Spritsail boats formed the first American one design dinghy class. In 1884 Dr Weld, a summer visitor to North Haven, Maine, designed a small open boat for pleasure sailing, rigged with a single spritsail of about 118 square feet, set on a mast stepped in the bow, similar to the Woods Hole boats. Dimensions were 14ft 5½in overall by 4ft 11in beam by 13½in hull draught, excluding the centreboard. The plumb stemmed hull had generous freeboard and was surprisingly fast. The doctor's design rapidly became popular and soon dozens of North Haven dinghies were scooting about the waters of Fox Island Thorofare every summer as the first of subsequent thousands of American racing dinghies.

Unfortunately the desire for speed led to adoption of a gaff sail, cat rig and the class became a strict one design. Shifting ballast was banned, but six pounds of lead was permitted in the wood centreboard and 350 pounds of inside fixed ballast made them stiff. Rules prohibited pot leading of bottoms during the twenty-four hours preceding a race and reefing was compulsory if ordered by the race officers. The first official race was unusual, at that time, in being won by a woman, Miss Ellen Haywood.

The North Haven dinghies were long lived and in 1920 John G. Alden, a noted yacht designer, lifted the lines and prepared plans to perpetuate the class, which continued to flourish into the 1960s.

Spritsail-rigged wherries were amongst the many types of small boats built all along the Maine Coast, mainly by fishermen-owners who turned boatbuilders during the harsh winter, constructing wherries, sloops, dories and double-enders for their own summer use and for sale to less skilled fishermen. Amongst noted builders around 1900, were Alan Ratcliff, and Freeman Ratcliff and his son Paris, who lived at the mouth of the Wessawesskeag river near Rockland, and turned

out many shapely and seaworthy craft which were in demand along the coast. Others were built and owned at Ash Point, a few miles north east of the Wessawesskeag, a typical coastal settlement living by hand lining, long lining, lobstering and tending fish weirs.

Ash Point fishermen made their own sails, and their smaller boats-dories, wherries and double-enders – were rigged with spritsails, some without a boom, others having a full length boom with jaws to the mast, and a few with a club boom two thirds to three quarters the length of the foot. These spritsails were always furled by unstepping the mast. Luther Hurd made many of the sails. The seamed-up cloth was laid out in a convenient meadow where the desired sail dimensions had been marked out with wood pegs, and was pinned and patted into shape under the critical gaze of the village experts, before being machined and roped.

They preferred mainsails which were flat at the leach and accepted a hollow leach profile to achieve it. Battens were not used. The luff was usually full near the throat.

Ash point owners were especially particular about their foresails, preferring fullness at the head and down the luff and leech, with a flat setting foot. This was achieved by fitting a headstick and a small sheeting club at the clew, and by careful sheeting.

The pointed-stern boats were primarily intended for rowing, though many were fitted with centreboards and spritsails. Sizes and hull forms varied but all had a flat bottom plank as keel, from six to twelve inches wide. An average

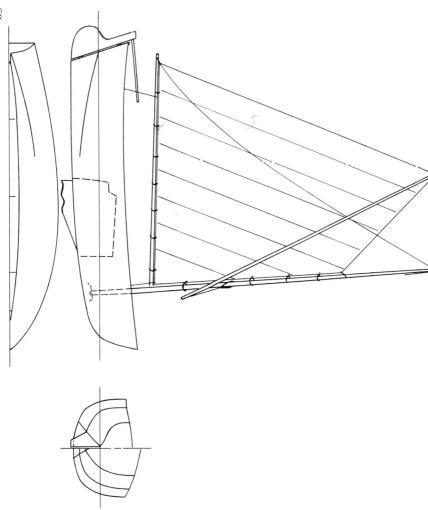

Figure 105. Maine wherry with spritsail rig. Built by Luther Hurd at Ash Point for rowing and sailing, fishing and general use. Note tuck formed by knuckle in after sections.

boat was sixteen feet long by four feet beam. As the two ends were built to be exactly alike the boats were locally known as double-enders.

The Ash Point wherries were also built with a flat keel plank and the bottom of the hull below water was of similar form to the double-enders but the sternpost was raked and the transom stern was usually half its depth and the wherry hull was slightly deeper aft than forward.

There were two principal types of wherry, intended primarily for rowing but often having a centreboard and spritsail, and the sailing wherry which was larger and intended for sailing, being always fitted with a centreboard and usually a gaff and boom mainsail, though some set spritsails (Fig. 105). These wherries were faster under sail than a Swampscott round-sided dory of similar length.

Luther Hurd owned one of the community's larger sailing wherries, lapstrake built of cedar by her owner from two driftwood logs he had salvaged about 1870. These were sawn in a Keag river tide mill to one inch thick boards. The frames were sawn from local hackmatak to finish about 1½in by 2½in when moulded, spaced about eighteen inches apart.

The lines show the sharp tuck or knuckle in the after sections, which is also found in the New Jersey beach boats.

This wherry had three rigs, of which the single spritsail is shown. This was probably the easiest and safest rig. Alternatively she could be rigged as a gaff sloop with single headsail or with a triangular 'leg of mutton' mainsail set on the spritsail mast when she was occasionally let to summer visitors.

She decked forward and aft and had narrow side decks, was fast and seaworthy off the wind but poor to windward. Ballast was about 1000 pounds of rock and a centreboard was fitted. The hull proved slow in rough water but would row well.

A typical double-ender, probably built by John MacDonald about 1895, was carvel planked on bent frames, had a centreboard and was rigged with a boomless spritsail with about a fourteen foot hoist. The rudder steered with yoke and lines.

She had unusually hollow waterlines at the ends and considerable rise of floor, but was fast and seaworthy and used for lobstering in all weathers. Some double-enders were steered with an oar.

Double-enders of more seaworthy type were built and fished from Matinicus Island, twenty miles offshore of the rocky coast of Maine. These were beamier and deeper sea boats, with plumb stems, hard bilges and flat floors. They were usually lapstrake built and had a false wood keel fitted under the constructional keel and shaped at its ends to blend with the end profiles. This suggests they were often left anchored off the beach when not in use. These boats had to contend with the big seas around Matinicus but were often rigged with a large spritsail, when they were steered with an oar over the stern.

The high point of the American 'outward bound' course for young people at Hurricane Island is a hundred mile, four day coastal expedition in bold hulled, pointed stern thirty foot open boats rigged with two spritsails, the fore larger than the main.

The boats are capable of being rowed by the crew of twelve, who carry all their gear and stores on board. Going 'off watch' is achieved by donning oilskins or another guernsey. Only the radar reflector at the foremast head reveals that this is the twentieth century as a pair of these spritsail sailers slide across the Maine coastal seascape alive with sun sparkle, a hint of haze dimming the pine and granite shores of Shoodic Head.

Long Island fishermen

On the south shore of Long Island, in the shallow bays around Westhampton, which were fresh water before Shinnecock and Moriches inlets opened to let salt water change the character of the bay fishes, local fishermen caught carp, white perch, bass and eels, and dug soft shell clams, the real 'steamers'. The fishermen's skiffs were carvel planked, about sixteen feet long, rigged with a single spritsail, or sometimes a gaff sail. Many had two mastholes so one sail could be furled and stowed in the boat and a smaller set in its place in stronger winds. The skiffs were occasionally raced and in a breeze used potato sacks full of sand weighing about two hundred pounds, as shifting ballast. Many of the races were held in Moneybogue Bay and others in the Bay proper. Skiffs were built by Charles Terry and J. Newton Hand of East Moriches, Elisha Lamb, William Nines, Parker Hallock and Joshua Penny of Center Moriches and by Samuel Wicks and Gilbert Smith of Patchogue; all of whom also built catboats and small sloops for fishing, or for pleasure sailing, which grew rapidly after 1890, when local settlement increased

St Lawrence and Alexandra Bay skiffs

The St Lawrence skiff is a clench planked, pointed sterned, sailing and rowing boat up to twenty-two feet long, of light and exquisite workmanship. It appears to have originated in the Thousand Islands region, where the St Lawrence River issues from Lake Ontario and much of its development took place at Clayton, New York State, during the late 1860s. Locally called 'skiffs', they were used for transport, shooting, rod and line fishing, rowing and sailing for pleasure. The hull lines were very finely formed yet a skiff could carry five or six people, if necessary. Many were used by guides to take parties of vacation sportsmen to and from the fishing grounds of the beautiful St Lawrence Islands; about 1800 of them scattered in a fifty mile long stretch of the river which divided New York State from Ontario, Canada.

During the 1850s Alexandra Bay was much sought by sport fishermen, using guides with double-ended skiffs, planked in pine and about fourteen feet long. These weere the crude prototypes of the later craft. Rapid expansion of the vacation business throughout America after the Civil War speeded development of summer resorts in many areas, and the desire of thousands for natural, outdoor recreation in rowing, sailing, camping, fishing, hunting and allied activities, established resorts in the Thousand Islands region. Skiff construction developed from the boats built in winter for their own use by the many fishing and hunting guides of the American and Canadian sides of the lake and river. A good skiff was vital to a guide as those with the best boats obtained the best custom and a refined boat could be rowed perhaps thirty miles each day, without fatigue. Besides rowing well, the skiffs had to be seaworthy enough to withstand the chop set up by strong winds off exposed places, such as the Forty Acre shoals off Gananoque, a favourite fishing ground. There is no record of a guide's skiff ever being involved in a fatal accident.

As rowing boats the skiffs did not need a rudder and when sails were added, the guides took to sailing them without one, by trimming the sheet and shifting the crew weight: an unusual method but one which can be practised in many traditionally shaped sailing dinghies with varying success. Skiffs were fast off the wind and guides often raced to the fishing grounds.

The St Lawrence skiff in its most refined form is credited to Xavier Colon of the small lakeside town of Clayton, New York who reputedly devised its shape and exceptionally light construction, which remains a hallmark of the type. As demand increased, several other boatbuilding businesses constructed them at Clayton and elsewhere in the area, but made little, if any, alterations to form or basic concept, though detail and finish varied.

Strangely, the St Lawrence skiffs were amongst the earliest mass produced boats, many thousands being built to very high standards. In 1873, A. Bain & Co. established a three storey boatbuilding shop at Clayton, principally to build skiffs, and were rivalled there by the St Lawrence River Skiff, Canoe and Steam Launch Co., who removed to Ogdensburg, New York, about 1900. J. G. Fraser, who had managed this company, left to found the Fraser Hollow Spar and Boat Co. at Greenport, Long Island, which built four sizes of skiffs, besides thousands of masts and spars. Vacationers carried the skiffs reputation elsewhere and scores of the beautifully finished hulls were annually exported from Clayton to American and European resorts.

The later skiffs were from 16 to 22 feet long by an average 3ft 6in beam with a weight of 150lbs. Stem and sternpost were straight and almost vertical, with a very sharp turn into the keel. The lines were virtually those of a developed type of canoe, though the design seems not to have been influenced by canoes. Hull construction was usually quarter inch thick lapstrake cedar planking over small, steam bent timbers. Trim was mahogany.

A single, boomed spritsail rig was adopted during the early development of these skiffs, saving much rowing for professional users and increasing enjoyment for pleasure use. Spritsail area varied from twelve square yards in a twenty-two footer to six square yards for a sixteen foot skiff. The short mast required no shrouds but some skiffs had a forestay. The mast passed through a hinged ring on the beam at the aft end of the short foredeck. The sail was laced to mast and boom and the sprit extended from about a foot above the boom, where its heel was lashed to the mast by a rope snotter. The rig could be quickly stepped and unstepped.

In 1882 Montraville Atwood, a plumber of Clayton, devised a centreboard which folded in three blades, operated by a lever on the pivot bolt. This retracted into a case of about half the size

Plate 79. St Lawrence River sailing skiffs manoeuvring before the start of a race. These light spritsail-rigged sailing and rowing boats are usually sailed without rudders by trimming the position of the crews weight and remain an exacting test of sailing skill. *Photo – Joe Young Jr.*

Figure 106. Sailing a St Lawrence skiff by use of weight location, centreboard and set of sail.

Sailing a rudderless St Lawrence Skiff – by use of weight location, centreboard and set of sail

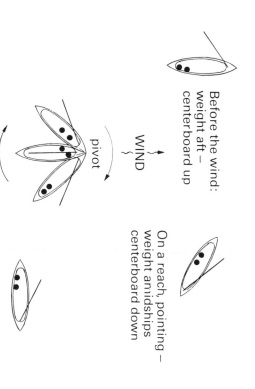

Before the wind: weight aft – centerboard up

WIND

pivot

On a reach, pointing – weight amidships centerboard down

To come about:
weight forward quickly with centerboard up – snap sail in and over when about, centerboard back down & weight aft.

P.S. To gybe, haul in sail, push over boom and quickly throw weight in opposite direction to counter balance – centerboard up and weight in stern – also unhook sheet so it can run more freely.

required for a convenient plate of comparable area and was used in most skiffs and in many sailing canoes.

Rudders are not usually fitted to the sailing skiffs. To steer a course the boat is trimmed by the crew shifting his weight so that correct adjustment is achieved between wind pressure on the sail and the immersed profile of the hull. To come about, the sheet is got in, the centreboard is raised and the crew weight is simultaneously moved quickly forward and to leeward, to depress the bow and raise the stern, allowing it to swing round. Momentum carries the boat to a new tack. The board is then lowered and the crew move quickly amidships, often by walking, then trim their weight to bring her close to the wind.

In a strong wind the crew movements are slow and deliberate; too fast a movement forward results in shipping water over the bow and lee side and can lead to swamping. Sailing to windward in a breeze, a spare sprit is often lashed across the gunwales as an aid to 'hiking', as Americans term sitting out.

In lighter conditions they must be quick, particularly when tacking. The sheet is gathered and the centreplate jerked up by its handle as the crew move swiftly forward as far as possible, causing the boat to luff sharply and allowing the stern to swing round. As the sail fills on the new tack, speed in moving aft and lowering the centreboard are essential to keep way on.

Running with wind on the quarter, the crew sit almost aft. With the wind dead aft he gets as far aft as possible. The mainsheet is also played but is never made fast as these long, narrow and shallow boats are very tender and careful watch is kept for squalls whipping down from the islands. Many will not use the sheet lead block clipped to the lee gunwale in some skiffs to flatten the set of the sail, preferring to hold the sheet as a single part.

When gybing the centreplate is raised and the crew sit in the extreme stern. The sheet is got in carefully and quickly to swing the bow. When it has swung sufficiently to catch the wind the crew weight is shifted to windward and the sheet cleared as the sail swings over, to be paid out smoothly to avoid capsizing when the sail fills to leeward.

If weight concentration aft is insufficient, the skiff will not gybe as the bow will not swing, being offset by wind on the sail. In these conditions the skiff must be tacked round.

A skilled crew can handle a skiff as though she had a rudder, but this is only possible in smooth water. For more boisterous conditions a rudder is sometimes fitted and later skiffs were equipped with these for sailing, operated by yoke and tiller lines.

If a skiff is filled or capsized the mast is unshipped and secured to the bow or stern painter before righting, so it cannot drift away. The skiff is bailed out by the swimming crew who climb on board over one end and re-step the rig. A long-handled pot was often carried as a bailer, enabling them to scoop out water over the gunwale.

The heyday of the skiffs was probably between 1875 and 1900. Every summer cottage in the islands needed at least one for communications and general purposes. Summer guests were often

Figure 107. Method of 'coming about' in a St Lawrence skiff.

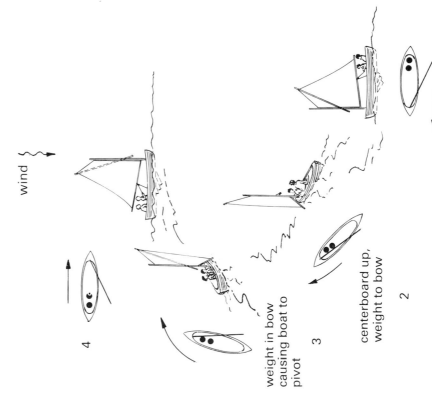

To 'come about' in a rudderless St Lawrence Skiff

wind

4

3

weight in bow causing boat to pivot

2

centerboard up, weight to bow

1

rowed or sailed to the nearest rail head or to church on Sundays and vacation houses obtained groceries and other essential supplies by skiffs, under oars or sail. Many amateur owners of skiffs fished and cruised in them, often making passages of fifty miles a day with favourable winds, camping at night beside the clear waters amongst the rocks and pines.

Racing

Rivalry between the Canadian guides from Gananoque and Americans from Clayton was expressed in annual regatta racing. Regattas for skiffs were held at Brockville, Clayton and Ogdensburg and races often attracted twenty entries, with large crowds of spectators and tremendous enthusiasm by American and Canadian sailing people. But by the end of the century professional participation and cash prizes had killed the sport and for a time after 1900 a sailing skiff was a rare sight on the river.

Although the skiffs were displaced for many uses by the motor boat, thousands continued in use and numbers were raced by amateurs, ideally in fresh south-west winds and over a figure of eight course called the 'corkscrew', typically around Papoose and Whisky Islands.

Some wealthy sportsmen owned 'batswing' skiffs which were a development of the guide boat type prior to 1910. They were exclusively racing boats carrying a large sail, battened to stand flat.

During the 1930s increasing use of the outboard motors brought a further decline in use of skiffs, whose fine form and pointed stern were unsuitable for efficient outboard propulsion. However, the

resurgence of interest in traditional craft built and used in natural ways has been extended to the St Lawrence skiff and many enthusiasts are refitting and using them again, encouraged by surviving boatmen of earlier days and by the activities of the Thousand Islands Museum at Clayton; a treasury of skiff lore and preservation.

The Quebec pilot boat

The Quebec pilot boat of the lower St Lawrence River, Canada, was a widely used small boat type until the beginning of the twentieth century. These open boats originated with the French settlers and remained little changed except for the three masted spritsail rig.

The lower St Lawrence was a large, tide racked estuary demanding a seaworthy boat to face frequent rough conditions and, apart from boarding pilots, they were also used for fishing, salvage and light cargo carrying. They were built up to the maximum size which could be hauled ashore and handled aground by the crew, twenty-eight to thirty feet being the usual length. Beam was about a third of length and the bow and stern waterlines were fine below water but full above, producing a buoyant bow and stern. The bottom rose at an angle of about fifteen degrees and the bilge radius was small. The straight keel projected about nine or ten inches below the garboards; unusual in a craft built for beaching, and an iron bar was shackled to the gunwale to act as a leg when aground. Its lower end had a shoe to press on mud or shingle.

Construction was strong and heavy, usually carvel planked. If clinker, it was very crude but a local characteristic was the full thickness of plank being carried over the lands.

The three masted spritsail rig enabled sails to be set with a small crew; it was a simple, effective rig with a low centre of effort. The foremast stepped through a short foredeck, the mainmast through the amidships thwart, and the mizzen on the inside of the transom off the centre line to allow the tiller to traverse. This does not seem to have impaired sailing qualities and many boats of this type were fast, besides being stiff and weatherly. The stone ballast could be partly shifted to windward during a long tack in a fresh breeze.

The foremast was tallest, descending in height to the mizzen. A foresail set on a short bowsprit and all sails had single part sheets. Reef points were not fitted and in very strong winds the mainsail was handed. Then, if the breeze 'She blow some up', the jib was taken in and the mizzen sprit unshipped, leaving it a flapping triangle. If it blew harder the sprit of the foresail was removed, but by then conditions would prevent the boat from doing her work properly and she would usually make for shelter.

Naval sprits and lugs
The United States Navy used spritsail and lug rigs in many of its ship's boats until the 1920s. In 1880 the Navy was in decline, but a conference attempted to standardise the boats used in the service. All pulling boats were expected to be effective under sail and officers expressed preference for sliding gunter rig for all light boats carrying men, because of the rig's safety, efficiency, handiness and observed freedom from

accident. Most regarded the standing lug as an excellent boat rig, faster than gunter, but less safe and handy.

However, contrary decisions were made and for the larger boats such as the fifty foot launch, complete sloop (cutter) and even a schooner rig were adopted in mistaken attempts to retain sailing navy tradition as long as possible in a steel and steam age. Many officers preferred and proposed standing lug, or a dipping lug foresail and standing main for these boats which might be sent away with a surveying party for up to three weeks, or carry passengers or provisions across an exposed channel perhaps thirty miles wide.

The twenty foot cutter and whaler were given spritsail rig for simplicity and ease of stowing the gear. they were used as lifeboats aboard small ships.

The twenty foot cutter set the moderate area of 143 square feet and the twenty foot whaleboat 137 square feet, and both boats had crews of five men in naval service.

The 1900 programme of twenty-eight, thirty, thirty-three, thirty-six and forty foot steam launches (known as cutters or steamers) were rigged with two masts and standing lugsails; the forward sail being boomless so it could be set and tacked with the funnel raised, though this was usually struck for the rare occasions when these boats were sailed. The rig was probably useful in exposed anchorages where boats had to steam long distances, and their low speeds (only six knots in the twenty-eight and thirty foot types) and often unreliable engines, could be backed up by the sails on a reach or in fair winds. These craft were used for towing ships boats and to carry personnel. The forty footers could carry sixty men at nine knots.

Sails persisted in the 1915 programme which included forty and fifty foot motor sailing barges whose flat bottoms and bluff hull forms never allowed them to sail but made them capable of transporting two hundred seamen or up to twenty tons of stores.

A new type of twenty-eight foot whaleboat was introduced, reverting to the well rounded heel of sternpost which restored the traditional whaleboat handiness in turning. These whalers were rigged with two gunter lugsails which were little used.

Even the eighteen foot catamaran rafs used for painting alongside and other odd jobs were provided with a single boomless spritsail, though it is difficult to imagine when it was used. These hulls were examples of establishment thoroughness in detail, considering their purpose, being built of white cedar with uncaulked, fitted seams; the hulls were bound by galvanised steel hoops, barrel fashion.

Spritsails in Alaska

Spritsail-rigged gill net boats maintained a tradition of fishing under sail and oar in mid-twentieth-century Alaska, where Federal regulations prohibited the use of powered craft for fishing salmon in the amazingly productive Bristol Bay until 1951.

Bristol Bay lies at the south eastern end of the Bering Strait, bounded to the south by the long mountainous arm of the Alaska Peninsula but open to the west. It includes the area from Cape Newenham to Cape Menshikoff, and was the most productive waters for red or sockeye salmon. As many as 24 million fish were netted in a year worth 30 million dollars even then. The gill net was the only legal fishing gear in Bristol Bay, used as a drift net. Residents of two years could also set them as stake nets in shallow water. Five salmon rivers issue into Bristol Bay: the Togiak, Nushagak, Naknek-Kvichak, Egegik and Ugashik. Each produced runs of salmon which, in season, were taken at their mouths in gill nets set and held by hand and worked from small rowing and sailing craft rigged with a single spritsail. The short season of this prolific fishery made this practice economic, and it was continued by a law prohibiting the use of power boats, which remained in force until 1951. The River Togiak was reserved for fishing by local inhabitants.

Early gill netters were rowing boats, when fish were plentiful and fishermen could make a full haul a short distance from their landings. The Bay has dangerous sand bars and banks extending miles seaward. The tidal range is the world's third largest and currents are strong and erratic. Many gill netters were swamped, capsized, went ashore and broke up, and hundreds of fishermen were lost over the years

Commercial fishing on Bristol Bay was first recorded in 1880 when the Alaska Commercial Company were salting 800 to 1200 barrels of salmon from the Nushagak River, where they had a trading station at Fort Alexander. Their enterprise was followed in 1884 by the Arctic Packing company, who established a cannery, closely followed by the Alaskan Packing

Company, and in 1886 by the Bristol Bay Canning Company at Dillingham, then by many others.

Salmon fishing also flourished further south in the large rivers of the states of Washington and Oregon, and in adjacent British Columbia. The vast quantities of fish to be caught on this West Coast and extent of the canning operations demanded large numbers of small fishing boats of shallow draught and simple rig and construction.

Form and construction

Early boats were twenty-two or twenty-three feet long, which increased to about twenty-eight feet as an optimum, with many thirty feet long. It may be that the pointed stern design of the gill netter resulted from the early boats being built on the then remote north west coasts of North America by ships carpenters, and others familiar with ships' boats.

The Bristol Bay gill netters reputedly originated from San Francisco where in 1868 J. J. Griffin built a boat of this type for a fisherman named Greek Joe. Next season another similar boat appeared on the lower Columbia River and afterwards the type was built in numbers in the San Francisco area and on the Columbia, where the cannery owners rented the boats to the men working them and the large numbers in use led to the building of several standard types by various firms, to lower building costs, which in 1880 was about $220 for an undecked boat and $240 for a decked craft.

Eventually the gill netters were built as stock boats, often at yards owned by the salmon

packers, such as that of the Columbia River Packers Association at Astoria. However, there were many different designs and each was used to build large numbers of gill netters.

The packers' gill netters were numerous and beamier than most. Hulls built for Libby were narrow, as were those for the Nakeen or squaw Creek firms.

It is estimated that over 15,000 Bristol Bay gill netters were built between the 1880s and 1954 and all were numbered for identification, usually with prefix initials denoting ownership e.g. 44 APA, meaning Alaska Packers Association boat number 44.

The Standard Bristol Bay gill net boat was a 28ft by 8ft 9in, beam pointed sterned, shoal draught boat, rigged with a single boomed spritsail under which she was a moderately good sailer, best loaded in a breeze. The boats were built to carry a load of salmon and nets, to have reasonable motion and to survive the breezy weather of the large, exposed and shallow bay.

The beamy hull had a fine entrance and run and fairly firm amidship sections, with some rise of floor and a well rounded deckline forward and aft giving considerable flare above water at bow and stern. At first the boats were open but by the mid 1870s short end decks and side decks were fitted and the cockpit coamings were rounded at each end, the mast stepping in a metal clasp against a strong thwart at the forward coaming. The hull drew only eighteen inches light and the rudder did not project below the keel, but a large rectangular centreplate enabled them to sail to windward.

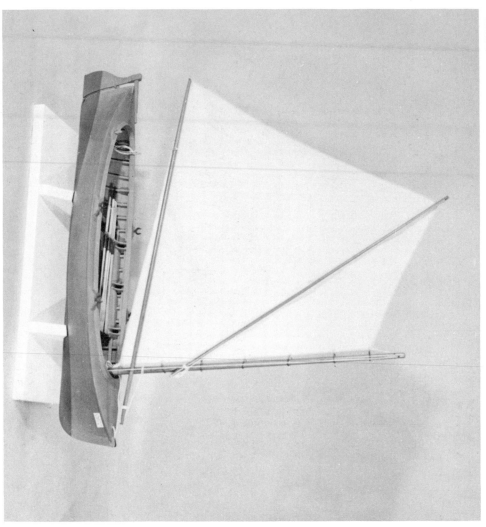

Plate 80. Model of a Columbia River salmon boat, showing the type around 1885. Note the spritsail boom secured by a snotter set taut against the mast, with the tack of the sail below it. These centreboard boats were often rowed when working the nets. *Photo – Smithsonian Institution.*

Handling

They were good carriers; it took eight hundred pounds to immerse a typical gill netter one inch. The limited sail area, generous freeboard and healthy sheer made them good sea boats and the flat amidship sections made them stiff in a breeze.

The full shouldered hull slammed heavily into a head sea and threw sheets of spray, and a good pump was necessary with the large cockpit. The gill netters were strongly but inexpensively built. Planked in Oregon pine on steamed timbers, with larch keel, stem and sternpost. They were strongly but plainly constructed, however they were usually neglected and often abused by their crews, who had no concern for their condition. However, many lasted ten or twelve years and easily amortised their cost. 'Finn built' gill netters working Bristol Bay probably originated from the Finnish community at Astoria and were notably shapely and strongly constructed. The strong local winds dictated a modest sail area and the boats had to be frequently rowed in calms, or to set or recover nets. The sail had a moderate luff length, a long boom and short head. It had no reef points and in strong winds the sprit was unshipped, converting it into an inefficient trysail, suitable for reaching or running but of little use for windward work. They could be made to heave to under this rig which was improved if the peak was tied to a mast hoop. The boom could be readily unshipped, but stepping the mast and rigging the sail was trying in a seaway or strong winds. When the sprit was set up its snotter was rigged so that a sharp pull on it would free the sprit to fall and so shorten sail in a squall. When the net was to be shot the sprit was usually taken down, leaving enough canvas to keep the boat moving while the gear was shot. In calms she was rowed. The boat could be sailed single handed while the other man overhauled the nets. Gill netters were slow in light airs and difficult to put about due to the parallel immersed profile. In stronger winds they carried considerable weather helm, which could be eased by trimming them slightly by the stern. A few set a foresail to the stemhead and some sailed well. An unconverted boat used for pleasure sailed forty miles in eight hours.

The fishermen worked for the cannery companies and many agreed to work day or night, seven days a week if necessary, though they were not generally expected to work on a Sunday. Many nationalities were represented in the gill netter crews and life in the fishing camps could be tough. Often the boats were fishing for six days, with little rest for the crew of two or three, who slept forward under the canvas tilt. Their day commenced about three in the morning when the mast was raised and clamped in place, the spritsail was set and the boat stood away for the fishing ground, perhaps in one of the channels of a rivers mouth.

In Bristol Bay the gill nets were seventy-five fathoms long and twelve feet deep, up to nine hundred feet of net being set. the bottom rope was leaded and the head rope was corked and had wooden floats at intervals, about twenty-five inches apart. The mesh was sufficiently large to allow a salmon to put its head through, but not its body, so the head was caught by the gills. The

nets might be set for only one hour or several but when the floats started moving the men knew it was filling with fish and it was hauled over rollers, one for the headrope and one for the footrope. The net was bundled into the net space aft, with the gilled fish still in it, to be picked out by hand, aided by a small hook. The fish were placed in pounds and when the net was cleared it was re-shot if the boat had not drifted from her fishing ground.

Some canneries had fish receiving scows anchored at various places along river, close to the best fishing grounds, so the boats could sell the catch without having to sail to the canneries. Two or three thousand salmon was a full load for a gill netter, depending on size of fish, the weather and distance from the scow or cannery. When alongside the scow the sail was dropped and cast off from the boom, to be stowed on the foredeck. The mast, sprit and boom were unshipped and the fish was pitched to the scow with a 'pew', or fork, being tallied on board and credited to that boat's crew. The boat was washed out and her crew had a hot meal on board the scow; the only one of the day as they lived on snacks the rest of the time.

With the latest reports of fish movements and catches they sailed again to shoot the nets, one man on watch and the other sleeping for an hour or so before changing places and hauling the nets.

Fishing usually finished at six in the morning on Saturdays and that day and Sunday were occupied mending and dipping nets for preservation, drying them and making any necessary repairs to the boat. They slept in shore bunks, replenished supplies and found the usual amusements of remote nineteenth-century communities.

Bristol Bay was subject to strong winds and sudden storms. If caught, a gill netter tried to ride it out using her nets as a sea anchor.

In May 1880 over twenty fishermen were lost in a gale while gill netting salmon. As the storm occurred immediately after a strike by the fishermen, most boats and men were fishing, which led to higher casualties than might have been sustained in normal working.

The Columbia River fishermen had a one-day annual regatta with gill netters sailing for the Java Cup, the winner being regarded as 'King of the Fleet'. Cannery companies owned fleets of old sailing ships which carried men, stores, and equipment to Bristol Bay, to return with canned fish, enduring much bad weather in the Gulf of Alaska and ice in the Bering Sea. Often it took forty days or so to sail from Astoria, Seattle or San Francisco to Bristol Bay, and a voyage of sixty-three days is recorded for one of these unhandy square riggers.

Decline of the gill netters

Gasoline engines were installed in large numbers of gill netters on the Columbian river but continued to be prohibited in the Bristol Bay fisheries until 1951. The reason for the long standing prohibition on power boats seems uncertain, but it may have been the possible expense to the fishing companies for the comparatively short season of use, and the supply of cheap labour.

In later years gill netters were towed from the cannery to the fishing grounds by a powered 'monkey boat' at the commencement of the season, and returned the same way at its close. Their catch was collected daily by a powered cannery tender which stationed herself in the centre of the fleet to receive salmon by the thousand. Strangely, this fleet of sailing workboats reached a heyday around 1948, when every salmon caught in Bristol Bay was still hand hauled by sailing fishermen using hundreds of gill netters.

When the federal government relinquished control of Alaskan fisheries to the state government, the rule against powered fishing vessels was lifted and the hundred and fifty sailing gill netters of a type which for about seventy years had been the mainstay of the salmon industry, were obsolete. Some were sold for conversion to power or sailing pleasure craft: many were left to rot.

An unusual split spritsail rig was set by the sixteen foot *Sea Serpent* which raced a fifteen foot centreboard dory named *Mermaid* from New York to the Lizard in 1891 (Fig. 108). The upper part of the mainsail was apparently set by halyards at the masthead, and the sprit end and was sheeted to the boom end. When this was stowed the boat was left under a low trysail. The *Sea Serpent's* hull form was similar to some New England lobster boats. She won the race; the *Mermaid* being picked up by a ship six hundred miles off the Irish coast.

The strangest spritsails in North America were carried by the 'ice schooners' of the eskimos:

cargo sledges fitted with a crude spritsail which was often made from a Hudson's Bay Company 'point' blanket, set on a driftwood mast and sprit lashed to the sledge and sheeted to an outrigger also used as a tiller by the 'helmsman' who alternately ran astern of or rode on the craft, which could make surprising speed on a reach or with a free wind and smooth snow or ice humming under the runners.

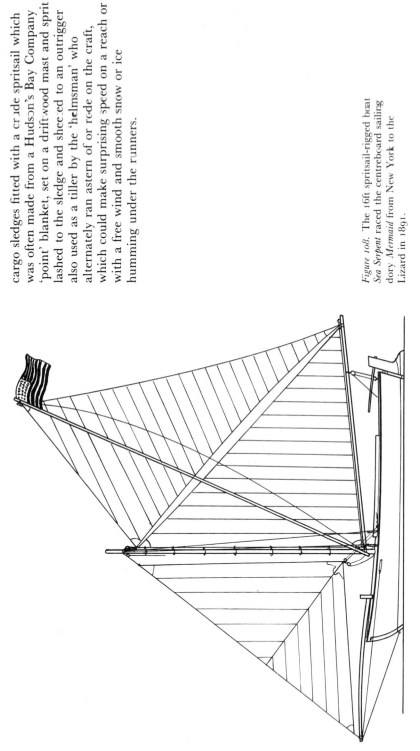

Figure 108. The 16ft spritsail-rigged boat *Sea Serpent* raced the centreboard sailing dory *Mermaid* from New York to the Lizard in 1891.

Glossary

The descriptions given are intended only to explain the terms in relation to the contents of this book. This is not a general glossary of nautical terms.

Abaft. At the after side of, or further aft than a part of the craft. For instance, 'Abaft the mast', 'Abaft the main hatch'.

Bayou. Term for shallow waterways of the coastal areas or the American states of Louisiana, Mississippi, north-west Florida and part of Texas.

Becket. Strictly an eye in the end of a rope. Also used as a term for an arrangement of a rope snotter for the heel of a sprit, using a rope with an eye and a toggle to secure it around the mast (see also *snotter*).

Belay. To belay a rope. To make it fast to a cleat, belaying pin, etc.

Brails. Ropes which gather the leach of a spritsail to the headrope and the luff, or the leach of a loose footed gaff sail if fitted with brails, to the gaff and the luff. A sail is 'brailed up' as a temporary method of reefing or when anchoring or mooring the craft.

Bullseye fairlead. A hardwood or plastic eye through which a rope leads. Particularly used as fairleads for headsail sheets.

Bumkin. A spar protruding from the stern of a craft to support a standing backstay, or the sheet of a mizzen or mainsail.

Burton. A tackle having two single blocks with a hook block in the bight of the running part. Often used as a purchase in the halyards and running backstays of lug, spritsail or gaff rigged craft.

Buss Sail. A squaresail hoisted on a yard and set by the North Sea herring busses of Holland and England. These sails retained many aspects of the early seagoing squaresail into the nineteenth century, when busses were still sailing from some Dutch ports. The sail could be set close hauled for windward sailing and had some of the characteristics of the dipping lugsail.

Cap iron. The iron band at the masthead (Cap). Sometimes also has an eye for the topmast (see *Spectacle Iron*).

383

Caveata Line. The concave line cut around the sheer of a yacht or other craft as decoration. Usually gilded or painted.

Clencher. Clencher or clinker planked. Clinker built. A hull constructed with relatively thin planking having the seams overlapped and fastened with clenched nails (see the book *Clinker Boatbuilding* by John Leather).

Coaming. The vertical watertight member surrounding a hatch, cabin top or cockpit.

Copers. Traders in liquor and tobacco using a sailing craft, often a fishing smack. Usually Dutch or Belgian and operating principally in the North Sea in the days of the large fleets of sailing fishing craft which spent much time at sea. Also a trade carried on with small craft in the Sound between Denmark and Sweden, in the sailing ship era.

Cutch. The distillate from the bark of an indian tree, used for tanning sails, nets or other fabric, for preservation.

Cranky. Adjective for a craft having little stability. Also *tender*.

Cutter. A fore- and aft-rigged craft having one mast setting a gaff or Bermudian mainsail, staysail and jib. May also set a topsail if gaff rigged. Some old cutters also carried squaresails.

Dumb sheave. A semi-circular hardwood block fitted inside a slot through a masthead or end of an outrigger or bowsprit. Grooved to allow a rope halyard, sheet or outhaul to pass smoothly over it. Constructed thus to avoid the halyard or sheet jamming, as might occur with a rotating metal sheave.

Fall (of halyard). The hauling end or part of a halyard.

False Keel. A wooden additional keel fastened under the keel proper to increase lateral resistance for sailing or to take chafe when grounding.

Fast. Adverb or adjective to describe catching a net or rope on an underwater obstruction. 'To come fast', 'To get fast'. A 'fast': noun for an underwater obstruction.

Fid. In rigging, the metal pin securing either the heel of a topmast against movement or the heel (inboard end) of a bowsprit against the bitts.

Fish pieces. Wooden strengthening pieces on each side of a large lugsail yard in way of the slings, where the halyard is attached. Fish pieces were usually fastened to a yard with rope bindings.

Gammon Iron. The iron band fastened to the stemhead, through which the bowsprit passes.

Garboard. The plank or strake next to the keel.

Hackmatack. A tree similar to larch, grown in North America. The roots were often used to cut knees for ship and boat building.

Headstick. A short spar spreading the head and load from the halyard on the head of a topsail. A term particularly applied to the topsails of English east and south coast sailing barges.

Horse. A metal or rope traverse on which a traveller for a sheet slides to enable the sheet to fall to leeward on each tack and obtain the best set for the sail.

Houari. A two masted rig, possibly of Mediterranean origin. The sails were of almost similar size, usually high peaked lugsails resembling or being gunter lugs, often without booms. A craft carrying that rig.

Hoy. A cargo and sometimes also passenger carrying coastal sailing vessel on a regular passage service between ports. A term particularly used in the coastal trade of the English counties of Essex, Kent and Suffolk.

Jigger. A mizzen sail, usually small and triangular in shape.

Lands. The overlap of the planks of a clinker-planked craft and the name of the lower edge of each strake of planking.

Lapstrake. The North American term for clinker planking (see *Clencher*).

Lateen. The triangular, high peaked sail of Indian Ocean and Mediterranean sailing craft. Set from a long yard hoisted on a short mast. Probably one of the oldest types of sails.

Lazyjack. A line or lines leading from a topping lift to or under a boom to gather the sail when lowering or hoisting.

Leg of Mutton sail. A triangular sail of low hoist and relatively long boom. Often fitted with a small headstick (see also *shoulder of mutton sail*).

Levee. An embankment or wharf. A term of the southern United States, the inland rivers of the south and mid west, and of the Pacific coast.

Lignum Vitae. A very hard and durable hardwood.

Lute stern. An early form of counter stern in small craft. The side planking was carried beyond a transom and, in profile, ended in a concave arc, reaching from the waterline to meet the deck. The transverse ending was planked-in to form a watertight counter.

Mast lacing (Luff lacing). A continuous rope lacing attaching the luff of a sail to a mast.

Oakum. A caulking material made from natural fibre rope. Used for caulking hull, deck and other seams.

Peak. The upper aft corner of a gaff, lug or spritsail is termed the peak. To peak a gaff, a yard, a sprit, or a sail, is to raise this upper corner when the sail is set.

Pirogue (Periauger). Simple small craft of Louisiana coastal waters. Cut from a single log and rowed, poled or sailed with a small spritsail. Used for fishing, fowling or light transport. Alternatively, from settlement to the early twentieth century, a New England type of two masted craft with a pointed stern, not setting a jib and having the foremast stepped well forward. A rig possibly of dutch origin.

Reef points. Short ropes termed 'points' sewn strongly to the sail on both sides, with reinforcement as necessary, in rows across the sail at the positions of reefs. The luff and leach of the sail are pulled down to a boom with reef pendants or earings which pass through cringles at luff and leach. The halyards are slacked off for the depth necessary for the reef and the slack of the sail is then reefed by carefully bunching it together, commencing at the centre of the foot and working outwards, tying the two opposing pairs of reef points under the footrope of the sail (never under the boom) tightly with a reef or a bow knot.

Rise of floor. The angle of rise of the bottom of a craft from the centreline, relative to a level line.

Robands. 'Rope bands'. Used to attach sails to masts and spars (see Fig. 13).

Rocker. The longitudinal curve of the underside of a keel or the bottom of a craft.

Seizing. To bind one rope to another with fine line or twine.

Sharpie. A flat bottomed craft of North

American origin having a shallow, single chine hull and usually narrow beam. Transom or pointed stern. Used for fishing, pleasure or carrying light cargo. A variety of rigs were used, usually set on two masts.

Sheer. The profile curvature of the upper edge of the sheerstrake of a craft, from stem to stern.

Shoulder of mutton sail. See *leg of mutton sail*.

Skiff. A name for a variety of boat types. For instance; a light, often fast, rowing boat of the English River Thames; a gill net fishing boat of Alaska and British Columbia salmon fisheries; sailing and rowing pleasure craft of the St Lawrence River, U.S.A. and Canada; the small boat belonging to an Essex bawley, fishing vessel; and many other widely differing examples.

Smack. A decked sailing fishing or sometimes a cargo carrying vessel varying from about 28–80 feet long, from British and European ports. Rigs included cutter, ketch and dandy. Hull form varied but general characteristics were a counter, lute, or transom stern, a straight, plumb stem, flush deck, crew accommodation aft, fish hold or wet well amidships, gear store forward. A powerful and weatherly type of craft usually engaged in trawling, line fishing, spratting, shellfish dredging or salvaging.

Smooth. (of waves). A momentary easing of the force of seas or surf.

Swatchway. A shallow, navigable passage through a sand or mud shoal.

Sneak Box. A shallow hulled gunning boat originating on Barnegat Bay, New Jersey, U.S.A. Later developed for pleasure sailing and racing.

Snotter. A form of rope strop or other arrangement of rope to secure the heel of a sprit to a mast.

Spectacle iron. An iron band at the head of a lowermast, which has an eye through which the heel of a topmast passes to the trestletrees.

Steeved down. To steeve down a bowsprit. To set a spar down by applying a downward pull from a purchase to its outer end.

Stiff. Adjective for a stable craft, one which will not heel easily.

Strike. To strike a mast. To lower a mast in a tabernacle, or a topmast from aloft.

Strop. An elongated band of rope used for connecting a spar to a halyard, a sprit to a mast, or for placing around an object to be lifted, or seized around a block.

Throat. The upper forward corner of a gaff, lug or spritsail.

Tine. An arm of a grapnel anchor.

Topping lift. A rope, ropes, a purchase or a combination of these used to raise or lower a boom.

Treenails. Hardwood dowels for fastening planks to frames and sometimes other hull members to each other. The treenail is driven tightly in the hole and the end is split and wedged, then cut off flush. An old form of boat and ship fastening now almost obsolete but which is surprisingly durable, but time consuming in construction.

Tumblehome. An inward curve or rake of a crafts side above water. Usually amidships and aft.

Tye. In lug rig the rope or chain leading from the yard through a mast sheave to the upper block of a purchase, the whole forming a halyard.

Vang. A rope or wire rope, usually having a purchase at the lower end, used to transversely adjust the trim of the peak of a spritsail or gaff sail, or to steady it at anchor in bad weather.

Whip. A single rope halyard, tye or lift ending in a single block with a simple purchase for hoisting.

Yard. The spar at the head of a lugsail or a squaresail.

Index

Aberystwyth, 234–236
  Fishing Boats, 234–236
  Herring Gigs, 235
Active, 196
Adams, George (of Dartmouth), 203
Aid, 300
Ainger, Peter (of Manningtree), 308
Alaska Gill Net Boats, 376–380
Albion, 131
Albion II, 123
Albion, 123
Albert Victor, 132
Aldeburgh, 281, 296–299
Alden, Samuel (Boatbuilder of Duxbury), 333, 334
Alexandra, 123
Allen, J., 105
Allen, Ratcliff and (Boatbuilders of Deal), 122
Almogolie (Swedish type), 58
Alnmouth, 254
Amazon, 118
Amble, 254
America, 292
Annan, 244
Aphrodite, 234
  Wharnmel Net Boats, 244, 246
Appledore, 221, 222
  Ferrymen, 222
Ash Point, 367–369
  Fishermen, 367–369
Axe, 272

Bacton, 270, 276
'Bafer' rig, 96
Bamburgh, 354
Band of Hope, 158, 254
Bargozzi (Venetian type), 34

Barnstaple, 221
Bay Head, 346
Bayly, J. (Boatbuilder of Deal), 122
  Michael (Boatbuilder of Deal), 122
  Thomas (Boatbuilder of Deal), 122
Beach Yawls, 279–281, 283–285, 287–292
  Companies, 281–284, 287, 292, 293
  Punts, Norfolk and Suffolk, 294–299
Beadnell, 254
Beatrice Annie, 189
Beeching Brothers (Boatbuilders of Great Yarmouth), 284
Beer, 187
  Luggers, 187–190
Beesands, 203
Beetle, James (Boatbuilder of New Bedford), 325
Belfast Lough Yawls, 237
Belinda, 167
Belton family (Boatbuilders of Worthing), 167
Belton, Thomas (of Worthing), 167, 168
Ben, The, 173
Bideford, 221
Biloxi, 358, 360, 363
Bird of Freedom, 159
Bishop, Nathaniel, 348
Bisquine (French lugger), 25, 26
Bittern, 283, 293
Blackpool, 242
Blakeney, 276–278
Blencathra, 159
Bluejacket, 139
Bluenose (modern spritsail boat), 38
Blyth, 254
  'Foy Boats', 254, 255
Bolger, Philip (Designer), 38
Bombay Sailing Boats, 25
Bonny Kate, 158
Boothbay, 341

Bosham, 181
  Luggers, 184
Boston, 336, 338
Cape Cod, 335, 364, 365
Caprice (later *Bream*), 179
Boulmer, 254
Braund, James (of Bucksh Mills), 220
Braunton, 221
Bream, 179
Brett, Howard (Boatbuilder of Cley), 276, 279
Bridgwater, 223, 227
Bridlington Cobles, 265
Brightlingsea, 302
Brighton (Boatbuilders of), 167
  Fishermen, 148, 164
  Hog Boats, 164, 166
  Luggers, 166, 167
Britannia, 159
British Columbia Gill Net Boats, 377
British Queen, 136
Bristol, 310
Bristol Bay, 376–380
Bristol Bay Gill Net Boats, 377–380
Brixon's Pride, 132
Broads Wherries, 312, 313
Broadmeadows, William (Sailmaker of Bridlington), 265
Brockville, 374
Brothers, 277
Brue, 222
Buckett, James (of Brighstone), 173, 174
Bucksh Mills, 220–221
Burgoyne, Alfred (Boatbuilder of Kingston-on-Thames), 38
Burnham (Somerset), 226–228

Cambridge (Boatbuilder of Filey), 264
Came, Tom, 228
Carver, F. J. and Son Ltd. (Boatbuilders of Bridgewater), 227
Casey (Boatbuilder of Nyrush), 239
Catboats, 331
Centennial Republic, 348
Chant (Boatbuilder of Salcombe), 205
Charlestown gigs, 213
Chase, Enoch (of Seabrook), 337
Chatham, 318
Chichester Harbour, 181, 184
Christabel, 152
Chudleigh, Tom (Boatbuilder of Scilly Isles), 217
Cley, 277, 278
Clayton, 370, 374
Clovelly, 219
  Luggers, 219
  'Picarooners', 220
Cobles, 247, 248, 255, 258, 260
  at Boulmer, 248, 249
  Construction of, 249, 250
  Crab, 261
Flamborough, 249
Fishermen, 253, 254
  'Five man boats', 258, 260, 261
  Launching and beaching, 249, 253
  'Mules', 259, 260
  in 20th Century, 267
  Rig, 250, 251, 252
  'Sploshers', 259
Cock Robin, 199
Cohasset, 336
Colon, Xavier (Boatbuilder of Clayton), 370
Columbia, River fishermen of, 380
Conant, Harry, 193, 194

Consolation, The, 168
Cooke, Edward W., 314, 318
Combwich, 223, 226–229
Conger, 181
Cotton, Rufus (of Atherford), 174
Cosmopolite, 120, 147
Cosmopolite II, 170
Cowes watermen, 175
   boats of, 175
Cozens, family (of Weston), 179
Crab Boats (of Norfolk), 270, 271, 272, 274
   fishermen (of Norfolk), 270, 274, 275
Craster, 254
Creef, Washington (Boatbuilder of Roanoak
   Island), 353
Cresswell, 254
Cromer, 270, 277
   hovellers, 277
   Pinkers, 277
   'Great Boats', 277
Crosby, family (Boatbuilders of Osterville,
   Massachusetts), 366
Crossley, Sir Savill, 293
Crotchet, 105
Crotch Island (Boatbuilders of), 338
Cruti, Giacomo and family (Boatbuilders), 361
Crystal Spring, 158
Cuckoo, 208, 211
Culler, R. D. (Designer), 41
Cullercoats, 254
Curraghs (or 'Canoes'), 240

Dack, Tom (Boatbuilder of Wells next the
   Sea), 276
Dart, 132
Dartmouth, 203
   fishing boats, 203
Deal, luggers. First Class, 113, 121
   construction of, 118
'Cats', 122
Cutters, 117
Galleys, 139, 141
Galley Punts, 141 *et seq.*
   'Great Galleys', 141 *et seq.*
Foresail and Mizzen punts, 137
'Half boats', 122
Pilots, 132, 134, 135, 147
Launching and beaching, 115–117, 139
Dell Quay, 181
Dobles, 318, 320
Dora, 244

Dory, 223, 364
Doughty, David (of Great Island), 331
Dublin Bay skiffs, 237
Dunball, 223, 229
Dungover Fishermen, 136
Dusters (of Hull and Grimsby), 267–269
Duxbury, 332, 334

Eagle, 301
Eakins, Thomas, 350
Earl of Eginton, 134
Early Morn, 118, 134
Eastbourne Boatbuilding, 159, 160
   Fishermen, 148, 157, 160, 162
   Fishermen, Names of, 158
   Luggers, 157, 159, 160
   'Shinamen', 158
   Punts, 158, 159
Ebenezer, 136
Eclipse, 136
Egg Harbour, 349
Eileen, 231
Emery, Robert (Boatbuilder of Sheringham),
   276
   Lewis (Boatbuilder of Sheringham) 276
Empress, 231
Emsworth, 181, 183
   Fishermen, 183, 184
   Luggers, 183
Endeavour, 136, 142
Englands Glory, 125
Englands Rose, 193, 194
Eresby, Lord Willoughby De, 151
Eskimos 'Ice Schooners', 381
Essex Luggers, 300, 301
Eurydice, 135, 174

Falmouth, Oyster punts, 212, 213
   boatbuilders, 213
Falmouth gigs, 213, 216
Fan Tan, 105
Faun, 132
Felixstowe, 267
Feltham (Boatbuilder of Portsmouth), 183
Ferris, Richard (Voyage of), 310
Fife (Scottish lugger), 70
Filey cobles, 264
Mules, 260, 263
Finnis, George W. (Sailmaker of Deal), 123
   Philip (Sailmaker of Deal), 120

Flamborough cobles, 264, 285
   mules, 260
Flatners, 222–229, 231, 234
   'Gore Boats', 223, 227, 228
   'Bay Boats', 223
   Weston-super-Mare type, 229–231
Flora, 135, 136
Fly, 132
Foregirt (see Vargood), 21, 189
Foresters Pride, 132
Fort Pierce, 345
Forte, 174
Fowey gigs, 213
Fox, 127, 301
Fred Archer, 159
Free Will, 159
Frentz, Henry, 359
Friends, The, 194
Friends Goodwill, 315
Friend of all Nations, 118, 135

Galilee, 342
   Fishermen, 343
Galleys (Isle of Wight), 173
Galleys (Deal), 139, 141
Galley Punts (Deal), 120–121, 141, 143
Galway, 239
Gananoque, 370, 374
Gamel, 174
Gardner, Henry (Boatbuilder of Deal), 136
John (Maritime Historian), 366
Garland, 123
Gausden, George (Boatbuilder of
   Eastbourne), 159, 160, 162
   and Sisk (Boatbuilder of Eastbourne), 159
Genesta, 334
General Havelock, 141
Georgiana, 136, 293
Giacomo, 360, 361
Gibbs, Kenneth (Designer), 101
Gigs (Pensacola), 356–358
   (Solent), 174
   (Warrington), 356–358
Giles, Morgan F. (Designer), 87
Gipsy, 142
Gleotogs (Irish type), 239
Gloriana, 287
Good Hope, The, 168
Good Intent, 318
Gorleston, 281

Gorran Haven, 208, 211
   Fishing Boats, 208, 211
Gray, John B. (Boatbuilder of Racoon
   Creek), 349
Gravesend watermens wherries, 310, 311
Great Galleys (Deal), 120
Green Harbour, 336
Greyhound, 292, 362
Grimsby, 276, 277
Gun Punts, 305, 307, 308, 347
Gunners Pride, 304
Guthorn, Peter J. (Author), 345

Haidai, 230
'Half and Halfer', 278
Hallsands crabbers, 203–205
Happy Go Lucky, 142
Happy New Year, 287, 289, 290, 297
Happy Thought, 159
Hampton Boats, 357–339, 341
Hartlepool cobles, 257, 258
Harrisor, John (of Deal), 122
Hastings fishermen 148–150
   Boatbuilders, 151, 152
   Punts, 148
   Luggers, 148–151, 154–156
Hausley, 254
Hawke, 300
Hatch Boats, 318
Hayle gigs, 213
Hayling Island, 181
Hayward, Thomas of Deal), 122
   Isaac (of Deal), 122
   Thomas and Son (of Deal), 118
Hazlebank, 146
Heart of Oak, 289
Heathen Chinee, 103
Henry Connett Skiff, 358
Hingham, 336
Hipsey, Charles (of Maldon), 307
Holloway (Boatbuilder of Whitstable), 108, 110
Hook, Robert (of Lowestoft), 289
Hookers, 239
Hope, 120, 142
Hope crabbers, 205, 208
Hope, Linton (Designer), 97
Hopwood, Hergreaves (Boatbuilder of
   Flamborough), 265
Holy Island, 253
Holyhead, 240, 241
Homer, Winslow, 363

Hornsea cobles and crab boats, 266
Howard, John (Designer and builder), 305
Howland, Lewellyn, 330
Hull (Massachusetts), 336
Huntspill, 228
Hurd, Fred (of Eastbourne), 160
Hurrell, Harry (of Hope), 205
Hurricane Island, 369
Husk (Boatbuilder of Wivenhoe), 216
Hussey, Frank, 314
Hutchinson (Boatbuilder of Worthing), 167

Increase, 288
Ingolf, 127
Industry, 136, 150
Inishbofin, 239
Instow, 222
Ipswich, 267
Ira, 205
Iron Crown, 125
Islander, 330
Itchenor, 161

Jack, 304
James and Thomas, 123
Jewel, class, 97
John Bull, 283, 287
Johns, William (of Appledore), 222
Jolien (Danish type), 31
Juniper, 219

Kaffenkahn (Stevenkahn, Mollenkahn), 30, 31
Kahn (German barge), 30
Kaperboats (Danish type – see also Almogiolle), 58
Keel Boats, 254
Kellog, Elijah (of Harpswell), 337, 338
Kessingland, 281, 293
Kathleen, 135
Kilner, Ashton and (Boatbuilders of Poole), 105
Kilve, 228
King William IV, 318
Kingsdown Galley Punts, 142
Luggers, 113 *et seq.*
Kingston (Massachusetts), 332, 334
Kolek (Malayan type), 27, 28

La Gracieuse, 279
Lady Bounder, 132
Lady Eleanor, 159

Lady Ross, 136
Lamaneurs (of Dunkirk), 28, 29
Langley, Morris (of Deal), 122
Langstone punts, 185
Harbour, 181, 185
La Reine, 97, 99
Laten sail, 18, 23, 25, 26, 31, 54, 68
Lavers (Boatbuilders of Exmouth), 189
Laura, 180
Leather, David (Boatbuilder and Designer), 38, 349
Leigh, 315, 316
Leopard, 349
Leslie, R. C. 193
Little Florence, 159
Liverpool, 240, 242
Gigs, 240-242
Lizard, 135
Lincolnshire fishermen, 266
London fishermen, 310, 314, 316
Long Branch, 342
Boatbuilders of, 344
Long Island, 369
Fishermens skiffs, 369
Longford, Robert (Boatbuilder of Pensacola), 357
Lottie, 222
Louise, 136
Louisiana pirogues, 363
Lowestoft, 280, 281, 289-291
Lutworth, 152
Lugsail split, 69

Lugsails:
Arrangements of, 16, 62
Balanced lugsails, 31, 33
Bending sail, 64
Boat handling, 66
in France, 19
Greek cargo luggers, 33
Gunter lugsail, 23
Halyards for, 64, 65
Methods of use, 21
Origins of, 17, 19
Resurgence of interest in, 37
Sailmaking, 41
Set with main and peak halyard, 34
Three masted luggers, 21

Lugsails, Balanced
Arrangement of, 87
As mizzen, 91
Boat handling, 89

Fully battered lugsails, 103, 105, 106
Halyards for, 88, 89
Reefing, 89
Sheet, 89, 91
Tacking, 89

Lugsails, Dipping
Arrangement of, 66
For gigs, 72, 74
Halyards for, 68, 69
Modern version, 75, 77
Reefing, 70
Tacking, 68, 69, 72

Lugsails, Gunter
Arrangements of, 92
Battens for, 96, 101, 103
Brails for, 93
Gibbs, Kenneth, gunter rig, 101
Gunter irons, 92, 93
Gunter latten, 102
Gunter spritsail, 97
Halyards for, 92, 94, 95
Handling, 95
Jaws for yard, 94, 95
Luff lacing, 96
Mast track for 94, 101, 103
Reefing, 95, 96
Roller Reefing, 101

Lugsails, Standing
Arrangements of, 78
As mizzen, 81
Boom for, 78, 80
Brail for, 79
Comparison with gaff sail, 85
Dipping yard, 80, 82
Foresail of the *Procyn*, 108
Halyards for, 79, 80
In racing dinghies, 86, 87
Reefing, 80, 81, 109
Scotch-cut, 81, 82
Setter rig, 87
Sheet, 79, 80
Tack purchase, 89

Mackenzie, Landseer, 103
McMullen, R. T., 108-110
Maine, wherries, 367, 369
Builders of, 367-369
Maldon, 304, 307, 309, 318
Mallard, 162
Manningtree, 308, 309
Maria, 301

Marlow, Thomas (Sailmaker of Deal), 123
Marske, 258
Marten, Carl (Designer), 106
Marthas Vineyard, 325-329, 330, 331, 364
Mary, 196
Mary Blane, 135
Matapa (type of Somali coast) 28, 29
Matilda, 183
Matinicus Island, 341, 361
Matthews, Henry (of Eastbourne), 162
May and Thwaites (Boatbuilders of Hove), 166
Medway huffers boats, 320, 321
'Melon Seed' type, 349
Mermaid, 380
Mersea Hard, 303
Mersey, 240-242
Miami, 345
Mocket, Richard (of Deal), 122
Morecambe Bay, 242
Moriches, East and Center, 369
Mounts Bay gigs, 216, 217
Mousehole gigs, 213, 216, 217
Moville yawls, 237
Mullet, 177
Mundsley, 270, 276
Mystery, 121
Mystic Seaport, 366

Naggar (of river Nile), 29, 30
Nantucket, 325
Nauvoo, 342
fishermen, 343
New England, lobster boats, 380
wherries, 229
New Bedford, 329
Newbiggin, 254
Newhaven luggers, 162
pilots, 162
New Jersey beach skiffs, 229
Newport, 282
Newlyn gigs, 213, 216
New Moon, 152
New Orleans luggers, 358-363
builders of, 360, 361
Newquay gigs, 213, 218
Newton, 254
Nichols (Boatbuilder of Deal), 142
Nichols, James (Boatbuilder of Deal), 129, 139
Nick of Time, 159
Nil Desperandum, 283, 287
Nomans Land, 325-331

Nomans Land fishing boats, 325–331
Norfolk 'canoes', 278, 279
Norman, 84
Normania, 216
North Carolina fishing boats, 351, 354–356
North Haven, 366, 367
North Repps, 278
North Star, 118
North Sunderland, 254

O'Donnell, John (Boatbuilder of New Docks), 239
Ogdensburg, 374
Oregon gill net boats, 377
Ossie, 298, 299
Our Boys, 142
Our Lassie, 162
Overstrand, 270, 278
Overton, 242
Oyster, 304
Ox, 127

Padstow gigs, 213, 218
Pakefield, 281–282, 293
Palling, 281–283
Pamlico Sound, 351
Panther, 151
Papoose, 85
Paradox, 159, 160
Parret, 222, 223, 227–229
Pascagoula, 363
Patchogue, 369
Patey, Harry (of Hallsands), 204
Payne (Boatbuilder of Southampton), 177
Peace and Plenty, 158
Pearson, Charles (of Deal), 135
Pegg, 'Go Farther' (of Sheringham), 276
Pensacola, 356
gigs, 356–358
Penzance gigs, 213, 216, 217
Perrine, J. H. (Boatbuilder of Barnegat), 348
Perry, Richard (Sailmaker of Birkenhead), 94
Perseus, 108, 110
Pet, 159
Peter Boats, 313–316, 318
Peters family (Boatbuilders of St Mawes), 216, 217
Petingill, John (Boatbuilder of Crotch Island) 338
Phoenix, 288
Pill, John (Boatbuilder of Gorran Haven), 211
Richard (Boatbuilder of Gorran Haven), 211

Pilgrim, 136
Pin Mill, 267
Pinks, 316
Pirogue (American type), 363
Plugh, John (Boatbuilder of Brighton), 167
Plymouth (Massachusetts), 332, 334, 336
Bay lobster boats, 332–336
Polperro, 208
fishing boats, 208
Poole Harbour, 85
fishing boats, 185
Popham, F. W. Leybourne, 159
Pophyn, 110
Porthscato, 213
Portsmouth, 169 et seq.
Powell, J. (Sailmaker of Grimsby), 269
Pram (type of Hjerting, Denmark), 31, 32
Price, Thomas (Boatbuilder of Weston-super-Mare, later of Pill), 230
Pride of the Sea, 118, 135
Pride of the West, 231
Princess, 139
Princess Mary, 136
Princess Royal, 135, 289
Procyon, 108, 109
Pucan (Irish type), 238, 239
Puritan, 334

Quebec pilot boats, 374, 375
Queenborough, 318
Queen of Sheba, 118
Queen of Sussex, 159

Raddings, Bill (Sailmaker of Bridlington), 265
Rail gunning skiffs, 349, 351
Ranger, 301
Ransom, Edward A. (Boatbuilder of Kingston, Massachusetts), 334, 336
Raters, 82, 84
Rattenbury, Jack (of Beer), 187
Redcar cobles, 258
Redjacket, 287
Red Lancer, 85
Reindeer, 283, 287, 290, 292
Reliance, 283
Remus, 160
Rennjolle, 106
Renown, 118
Reynolds, Stephen, 196, 198, 201, 202
Roanoake Island, 351, 353

Robands, 48
Robin Hoods Bay, 258, 260
Robin Hoods Bay 'five man boats', 260
Rochester, 318, 321
Rockland, 341
Romulus, 160
Rondo II, 38, 40
Rover, 159
Royal Sovereign, 292
Rua Pet ('Type of the Gulf of Siam), 25
Runswick cobles, 258
Runton, 278
Rye, 148
Ryde, 169 et seq.
Ryde watermen, 175

St Helens Road, 171
St Ives gigs, 216, 218
St Lawrence skiffs, 370–373
builders of, 370, 371
Sacoleve (Greek type), 19, 54
Salem, 294
Saltburn cobles, 258
Sandsend cobles, 258
Sandy Hook, 342
Sarah, 203
Saxon, 141
Scarborough cobles, 258, 259, 261, 263, 264
Scilly Isles gigs, 213, 216–218
Scituate, 336
Scout, 301
Seabright skiffs, 342–345
Seahouses, 254
Seaman, family (Boatbuilders of Pamrapo and Nauvoo), 345
Seaman, Hazleton (Boatbuilder of West Creek), 346
Seaman's Hope, 141
Sea Serpent, 380, 381
Seaview, 175
Settee rig, 87
Shaldon, 202
Shallops, 325
Shamrock, 231
Sheringham, 270, 276, 277
'Great boats', 277
Sidall, Baker (Boatbuilder of Flamborough), 265
Sidmouth, 190, 191
luggers, 190–195, 199, 200
Fishermen, 190–202
beaching at, 195, 196

Silver Spray, 230, 231
Simmonds (Boatbuilder of Penzance), 216
Sisk, Tom (Boatbuilder of Eastbourne), 159
Sisters, 289
Skinningrove cobles, 258
Skovshoved boats (of Denmark), 58
Smack boats, 364, 365
Smakkejolle (of Danish Lillebelt), 36
Sneak Box, 346, 347–349
Snotter, 16, 46–48, 52, 53
Solent, 169 et seq.
Solitaire, 334
Solway Firth, 242–244
Sophia, 293
Southampton, 169 et seq.
fishing boats, 175, 176, 180
South Shields, 254, 255
pilot cobles, 257
Southwold. 280, 281, 291–293, 296
Spars, 45
Spread Eagle, 312
Sprit, 16, 46, 54
Spritsail Arrangements of, 16, 45, 46, 47, 50
Extent of use, 21
Danish spritsail, 36
Divided rig, 61
Dutch sprit arrangements, 58
Half sprit, 19
Mizzen, 53
Mizzen boom, 52
Origins of, 17, 19
Reefing, 52
Resurgence of interest in, 37, 45
Sailmaking, 41, 45
Sheeting, 50
Brail for, 49, 54
Three-masted rig, 36, 38, 40, 50
Two-masted rig, 50, 53
Spurn Point crab boat, 266, 277
Staithes, 258, 259
Stanton, William (Pilot of Deal), 127, 132, 134, 146
Starling, William (Boatbuilder of Blakeney), 276
Staunch, 142
Stella, 304
Stolford, 228
Stretcholt, 223, 229
Strood, 318, 320
Success, 118, 294
Sunderland, 254

Sunderland cobles, 257
  'Foy boats', 255
  Point, 242–244
  Point, Tank boats, 242, 243
  Point, Whammel boats, 243
Surprise, 270
Swiftsure, 283, 287, 292
Sycamore, Capt. Edward, 103
Sylvia, 204

Tabernacle, 62
Tancook whaler, 341
Tatchell, Percy, 101
Taw, 221, 222
T.C., 266
Tchektima (Turkish type), 56
Teignmouth, 202
Tenby, 231
  luggers, 231, 232
Terri II, 75, 77
Thames skiffs, 309
  wherries, 309–311
Thorpness, 281
Though, 290
Tiddy, Samuel (Boatbuilder of Scilly Isles), 217
Tiger 198
Tollesbury, 304

Topsail, with spritsail rig, 58
Torridge, 221, 222
Trabacola (Greek type), 34
Trackonderi (see also Trehendire), 56
Treffery, 216
Trimingham, 270
Triton, 180
Turkish Knight, 169
Tutt, Frederick (Boatbuilder of Eastbourne) 151
Tyne 'Foy boats' 255
  'Foy boats' builders of, 255
  pilot cobles, 257

Uma, 175
Undaunted, 141
United States naval boats, 375, 376

Van Kook, 125
Vargood (see Foregirl), 21, 27, 189
Vesper, 136
Victoria, 136
Victory, 167
Vixen, 334

Walmer galleys, 139
  galley punts, 142

luggers, 113 et seq.
Walmsley, Leo (Author), 261
Wanderjolle, 106
Walton-on-the-Naze, 301, 302
  fishing boats, 301, 302
Warrington 356
  pilot and fishing gigs, 356, 358
Washington gill net boats, 356, 358
Watson, James (Boatbuilder of Clarks Island),
  334
  Nathan (Boatbuilder of Kingston,
  Massachusetts), 333
Watts, John (Boatbuilder of Weston Super Mare),
  231
Wells, 276, 277
West Hartlepool cobles, 257
West Mersea, 302–305, 307, 309, 315, 318
  One Design class, 91
  fishing boats and fishermen, 176–180
Weston-super-Mare,
Wexford, 232
  cots, 232, 234
Wheezy Anna, 304
Wherries of Spithead, 169, 171
  smuggling, 173, 374
Whitby cobles, 258, 259, 263

White Slave, 162
Wight, Isle of, 169 et seq.
Wilkins, George and Henry (of Pawlett), 226
Williams, David and Sons (Boatbuilders of
  Aberystwyth), 235
Winnie, 304
Winterton, 281, 282
Withernsea cobles and crab boats, 266
Wittering, 181
Wivenhoe, 390
Wolverine, 300, 301
Woodham, 171, 173
Woodhouse family (of Overton), 243
Woods Hole boat, 365, 366
Woolley, Bob and Tom (of Sidmouth), 197, 202
Worthing, Boatbuilders of, 167
  luggers and fishermen, 167, 168
Wyatt, William (Boatbuilder of West Mersea)
  304, 305

Yawls, Yorkshire, 262
Yeo, 222
Yarmouth, Great, 266, 267, 280, 283, 290, 291
  cobles, 267
  boatbuilders of, 283
Young Prince, 287, 293
Young Reliance, 283, 293